James Donkor Afoakwah

The Nathan-David Confrontation (2 Sam 12:1-15a)

A slap in the face of the Deuteronomistic hero?

Bibliographic Information published by the Deutsche Nationalbibliothek
The Deutsche Nationalbibliothek lists this publication in the Deutsche Nationalbibliografie; detailed bibliographic data is available in the internet at http://dnb.d-nb.de.

Zugl.: Tübingen, Univ., Diss., 2014

Library of Congress Cataloging-in-Publication Data
Afoakwah, James Donkor, 1967-
 The Nathan-David confrontation (2 Sam 12:1-15a) : a slap in the face of the Deuteronomistic hero? / James Donkor Afoakwah. - 1 [edition].
   pages cm
 ISBN 978-3-631-66186-4
 1. Bible. Samuel, 2nd, XII, 1-15–Criticism, interpretation, etc.. 2. Nathan (Biblical prophet). 3. David, King of Israel. I. Title.
 BS1325.52.A36 2015
 222'.4406–dc23
                        2015016741

D 21
ISBN 978-3-631-66186-4 (Print)
E-ISBN 978-3-653-05849-9 (E-Book)
DOI 10.3726 978-3-653-05849-9

© Peter Lang GmbH
Internationaler Verlag der Wissenschaften
Frankfurt am Main 2015
All rights reserved.
Peter Lang Edition is an Imprint of Peter Lang GmbH.

Peter Lang – Frankfurt am Main · Bern · Bruxelles · New York · Oxford · Warszawa · Wien

All parts of this publication are protected by copyright. Any utilisation outside the strict limits of the copyright law, without the permission of the publisher, is forbidden and liable to prosecution. This applies in particular to reproductions, translations, microfilming, and storage and processing in electronic retrieval systems.

This publication has been peer reviewed.

www.peterlang.com

The Nathan-David Confrontation (2 Sam 12:1-15a)

Acknowledgement

The journey that has culminated in the publication of this book begun as a surprise and has progressed with the help and under the guidance of many loving and well-meaning companions along the way. I would like to express my sincere gratitude to the numerous personalities who have been a gift to me at various stages of the journey and the development of this work. His Eminence Peter Cardinal Turkson initiated the journey with his acquisition of a *Propaganda Fidei* scholarship for me to Study in Rome. At the end of that phase he linked me up with Prof. Dr. Peter Hünermann, through whose effort the Diocese of Rottenburg/Stuttgart welcomed me into her pastoral embrace and accorded me every necessary aid to complete my studies. To the Bishop, Dr. Gephardt Fürst and the personnel of *Hauptabteilung* IV, I say, thank you for the acceptance and the trust reposed in me and Archbishop Mathias Nketsiah of Cape Coast for allowing me the needed time for my sojourn in Germany.

Prof. Dr. Walter Groß has not just been my moderator but a *Doktorvater* in every ramification of the word. Herr Groß began his pension before the completion of this work but still accompanied me like the son of his old age, with meetings at short notice, prompt reading of the different parts of the work and encouraging words at the deepest moments of the journey. Herr Groß, this book is a personal, pension gift to you.

Prof. Dr. Ruth Scoralick assumed the responsibility of the second moderator and carried out that responsibility in record time. To you I express my sincere appreciation. As if one Professor Emeritus was not enough for me, I was blessed with two others; Prof. Dr. Ottmar Fuchs and B. J. Hilberath, under whose paternal but scrutinizing glance I sat for the final Exams – *Rigorosum*. Thank you, Herrn Fuchs and Hilberath, for the opportunity to learn from you at the various seminars and your paternal collegiality at the *rigorosum*.

Msgr. James Myers of the Archdiocese of Cape Coast has taken the time to read through the work, correct the language and offer challenging comments that helped yield the present result. Monsignor, I am grateful to you as my English Master in the minor seminary and proof-reader of my thesis. Whenever I was at my wit's end with my computer knowledge, Frau

Giuseppina Modica came to my rescue with her secretarial services. Giusy, accept my thanks for your silent, almost invisible aid.

The Italian parishes of Beato Carlo Steeb, in Reutlingen and San Bruno in Metzingen were a piece of home for me despite being far from home. My dear Parishioners, I am blessed to have had you in my life during the period of my studies. Despite the scarcity of time for pastoral work, you accepted me into your midst and into your families. Thank you for the experience of real love among you. Frs. Anthony Sackey and Richard Techie-Quansah, my brother Ghanaian priests who are also studying here in Germany; your unwavering, fraternal support and sharing with me in good and in bad times have worked an anchor-effect in my academic, moral and pastoral life. To you and the many nameless others, I render my heartfelt gratitude.

Finally, my sincere thanks to Jacob James Donkor (who did not live to see the completion of this work) and Joana Donkor, my parents, my brothers and sisters; James, Mary, Georgina, Isaac, Cecilia, Emmanuel, Gloria, Michael, Francis, William and Anthoinette. Together with you I have learnt to live, to love, to offend, to be offended, to forgive, to be forgiven and to grow. Thank you for your love. To God be the glory.

To
Jacob James Donkor,
Peter Cardinal Turkson, Walter Groß
and all the priests of the Archdiocese of Cape Coast.

Table of Contents

Abbreviations XIII

Text and Translation of 2 Samuel 12:1-15a XV

Introduction 1

Chapter 1. Panoramic view of 2 Sam 12:1-15a 5
1.1 The mediate context 5
1.2 The immediate context 8

Chapter 2. Status Questionis 19
2.1 The Literal Critical Approach (diachronic) to
    2 Sam 12:1-15a 22
2.2 The Succession Narrative; an anti-monarchical document? 34
2.3 The parable of Nathan as part of the DtrH 48

Chapter 3. The Deuteronomistic History (DtrH) 51
3.1 The Succession Narrative and the Deuteronomist (Dtr) 67
3.2 2 Sam 12:1-15a and the dtr 70
    3.2.1 Samuel and Saul 76
    3.2.2 Ahijah and Jeroboam 78
    3.2.3 The unnamed prophet and Ahab 79
    3.2.4 Nathan and David 80

Chapter 4. The text of the narrative 85
4.1 Structure; 2 Sam 12:1-15a 88
    4.1.1 The story: vv. 1-4 91
    4.1.2 Analysis 91
    4.1.3 Interpretation 93
4.2 The judgment: vv. 5-6 100
    4.2.1 Analysis 100
    4.2.2 Interpretation 102
4.3 The prophetic word: vv. 7-12 106
    4.3.1 The Prologue: vv. 7-9 107
    4.3.2 Analysis 107

	4.3.3	Interpretation 109
	4.3.4	The oracle of doom: v. 10-12 117
	4.3.5	Analysis 117
	4.3.6	Interpretation 118
4.4	The concluding words: vv. 13-14 124
	4.4.1	Analysis 124
	4.4.2	Interpretation 127
4.5	Summary 134

Chapter 5. The David of the Dtr and the parable of Nathan 137

5.1	The Kingship of David in the OT Tradition 140
5.2	The kingship of David in the light of Nathan's oracle 149
	5.2.1 The rise of David; 1 Sam 16-2 Sam 8 150
	5.2.2 The anointing of David and entry into the court of Saul 154
	5.2.3 Divine protection of David against Saul 156
	5.2.4 The elimination of Rivals to the Throne 162
	5.2.5 The Promise of an Everlasting Kingdom: 2 Sam 7 169
	5.2.6 David at the height of his reign – 2 Sam 8-20 171
	5.2.7 The last days of David: 1 Kings 1-2 175
5.3	The image of David that emerges from the narrative 178

Chapter 6. The prophet Nathan in the dtr corpus 183

6.1	2 Sam 7; an overview 186
	6.1.1 2 Sam 7; description and interpretation 196
6.2.	2 Sam 12 213
	6.2.1 2 Sam 12; description and interpretation 215
6.3	1 Kings 1 235
	6.3.1 1 Kings 1: an overview 236
	6.3.2 1 Kings 1; description and interpretation 244
	6.3.3 The Exposition: v. 1-4 244
	6.3.4 Adonijah's presumption: v. 5-10 246
	6.3.5 The counter plot: v. 11-14 250
	6.3.6 The successor is named: v. 15-37 252
	6.3.7 Solomon is King: v. 38-40 257
	6.3.8 Report by Jonathan Ben Abiathar: v. 41-49 262
	6.3.9 Adonijah's capitulation: v. 50-53 266

6.4 Synthesis..267
6.5 The Nathan narratives seen together 271

Chapter 7. Conclusion: The parable of Nathan; a slap
in the face of the dtr image of David?...281

Bibliography..291

Abbreviations

AB	Anchor Bible Series or Commentary
BBB	Bonner Biblische Beiträge
BETL	Bibliotheca Ephemerides Theologicae Lovaniensis
BH	Biblical Hebrew
BTS	Biblisch-Theologische Studien
BZAW	Beiheft zur Zeitschrift für die alttestamentliche Wissenschaft
CBET	Contributions to Biblical Exegesis & Theology
CBQ	Catholic Biblical Quarterly
CH	Court History
Dtr	Deuteronomist or the Deuteronomistic author or writer
DtrH	Deuteronomistic History
FAT	Forschung zur Alten Testament
FCB	The Feminist Companion to the Bible
FRLANT	Forschungen zur Religion und Literatur des Alten und Neuen Testaments
HS	Heiligenkreuzer Studien
HThKAT	Herders theologischer Kommentar zum Alten Testament
JSOT	Journal for the Study of Old Testament
JSOTSup	Journal for the Study of Old Testament Supplement Series
KAA	Kölner Anglistische Arbeiten
LXX	The Septuagint – Ralf's Edition
ÖBS	Österreichische Biblische Studien
PdÄ	Probleme der Ägyptologie
SBA	Stuttgarter Biblische Aufsatzbände
SBL	Society of Biblical Literature
SBT	Studies in Biblical Theology
SBTS	Sources for Biblical and Theological Study
SFEG	Schriften der Finnischen Exegetischen Gessellschaft
SJOT	Scandinavian Journal of the Old Testment

SN	Succession Narrative
STTAASF	Suomalaisen Tiedeakatemian Toimituksia Annales Academiae Scientiarum Fennicae
ThR	Theologische Rundschau
VT	Vetus Testamentum
WBC	Word Biblical Commentary
TS	Theologische Studien (Zürich)
ZAR	Zeitschrift für Altorientalische und Biblische Rechtsgeschichte

All other abbreviations follow the list in the *Abkurzungen Theologie und Religionswissenschaften nach RGG*[4] (UTB 2868), hg. von der Redaktion der RGG[4], Tübingen 2007.

Text and Translation of 2 Samuel 12:1-15a

Hebrew		English
וַיִּשְׁלַח יְהוָה אֶת־נָתָן אֶל־דָּוִד וַיָּבֹא אֵלָיו וַיֹּאמֶר לוֹ שְׁנֵי אֲנָשִׁים הָיוּ בְּעִיר אֶחָת אֶחָד עָשִׁיר וְאֶחָד רָאשׁ:	1	(Then) Yhwh sent Nathan to David. He came to him and said to him; "There were two men in one city, the one rich and the other poor.
לְעָשִׁיר הָיָה צֹאן וּבָקָר הַרְבֵּה מְאֹד:	2	The rich man had very many flock and cattle,
וְלָרָשׁ אֵין־כֹּל כִּי אִם־כִּבְשָׂה אַחַת קְטַנָּה אֲשֶׁר קָנָה וַיְחַיֶּהָ וַתִּגְדַּל עִמּוֹ וְעִם־בָּנָיו יַחְדָּו מִפִּתּוֹ תֹאכַל וּמִכֹּסוֹ תִשְׁתֶּה וּבְחֵיקוֹ תִשְׁכָּב וַתְּהִי־לוֹ כְּבַת:	3	but the poor man had nothing except one little ewe lamb which he had bought. He took care of it and it grew up together with him and with his children: it used to eat of his morsel, drink from his cup, lie in his bosom and it was like a daughter to him.
וַיָּבֹא הֵלֶךְ לְאִישׁ הֶעָשִׁיר וַיַּחְמֹל לָקַחַת מִצֹּאנוֹ וּמִבְּקָרוֹ לַעֲשׂוֹת לָאֹרֵחַ הַבָּא־לוֹ וַיִּקַּח אֶת־כִּבְשַׂת הָאִישׁ הָרָאשׁ וַיַּעֲשֶׂהָ לָאִישׁ הַבָּא אֵלָיו:	4	Now, there came a traveller to the rich man, and he loathed (pitied) to take from his flock and cattle to prepare for the wayfarer who had come to him. Instead he took the lamb of the poor man and prepared it for the man who had come to him.
וַיִּחַר־אַף דָּוִד בָּאִישׁ מְאֹד וַיֹּאמֶר אֶל־נָתָן חַי־יְהוָה כִּי בֶן־מָוֶת הָאִישׁ הָעֹשֶׂה זֹאת:	5	Then David's anger was greatly kindled against the man. He said to Nathan; "As Yhwh lives, the man who has done this deserves to die;
וְאֶת־הַכִּבְשָׂה יְשַׁלֵּם אַרְבַּעְתָּיִם עֵקֶב אֲשֶׁר עָשָׂה אֶת־הַדָּבָר הַזֶּה וְעַל אֲשֶׁר לֹא־חָמָל:	6	and the Lamb, he shall restore fourfold, because he has done this thing and he had no pity."
וַיֹּאמֶר נָתָן אֶל־דָּוִד אַתָּה הָאִישׁ כֹּה־אָמַר יְהוָה אֱלֹהֵי יִשְׂרָאֵל אָנֹכִי מְשַׁחְתִּיךָ לְמֶלֶךְ עַל־יִשְׂרָאֵל וְאָנֹכִי הִצַּלְתִּיךָ מִיַּד שָׁאוּל:	7	Nathan said to David, "You are the man! Thus says Yhwh, the God of Israel: I have anointed you king over Israel and have rescued you from the hand of Saul.

XV

Hebrew		English
וָאֶתְּנָ֨ה לְךָ֜ אֶת־בֵּ֣ית אֲדֹנֶ֗יךָ וְאֶת־נְשֵׁ֤י אֲדֹנֶ֙יךָ֙ בְּחֵיקֶ֔ךָ וָאֶתְּנָ֣ה לְךָ֔ אֶת־בֵּ֥ית יִשְׂרָאֵ֖ל וִֽיהוּדָ֑ה וְאִ֨ם־מְעָ֔ט וְאֹסִ֥פָה לְּךָ֖ כָּהֵ֥נָּה וְכָהֵֽנָּה׃	8	I have given you your master's house and your master's wives into your bosom and (I have given) you the house of Israel and of Judah; and if that were too little I will add as much more.
מַדּ֜וּעַ בָּזִ֣יתָ ׀ אֶת־דְּבַ֣ר יְהוָ֗ה לַעֲשׂ֣וֹת הָרַע֮ בְּעֵינוֹ֒ אֵ֣ת אוּרִיָּ֤ה הַֽחִתִּי֙ הִכִּ֣יתָ בַחֶ֔רֶב וְאֶ֨ת־אִשְׁתּ֔וֹ לָקַ֥חְתָּ לְּךָ֖ לְאִשָּׁ֑ה וְאֹת֣וֹ הָרַ֔גְתָּ בְּחֶ֖רֶב בְּנֵ֥י עַמּֽוֹן׃	9	Why have you despised the word of Yhwh, to do what is evil in his sight? You have struck down Uriah the Hittite with the sword and his wife you have taken for yourself as your wife but him you have killed with the sword of the Ammonites.
וְעַתָּ֗ה לֹא־תָס֥וּר חֶ֛רֶב מִבֵּיתְךָ֖ עַד־עוֹלָ֑ם עֵ֚קֶב כִּ֣י בְזִתָ֔נִי וַתִּקַּ֗ח אֶת־אֵ֙שֶׁת֙ אוּרִיָּ֣ה הַחִתִּ֔י לִהְי֥וֹת לְךָ֖ לְאִשָּֽׁה׃ ס	10	And now the sword shall never depart from your house because you have despised me and have taken the wife of Uriah, the Hittite to be your wife.
כֹּ֣ה ׀ אָמַ֣ר יְהוָ֗ה הִנְנִי֩ מֵקִ֨ים עָלֶ֤יךָ רָעָה֙ מִבֵּיתֶ֔ךָ וְלָקַחְתִּ֤י אֶת־נָשֶׁ֙יךָ֙ לְעֵינֶ֔יךָ וְנָתַתִּ֖י לְרֵעֶ֑יךָ וְשָׁכַ֥ב עִם־נָשֶׁ֖יךָ לְעֵינֵ֥י הַשֶּׁ֥מֶשׁ הַזֹּֽאת׃	11	Thus says Yhwh: I will raise up evil against you from your own house; and I will take your wives before your eyes, and give them to your fellow and he shall lie with your wives in the sight of this very sun.
כִּ֥י אַתָּ֖ה עָשִׂ֣יתָ בַסָּ֑תֶר וַאֲנִ֗י אֶֽעֱשֶׂה֙ אֶת־הַדָּבָ֣ר הַזֶּ֔ה נֶ֥גֶד כָּל־יִשְׂרָאֵ֖ל וְנֶ֥גֶד הַשָּֽׁמֶשׁ׃	12	For you did it in secret but I will do this thing before all Israel and before the sun.
וַיֹּ֤אמֶר דָּוִד֙ אֶל־נָתָ֔ן חָטָ֖אתִי לַֽיהוָ֑ה ס וַיֹּ֨אמֶר נָתָ֜ן אֶל־דָּוִ֗ד גַּם־יְהוָ֛ה הֶעֱבִ֥יר חַטָּאתְךָ֖ לֹ֥א תָמֽוּת׃	13	Then David said to Nathan, "I have sinned against Yhwh". Nathan said to David, "Yhwh has, on one hand, caused your sin to pass over, you shall not die.
אֶ֗פֶס כִּֽי־נִאֵ֤ץ נִאַ֙צְתָּ֙ אֶת־אֹיְבֵ֣י יְהוָ֔ה בַּדָּבָ֖ר הַזֶּ֑ה גַּ֗ם הַבֵּ֛ן הַיִּלּ֥וֹד לְךָ֖ מ֥וֹת יָמֽוּת׃	14	Nevertheless, because you have by this deed utterly scorned the enemies of Yhwh, the child that is born to you, on the other, shall surely die."
וַיֵּ֥לֶךְ נָתָ֖ן אֶל־בֵּיתֽוֹ	15	Then Nathan went to his house.

Introduction

The story of David occupies a very prominent position in the history of Israel, and the unity of the Biblical narrative, where it constitutes the core and reference point for both the Old and the New Testaments. From this perspective the person and image of David never lack admiration or critique. The more one gets immersed into the narrative about the royal family of David the more one gets inundated by a rich minefield of exegetical literature. The recent work of Walter Dietrich, *Forschung an den Samuelbüchern im neuen Jahrtausend*, has shown that there are more than thirty-seven major exegetical research works on the first and second books of Samuel in the last decade alone. This interest does not in any way dwindle with the passage of time; it rather grows in leaps and bounds. In line with this growth in interest, I have also chosen to enter into the exegete's favourite text – the story of David's family or succession,[1] but my interest lies in only a very small portion of that great story. It is the intriguing manner in which the Deuteronomist (dtr) author uses the prophet Nathan in his development of the character and story of David and, in so doing, in his complex ideology and theology that captivates my attention. The author paints the picture of a man who is worthy of emulation, the yardstick with which he measures all the kings of Israel and Judah, but at the same time allows the prophet to denigrate him in a manner befitting only the worst kings in the history of Israel (Ahab and Manasseh). The story in question is the parable of Nathan and its subsequent oracle or prophecy of doom against David and his house (2 Sam 12:1-15a). A confrontation between a prophet and a king is in no way unusual in the history of Israel, but when that king involved is no other than David, then that event becomes unusual if not extraordinary. The characterization of David in Biblical tradition is the ideal that one can aspire towards; the faithful king who walked before Yhwh "with integrity of heart and uprightness" (1 Kings 9:4), the bearer of the promise of an eternal dynasty (2 Sam 7) and the yardstick with which all other kings before and after him are judged. It is in 2 Sam 12 and only here does David stand accused

---

[1] L. Rost, *The Succession to the Throne of David*, Sheffield, 1982, p. 65.

of adultery and murder and faces a condemnation that endangers his life and that of his dynasty.

The typical exegetical attitude towards this pericope has been to follow the literal critical method that considers the parable a later addition to the history or the redactional critical approach which sees different levels of redaction in the pericope. Modern thought does not very much wean itself from the traditional historico-critical approaches, for it cannot do otherwise, because there is no method that is absolutely right or absolutely wrong.[2] It is the results of the various methods put together that provide the reader with the necessary foundation upon which to decipher the sense of the Biblical text. The most radical approach of our day towards the parable of Nathan has been that of John Van Seters, who proposes a late exilic writer (the Court Historian), who has forced the parable into the completed work of the DtrH to sabotage the otherwise perfect image of David; the just and righteous king, created and defended by the dtr author, with the ultimate aim of undermining the development of the promise of an eternal dynasty to the house of David in 2 Sam 7 into the expectation of the Messianic rule of that royal house.[3] This mind-tickling hypothesis naturally arrests the attention of the reader and widens the horizon of interest in the pericope.

Evidently the initial question that a narrative arouses in its audience is about what determines the direction of the ensuing research. If the intriguing question is: Which author could have inserted such a negative material into an otherwise predominantly positive narrative? Then one is very likely to seek answers outside the text since one postulates the existence of two separate narratives, a positive and a negative, and, therefore, two separate authors. My aim and interest in the parable is not the question of who may have written it, the subject of source criticism, but what role the pericope plays in the over-all history of the Dtr from the point of view of the position where it has been placed by that particular author in his work. My initial premise is that the dtr author or school of thought has adopted the parable from the many sources that were available to him at the moment of compiling the history and has reworked it in such a manner that it fits very well into the composite whole that is termed "the deuteronomistic

---

2   T. Römer, *Das DtrG und die Wüstentraditionen*, p. 58.
3   J. Van Seters, *In Search of History*, p. 290.

history" (DtrH). Thus, I am looking at the parable from the End Text Perspective; as an integral part of the DtrH of Deuteronomy – 2 Kings, keeping in mind the historical process that may have influenced its formation. The direction of my work is the examination of the purpose that this apparently negative text serves in the work of the Dtr so that the author did not find it too odious, detrimental or even counter-productive to the goals of his project. This position is very much influenced by the fact that 2 Sam 12:1-15a can neatly be lifted out of its context without any noticeable break in the flow of the narrative except that the homicides committed in the house of David and Absalom's revolt will be stripped of their theological interpretation and 1 Kings 1-2 will hang in mid-air with the protagonist and heir to the throne of David rising out of the blue. With the position and content of 2 Sam 12, the narrator perfectly fills in the gaps that may have arisen and propels the account into the future when succession to the throne of David takes centre stage.

One will have to agree that the presentation of David as a character in the narrative and as a father and king who is the hero of the complex history, is in many instances very ambivalent. It is, however, in this ambivalence that the author succeeds in creating an enigmatic character of the perfect hero in his imperfection as a human being borne only on the wings of divine grace and mercy. He is, in fact, like a mirage; it is all the farther away when you think that you have gotten to it. This characteristic style in the presentation of the central figure of the epoch so much endears the narrative to the exegete that it is at the very moment when one thinks that one has discovered a new key to the understanding of the story that one realizes that someone else has been there before, and yet the interest does not die out.

This book is composed of six chapters with an introduction and a general conclusion. The first chapter seeks to situate the David-Nathan confrontation in its mediate and immediate narrative contexts with the purpose of focusing attention on its unique stylistic position that gives rise to the discussion of whether it fits into its environs or not. This question leads the reader automatically to the second chapter, which deals with the state of the issue or the nature of the discussion surrounding 2 Sam 12:1-15a; the *Status Questionis*. Chapter three takes an excursion into the Deuteronomistic History, the major work to which the parable of Nathan and its resultant oracle belong, while the fourth chapter zooms into the narrative text of 2 Sam 12:1-15a, subjecting it to critical observations and analyses based upon the historical and literal critical methods in a synchronic manner, without losing sight of the fact that the pericope belongs to a larger narrative block. The fifth chapter takes up the theme of the image of David presented in the larger work of the Dtr in order to facilitate a comparison with the presentation of that same character in 2 Sam 12 with the prophet Nathan playing the role of the judge; the agent who pronounces the prophecy of doom against the otherwise perfect hero of the narrative. Reasoning along the same wavelength, the sixth chapter seeks to find out the missing link in the narrative; what David and Nathan have in common or the inseparable force that binds the two characters so firmly together as to warrant not only the audacity of Nathan to stand out against David, but also the king's humility in succumbing to the prophetic authority. This, invariably, demands an analysis of the three Nathan pericopae which are all enacted at the palace of David, with the king as the object of all three prophetic addresses. The work emphasizes the multifaceted role of Nathan at the royal palace as a messenger of Yhwh, a trusted personality at the court, a spiritual guide and a faithful defender of the dynasty. It is in the complexity of these roles that his prophetic rebuke of David reveals its corrective quality of bringing the erring king back to his God. This strong and corrective word of the prophet does not in any way imply an outright rejection and if it is to be assumed that a late writer has sought to purport this, then that writer may only have succeeded in shooting himself in the heels.

Chapter 1. Panoramic view of 2 Sam 12:1-15a

The context of 2 Sam 12:1-15a is so unique that it hardly escapes the attention of the casual, let alone the critical reader of biblical narratives. The mediate context is, obviously, the Ammonite campaign of 2 Sam 10:1-11:1 and 12:26-31 within which the author or redactor situates what is identified as the David-Bathsheba-Uriah sequence (11:2-27). The author concludes with the prophetic intervention of Nathan, with its aftermath, and then takes his reader back to the original story from where he had left off. This gives a broad framework or a panoramic view, which I would call the mediate context of the Nathan-David confrontation. Within this framework is located the David-Bathsheba-Uriah sequence that I will term the immediate context and will single out, in so doing, the prophetic intervention of 12:1-15a as a kind of double redaction or a separate level of redaction. The passage can neatly be lifted out of its context without doing any harm to the narrative sequence. It will, however, do an ideological damage to the global understanding of the text that is so-called "Succession Narrative" or "Court History" of David (hitherto SN and CH respectively) and the whole corpus of the Deuteronomistic work, which stretches from Deuteronomy to the second book of Kings (DtrH).[4]

1.1 The mediate context

The tenth chapter of the second book of Samuel opens with the death of the king of the Ammonites, Nahash, and his succession by Hanun, his son. To show loyalty (*hesed*), "David sent envoys to console him (Hanun) concerning his father" (2 Sam 10:2). The Ammonite princes interpreted this action as an act of espionage, resulting in the maltreatment of the envoys. David had recourse to the "*hesed*" which Nahash had shown him and his desire to reciprocate with the son as the reason for sending the

---

4   In this work the siglum DtrH will be used to designate the work of the Deuteronomist in correspondence to the German DtrG, as the basic work or history narrated by the sixth century exilic author or the complex whole of the Deuteronomistic work stretching from Deuteronomy to 2 Kings.

envoys. Such a protocol between two rulers coupled with the usage of the word *"hesed"* points to a covenant relationship or a bond of friendship. It is difficult to establish when such a relationship might have been initiated between David and Nahash. A relationship of this kind between the two rulers may, however, be a possibility; after Saul had gained his acceptance as king of Israel to the detriment of the Ammonites in 1 Sam 11, Nahash may have courted the friendship of David, Saul's rival, in order to end the Israelite threat to his people. This seems to be confirmed by the fact that another of his sons, Shobi, was among the delegation that welcomed David to Mahanaim while he was fleeing from Absalom (2 Sam 17:27-29). The dating of these two encounters has been the bone of contention for some time and has given rise to the chronological argument that seeks to date the meeting with Shobi before the encounter with Hanun, ascribing the *hesed* to the meeting at Mahanaim. I would like to maintain, from the point of view of the end text, that the relationship between David and Nahash preceded these two events and would rather consider these encounters as the result of that friendship. David's dispatch of a delegation then will be in keeping with the established protocol in order to keep relationships intact.[5]

Nahash was the enemy of Saul and regarded David an ally against a common enemy. Hanun and the Ammonite princes would object to this contract because the common enemy was no more and David had now become the king of an emerging power that threatened the very existence of the Ammonite nation. Logically, the alliance with the other regional rulers was formed to neutralize the growing power of Israel in like manner as Nahash had aligned himself with David to offset Saul's onslaught against Ammon. The treatment of David's emissaries had a special significance for the Semitic people as a symbolic gesture of humiliation. According to McCarter, the removal of the beard symbolically deprives a man of his masculinity. Cutting off the skirt may be a palliative for castration, as it bares the testicles; and combining the two constituted a peculiarly appropriate punishment for the

---

5   P. K. McCarter, *II Samuel*, AB 9, p. 270. McCarter quotes Moran to support the position that David's sending of emissaries was a requirement of the established protocol at the death of a treaty partner.

supposed spies whose secrets had been exposed.[6] Physical nudity or nakedness seemed to have been considered the height of disgrace and shame in the Ancient Orient as expressed by Isaiah in his description of the conquest of Egypt and Ethiopia (Cush); both the young and old would be led away naked and barefooted, with buttocks uncovered (Isaiah 20:4).

Having humiliated the messengers, Hanun formed a coalition with (*hired*, *cf.* 10:6) the Aramaeans. Hadadezer, the Aramaean king, entered into this alliance for the possible advantage of fighting a common enemy to his own rising power.[7] David had, by this gesture, received the necessary spark to ignite the power keg on which the neighbouring states sat. In three sweeping battles the Ammonite-Aramaean campaign was concluded with outright victory to the Israelite army. The war is splendidly described in full detail. The first of them was joined at the entrance of Rabbah. The two-pronged attack of Joab and Abishai routed the Aramaeans and caused the Ammonites to take refuge in their city (2 Sam 10:6-14). In the second encounter, a reinforced Aramaean side was regrouped at Helam. This time David himself led Israel to war and won a decisive battle (vv. 15-19). The Aramaeans made peace and became subjects to Israel. The die was cast for the final onslaught, which was the siege of Rabbah. The narrator begins the account in 11:1 but interrupts the narrative with the David-Bathsheba-Uriah sequence and resumes it in 12:26-31 with the capture of the city by David himself upon the request of Joab.

The siege of Rabbah occurred "In the *spring* of the year, the time when kings go out to battle...." (2 Sam 11:1). The text reads *turning* (litšûbat), but Josephus specifies it as the *spring*.[8] The actual duration of the siege is not known except that it lasted long enough for David to commit adultery with Uriah's wife, learn of her pregnancy, get the soldier killed in the battle

---

6 McCarter, Idem.
7 In *Antiquities* 7.121, Josephus states that the Arameans "sent a thousand talents to the Syrian king of Mesopotamia". Recent commentators would, however, not like to think of an outright hiring but a coalition of interest to Zobah as the Ammonites might not have had the resources to hire an army of such nature as outright mercenaries. Cf. McCarter, op. cit., 274.
8 Josephus, *Jewish Antiquities*, 7.129. The Chronicler uses the same verb as 2 Sam 11:1 but the feminine singular.

for Rabbah and marry the widow, who bore him a son. It may not be right to insist that the events happened in this chronology. What is clear is that the author has used the Ammonite war as the reason for Uriah's absence from home and the vulnerability of Bathsheba as well as the easiest means at the disposal of the king to eliminate Uriah for the purpose of covering up his crime.

2 Sam 11:1 forms a coherent narrative with 12:26 in which the latter constitutes a logical sequence to the former as the final battle with the Ammonites that took place in the spring. To all intents and purposes, the David-Bathsheba-Uriah episode is an insertion into this war narrative. The writer of the story has picked the archival Davidic war document as his setting to narrate the episode of palace romance, intrigue and murder. The warrior-king remains at home while his soldiers march to war. Jonathan Kirsch is very apt in his description:

> Some of the old fire had gone out of David, or so the Bible seems to suggest. He was now well into middle age, and apparently he was no longer willing to endure the discomforts and dangers of a long march and a hard campaign in the enemy territory. So he sent Joab and the army to fight, and he remained behind in the royal palace in Jerusalem. But as it turned out, David still burned with the white-hot sexuality that had always made him so compelling to both men and women.[9]

Thus the mediate context of our theme is clearly carved out; 10:1-11:1 (A) and 12:26-31 (A¹). The author has craftily made use of an independent war narrative as a frame-work to recount the complex and intricate palace romance between the monarch himself and his future favourite wife and mother of the successor to the throne, Solomon.

1.2 The immediate context

Having prepared the stage for the episode, which Gressmann would call a novella,[10] the narrator swiftly leads his readers into a classic story of love, romance, cunning, treachery and murder in high places. While Uriah and the valiant men of Israel are battling the Ammonites to salvage the dignity of their nation, the king commits adultery with the wife of one of

---

9   J. Kirsch, *King David*, p. 184.
10 H. Gressmann, Oldest History Writing, p. 26.

his soldiers and plots the same soldier's death. The sin of David is heightened by suspense in the fact that the innocent Uriah carries his own death sentence from the king, whom he faithfully serves, to the commander who executes it.[11] The narrative reveals the dark side of the character of David; the otherwise righteous king, who is supposed to defend the poor and the oppressed, misuses his royal power and authority to the detriment of a loyal subject and one of his own generals at that. Appropriately, the drama seems to end with the Lord taking notice of the abominable act of David and his striking the child born from it with a mortal illness. Here again 2 Sam 12:15b flows coherently from 11:27b. Without 12:1-15a, the story proceeds from the displeasure of the Lord (11:27b – B) to the striking ill of the son born to David by Uriah's wife (12:15b – B^1) and subsequently to the birth of Solomon. If 12:1-15a (C) is lifted out from the narrative the sequence will remain undisturbed and the flow of the story syntactically coherent.

For some reasons that call for a re-reading of the text, the author breaks the flow of the narrative with a divine intervention mediated by the prophet Nathan (12:1-15a). This is very uncharacteristic of both the mediate and immediate contexts or even of the whole narrative that is termed "David's Succession Narrative" (2 Sam 9-20, and I Kings 1-2). In these chapters God is portrayed as a silent observer in the unfolding of the events, but here he is an active player through the medium of a prophetic figure.[12] Remarkably, the pericope begins with God sending Nathan to David and ends with Nathan going to his house. Besides this encounter, the only other

---

11 The motive of Uriah carrying his own death warrant is demonstrated by the Illiad (6. 168-190) where King Proteus suspecting Bellerephon of adultery with the queen, sends him to the king of Lycia, the father of the queen, with a coded message to put the young man to death. In the Biblical episode, we may even wonder the level of literacy of the players in the drama at that time. There remains the probability that all the three players may have been illiterates; David, Joab, Uriah. Hence the secret was a secret so long as the scribal witness kept it as such.

12 Von Rad identifies this as one of the three theologically explicit passages in the Succession Narrative that help the reader to associate God's judgment with the succession of blows that befell the house of David. The others are: 2 Sam 12:24 and 17:14. These verses would seem to say. "God has taken note and would act at the appropriate time". Cf. P. K. McCarter, *II Samuel*, p. 298.

times we hear of Nathan in the narrative are in connection with the promise of a lasting house to David (7:1-17), the ambivalent naming of Solomon, an apparent narrator's remark (12:24-25), and later in 1 Kings 1:11ff to push for the succession of Solomon. Thus the encounter between David and the prophet Nathan is isolated within its surroundings, but has great resonances on the subsequent events. This the impression of different levels of redaction within the same narrative; the war report as a framework, the adultery with Bathsheba and murder of Uriah as the main insertion, and the encounter with Nathan the prophet a second level of insertion.

Some modern translations of the Bible, such as the New Revised Standard Version, probably following the Septuagint (LXX), read 2 Sam 11:27b with 12:1 as in the 1979 Rahlfs' edition. Even though such a position might appear to give good grounds for a textual unity, I prefer to read the two verses separately and in line with the masoretic text (MT) and note without entering, at this stage of the work, into the question of the historical background to the division of the Biblical text into chapters and verses. The MT has a clean break after 11:27b, marked by the *petuḥa*, and proceeds with the proper name of the subject of the verb "send" (Yhwh) to signalize a fresh start or at least a new paragraph beginning with 12:1.[13] This highlights the textual beauty of the narrative as we have it. Whatever argument one puts forth to justify the shift from 11:27 to 12:1 can also be expressed in favour of the swing to 12:15b. Chapter 11:27b breaks off the succession of *wayyiqtols* with a qatal (ʿāśāʰ) indicating the break with the sequence of events for the provision of background information. This, coupled with the introduction of a completely new character (Yhwh) into the narrative, provides a moral conscience to the otherwise tacit narration of events in the whole chapter and sets the stage for an expected *wayyiqtol* of consecution (וישלח) depicting Yhwh's reaction as a consequence to the actions of David. Both 12:1 and 12:15b exhibit the distinctive semantic nuances of Biblical Hebrew that could be expected in this context; they all begin with Yhwh as the subject of a *wayyiqtol* (וישלח & ויגף respectively) constituting a logical sequence to 11:27.

---

13 I am of the view that the author would have used pronouns in 12:1 if he intended to continue the narrative as presented by the versions. We will pick up and develop this argument in the fourth chapter of this work.

12:1 → וַיִּשְׁלַח יְהוָה אֶת־נָתָן אֶל־דָּוִד
"Thus Yhwh sent Nathan to David..."[14]

12:15b → וַיִּגֹּף יְהוָה אֶת־הַיֶּלֶד אֲשֶׁר יָלְדָה אֵשֶׁת־אוּרִיָּה לְדָוִד וַיֵּאָנַשׁ
"So Yhwh struck the child that Uriah's wife bore to David, and it became ill..."[15]

The question that might call for consideration is: "What does Yhwh do when he is not pleased with someone or about something?" Biblical tradition abounds in moments when God sends afflictions or prophets to express disgust at morally unacceptable situations. In Gen 38:7 the Lord supposedly put Er to death because he was wicked (רע) and did the same with Onan because "what he (Onan) had done was evil (רע) in the eyes of Yhwh" (v. 10). The ten plagues of Exodus 7-13 are clear examples of how God reacts to a stiff-necked disobedient monarch. In this instance, God sends the plagues through the practical actions of his messenger, Moses. In 1 Kings 22, the Lord sends Elijah, his prophet, to confront Ahab, who has killed Naboth, through the machinations of Jezebel, and has crowned the misdeed by taking possession of the property of the deceased; the victim of a travesty of justice. The books of Samuel do not lack examples of the two methods as *modus operandi* of the Lord in similar situations. On one hand, when Saul breached the word of the Lord by preserving Agag, king of the Amalekites, and the best of the things devoted to destruction, the Lord sent the prophet Samuel to denounce him (Saul) and announce his rejection as king of Israel (1 Sam 15). On the other, Yhwh gave David a choice among three punishments for the census he had taken of the people[16]; an apparent declaration

---

14 Most modern translations maintain the simple translational value of waw as a conjunction (and) but in this instance a little more in addition will be required as in the case of the Einheitsübersetzung (*Darum*), The New American Standard Bible (*Then*) and La Nuova Diodati (*Poi*).
15 Almost all the major translations stick to the normal sense of *waw* as "and" but a consecutive value translates better the global sense of the text. La Nuova Diodati as well as the CEI edition of 2008 beautifully capture this idea with their use of "*ma*" (but) in 11:27b and "*quindi*" (therefore) in 12:15b. "... Ma ciò che Davide aveva fatto dispiacque all'Eterno. Poi l'Eterno quindi colpì il bambino che la moglie d'Uriah aveva partorito a Davide, ed egli si ammalò".
16 The background to the census is very difficult to explain. The received text attributes David's order for the census to divine instigation and command on account of Yhwh's wrath against Israel for an unknown reason (24:1). The Chronicler might have grappled with this fact and not finding a satisfactory

of the king's reliance on the military might of the people instead of an abandonment to divine protection (2 Sam 24:10-17).[17] In a matter of x – עשה רע – בעיני יהוה (x – doing what is evil – in the sight of Yhwh) the reaction can go in different directions; either by prophetic judgment that will take place in the future (1 Sam 15, 2 Sam 12:1, 1 Kings 22), by plague through an agent (Ex 7-13, 2 Sam 24:12) or by a direct punishment that is considered a divine intervention (Gen 38:7, 10, 2 Sam 12:15b[18]). In the present case, the redactor of the narrative has craftily placed one after the other the two modes of punishment each of which fits very well into the context, but without excluding the other; the prophetic judgment, which will be fulfilled in the future, and the death of the child as its immediate sign (cf. 4.4.2).[19]

McCarter, in fact, accords the whole block of material, stretching from chapter ten to twelve, a functional role of a theological preface[20] to the subsequent tragic events in David's house. Schwally, however, had already in 1892 opined that v. 15 is a continuation from v. 27a and that 27b-12:15a are reminiscent of later prophetic materials.[21] In like manner, Nowack doubts the originality of 12:1-15a to what precedes and what follows. If we leave it out, we get a very good connection, joining 11:27b to 12:15b: *The thing was evil in the sight of Yahweh, and Yahweh smote the child which the wife of Uriah bore to David.*[22] Nowack finds it reasonable

---

answer to the contradiction changes the subject of יסת (he incited, or instigated) from Yhwh to Satan (1 Chr 21:1) so that David sins against Yhwh under the instigation of Satan.

17 The case of the same Nathan going back to David to counteract his own words regarding the building of a house for God at the behest of Yahweh can be cited (2 Sam 7:1-17).
18 This is the impression that will be created if one jumps from 11:27b to 12:15b; the death of the child as the just response of Yhwh to the evil done by David.
19 The death of "the child born to David by the wife of Uriah" will be explained in 4.4.ii. as the sign of the oracle of doom which was generally to be fulfilled in the future.
20 P. K. McCarter, *II Samuel*, p. 276.
21 F. Schwally, ZAW 12, 1892, 155-56), as in WBC, p. 160. Schwally cites I Kings 20:35-42, Isa 5:1-7, Jer 3:1 and Hag 2:10-14 and concludes that 2 Sam 11:27b-12:15a belongs to a similar category of narratives of a later epoch. A similar stance is taken recently by Dietrich, Würthwein and Veijola.
22 D. W. Nowack, *Richter, Ruth und Bücher Samuelis*, p. 194.

in supposing that the early narrative was content with pointing out that the anger of Yahweh was evidenced by the death of the child and that a later writer was not satisfied with this, but felt that there ought to have been a specific rebuke by a direct revelation, hence, the Nathan intervention. I share the view of Nowack and the numerous others who follow this line of thought, but I am also convinced that there is more to the insertion of the confrontation of Nathan with the king than just providing a space for a prophetic intervention in the tradition. The "later writer" whom I identify in this work as the Deuteronomistic writer has inserted this prophetic episode at this moment in the account to give meaning to the events that will develop later in the narrative future (2 Sam 13-19) through the efficacious word of a particular prophet, Nathan. McCarter proposes a theory for the textual unity by ascribing the David-Bathsheba-Uriah sequence to a prophetic writer who inserted his finished work into the archival frame and prefaced it to the Absalom revolt as its interpretation.[23] I am in accord with McCarter in regarding the sequence as a composite unit from a probable prophetic source and an insertion into an archival document but will not be too quick to ascribe the narrative in its current form to an unknown prophetic writer. The encounter between David and Nathan in this episode is so programmatic to the SN as a whole that it could not have existed without it. At the same time, the theological undertones of the pronouncement of punishment for sins committed against Yhwh and Yhwh's abundant mercy expressed in forgiveness are very appropriate for the exiled nation of the sixth century and akin to the work of the Dtr. The narrative is composite and may have originated from a prophetic cycle, but it is the hand of the Dtr that has made it what it is.

What we have inherited in the masoretic text is a uniform material stretching from chapter ten to twelve, which I have termed the mediate context. On a closer inspection, the text, viewed as an archaeological field of investigation, reveals three strata of materials which have been assembled together to produce a single unit and is therefore composite in nature. I will like to demonstrate the various strata that constitute the block with the help of a graphic reconstruction:

---

[23] P. K. McCarter, *II Samuel*, p. 306.

```
        A                                              A¹
    ┌───────┐                                       ┌───────┐
    │ 2 Sam │                                       │ 2 Sam │
    │10:1-11:1│     B                      B¹       │12:26-31│
    └───────┘  ┌───────┐                ┌───────┐   └───────┘
               │ 2 Sam │                │ 2 Sam │
               │11:2-27│       C        │12:15b-25│
               └───────┘   ┌───────┐    └───────┘
                           │ 2 Sam │
                           │12:1-15a│
                           └───────┘
```

A → War with the Ammonites: David *sends* Joab and the men (10:1-11:1)

    B → David and Bathsheba: David *sends* for Bathsheba (11:2-27)

        C → David and Nathan: Yhwh *sends* Nathan to David (12:1-15a)

    B¹ → David and Bathsheba (Nathan); the death of the son (12:15b-25)

A¹ → Victory of Israel over the Ammonites; Joab *sends* for David (12:26-31)

The panoramic view picks out three possibly independent strata of materials that have been assembled together by an author to tell a story in a composite manner. That there was war between Israel and Ammon is a normal aspect of the natural process of growth among two neighbouring nation states in ancient times. Any attempt by Israel to increase her territory towards the east meant an inevitable encroachment upon the sovereignty of Ammon and the latter's desire to expand towards the west would fall into the same category. The only thing that could have prevented war between the two neighbours was the existence of a peace treaty like the one that supposedly was established between David and Nahash to which David alludes in 2 Sam 10:2. As it was consummate with ancient monarchical propaganda, accounts of various wars were kept in the archives of the palace or temple. Thus the narrator of the biblical stories may have had access to some kind of materials of this nature from the archives of the kingdom given that they were extant.[24] In any case, the manner in which the narrator has split the war account into two and inserted the palace romance is, in my opinion, an indication of a pre-existing war document. The second stratum carefully picks up the story-line that delineates the pedigree of Solomon (2 Sam 11:1-27, 12:15b-25). If Solomon inherited David as king of Israel, from the narrative point of view, there will be no doubt that his parentage was of public interest. Above all, the rivalry that surrounded his enthronement (1 Kings 1) could have sustained the interest in the story of the new king's family background in both directions as a negative publicity or a legitimization of his reign. Should the negative aspects of the story have filtered out into the public domain it could never have beeen ironed out under the false pretense of loyalty to the king and would have remained an established part of the history. A later writer with such a story at his disposal, whether oral or written, would have the liberty to reproduce it as it was or to alter it to suit his own purpose.

The third stratum (2 Sam 12:1-15a) which has caused a lot of discussions over the years might also have purposely been fixed at its present location as the consequence to the palace romance.[25] It does, however, not

---

24 M. Noth, *Überlieferungsgeschichtliche Studien*, p. 62. Martin Noth states that the Dtr author had information about Saul, David and Solomon at his disposal and did not have to compose the materials himself. This takes it for granted that the materials were handy. There is no particular reason why the author would not resort to such a source of material if it was extant. What is difficult to assume is the existence of such annals in the early monarchical period. The probability would be that different interest groups, like the prophetic schools, kept materials that served their purpose.

25 Regine Hunziker-Rodewald notes that the structure of 2 Sam 10-12 portrays a *Mehrfachtransparenz in verschiedenen Erzählfenstern* that develops in three levels the theological concept of sin and punishment. In the first level David is drawn into a failed diplomatic relationship (10:1-19, 12:26-31) which leads to a war from which David emerges the victor. The second window opens with David embroiled in a crisis of adultery that leads to the insinuated death of Uriah, the wronged husband (11:1-12:25). The story parallels the first window but portrays David as the culprit who still emerges victorious as regards the birth of Solomon. The third window (12:1-15a) focuses on a *religiös-rechtlicher Art*. Here, the failed behaviour of the second window is with the help of a parable judged as sin with the death penalty as its result. The language and direction of this centre piece (12:1-15a) is doggedly theological and will later be made

need to be later than the writer who placed the romance into the framework of the Ammonite war. The parable of Nathan (2 Sam 12:1-4), the preamble to the oracle (v. 7-9), and the double oracle of doom (v. 10-12) look back upon the whole life story of David and project it into the future in a bird's eye view, summing it up by so doing. The encounter between David and Nathan serves not only as a hinge upon which the narrative hangs and oscillates but also as a propelling factor of the whole. It is a necessary moral intervention flowing from the fact that the author, in section B→B¹, has not portrayed David as a despot, but rather as a culprit, caught in a tight corner. The encounter with Nathan portrays David as a very pious servant of God who knows when and how to bow to the divine ruling in repentance and is acceptable to God. At the same time it makes clear the relationship between God and his people; not even the great King David himself can escape divine punishment for his sins, but the mercy of God lasts forever despite human weakness and failure. This dominant message of the narrative is revealed only through the instrumentality of the prophet of Yhwh as the mediator between the king and his divine benefactor. He exercises an authority over and above the king and can bring him to acknowledge his guilt. Such a material would have been cherished and protected within the prophetic circles or schools.[26] The question that remains unanswered is, "Which author may have placed it at its present location as part of the elaborate scheme and programme of the project that seeks to provide meaning to the historical enigma of Israel in exile?" Since the author of the Chronicles knew of the tradition but chose to avoid narrating the double crime of David; adultery and murder, 1 Chr 20:1-2, the current author could also have done the same, but he chose to do otherwise. In this work, I will defend the theory that the deuteronomistic author (without going into the various stages of redaction) has carefully reworked

---

clear (in the light of the death of Amnon, Absalom, Adonijah and the Absalom revolt) that it is all about the theme of Sin and its meaning in the context of the dynasty. David and his dynasty emerge out of this third conflict with a negative promise. Cf. Die Beiden Söhne, Sprache, Sinn und Geshchichte in 2 Sam 10-12, in C. Schäfer-Lichtenberger, *Die Samuelbücher*, p. 97.

[26] Prophetic schools have existed as early as the days of Samuel and Saul, according to the Biblical tradition; 1 Sam 10:10, 19:20. The phenomenon continues especially in the days of Elisha, 2 Kings 2:3, 5.

a narrative material that he may have picked from a prophetic source and inserted it into the history that he had set himself to narrate (DtrH). In doing so, he has deftly re-touched the material to make it fit perfectly into the whole on both ideological and semantic levels.

A graphic presentation of the David-Bathsheba-Uriah sequence

a. The single blocks

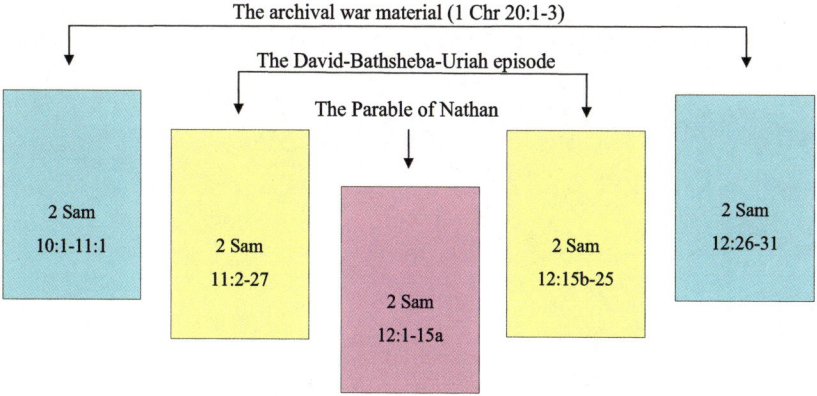

b. The blocks as they are presented in the sequence

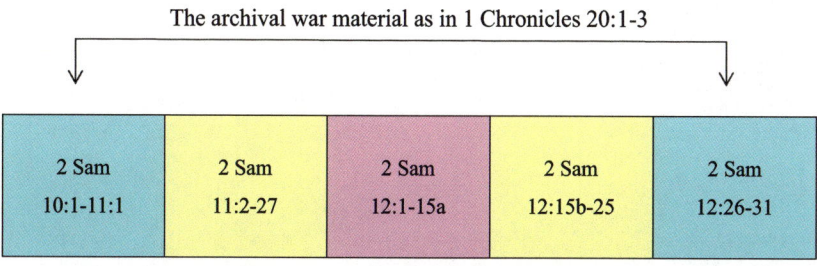

Chapter 2. Status Questionis

The epoch-making thesis of Martin Noth in the mid-twentieth century has made a great impact upon the study of the sources of Biblical traditions. It was Noth who first coined the term "Deuteronomist" as the author behind the tradition stretching from Joshua to 2 Kings because of the writer's affinity in language and world view to the Deuteronomistic law and to the paranetic speeches that frame it.[27] He identified this author with the siglum *Dtr* and the completed work he termed "deuteronomistische Geschichtswerk", *DtrG*, translated into English as Deuteronomistic History – *DtrH*.[28] This author (or group of writers, as will come to be known later), made a great capital of the image and role of David in the over-all plan of Yhwh for His people in the unfolding of the history. The image of

---

27 Martin Noth, *Überlieferungsgeschichtliche Studien*, Dritte Auflage, p. 4.
28 It is speculated that after the fall of Samaria and the deportation of Israel to Assyria in 721 BC certain groups of refugees, especially from prophetic circles, who fled to Judah, carried along with them traditions that emphasized the worship of Yhwh alone as the condition for survival against the growing threat of the rising super powers. The new ideologies that developed alongside this mode of thinking attracted the sympathy of Levites, nobles, priests, etc (so, Norbert Lohfink, *deuteronomistische Bewegung*, p. 359) who began a project of compiling the history of Israel with a strong emphasis upon obedience to the law as the condition for survival. The morale of the group was boosted by the discovery of a copy of an earlier form of Deuteronomy (11-26?) in the temple and the reform that King Josiah undertook in obedience to the law in 622 (2 Kings 22). This reform was embraced as the heroic act of repentance and reconciliation that was to temper the wrath of Yhwh with mercy and the King became the hero of the group which now grew into a movement that is in contemporary Biblical studies known as Deuteronomism or Deuteronomistic Movement or School. The name "Deuteronomist" was coined by Martin Noth in his *Überlieferungsgeschichtliche Studien* and refers to "an author" (p. 11) of the 6th century who considered the catastrophe of Israel as a nation and the destruction of Jerusalem as a foregone conclusion; a just punishment from Yhwh. The work of this writer, according to Noth, begins with Deuteronomy and runs through to the Second Book of Kings; with the Deuteronomic law as the basic and governing principle of the whole history, hence deuteronomistische Geschichtswerk (DtrG) or Deuteronomistic History (DtrH). Where Noth identifies a single author, modern research posits a group of writers or a Deuteronomistic School that carried out the work in stages possibly before, during and after the exile.

King David, the founder of the Jerusalem dynasty, which emerges from the DtrH and indeed from the entire biblical tradition, is one that commands admiration, if not envy. He is referred to as the servant of God (2 Sam 7:5 cf. Ps 89:20), a man after God's own heart (1 Sam 13:14), the bearer of the promise of an eternal kingdom (2 Sam 7:16), a king who walked in the ways of the Lord without turning left or right (1 Kings 15:5?); an idealised perfection of a king who then becomes the yardstick with which to measure subsequent kings of Israel and Judah. This image is virtually tainted by David's adultery with Bathsheba, the wife of Uriah, at the time when the soldier is at the war front, defending the honour of the kingdom, and the subsequent murder of the same upon the explicit instruction of the king (2 Sam 11). The debasement of David culminates in the confrontation with Nathan, who brings the king to his knees with the double prophecy of doom (2 Sam 12:1-15a) captured as the single stain on the otherwise purely white page of David's life; *"For David did what was right in the eyes of Yhwh and did not turn aside from anything that he commanded him all the days of his life, except in the matter of Uriah the Hittite"* (1 Kings 15:5).

Logically, the status of chapters 11 and 12 has been in the limelight of exegetical discussions over the years with three basic questions generally surfacing: Do these two chapters fit into the unity of the material within which they are found? Who may have composed the narrative found in them? And what purpose do they serve? These questions can adequately be answered only in the context of the broader narrative within which the chapters are found. In the *Überlieferungsgeschichtliche Studien*, Martin Noth employs the redactional critical method to his study of the Books of Samuel and places them within the overarching Deuteronomistic historical work. He posits that such narrative traditions like the rise of David and the question of succession to his throne, among others, predate the Dtr and that author only had to re-order, present and preserve them in his work.[29] The block of material stretching from 2 Sam 9-20 and 1 Kings 1-2 has been variously termed *"Succession Narrative"* (in line with the thinking of Martin Noth and the subsequent research of Leonhard Rost) or *"Court*

---

29 M. Noth, Überlieferung, p. 62.

History" (as John Van Seters would have it). The corpus narrates the story of the succession to the throne of David or the family life at the court of the Jerusalem dynasty. A good number of researchers postulate that the Succession Narrative is a Solomon-friendly narrative stemming from the early years of Solomon's reign.[30] If this were the case, the narrative would require not only a Solomon-friendly but also a David-friendly material to establish the background to the successor of the celebrated throne. Thus 2 Sam 11 and 12 fall completely out of tune with the surrounding narrative and even run the risk of presenting Solomon as the illegitimate son of David and Bathsheba. This difficulty makes the presence of 12:1-25 a necessity but that only succeeds in saving the dignity of Solomon by presenting David in a bad light. In a work like the SN, where the natural course of events is subtly made to define Divine will, it is only here (12:1-15a) that David stands directly condemned by a prophet. The prophetic oracle of judgment pronounced by Nathan denigrates the character of the principal actor whose status the author has gone to every extent to purify in order to keep him blameless. Could one and the same author idealize a character and turn round with the same vigour to smear him in such an outright manner? What driving force could there have been for such an apparent double standard? Following the example of Nowack, many textual analysts would appeal to a secondary addition to the text for an explanation or even a double redaction.[31]

The proponents of the "Court History" (CH), on the other hand, consider the narrative a late work possibly of the post-exilic period of an anti-monarchical group to counteract the idealization of David.[32] It is a unified

---

30 L. Rost, Succession, p. 105, Other modern researchers like Roger N. Whybray (Succession Narrative, p. 53), Arnold A Anderson (2 Samuel p. 166) and Erhard Blum (Geschichtschreibung, p. 22–23) among others share this position.
31 D. W. Nowack, *Richter, Ruth u. Bücher Samuelis*, p. 194: Already in 1902, Nowack had relegated the Nathan pericope of 2 Sam 12:1-15a to the level of a later addition with a further notice that the Nathan-David dialogue itself had seen various stages of redaction.
32 This is the direction of John Van Seters especially summed up in his contribution, *The Court History and DtrH; Conflicting Perspectives on the House of David*, in Albert de Pury – T. Römer, Die Sogenannte Thronfolgegeschichte Davids, OBO 176 (2000) 70-93.

text with the aim of sabotaging the monarchy in general and King David in particular. It is a post-Dtr addition to the history of David from the postexilic period. In this period, the theme of divine promise to David in 2 Sam 7 tended to develop into an "eternal covenant" with strong messianic overtones and the Court History emerged as an anti-thesis, an antimessianic tendency in certain Jewish circles to counteract this development.[33] The reactions of various authors in the past decades to the two chapters and especially to 12:1-15a demonstrate how perplexing and nagging this short narrative piece is and can be. From whichever angle one would like to look at the material the analyst should of no account lose sight of the fact that whether SN or CH, the work belongs to a bigger unit that is identified as the deuteronomistic history (DtrH).

Various methodological approaches have been employed in the bid to answer the nagging questions posed by the confrontation between Nathan and David and naturally, different conclusions have been drawn depending upon the particular method used and the interest of the exegete in question. The one point at which most exegetes converge is the fact that whatever method one chooses, the single units of the text must be identified before one can effectively analyse it. Thus literary criticism becomes the currently undisputed base and foundation upon which all other methods build.[34]

2.1 The Literal Critical Approach (diachronic) to 2 Sam 12:1-15a

The literal critical method studies the text-witness from the point of view that a given text has, over the years, been worked upon by various authors and redactors who have left their visible marks on it. Among such notable signs are doublets and repetitions in a seemingly unified text, conflict of names of persons or of places, unmotivated change of characters or subjects and parallel texts, which depend one upon the other. The literal critic considers such contradictions and inconsistencies as indications of the process

---

33 J. Van Seters, *In Search of History*, New Haven & London, 1983, p. 290.
34 W. Richter considers literary criticism as the first in the rung of methods used in the analysis of the Biblical text. The separation of the single units is obligatory and a necessity for a meaningful critical research into the text at our disposal. cf. W. Richter, Exegese, p. 33 and J. Werlitz, Studien, pp. 43–44.

of growth within that text.[35] Consequently, literal criticism begins with a diligent separation of the composite parts of a text to find out which unit is old and which young. The result is the reconstructed unity of small passages that can be identified as "original" and the later additions that are considered redactions; second or third degree. The methodology of the literary critic, simply put, is the ascertaining of the internal arrangement of a chosen text to find out its themes, structure and literary units with the view to finding their relationships, whether thematic, formal, chronological or haphazard. This might lead to the discovery of a conflation of terminologies, logical or thematic, and inconsistencies within the text that may be the result of an interruption, digression or a sudden change in style.[36] In such an instance, the basic idea of a text could be abandoned, lost or reaffirmed later. In many instances, what constitutes a binding ligament of a late text to its environment may be an introduction, conclusion, a framework or just a carefully worded sentence or two that depend upon the artistic competence of the sacred writer for their expected effect.

The work of **Julius Wellhausen** is often seen as the culmination of Old Testament critical scholarship of the two centuries preceding him, and this is particularly true in the realm of double narratives in his *Prolegomena zur Geschichte Israels* (1883).[37] We can, therefore, talk of literary criticism as a separation of sources, with regard to the Pentateuch, in line with the thought of the Wellhausen school or classical literary criticism in the manner in which Wellhausen applied the method to Biblical studies and thus to the history of Israel. He is to all intents and purposes a pioneer in the application of the method to the study of the Bible as a whole without it being his brain child.

In consonance with the prevalent tendency of Biblical scholarship, consummate with the current of his day, Wellhausen considers our block of narratives as a unified work with identifiable internal inconsistencies due

---

35 Klaus Koch defines Literary criticism as "Biblische Bücher analysieren unter Beachtung von fehlender Gedankenverbindung, Doppelungen, Widersprüchen und individuellem Sprachgebrauch mit dem Ziel, den Anteil der einzelnen Verfasser und Redaktoren sowie Ort und Zeit der Entstehung genau abzugrenzen" (cf. *Formgeschichte*, p. 87).
36 N. Habel, *Literary Criticism*, p. 6–7.
37 A. Nahkola, *Double Narratives*, p. 12.

to various stages of redaction. In his view, 2 Sam 12:1-15a provide a very good example of difficulties in Biblical texts that result from redactions and the loss of text parts in the process of transmission. With v. 13 as his point of departure, Wellhausen isolates vv. 10-12 as a later addition to the text that rather disrupts the flow of the narrative and constitutes a discordant note in the block on the basis of the following reasons:

a. v. 13 is too abrupt to be the natural follow-up to vv. 10-12.
b. v. 13 would smoothly follow v. 9 without the interruption of vv. 10-12.

He finds the sudden change of mood and tone in the message of Nathan too abrupt and consequently, unnatural. How could the prophet in one and the same breath pronounce judgment and forgiveness just for the fact that David acknowledges his guilt? He draws attention to the dialogue of Saul and Samuel in a similar circumstance in I Sam 15:24 and posits the loss of a part of the discourse as a reason proven by the *"pisqa"* in the middle of the verse (v. 13).

Wellhausen further notes that, whereas the גם (*gam*) of v. 13b is a logical and direct response to the words of David, in v. 13a the לא תמות (*lo tamuth*) at the end of the verse, however, does not reflect in any way the death threats of vv. 10-12. Besides, v. 14 puts the death sentence on the child while the double threat of vv. 10-12 is to come upon David. Finally, he suggests that העביר חטאת is meaningful only in the context of לא תמות and the death of the child, predicted in v. 14 as a transfer of the punishment. Without vv. 10-12 v. 13 follows naturally from v. 9, but 10-12 have no basis without their actual and direct fulfilment in the subsequent chapters; Absalom's revolt. The double oracle of vv. 10-12, therefore, depends upon the revolt of Absalom; it breaks the flow of the narrative and is definitely a secondary addition to the text.[38]

The presence of the *pisqa* in the middle of the verse does not necessarily need to be interpreted as an indication of an extinct piece from the verse. It could be a logical separation of two distinct and complete sentences without breaking the flow of thought. It is not for nothing that most manuscripts, including the LXX, omit the interval. The risk here is that one could lean so much on one side or the other as to make a capital of a non-existent

---

38 J. Wellhausen, *Bücher Samuelis*, p. 184.

reason and lose the sense of the text as a whole. What matters here is that the Biblical author is using the material at his disposal to transmit a fact in his own manner and words. What we might have to look at is what he intends to carry across to his audience with the swift pronouncement of forgiveness based upon the acceptance of guilt and what that would mean to his historical audience.

The לא תמות (you shall not die) of v. 13 certainly raises the eyebrows of any careful reader of the text. In the oracle, the prophet does not refer to the death of David on account of his sins. It is, therefore, awkward that he absolves him from a death penalty. From the onset, Wellhausen's argument is sound, but it loses its credibility and force if one considers the text synchronically. David is guilty of two basic sins; adultery and murder. Either of these two sins carries the death penalty as a just punishment according to Israelite law (Ex 21:12, Deut 22:22). The direct audience of the double oracle of doom, David, might have been very much aware of the enormity of his sins even as the larger audience; the exilic Jew.[39] In any case, by pronouncing judgment upon "the man" of the parable, David had condemned himself to death and warranted the absolution of the prophet. That the child born to David out of the adultery should die may also not be out of place. In the first oracle (v. 7b-10) the sword would not depart from the "house" of David and in the second (v. 11-12) evil would be brought upon the same "house". The innocent little baby forms part of that house and is a result of the sin in question. His death is, therefore, not contradictory to the oracles of doom even if one finds it unjust.

The earlier part of the 20th century saw a great stride in the study of Biblical literature. The work of Wellhausen triggered a high degree of interest in the Nathan pericope of 2 Sam 12 leading to **Friedrich Schwally's** apt comments that v. 15b provides no indication of a knowledge of the double oracle of Nathan and that the character of Nathan himself in this chapter is too much at variance with his role in I Kings 1.[40] **Wilhelm Nowack** questioned the unity of the narrative that deals with the succession of David along the lines of Wellhausen. He identified 2 Sam 12:1-15a, not only as a

---

[39] The law prescribes death for the sin of adultery as well as murder: Lev 20:10, Num 35:16-27, Deut 19:12-13.
[40] F. Schwally, *Der Profet Nathan*, p. 153.

later addition to the narrative, but also as exhibiting various stages of internal redaction. In his opinion, vv. 1-15a are the work of a later hand that did not consider the death of the child sufficient punishment for David's misdeed against Uriah and, therefore, added the dialogue to concretize the punishment. This was necessitated by the fact that David's behaviour in vv. 15bff does not portray any sign of repentance and humility on the part of David but only penance for the sake of obtaining mercy from God. Even though vv. 1-15a have the same motif, the text is constructed by different authorial hands and the interpolation of v. 10-12 was later added to the block to make the series of murder in the house of David and Absalom's revolt the appropriate punishment for the adultery with Bathsheba. All the same, the inconsistency in the text is not resolved by these additions because Nathan's absolution of David from death (v. 13) does not have anything to do with the threat of vv. 10-12 nor does it change the import of the death of the child (v. 14) as the only punishment meted out to David.[41] **Hugo Gressmann** further identified the existence of a loose collection of short individual component narratives like sagas, historical narratives, anecdotes, annals, legends and prophecies in the books of Samuel. He was fascinated by the uniqueness of the David-Bathsheba episode and singled it out as a single unit that he termed a *"novella"* and the appearance of Nathan on the scene as a later addition based on an old motif with a new twist.[42] The war narrative, states Gressmann, is an older tradition that the author has used as a frame work and into which he has inserted the novella. So far, all the literal critics are in accord on the point that the encounter between David and Nathan (12:1-15a) is the work of a later writer and that vv. 10-12 were still later added to the episode.

In this climate of intellectual fertility, **Leonhard Rost**, in 1926, would find a harmony between *Wahrheit und Dichtung* (fact and fiction) in what he would appropriately call the "Succession Narrative", as in the case of the work of any *künstlerisch empfindenden Geschichtsschreibers* (artistically sensitive history writer). Rost was very much influenced by the work of his contemporary, Gressmann, but followed a different line of thought

---

41 D. W. Nowack, *Bücher Samuelis*, p. 194.
42 H. Gressmann, *Geschichtsschreibung und Prophetie*, p. XIff (cf. also *Narrative and Novella*, p. 9ff).

in finding the existence of a few extensive unitary narratives put together in the books of Samuel and Kings. In his view, 2 Sam 9-20 and 1 Kings 1-2 form a single unit recounting the story behind the succession to the throne of David written by a member of the royal court, possibly, in the early years of Solomon's reign. In a later work in 1982, he rightly and carefully retraces the "history" with 1 Kings 1 as his starting point. With Solomon as the hero and successor to the throne of David, Rost works backwards through the story at the background of the succession (2 Sam 13-20) to the background of the hero (2 Sam 11-12).

Rost thinks along the same wavelength as his predecessor, Wellhausen, but goes a step further in his coming to the conclusion that it is not just the double prophecy of doom in 2 Sam 12:10-12 that is to be considered a secondary addition to the text, but rather the oracles of vv. 7b–10 and 11-12 are both a later addition to the Succession Narrative.[43] Comparing the parable of Nathan to that of the widow of Tekoa, Rost posits that the narrator of the latter (2 Sam 14) "clings fast to the basic idea of the story, namely, the necessity in certain circumstances of stopping a blood feud in order to preserve a line weakened by fratricide."[44] In the former, however, he finds the obvious interest in the poor man in so far as he is the owner of the sheep and the emphasis is on the rich man's action of robbing the poor man of his lamb rather than on the suffering of the poor man. Strangely enough, the subsequent punishment is based upon the death of Uriah by the sword. "Hence it is hardly probable that... the same narrator could have handled the basic idea of that parable so cavalierly. As a consequence we will have to delete vv. 7b-10."[45] The second threat (vv. 11-12), Rost further notes, finds an exact fulfilment when Absalom approached his father's concubines upon the advice of Ahitophel and must also be deleted, being a later insertion.

In the opinion of Rost, the long-winded speeches weaken the impact of the parable and its blazing judgment which are followed by the short crushing "You are the man." David's acknowledgement of his guilt; *I have sinned against the Lord*; (v. 13) warrants the promise of forgiveness and

---

[43] L. Rost, *Thronnachfolge Davids*, p. 99.
[44] L. Rost, *Succession*, p. 75.
[45] L. Rost, *Succession*, p. 75.

the death of the child because he has despised the Lord (v. 14) suffices as his punishment. Rost concludes: "We can thus see that the Nathan pericope in chapter 12 includes vv. 1-7a, 13-15a."[46] As his point of departure is 1 Kings 1 and the succession of David his aim, Rost logically adds vv. 15b-25 to this block as providing the background to the hero of the narrative, Solomon. He thus isolates vv. 7b-12 as the work of a redactor.

Rost considers the death of the child rather inconsistent with the sense of the parable, because the sheep as the victim of the parable corresponds to the woman in the real life situation, not the child (nor Uriah). The redactor of the text has sought with the death of the child to emphasize that the sin of David has been forgiven and its guilt already punished. Therefore, Solomon's birth as the high point of the story could be announced on the joyful note; "*Und Jahve liebte ihn*" (And Yahweh loved him).[47] Gerhard von Rad recognizes three prophecies of doom in the episode by the addition of the death of the child to the list and affirms that "of the three prophecies of doom (vv. 7-10, 11-12, 14), probably only the last is original: God will forgive David his sin, but the child must die."[48] He, however, does not devote much time to our pericope as he focuses on the SN as a whole.

Identifying an insertion is one thing but deleting it is another. What will be left of the Biblical text if every so-called secondary material is deleted? Who judges what material is to be considered secondary and upon what criteria; objective or subjective? Separating an insertion from an "original" material calls for a clear identification of what is added, written, and what was before, oral. Traditions as sources in Biblical scholarship are some of the most slippery areas of study as they are very difficult, if at all possible, to identify and to separate. Oral and written traditions could exist at one and the same time and develop parallel to each other without any difficulty at all. Moreover, the Biblical material, whether oral or written, predates the Biblical writer himself, and how he presents it is his personal ingenuity as a writer. The modern scholar equipped with modern technology has to tread his ground with great care as one can not easily enter into the mind-set of the ancient writer.

---

46 L. Rost, op cit., p. 77.
47 L. Rost, *Thronnachfolge*, p. 98.
48 G. von Rad, *Hexateuch*, p. 179.

Rost rightly compares the story of the widow of Tekoa with the parable of Nathan, because they are of the same genre and are found in a single corpus, but concludes that the two stories could not have been produced by a single writer. In his view the author stuck diligently to the basic idea of the second story (2 Sam 14), but handled that of the first (2 Sam 12) "cavalierly". On one hand, the family of the widow is both the culprit and the victim. The narrative makes it clear that the murder occurred in a fight but does not indicate whether it was calculated or accidental. She now petitions the king to put aside the just operation of the law by pardoning her fratricidal son in order to save her endangered family line. The practical effect of the story was to secure the king's pardon for the estranged prince, Absalom, and ensure his reinstatement. The parable of Nathan, on the other, portrays David as the culprit and Uriah the victim. The underpinning is the unscrupulousness of the rich man who does not only take (steal) from the poor without remorse but also kills with impudence. The purpose is to get the king pass judgement on the rich man and convict himself in so doing. The deftly narrated story achieves its purpose within a very short narrative space as compared to the later story of the widow of Tekoa. The parable of Nathan does not fail in any way in serving its purpose.

It must be noted that the apparent inconsistencies in the story come about only in its application to the real life situation of the primary audience. This would mean that one considers the narrative an allegory. The modern analyst creates the problem for himself if he decides to let the story fit into his modern models. If the writer intended to compose an allegory, he could very well have done that. The question that arises is whether the parable has always been in the form we have it today or that a later writer took over the story and expanded it to fit into his programme. It is probable that a later writer has reworked an older material by reshaping it to fit into a broader whole, rather than the material itself being a later composition.

Rost further finds the two prophecies of doom rather long-winded, a disruption in the flow of the narrative and inconsequent upon David's acceptance of his guilt and his absolution by the prophet. In this sense he technically distances himself from his predecessor, Wellhausen. Where the former would seek an intervening discourse that may have over the years been lost, the latter would quickly join the verses (v.7a and 13) together as a natural and logical follow up. The veritable question is: Are the two oracles pronounced by the prophet Nathan just long-winded and serving only to weaken the crushing impact of the blazing "*You are the man*" and its subsequent candid response "*I have sinned against the Lord*", as purported by Rost? In a logical sequence, the conclusion can always be proven if it is deduced before the premises are constructed. Once the starting point of Rost is the succession of Solomon to the throne of David, the oracles come to be seen as a preparation for that event. Solomon was a young, hitherto unknown prince who emerged as the heir after all the other elegible princes had removed one another or got sidelined to pave the way for the young son to sit on the throne of his father. The royal blood-bath is explained as a retribution for the sins of David put into the mouth of the prophet Nathan by a later redactor of the text, a member of Solomon's court, as a preparation for the appearance of the young prince on the scene. The argument holds water but loses sight of a very significant point; the form of prophetic oracles in the DtrH. Does this so-called monarchy-friendly writer of Rost have anything to do with the Dtr? The SN as a unity is found within a bigger unit of texts with its own definite plan and programme that extends wider than just the succession to the throne of David even though the Davidic dynasty plays a central role in the work that is referred to as the deuteronomistic history (DtrH). I will pick up this issue in the third chapter of this work.

Rost's position that the death of the child is inconsistent with the sense of the parable is a very legitimate remark except that the death of the child does not need to be consistent with the parable as it has nothing directly to do with it. The child has no correspondence in the parable; he is the result of the adultery committed by David, and not the stolen and slaughtered object of the parable (the lamb). The parable, as we have it, is tailored to capture the adultery (stealing) and killing (murder) perpetrated by David, not the result of that criminal act. The death of the child is particularly and emphatically proclaimed only at the end of the encounter as part of the punishment that would come upon the house of David. It is unfortunate to the modern mind that the innocent child had to die for the sins of his father but so was the case. In the mind-set of the ancient Semitic world is the child, the result of the sin and an embodiment of it. His death would play a very important role in the expiation of the sin, generally, and in this particular case, as a punishment for it. The announcement of the birth of Solomon in vv. 24-25 comes almost as an appendix to the text and not as the central message of the narrative. Much as we do not have to play down the stylistic flare of the biblical author in keeping his audience in suspense and releasing the necessary information only at the rightful moment, I will definitely not toe the line of Rost in making the two verses the climax of the whole narrative. The birth of Solomon is, arguably, a major point of the story but it does not constitute the climax of it as it recedes into the background. Such a view will make the narrative a biography of Solomon instead of the failed behaviour of David in contrast to God's faithfulness and mercy towards His servant.[49]

The literal critic is certainly right in identifying discordant notes in the parable of Nathan and its application in the real life situation; the lamb dies in the parable but Bathsheba lives in the real life. In her stead, Uriah is murdered and the child dies as a punishment. If one wishes to do justice to such inconsistencies then the questions posed by Werlitz in his analysis of discordant notes in Biblical texts[50] must be carefully considered. The following are some of them:

1. Does discord in a text prove without doubt a historical development within it?
2. Does every discord point to a process of redaction?
3. Is incoherence a sign of the growth in a text or the weakness of a writer or a legitimate stylistic effect worked out by a particular writer?
4. Does the swift change of characters always denote a redaction? (What about the ingenuity of the author?)

---

49 The whole Issue about the death of the child is also the question of the legitimacy of Solomon as the heir to the throne of David. If the child lived, then who was he? If he died then he could not have been Solomon. P. K. McCarter maintains that 12:25-31, like 10:1-19 and 11:1, derives from contemporary (Davidic) annalistic sources and was probably added to the David-Bathsheba-Uriah story by a prophetic writer who then affixed the whole (chapters 10-12) to the account of Absalom's rebellion (chapters 13-20) as a kind of theological preface despite being anachronistic since the siege of Rabbah may have taken place after Absalom's revolt. Cf. II Samuel, pp. 275–276.
50 J. Werlitz, *Studien zur Literarkritischen Methode* (BZAW 204) Berlin, 1992, p. 46.

Between the time of Rost and what we may consider the next big name on the rung of literary criticism, Ernst Würthwein, appeared the groundbreaking work of Martin Noth, who identified an authorial unity of texts stretching from the books of Joshua and Judges through Samuel to Kings. This anonymous writer or group of redactors he called the "Deuteronomist" (Dtr) because of the close resemblance in thought and language to the Deuteronomic law and the admonitory speeches that precede that law.[51] This writer, states Martin Noth, had a rich variety of material covering the reigns of Saul, David and Solomon, such as "the story of the rise of David and the story of the question of David's succession[52], compiled long before him and all at his disposal. The task of a good author in such a circumstance then would be to organise or reorganise the materials by trimming the edges to fit into his preferred scheme or programme. So was the project of the Deuteronomistic author or school that produced the "Deuteronomistic History" (DtrH). The identification of the work of the Deuteronomist (DtrH) as a unified narrative within which the SN is located provided Würthwein with an added advantage over his predecessors.

Equipped with the propositions of Rost and Noth, **Ernst Würthwein** works with the background information of the existence of a DtrH within which is located the SN. He sums up the works of Rost and von Rad as follows; *the whole purpose of the SN, written at the beginning of the reign of Solomon by a member of his court, was "ad maiorem gloriam Salomonis".*[53] In the David-Bathsheba-Uriah episode the author expertly keeps his disapproval at the background and weaves the story through to its high point "...and she bore a son, and he named him Solomon" (2 Sam 12:24). The rest of the verse with v. 25, he considers a secondary addition coming from a monarchy-friendly source.

Würthwein considers Uriah carrying his own death warrant common place in legends, fairy tales and dramas in which the author of the letter is the despot who seeks the death of his trusting messenger and, at the same time, the perceived adversary. In this wise, David is portrayed as an

---

51 M. Noth, *Überlieferungsgeschichtliche Studien*, p. 4.
52 M. Noth, *Überlieferung*, p. 62.
53 E. Würthwein, *Thronfolge*, p. 7.

oriental despot.[54] There is nothing positive in the whole SN with its succession of murders and intrigue that reaches its apex in the shrewd moves of Bathsheba and Nathan coupled with Solomon's elimination of his opponents to the throne.[55]

Würthwein names 2 Sam 12:1-15a among the materials that he considers pre-dtr but with nomistic or prophetic additions for the purpose of transmitting them in a new light.[56] In an earlier work, he strikes out the Nathan pericope from the SN as a later political work based upon an older tradition with a theological purpose; the king has repented and God has forgiven him.[57] He thus differentiates the anti-monarchical SN that he, like his predecessors, dates in the early years of the monarchy from the pro-Davidic exilic theological concept of the ideal king.[58] Würthwein intimates that the idealisation of David is later than the SN and SN has the aim of discrediting David, his sons and Bathsheba, his favourite wife.[59]

Familiarity with Biblical narratives regarding the stature and role of David as compared to that of Solomon in the history of Israel raises a basic and logical question: Who at all will belittle David in such a manner *ad maiorem Salomonis gloriam*? Reacting to this question, Würthwein suggests that the idealization of David is a late exilic concept and does not reflect the *status quo* at the time of Solomon's reign. Granted that this was the situation, elevating one to the detriment of the other would rather promote an anti-David tendency that would eventually have led to an anti-monarchy. Neither is it easy to accept Würthwein's view of the oriental despot in the case of David. The narrative makes David cunningly scheme to secure a legal paternity for the son of Bathsheba and resort to a detached violent approach to settle the issue only when he had drawn a blind. It is highly doubtful that an oriental despot of the calibre of David, if he were, would have gone through that kind of trouble to cover up his

---

54 E. Würthwein, *Thronfolge*, p. 23.
55 E. Würthwein, *Thronfolge*, p. 69.
56 E. Würthwein, *Deuteronomistischen Geschichtswerk*, p. 6.
57 E. Würthwein, *Thronfolge*, p. 25f.
58 W. Oswald, *Nathan der Prophet*, p. 98.
59 E. Würthwein, *Deuteronomistischen Geschichtswerk*, p. 50. In recent years, John van Seters has emerged as a lone warrior and proponent of this view point.

misdeed. The stand-point of Würthwein, however, throws a different light on the issues at stake:

a. the whole SN is anti-monarchy
b. the Nathan pericope, 12:1-15a, pre-dates the dtr but is a later addition to the SN and
c. vv. 24b-25 are secondary.[60]

Is the SN really an anti-monarchical document? If the pericope, 12:1-15a, is a later addition, then who might have incorporated the text into the narrative, and for what purpose? These questions have in the past as well as in recent years occupied the attention of many a textual analyst, beginning with the remarks of Schwally in 1892 that the presence of the pericope in its present location makes the whole text absurd. The fasting of David to implore divine mercy upon his dying son is inconsistent with the knowledge of the prophecy of Nathan that the child would die. The only acceptable explanation for this absurdity, in the opinion of Schwally, is that a late text has been forced into an earlier composition.[61] An attempt to answer the question of authorship of the pericope would require a quick look at the SN as a part of the Biblical tradition that we have inherited.

2.2 The Succession Narrative; an anti-monarchical document?

The early literary critics, like Wellhausen and Rost, do not concern themselves with whether the SN is pro or anti-monarchical; it is the presentation of historical events with a few later explanatory additions here and there. For Wellhausen, the textual unity is disturbed by the addition of 12:10-12. But once these verses are understood as a later interpolation the problem is easily resolved; chapters 13-20 constitute the heart of the narrative, while 10-12 introduce the son who would later emerge as the successor to the throne of David. The story line then narrates how the succession

---

60 Würthwein argues that the phrase "Yahweh loves" is too young to be an original part of the SN; Hosea and Jeremiah use the term for God's love for his people Israel. For individuals in the OT there are only two examples; Solomon and Cyrus in Isaiah 48:14. cf. *Thronfolge*, p. 29.
61 F. Schwally, *Der Profet Nathan*, p. 155.

slipped through the hands of Amnon, the rightful heir, to the next in line, Absalom, the usurper, to Adonija, the proud and, finally, to Solomon, the chosen one.[62] He affirms that 2 Sam 9-20 and 1 Kings 1-2 are the work of a single hand with a very good historical source material that aided the production of an objective work with a purposeful interest in particular details.[63] Rost shares the view point of his predecessor but adds 12:7b-9 to 12:10-12 as a later addition to the text.

Würthwein, on his part, sees nothing positive in the whole SN. The material presents nothing but violence, murder and intrigue in the house of David and in the early stages of the monarchy. The image of David that emerges out of the SN is the "oriental despot", whose will must be carried out even if it is at the cost of other people's lives. Strangely enough, Würthwein states, emphatically, that the narrative was to the glory of Solomon. The implication of this assertion will be that the SN is anti-David but pro-Solomon. In recent years only a few scholars seem to share this opinion but those who do so go further than those before them without necessarily identifying themselves with the literal critical method. One such modern proponent of this view is John Van Seters, (a historical critic) who prefers to call the work "Court History" instead of Succession Narrative.[64]

John Van Seters contends that the Court History is a unified work that was later added to the DtrH.[65] The Dtr epitomises David as the just and righteous ruler completely obedient to God and a model of all subsequent kings of Israel. Therefore, his inconsistent behaviour in the Court History cannot have existed before the dtr corpus. The theme of the work is anti-traditional with the fundamental purpose of calling into question the traditional royal ideology of the Davidic covenant and the picture of the good king David which is basic to that ideology.[66] In the opinion of Van Seters, the Court History is a bitter attack upon the whole royal ideology of a "sure house for David" which simply had David peacefully succeed Saul

---

62 J. Wellhausen, *Hexateuchs*, p. 256–257.
63 J. Wellhausen, *Hexateuchs*, p. 259.
64 In two works of 1974 and 2000 Van Seters claims that this block of material is the court history of David with the question of succession forming only a small unit within it.
65 J. Van Seters, *In Search of History*, p. 282.
66 J. Van Seters, *Court History of David*, p. 22–23.

at the invitation of the northern tribes instead of the political scheming, assassinations and direct military action. David is portrayed in the Court History as a moral and spiritual weakling who does not fight the battles of Yahweh, but takes the wife of his brave warrior while the Ark is at the battle front; a man whose house is nothing but a den of turmoil and intrigue, infidelity and murder, hate and suspicion. Along the same path trodden by his father, Solomon dubiously succeeds David after a palace blood bath. If one should lift out the Court History from the Biblical narratives the dtr story will stand undisturbed with Nathan's promise of the dynasty coming after David's wars and in his old age and Solomon smoothly succeeding him to build the Temple, the moving factor and apex of that promise.

Van Seters explains that the Court History is a post dtr addition to the history of David from the post-exilic period. It is a product of an anti-messianic tendency in certain Jewish circles of that time to counteract the development of the divine promise to David in 2 Sam 7 into an "eternal covenant" with strong messianic overtones.[67] It is the figment of the imagination of an author contrived as a slap in the face of the otherwise impeccable dtr image of the ideal king David. The Court History is a clear anti-monarchical document of the exilic period. 2 Samuel 12:1-15a, maintains Van Seters, is the work of the same author of the David-Bathsheba episode and no amount of fiddling can make it a later addition or the work of a redactor. Nathan's intervention puts David on the same level as the other kings like Saul and Ahab, condemned by the Dtr for doing "what was evil in the eyes of the Lord".[68]

P. Kyle McCarter takes a different view of the issue. He finds in the SN an original Solomonic succession story to which chapters 10-12 were later added. "The introduction of the story of David and Bathsheba into the larger narrative in a position immediately preceding the old account of Absalom's rebellion was the contribution of a writer who interpreted the disastrous events of chapters 13-20 in reference to David's behaviour

---

67 J. Van Seters, *In Search of History*, p. 290: The messianism read into and out of the prophecy of Nathan could not be glossed over as it lies at the heart of the dtr theology of city and dynasty. Cf. G. Von Rad, *Old Testament Theology*, p. 341.
68 J. Van Seters, *Court History*, p. 73.

towards Bathsheba and Uriah".[69] Like Van Seters, McCarter maintains that unity of 11-12 as a later insertion into a finished work but, unlike Van Seters, he prefers to think of the David-Bathsheba-Uriah sequence (2 Sam 11:2-12:24) "as the wholly original work of a prophetic writer who inserted it into the archival frame and set the finished composition in front of the story of Absalom's rebellion, which it serves as an interpretative preface."[70] Where Van Seters posits a post-dtr, anti-monarchical writer, McCarter sees a prophetic writer who might pre-date the Dtr.

In two works; *King David, A Biography* and *David's Enemies,* **Steven L. McKenzie** agrees on the whole with McCarter that David's affair with Bathsheba is a later addition to 2 Samuel. Its present location is to produce a scheme of "sin and punishment" or "cause and effect" with respect to Absalom's revolt. He comes to this conclusion because the oracle of Nathan (12: 11-12) attests to an awareness of Absalom's revolt, but the latter has no allusions that attest to the former.[71] He assumes that the narrative block, stretching from 1 Sam 16-1 Kings 2, is apologetic in nature and sought to legitimize David by seeking to exonerate him from the death of his enemies who met a common fate. The narrative carefully presents David as wise and deeply religious with an over-estimated love for his sons. This leads to the lack of a strong fatherly figure which almost led to the destruction of his lineage but for the timely reaction of the aged David upon the promptings of the prophet Nathan. Thus the succession of Solomon to the throne of his father is in accordance with the divine promise and will. Unlike the surrounding narrative, 2 Sam 11-12 make no attempt to cover up David's guilt but frankly recount his crimes; they are "not apologetic, and in my judgment are a later addition".[72] McKenzie's position can not be taken from the face value and en block, because the narrative could be apologetic, but it does not have to be and even if it were, it would not necessarily have to distort facts to convey its message. There are definitely subtle elements spread throughout the narrative that call for admiration for David even in his deepest moments of guilt. Neither does the portrayal of awareness of the

---

69 J. P. McCarter Jnr., *II Samuel*, p. 298.
70 J. P. McCarter Jnr., *II Samuel*, p. 302.
71 S. L. McKenzie, *King David*, p. 160.
72 S. L. McKenzie, *David's Enemies*, p. 39.

events of the revolt in Nathan's condemnation of the king make the oracle of judgment a later addition to the text without denying a dtr authorship of the whole. It would be easier to argue that the hand that finally retouched the materials and re-arranged them into the form that we have today could only have been there after the events, but he may not necessarily have had to compose them himself.

Arnold A. Anderson holds the view that the SN in its original form was possibly produced in the early part of Solomon's reign and that its main purpose may have been to provide legitimization for the dynastic claims of the house of David as well as for Solomon's accession to the throne. Contrary to McCarter and McKenzie, Anderson opines that the narrative contained in chapters 11-12 forms a veritable part of the Solomonic apologia or propaganda. For an apology to be successful, it did not have to tell lies or distort facts; rather it had to appeal to what was already known or believed. At the same time, it had to reshape and supplement the shared information, beliefs and hopes. Thus the inherently detrimental David-Bathsheba-Uriah story could not be disregarded, for it would not go away. However, it could be retold in a less critical manner and be rendered innocuous by the addition of David's repentance, Yahweh's forgiveness and the punishment imposed. Thus the way was open for a future reversal of fortunes.[73] As part of the SN, 2 Sam 12:1-15a served the same end: David's adultery with Bathsheba and Uriah's murder could not be denied, but they had already been punished and, therefore, the dynasty as such was free from David's sin and consequences. Even before the succession becomes an important issue in the SN, the later successful claimant is hinted at by means of his name: Jedidiah.[74] Vv 24-25, in particular, contain an implicit promise of better things to come: *Yahweh loved Solomon.*

In this sense, Anderson is no different from **Roger N. Whybray**, who earlier in 1968 had contended that the SN was composed in the period of enlightenment brought about by the early monarchy by an author who was a contemporaneous, or nearly so, with the events he narrates.[75] That the

---

73 A. A. Anderson, *2 Samuel*, p. 166.
74 A. A. Anderson, Idem, p. 160. It must be noted that this name appears only here and is not clear whether it was a throne or a pet name for Solomon.
75 R. N. Whybray, *Succession Narrative*, p. 6.

composer does not conceal the faults of David, despite his obvious admiration for the king, and that he almost never directly states his own opinion of actions and of the personalities, but lets them speak for themselves demonstrate adequately his objectivity as a historian, even though his work, the SN, may not be considered history in the strict sense of the discipline, because the author has no interest in the public life and administration of the kingdom but the internal and personal life of the court of David.[76] The oracles of Nathan (12:10-12), even if they may not be an original part of the narrative, openly express the inherent theme of cause and effect in the royal blood bath.

Whybray describes the image of David that emerges from the SN as enigmatic and judges this effect as one of the greatest literary achievements of the genius behind the narrative. "Not only David's clemency and piety but even his greatness is similarly left an open question. David was, in the end, successful, though he had more than once come close to total failure, in the achievement of his political and military aims. He left behind him a strong kingdom and an assured succession."[77] As king and statesman, however, David shows the most absurd ineptitude: though accustomed to the role of a judge, he is ironically unable to distinguish between a true and fictitious story whether it is narrated by Nathan or the wise widow of Tekoa; he is totally blind to the fact that Absalom is steadily undermining his position (2 Sam 15:1-12), he is incapable of seeing the effect of his uncontrolled grief upon the morals of his soldiers until Joab points it out to him (2 Sam 19:1-8), and it is not accidental that it is only when he is old, feeble and a mere puppet in the hands of skilful statesmen that the danger of his refusal to name a successor to his throne is resolved (I King 1:11-40). On the flip side of the coin, he is a very brave and excellent soldier, with a sharp vision in taking strategic decisions such as his choice of Jerusalem as a capital of the nation and his flight before Absalom for the sake of the city and what it stood for. He was very pious in his resignation to God's will (12:16-23, 15:25, 31, 16:10-12) and magnanimous towards his opponents (16:5-14).

---

76 R. N. Whybray, *Succession Narrative*, p. 18.
77 R. N. Whybray, Op. cit, p. 36.

A close reading of the SN shows that the writer did not have any personal interest in Solomon as a person and king but as a successor to David and the firm establishment of the dynasty, despite the turmoil. It is his strong belief in the hand of Yahweh at work in the dynastic story of David that spurs him on in the whole project. The sensual and morally weak Amnon, the haughty, fratricidal and usurping Absalom and the presumptuous Adonija are all rejected while the innocent and unassuming Solomon finds favour with God. God fulfils his promise, despite human weakness and failure. For this reason Whybray rightly concludes that the work may have been written at a time when the stability and legitimacy of the regime were being threatened, as may likely have been in the first few years of Solomon.[78] That the SN with its candid description of events is a pro-monarchical document is a view that has acquired a great following in modern Biblical scholarship. The report of David's crime against the family of Uriah does not simply constitute an anti-monarchical tendency in the narrative; it presents the strong King David as a morally weak man struggling for perfection and depending upon the mercy of Yhwh to succeed as a man and as a king. The theological stunt of the story comes to the fore in the moment of showing the weakness of the human hero; it is Yhwh's tenacious grip that guides the story towards its fulfilment.

In a thirty-page article of the year 2000, **Thomas Naumann** argues that David's action of taking Bathsheba and killing her husband can not be used as a proof for the concept of the oriental despot as many try to make it seem. The story line makes it clear that David had acted wrongly; he had broken the law, and now sought with every means at his disposal to cover up his crime. The author of the story draws on the fairy tale motif of "*Das Glückskind mit dem Todesbrief*" (the lucky child carrying his death warrant) as David's last resort to eliminate Uriah. Such a motif in its classic Mesopotamian sense, as in the case of Sargon,[79] and the later European variant, as in the case of Shakespeare's *Hamlet*, portrays the victory of the "victim" (here Uriah?) and the failure of the diabolic plan of the despot (in this case David). The author adopts this art of narration, but turns the whole concept around to the advantage of David as a king, making his

---

78 R. N. Whybray, Op. cit., p. 53.
79 T. Naumann, *Exemplarische König*, p. 143.

plan achieve its aim in so doing. Uriah does not become the king in place of David as would normally have been the aim of the tale or legend; to rid the state of the diabolic despot. It is only when the story of Uriah is considered in the context of David's adultery that its true meaning stands out: even the King himself cannot be excused from taking another man's wife.[80] The story, moreover, does not simply end with the murder of Uriah and David's marriage to Bathsheba, but the arrival of the Prophet Nathan propels the story forward by bringing the guilty king to book. Some modern critics consider the Nathan episode a later addition, argues Naumann, as the fearlessness of Nathan reflects a more developed stage of Israel's prophetic stature like Isaiah or Jeremiah than the early days of the monarchy. Much as this position may be tenable the unity of the narrative in 11 and 12 makes it impossible for it to end with 11:27a. The adultery and murder serve as a dark page in the history that calls for the intervention of the prophet with v. 27b functioning as a hinge on which the whole story depends.[81]

The events of chapters 11and12 paint a picture of the two sides of the same coin; the mighty king without scruples and the humble man who bows down to the prophetic reproach. This picture emphasizes not only the ideal of the sinner, who repents from his sins, but also raises the prophetic function unto a high pedestal. The oracle of Nathan as well as the punishment of David smack of a dtr reformulation of a pre-dtr tradition of Uriah-Nathan-complex. The two chapters can easily be seen as a prophetic prologue to the Absalom revolt (13-20) that explains the crises of David's family and the state as a result of his sins and the subsequent prophecy of doom. At the same time David becomes a paradigm: not even the great David can escape divine punishment in the misuse of kingly power and that he is spared only because he submits to the prophetic word and guidance. This makes the Uriah episode acceptable in the DtrH as a precedence of political ethics in the prophetic perspective.[82] Thus in the opinion of Naumann, the SN is certainly neither anti-David nor anti-monarchy and the height of the admiration of David as a king is reached by the unity of the narrative in chapters 10-12.

---

80 T. Naumann, *Exemplarische König*, p. 149.
81 T. Naumann, *Exemplarische König*, p. 165.
82 T. Naumann, *Exemplarische König*, p. 166.

Erhard Blum, like his contemporary Naumann, will rule out every tendency to make the SN an anti-monarchical document or even a political propaganda *ad maiorem Salomonis gloriam*. The overriding tendency of the story as a whole is a fundamental friendliness towards David and Solomon. After a synchronic review of the narrative material, Blum concludes that the theme that runs through the story is not the succession to the throne of David but the existence and internal stability of the kingdom of David.[83] He reveals that both David and his sons strive far beyond their limits: David takes what is not his and kills to cover up while Absalom and Adonija exalt themselves much against the Biblical ideal and cause their own downfall in so doing (Prov 16:18, 18:12, 29:23). In contradistinction to this image is the humble and contrite David at the two lowest moments of his life: when Nathan slaps him in the face with the guilt of his crimes and as he flees before his own son. In both moments he authentically submits himself without any form of reserve to God and he is accepted. Out of the ordinary and, as such, highly commendable is the story of the warrior king who resigns himself into the hands of Yahweh, his God in the face of the threat of mortal danger from Absalom (15:25, 31; 16:10-12). Admirably, David acknowledges the impenetrable reality of God's active presence in human activities and his own limitations in the presence of this overwhelming power and greatness.

In holding this view, Blum hits the nail on the head, because internal evidence in the SN does not warrant an anti-monarchical let alone anti-David tag. Neither will one do justice to the narrative material about David, found in 2 Sam 9-1 Kings 1-2, if one restricts oneself to the theme of succession and ignores the fact that succession to the throne of David is part of a larger story; that of David and his monarchy in the context of the story of Yhwh and his choice of Israel. The story of the rise of David to the throne of Israel is the reality of a man who inherited a loosely organized tribal confederacy out of which he established a nation ruled for the first time by a stable dynasty under the guidance of the prophet of Yhwh. For that matter, the narrative preserves a high level of admiration for the man without seeking to brush over all his faults and weaknesses or sweep them under

---

83 E. Blum, *Geschichtsschreibung*, p. 22–23.

the carpet. The exilic author who assembled the various traditions and put them together to narrate the story of Israel has made use of not only the positive elements in the tradition that he dwells upon, but has also utilized the failings of his characters as a means to transmit his message of hope for the exiled people of Yhwh, faced with the dilemma of failure. It is in this light that the parable of Nathan becomes a very useful tool in the hands of the deuteronomistic historian.

The recent work of **Walter Dietrich**[84] has thrown much light upon the trend of the arguments surrounding the narrative and has shown how easy it is to end up in a labyrinth of arguments if one loses the focus of the corpus and its message and instead concentrates too much on small segments of the narrative. Out of the many contributions that Dietrich puts under the loop, I will settle on only two of them, **Thilo Alexander Rudnig** (2006) and **Wolfgang Oswald** (2008), because they directly affect my work and will leave out the others for the sake of avoiding a photocopy of the work that is available to the reader. Rudnig[85] identifies in the narrative of the succession to the throne of David a good variety of fragments, redactions and additions that have been woven together. As his point of departure for the growth of the texts *stehen vier verschiedene Quellenstücke* two of which present the laconic war accounts of the conquest of Rabbah (2 Sam 11:*1a + 12:29, 31b) and the quenching of Absalom's revolt (2 Sam 15a$\beta\gamma$b, 12b, 17:22abα1, 18:1a, 6, 9b, 15aαb, 16a, 17a), while the two others recount bluntly a report about David's successor, Solomon; his birth (2 Sam 11:2, 4a$\alpha\beta$b, 5, *27a + 12:24bα2) and his enthronement (1 Kings 1, 5, 7, 8aαb, 38,*39, 40a$\alpha\gamma$b). These fragments with their pro-Davidic and pro-Solomonic sentiments might date back to the early monarchy and may have been kept in the archives of the Jerusalem palace from the tenth century.[86] In the ninth century, continues Rudnig, these fragments received their earlier redaction into the actual succession narrative by the insertion of the

---

[84] W. Dietrich, *Von den ersten Königen Israels, Forschung an den Samuelbüchern im Jahrtausend*, zweite Teil (Theologische Rundschau 77, Jahrgang 2012 Heft 3) Tübingen, 2012, Mohr Siebeck, 263–316.
[85] T. A. Rudnig, *Davids Thron*, BZAW 358, Berlin, 2006, as presented by Walter Dietrich in Forschung an der Samuelbüchern, pp. 267–272.
[86] T. A Rudnig, *Davids Thron*, pp. 331–332, in W. Dietrich, *Forschung*, p. 268.

birth of Solomon into the Rabbah campaign followed by Absalom's revolt and Solomon's enthronement as king. The hand of this redactor, according to Rudnig, is to be seen in the addition of two verses; 11:*1a and 15: 1aα and his work remained until the late exilic and post-exilic period when the eighteen verses (according to Rudnig's own method of verse count from 2 Sam 10-20 + 1 Kings 1-2) were expanded into the current four hundred and thirty nine which were adopted by the late and post exilic writer and incorporated into the DtrH.[87]

Dietrich raises doubts about the certainty of identifying such small pieces of textual components that are spread over a whole block of narrative material. Among the many other critiques that he legitimately brings out against Rudnig's work, I find very meaningful the part that concerns the parentage of Solomon. From the face value of Rudnig's supposed earliest version (2 Sam 11:2, 4aαβb, 5, *27a + 12:24bα2) David would have had a sexual relationship with a nameless woman who bore the successor to his throne. This raises doubts about Bathsheba's motherhood of Solomon and, worst of all, risks making Uriah's son the son of David, a fact that is far removed from what the received text presents.[88] In the end, insists Dietrich, it is far better to read the SN as a unity than split it apart, even if one does so with admirable intelligence and exegetic-philological accuracy.[89] On my part, I find it difficult to accommodate the idea that a pro-Davidic and pro-Solomonic text will turn round to place the parentage of Solomon on such a precarious ground when the motherhood of Bathsheba has not been anywhere in dispute and whether one can argue with certainty that there was a palace archive in the 10th century Jerusalem. Despite the objections to Rudnig's conclusions, his work brings us back to the already accepted hypothesis that the dtr author gathered extant narrative materials and edited them to compose the history of Israel in the context of the exile and its aftermath.

Where Rudnig dissects the narrative into small pieces of different sources dating back to the 10th century, Wolfgang Oswald will lift the prophet

---

87 T. A Rudnig, Davids Thron, p. 336.
88 W. Dietrich, *Forschung an der Samuelbüchern*, p. 271, cf. Rudnig, *Davids Thron*, p. 48.
89 W. Dietrich, *Forschung*, p. 272.

Nathan completely out of the historical milieu of the early monarchy.[90] He systematically analyses the three Nathan chapters and comes to the conclusion that 2 Sam 7 *ist durch und durch dtr*[91] and that 2 Sam 12 as well as 1 Kings 1 constitute, in essence, a literary unity which is part of the SN written hundreds of years after the events with the personality of the prophet Nathan as the one who ensured that the first succession to the dynasty was legitimate and according to the will of God.[92] Oswald opines that the use of 2 Sam 11and12 and 1 Kings 1 as the frame work for the *Hofgeschichte*, 2 Sam 13-20, may have taken place in the late monarchical period and it is only then that the SN may have taken its actual shape. It is pro-monarchy, pro-David and pro-Solomon and the prophet Nathan plays a very positive role all through; he is the (fictional) personality who gives the story its divine legitimization. He helps David to free himself from the burden of sin that he has brought upon himself on account of the Bathsheba-Uriah-scandal, brings the news of God's love for the second son born out of the relationship with Bathsheba and reacts promptly when Adonijah threatens to sink the ship of state by helping the *Beloved of Yhwh* to power. All these have very little or nothing at all to do with the actual historical events of the 10th century and any attempt to situate him in the political and religious context of David's reign is an exercise in futility. He is simply a fiction of the literary works that wished to have a messenger of Yhwh at the court of David and in this function have assigned him different appearances. The different facets of the Biblical image of Nathan are in no way uncoordinated with one another,

---

90 W. Oswald, *Nathan der Prophet*, p. 275. In the subsequent paragraphs, I have benefited a great deal for the precise summary of Oswald's work from the literature review of Walter Dietrich, which subjects the pure authorial material to a critical analysis and sums it up in four pages (cf. *Forschung an den Samuelbüchern*, pp. 274–278).
91 Oswald argues among others that the oracle of Nathan in 2 Sam 7 qualifies as one of the reflective speeches of the leading figures of the history identified by Martin Noth (p. 84) The chapter links up perfectly with 1 Kings 1-2 as promise and fulfillment that is a hallmark of the DtrG (p. 86, 235). The encounter between Nathan and David in this chapter constitutes the theological and compositional foundation of the dtr work (p. 101) that presents David as the founder of the dynasty who did not build the Temple and therefore legitimize Jehoiachin's rule that lacked Temple or city (p. 84–85).
92 W. Dietrich, *Forschung*, p. 276.

as is often held, but rather produce a very consistent portrait. This development, however, does not stem from a single hand, but is composed on two levels; the first level which took place shortly before the end of the monarchy was 2 Sam 12 and 1 Kings 1 and in the late exilic period, 2 Sam 7.[93]

Dietrich points out that Oswald's thesis is based upon the literary-ideological nature of the personality of the prophet Nathan and thus hangs upon a thin thread of literary history. He proceeds by posing a number of questions prefaced by "what ifs" (*Was, wenn?*): What if 2Sam 7 is not completely dtr, but incorporates a pre-exilic account[94] and what if the basic narrative of 2 Sam 12 and 1 Kings 1 does not stem from the late monarchy? Where does the precise information about the Ark in the tent, and about personalities like Bathsheba, Abishag, Benaiah, Joab, Shimei, Zadok, and about the two plausibly competing parties for the crown come from? What about the ambivalence and contradictory tendencies in the text; is it not true that the three Nathan- chapters present a very different image of their characters which reflects a possible long tradition and literary history? Are the coup d'état of Nathan and the enthronement of Solomon with their ensuing bloody cleansing not too repulsive or, at least, too disturbing to be polished up by forcing a few sentences into the narrative which would have done more harm than good? Does Nathan's appearance in 2 Sam 12 not achieve the function of saving the honour of David and Solomon? Such pertinent questions are not taken into consideration by the work of Oswald;[95] Dietrich maintains and earns my unqualified support.

Dietrich concretizes the direction in which his critique of the various works he analyses is supposed to lead his audience by summarizing his own

---

93 W. Dietrich, *Forschung an der Samuelbüchern*, pp. 274–277. Oswald notes that 2 Sam 12 (without v. 7b-12) and 1 Kings 1 belong to the SN where Nathan is already identified as a prophet and predates the DtrG while 2 Sam 7 is deuteronomistic (*Nathan der Prophet*, p. 264). The Dtr took over the character called Nathan and developed his identity and stature to the ideal type of a prophet with which he works all through the history (pp. 234–235).

94 Dietrich reacts to this question with his own position that there was already a basic form of the dynastic oracle which was part of the Hofischen Ezählwerks of the first kings of Israel which contained an enthronement formula with the sentences in 7;12aβb, 15b (*Forschung*, p. 277).

95 W. Dietrich, Forschung, p. 277.

work; *David, Der Herrscher mit der Harfe*.[96] As his point of departure, Dietrich maintains that the books of Samuel developed from ancient sources that date back to the early monarchy with a three-level dtr redaction and a post-dtr expansion to which the songs of 1 Sam 2:1-10, 2 Sam 22, 23:1-7 as well as the appendix (2 Sam 21-24) were later added. In Dietrich's view, the process of the dtr editing of the books was not completed in the 6th but continued into the 5th century and engulfs the classic dtr texts, which are those influenced by Deuteronomy.[97] These earlier materials were made up of a number of single lists, songs, narratives and two narrative chains about David, the prey quarried by Saul, the fate of the Saulides and two novellas; the Absalom revolt and the birth and rise of Solomon. The most important step towards the development of the Books of Samuel, in the opinion of Dietrich, was the work of the *Höfische Erzähler* (court narrator) who made use of the ancient materials to recount the story of the early kings of Israel from 1 Samuel – 1 Kings (perhaps 1 Kings 12). The purpose of this work was not a Solomonic propaganda but a highly artificial and multifaceted historical work that was not only to narrate what happened in Israel at the foundation of the state but mirrors the themes and questions that were very pertinent at the time of the writer; How does God act in history? How could or should people in authority act according to his will? What happens if they do not? What is good and bad rule? What should characterize the ruler-subject, father-son or male-female relationship? These are some of the issues that the *Höfische Erzähler* develops with the help of his historical source materials and his answers are not placatory but sometimes divergent, ambivalent and even contradictory. His characters reflect the same sentiments; they demonstrate bright and dark sides. David is not only good nor is Saul only bad and figures like Michal, Abner, Joab, Absalom, Ahitophel, Bathsheba, Sheba and Nathan shimmer a duality of light.

---

96 W. Dietrich, Forschung, pp. 288–290. Dietrich refers his readers to the position he holds in his book; *David, Der Herrscher mit der Harfe*, pp. 26–65, which he summarizes here.

97 W. Dietrich, *Forschung an den Samuelbücher*, p. 289. Dietrich provides an elaborate list of the three levels of redaction that is, in his opinion, evident in the books of Samuel among which he ascribes 2 Sam 12:7b, 8, 10b & 13f to the DtrP. We will come back to this position of Dietrich in the next chapter where we will present his three levels of redaction with a table.

This portrays the quality of the author who is responsible for the work; a shrewd redactor, an experienced writer, a serious historian, a keen judge of human nature (*weiser Menschenkenner*) a thoughtful theologian and above all an artist.[98]

Dietrich is certainly right that there is a multitude of pertinent issues addressed in the narratives and especially in the narration of the story of King David and the succession to his throne. In fact, all the foregone epithets that Dietrich employs in describing the *Höfische Erzähler*, I vouch to say, can also be heaped upon the dtr historian who has gathered the varied documents and bound them together to compose the narrative of the history of Israel from the entry into the Promised Land to the exile and beyond. While the provenance of his source materials is and will remain the bone of contention to exegetes for generations to come, he has made use of the varied materials in the composition of a unified narrative with a definite scope and purpose that come to light if considered as a whole and not dissected into single pieces. It is against this background that the parable of Nathan can only and effectively be understood within the context of the DtrH if one wishes to unravel its hidden meaning and function in the Biblical narrative.

2.3 The parable of Nathan as part of the DtrH

The literature review has revealed that the problem of 2 Sam 12:1-15a has made its mark in Biblical scholarship by catching the attention of critics over the last two centuries. The legitimate comments of Schwally in 1892 may have paved the way for the current status of the pericope: vv. 15bff give no indication of a knowledge of the oracles of vv. 10-12 and the character of Nathan in this chapter sharply differs from his actions in 1 Kings 1.[99] Much as these comments are very true in themselves, they pose no problem to the understanding of the narrative as a whole if we look at the text not just from the mediate and immediate contexts that we have defined in the previous chapter, but as part of a whole that is called the deuteronomistic work or history (DtrH). The literal critical method does a very good job by breaking the text down into its different units in order to find out which

---

98 W. Dietrich, *Forschung an der Samuelbüchern*, pp. 289–290.
99 F. Schwally, *Der Profet Nathan*, p. 154ff.

parts are "original" to the tradition and which "later additions" to it. In the case of 2 Sam 12:1-15a, this method only leads us to the revolt of Absalom to which 2 Sam 10-12 function as a prologue and which in turn responds to the question of who succeeds David, hence the Succession Narrative. Remaining with the SN as the goal of the narrative has the tendency of leading one to conclude that it was an anti-David material (Würthwein), but at the same time written for the legitimization of Solomon (Rost and Würthwein).

A volume of modern research has followed this trend of categorizing the parable of Nathan under the theme of the succession to the throne of David and has ended up considering it either a pro- or anti-monarchical document. This can not be the case because, as Blum puts it, "the theme that runs through the narrative is not the succession to the throne of David but the existence and internal stability of the kingdom of David".[100] It is imperative for one to look further than just the SN in order to arrive at such a conclusion. The parable of Nathan is part of a unified work stretching from Deuteronomy to 2 Kings, composed to tell the story of Israel from her deliverance from Egypt through the conquest of the Land of Promise to its establishment as a nation under the reign of the dynasty of David and, finally, to the defeat and exile of the divided nation by an author or group of authors who had gone through the bitter experience of the exile. These authors sought answers to the questions of their day through the history of the people of Yhwh in order to launch a message of hope for their contemporaries. The parable of Nathan forms part of this message of hope and it is in this context that its meaning can be appreciated to the full. In this work, my scope is the DtrH and my perspective, the End Text. My stand is that 2 Sam 12:1-15a is part of the material that constitutes the SN, but the SN on its part is located within the DtrH, which implies that the dtr author has influenced its present nature and location in the Biblical narrative, as we have it today.[101] I will, therefore, take advantage of the findings of the literal critical method without forgetting that each block of narrative

---

100   E. Blum, *Geschichtsschreibung*, p. 22–23.
101   It is very interesting and absolutely relevant to look at the interconnectedness of Biblical narratives and ask ourselves what would become of 1 Kings 15:5 and the heading of Ps 51 if the David-Bathsheba-Uriah sequence is taken out of the tradition as the Chronicler has done (1 Chr 20:1-2)?

material has its own particular history but functions in conjunction with other parts of the whole and requires, for that matter, a synchronic reading.

From the outset, I consider chapters 10-12 as a composite block of three separate and coherent narratives that have been carefully put together with a fine binding seam by a refined author to fit into an over-all scheme or programme: the Ammonite war, the David-Bathsheba-Uriah sequence and the parable of Nathan. As has been noted in the first chapter of this work, the Chronicler did not deem the last two blocks of narratives meat to be included in his work and simply glossed over them, but the dtr author has inserted these narratives into his grand project and at their present location. Since, in my view, the single blocks acquire their importance and meaning only as part of the whole DtrH, I will turn my attention to this project or work in order to find out what light it throws upon our understanding of the parable of Nathan and its castigation of David, despite presenting him as the ideal king and the yardstick with which to measure the life and performance of all other kings in Israel and Judah.

Chapter 3. The Deuteronomistic History (DtrH)

The books of Deuteronomy through second Kings as they appear in the Biblical sequence tell the story of Israel from the plains of Moab at one end of the desert to the exile in Babylon on the other side of the same desert. In fact if one goes along with the division of the Bible as the Pentateuch (Torah) and the historical books or the former Prophets (Joshua-2 Kings) one would logically talk about the people of God outside the Promised Land and the same people within the confines of the Land of Promise. The tragic narration then will end where one began; the self same people outside the celebrated land with neither laws nor institutions, having lost their identity as a nation in exile, away from the land they have possessed as their own for about eight hundred years. There are different models of reading the text from Genesis to 2 Kings; as the Tetrateuch (Genesis – Numbers), the Pentateuch (Genesis – Deuteronomy) the Hexateuch (Genesis – Joshua), the Deuteronomistic History (Deuteronomy – 2 Kings) or the Enneateuch (Genesis – 2 Kings). The Masoretic Text makes the complex exercise simple in its complexity by dividing the whole Bible into three parts; *Torah* (Pentateuch), *Nebiim* (Prophets; Joshua – Malachi) and *Ketubiim* (Psalms – Chronicles).

The traditional method of reading the books of the Old Testament had for a long time been taken for granted that the first five books constitute a single unit simply identified as the Pentateuch (without going into the JEP hypothesis as the sources of the narrative materials found in these five books) to which Joshua came to be added since it is only in the conquest of the land that the march from Egypt comes to a close when the fulfilment of the promise made to Abraham, Isaac and Jacob is achieved. In consequence, the Pentateuch becomes the Hexateuch with the addition of Joshua.[102] The story, however, does not end there, it continues from Joshua

---

102 There is an abundance of arguments in this area that seek to explain in one way or the other how the Pentateuch or Hexateuch came into being. For instance, Eckart Otto posits that the priestly circle which in the fifth and early fourth century B.C., at the time of Esra, edited the Hexateuch could not accept the idea that Yhwh's plan of salvation for Israel was realized with

through Judges and Samuel to the second book of Kings for which reason one will end up with a narrative from creation to the conquest of the land and the loss of that same land, hence the Enneateuch (Genesis – 2 Kings).[103] It was in the second half of the twentieth century that the influential work of Martin Noth gave a new orientation to the analysis of the first nine books of the Bible by identifying the historical work of the deuteronomistic historian beginning from Deuteronomy and running through to the second book of Kings so that one will talk of the Tetrateuch (Gen – Num) and the DtrH.[104] With this great contribution of Martin Noth to the study of Scriptures, the book of Deuteronomy gained a special attention as the beginning of a carefully written work that comprises the block of narratives stretching from there to 2 Kings.[105] This work of history, notes Martin Noth, was the project of a man who had been moved by the calamities that had befallen Israel in the sixth century B.C. to seek meaning to the enigmatic questions of his day, making use of the traditions of his people that were available to him. In the opinion of Noth, it is the work of a single writer of the exilic period, who organized the various units of material at his disposal to constitute a continuous history of Israel, evaluating it with his own legalistic conception of the deuteronomic law

---

the conquest of the land. They thus separated the book of Joshua from the Pentateuch the closing event to which is the death of Moses. In this way, they succeeded in portraying the theological creed that Israel subsisted everywhere that people with links to the genealogy of that people lived and where the Torah of Yhwh, the Sinaitic code, was adhered to as the norm of life; (*Herrscherlegitimation und Rechtskodifizierung*, p. 81).

103   E. Blum, *Pentateuch – Hexateuch – Enneateuch*, pp. 67–68. Blum rightly adds that the narrative from Genesis to 2 Kings is so composed that there are various levels of continuity and links between the different stages in the development of the narratives such as songs, speeches and prescriptive texts, the coherence of time span from creation to the conquest of the land and its loss, and the systematic chronological data geared towards the exodus, the Temple building project of Solomon and its rededication by the Maccabees in 164 B.C., among others (cf. p. 70).
104   E. Blum, Op cit., p. 69.
105   Cf. K. Schmid, *Deuteronomium innerhalb der deuteronomistischen Geschichtswerke*, p. 194.

...as a norm for the relationship between God and people and as a yardstick by which to judge human conduct".[106] This author, commonly referred to as the dtr, had extensive sources for the reign of David and intervened with his own comments in this part of the history only rarely. He was "at one with the whole Old Testament tradition in seeing the figure of David, despite his weaknesses, as a model against which to judge the later Judean kings.[107]

Noth identifies a definite *terminus a quo* of the Dtr as 562 B.C.,[108] "when the history of the people of Israel in the ordinary sense was essentially at an end", but with the pardoning of Jehoiachin as a sign of hope, and ascribes all parts of the history which bear marks of an earlier date of composition to the old material adapted by him.[109] The purpose of the author was to reconstruct the history of his people, making use of the materials at his disposal, in order to provide an answer to the great question of his day: "Why a great nation with a merciful God should be reduced to a laughing stock languishing in captivity and suffering destruction?" He found the answer in the constant disobedience, apostasy and idolatry of the kings with the people, in spite of God's continuous admonitions. It is, therefore, divine justice. At the same time the author emphasizes the faithfulness and permanence of divine mercy that protected and ensured the continuity of the Davidic dynasty despite its human frailties, moral disappointments and failure as a sign of hope for the exiled people of Yahweh.

Christian Frevel has analysed in a monograph the views that have been expressed by various Biblical scholars on the theme of the DtrH either as the work of a single author (M. Noth) or a composite work that has seen various levels of redaction (Cross, Smend and the Göttingen model) and rightly concludes that the thesis of the DtrH is the most meaningful in Old

---

106   M. Noth, *The Deuteronomistic History*, p. 124.
107   M. Noth, Op cit., p. 86–87: Von Rad's subsequent studies has placed emphasis on the paramount position of the dynastic promise to David (2 Sam 7) in the dtr that holds out the hope in a future messiah – G. Von Rad, *Studies in Deuteronomy*, London (1956) p. 86.
108   Reinhard Kratz points out that the pardoning of Jehoiachin in 2 Kings 25:27 begins in the Babylonian lists from 592 B.C. but the mention of king Amel-Marduk (Evil Merodach) helps very much in scaling it down to 562 B.C. (cf. *The Composition of the Narrative Books of the Old Testament*, p. 157).
109   M. Noth, *The Deuteronomistic History*, p. 27: Von Rad prefers to date it from the freeing of Jehoiachin in 561 (*Old Testament Theology*, p. 335).

Testament scholarship of the last century. "I do not know of any German language textbook that is without a reference to Martin Noth's thesis in one or the other variation"[110], emphasizes Frevel. For our purpose, suffice it to say that a dtr author is behind the text before us. The said author did not necessarily have to compose it himself. He has taken over the independently composed materials and has set them together or re-arranged them to narrate his story of hope for the exiled Jew. Such an author may have been among the remnants left behind in the land of Israel who expresses his faith in Yahweh and his hope for Israel.

Noth's position constituted a radical revision in the literary critical view which held sway at that time in its assertion that the material found in the books of Joshua, Judges, Samuel and Kings grew into their present form as the result of a series of redactional processes over a period of time. Against this position, Noth posits the Dtr as an author and interpreter of history who assembled the various materials, edited them to fit into his informed framework and even imposed his theological and historical slant on them. The author then provided a new introduction and conclusion to an older form of Deuteronomy (Deut 1:1-4, 43, 31:1-32-32:44, 33:1-34:12) and prefixed it to his work as the beginning of the DtrH, that stands against the *Tetrateuch* or the so-called *Priestly work*.[111] In this work the resonating theme is the irreversible doom of Israel on account of her apostasy and idolatry, symbolised by Jeroboam in Israel and Manasseh in Judah, that incurs the inevitable wrath of God and the curses of the covenant: death, disease and captivity.[112]

---

110 C. Frevel, *Deuteronomistische Geschichtswerk oder Geschichtswerke*, p. 69. Frevel argues that the Dtr begins from Deuteronomy and includes Joshua which has no beginning of its own. He is an author who takes over extant materials, edits, reconstructs and gives meaning to them (pp. 61–62). Among the most important texts that bind together the whole story besides the chronologies are the *Geschichtrückblick* (historical retrospective view) of Deut 1-3, The speech of Joshua at the departure from Shittim, Jos 1:10-15, and his farewell address in 23:1ff, the farewell address of Samuel in 1 Sam 12 and Solomon's Temple dedication speech of 1 Kings 8:14-53 as well as the theological reflections on the fall of the northern kingdom of Israel in 2 Kings 17 (pp. 65–6).

111 F. M. Cross, *Canaanite Myth*, p. 274.

112 F. M. Cross, Op cit., p. 275.

There have been a number of attempts to challenge Noth's dating of the Dtr in the exilic period with Cross noting features in the text that demand a Josianic date with an exilic redaction. On one hand, Cross begins with a reference to the study of Von Rad which finds the theme of grace in the promise of an eternal dynasty to David as a basis for hope in the future messianic kingship of the house of David,[113] and on the other, Wolff's *Kerygma of the Deuteronomist*, which finds the hope of restoration as the result of a repentant Israel in certain passages of the dtr work such as; Judg 2:18, 1 Sam 12:1-24, 1 Kings 8:33, 35, 2 Kings 17:13.[114] Cross concludes that both positions, while identifying particular themes of the great collection, are, nevertheless, too simplistic and, therefore, inadequate as an explanation to the complexity of the theological lore in the work of the Dtr.[115] Instead of the position of these two, Cross identifies two phases in the development of the deuteronomistic work. The first phase, which he terms Dtr^1, revolves around two basic themes which run through the book of Kings. The first is the sin of Jeroboam in establishing a counter cultic centre to Jerusalem in Dan and Bethel leading to syncretism and cultic alienation of the two already politically-alienated kingdoms of Israel and Judah. The description of the sin is couched in a typical dtr parlance:

> [28]So the king took counsel, and made two calves of gold. He said to the people, "You have gone up to Jerusalem long enough. Here are your gods, O Israel, who brought you up out of the land of Egypt." [29] He set one in Bethel, and the other he put in Dan. [30] *And this thing became a sin, for the people went to worship before the one at Bethel and before the other as far as Dan.*[31] He also made houses on high places, and appointed priests from among all the people, who were not Levites. [32] Jeroboam appointed a festival on the fifteenth day of the eighth month like the festival that was in Judah, and he offered sacrifices on the altar; *so he did in Bethel, sacrificing to the calves that he had made.* And he placed in Bethel the priests of the high places that he had made... (1 Kings 12, NRSV)

The account ends with the typical dtr commentary or interpretation of the history that presents the exile as a foregone conclusion in; *"This matter became sin to the house of Jeroboam, so as to cut it off and to destroy it from the face of the earth"* (1 Kings 13: 34).

---

113 G. von Rad, *Old Testament Theology*, p. 341.
114 H. W. Wolff, Das Kerygma, 171-186.
115 F. M. Cross, *Cannanite Myth*, p. 279.

The persistent imitation of the sin of Jeroboam by the kings and people of Israel exhausts divine patience and exudes the consequence of Yahweh depriving Israel of his presence resulting in Israel being taken into captivity away from her land to Assyria (2 Kings 17:23). In contrast to the gruesome end of Israel on account of the sin of Jeroboam is posited a second theme of the Dtr, according to Cross: the faithfulness of David to Yahweh that runs through the books of Samuel and Kings. It may be expressed in a simple form in the refrain-like phrase:

לְמַ֙עַן֙ דָּוִ֣ד עַבְדִּ֔י וּלְמַ֙עַן֙ יְרוּשָׁלִַ֔ם אֲשֶׁ֥ר בָּחָֽרְתִּי׃

"...for the sake of David my servant and for the sake of Jerusalem which I have chosen."[116]

This promise of hope begins in the dynastic promise of 2 Sam 7 and runs through the books of Kings to the extent that even in the case of the Judean kings, who stand condemned, the Dtr does not fail to include the reference to the faithfulness of David as the basis for hope in a future restoration.[117] This element of hope reaches its apex in Josiah who alone of all the Kings of Judah receives an unqualified praise;

> He did what was right in the sight of the LORD, and walked in all the ways of his father David; he did not turn aside to the right or to the left (2 Kings 22:2) and before him there was no king like him, who turned to the LORD with all his heart, with all his soul, and with all his might, according to all the law of Moses; nor did any like him arise after him (23:25).[118]

The reform of Josiah makes the king the protagonist of the drama; the extirpation of Jeroboam's abomination, the renewal of the ancient covenant and the celebration of the Passover as a united Israel looked forward to the

---

116 1 Kings 11:12, 13, 32, 34, 36, 15:4, 2 Kings 8:19, 19:34, 20:6.
117 Solomon did not follow the ways of his father and did evil in the sight of the Lord but the kingdom would not be taken from his hands for the sake of David and of Jerusalem (1 Kings 11:34-36). In the same vein even Jehoram who walked in the ways of the kings of Israel and did that which was evil in the sight of the Lord is honoured with the unwillingness of the Lord to destroy Judah for the sake of David (2 Kings 8:18f). Cross sees in this elements of the royal liturgy as expounded in Ps 89:20-38 and in the prayer of David in 2 Sam 7:18-29.
118 F. M. Cross, *Canaanite Myth*, p. 283.

fulfilment of the promise to David. The insistence on the theme of hope implies relevance to the audience of the author, whom he calls upon to avail themselves "to the new possibilities of salvation through obedience to the ancient covenant of Yahweh and hope in the new King David, Josiah."[119] Thus, taking the cue from Noth, Cross places the primary edition of the history in the reign of Josiah, whose reforms, he maintains, it was compiled to support.

In the second phase, which he terms Dtr², there is the expressed threat of captivity without prior preparation, and concerns, especially, the kingdom of Judah. The event that led to it, according to Cross, was Manasseh's sin of syncretism and idolatry, even to the extent of setting up the image of Asherah in the temple of Yahweh, that caused the whole people to sin as Israel had done under Jeroboam.

> The LORD said by his servants the prophets,
> "Because King Manasseh of Judah has committed these abominations ... and has caused Judah also to sin with his idols; therefore, thus says the LORD, the God of Israel, I am bringing upon Jerusalem and Judah such evil that the ears of everyone who hears of it will tingle. ... I will wipe Jerusalem as one wipes a dish, wiping it and turning it upside down. I will cast off the remnant of my heritage, and give them into the hand of their enemies; they shall become a prey and a spoil to all their enemies[15] because they have done what is evil in my sight and have provoked me to anger, since the day their ancestors came out of Egypt, even to this day." (2 Kings 21:10-15, NRSV)

Cross notes the sudden and vague mention of "prophets" when there has been no prior indication of any such prophecy in the work of the Dtr whose emphasis has been the revival of the Davidic state by Josiah, and the reunion of the alienated half-kingdom of Israel and Judah.[120] In addition, a significant gloss is found attached to the account of Josiah's reform that levels the guilt of the exile at the feet of Manasseh, even though he ruled

---

119 F. M. Cross, *Canaanite Myth*, p. 285.
120 Erik Eynikel sees in the use of the plural "prophets" an indication that this condemnation had been pronounced many times already and that many more people were addressed than Manasseh alone. The audience then will be the whole people of Israel since the day their ancestors came out of the land of Egypt which is liable for what will happen. It is stock-taking of the entire history of the people in the land. Cf. *Portrait of Manasseh*, p. 241.

before Josiah: *Still the LORD did not turn from the fierceness of his great wrath, by which his anger was kindled against Judah, because of all the provocations with which Manasseh had provoked him* (2 Kings 23:26). Cross sees in this a retouching of the dtr work by an exilic writer to bring the work up to date in the exile, "to record the fall of Jerusalem, and to reshape the history, with the minimum of reworking, into a document relevant to an exiled people for whom the bright expectations of the Josianic era were hopelessly past".[121] Consequently, he dates this retouching to about 550 B.C. To sum up, according to Cross, the work of the Dtr[1] extends from Deuteronomy to 2 Kings 23 and dates to the time of Josiah (ca. 562 in accordance with Noth) with Dtr[2] extending it to 2 Kings 25 besides internal minor additions in ca. 550 B.C.

Following Cross, the investigations of the Smend school of thought, commonly known as the Block or Göttinger Model, contend that the primary deuteronomistic history (DtrG) passed through two other phases of redaction. A critical examination of Joshua and Judges by Rudolf Smend led him to posit a systematic reworking of the Dtr with the law as the chief motif.[122] To this he assigned the siglum DtrN. Walter Dietrich, a student of Smend, studied the prophetic material in *Kings* and identified a redaction of the history with formal and linguistic features linking it with classical prophecy but with an affinity to dtr thought. This redactor knew of the events of 587, cites Ps 79 (which is generally dated close to 587) and falls very much under the influence of Jeremiah and Baruch among others. This level of redaction he termed DtrP. Thus Dietrich considers the historical work of the dtr author (Deuteronomy – 2 Kings) as a composite block from three different hands extending from 580-560 B.C.[123]

---

121 F. M. Cross, *Canaanite Myth*, p. 285; Cross considers the closed options of Deut 4:27-31 and the promise of hope in 30: 1-10, together as the hand of a second editor distinct from the Dtr[1].
122 R. Smend, (1971) in P. K. McCarter, *II Samuel*, p. 7.
123 W. Dietrich, *Prophetie und Geschichte*, p. 143: Dietrich's dating is simply based upon the assumption that *DtrG kurz nach der Eroberung Jerusalems und, DtrN hingegen kurz nach der Rehabilitierung Johachins anzusetzen sind.*

NAME	SIGLUM	DATE OF COMPOSITION
Deuteronomistic History	DtrG	ca. 580 BC; shortly after the fall of Jerusalem
Prophetic Redaction	DtrP	Between DtrG and DtrN
Nomistic Redaction	DtrN	ca. 560 BC: shortly after Johoiachin's rehabilitation.

This seemingly complete study and summary of the DtrH does not in any way end the interest of exegetes and researchers into the origin and purpose of the work. Konrad Schmid in 1999 looks at the historical books from the point of view of the patriarchal and Moses narratives in Genesis and Exodus as part of the history of Israel from creation to the exile. The one thing that he finds clear and beyond doubt is the sequence of the history of Israel, as it is narrated in the first nine books of the Bible (the Enneateuch): the Patriarchal epoch, the Exodus, the desert march, the conquest of the land, the period of the Judges, and Kingship.[124] The narration of these facts, according to Schmid, has gone through a series of redactions that have produced the closely-knit complex of traditions found in the nine books from Genesis to 2 Kings "*als zusammenhängenden Überlieferungskomplex*".[125] The relationship of the books to one another is so intricately woven that it is not just that one follows the other but that the one takes the narrative strand from where the previous one left off in the history.[126] Deuteronomy, he continues, is styled as the last words of Moses with a strong emphasis on the Law before the entry into the Land of Promise. It is beyond any reasonable doubt that an older, "vor-Dtr" Deuteronomy, which was conceived either as the words of Moses or of Yahweh (Deut 6-26) as the rule of life for Israel, is programmatically pitched between the Exodus and the conquest of the Land.[127] An analysis of the concluding passages of Joshua (Jos 21:43-45), built around the words; dwell, surround and rest (שׁי׳, מסב׳ב, נוח), leads Schmid on to the conclusion that the author did not in any way have the Patriarchs of Genesis in focus, but the generation of Moses, who had been led out of Egypt as a

---

124 H. Schmid, *Erzväter*, p. 3.
125 H. Schmid, Op cit., p. 19 – "closely-knit traditional complex".
126 H. Schmid, Op cit., p. 1.
127 H. Schmid, Op cit., p. 95.

direct link to Deut 12:10. Jos 23 on its part modifies the yardstick of the law by linking up not only with Deut 12 but also Deut 5-11 and 31 while Jos 24:2-13 looks back to the promise to the Patriarchs of Genesis.[128] Thus the triple ending of Joshua, according to Schmid, is the work of a redactor to link up Joshua with the books before it i.e. the Pentateuch. At variance with Noth and the majority of exegetes, Schmid does not posit a DtrH enshrined in Deuteronomy – 2 Kings, but rather finds behind Exodus – 2 Kings a great authorial work of a theological school, a popular movement, a single man, a long theological trend or the expression of the late exilic thought that is simply tagged "Deuteronomistic".[129] Where Martin Noth posits a single author and genius who was based in Mizpah and sought answers to the calamity of his day, hence the *"Ätiologie des Nullpunkts"*, Schmid rightly finds in the Dtr a school-of-thought or a movement, but his view that the work of that author begins from Exodus is and remains hypothetical.

In his bid to establish the compositional *Knoten* (ties or bonds) between Joshua and Judges, Erhard Blum discovers the dtr concept of the conquest of the land set forth in Jos 21 under the leadership of Joshua: the whole land is conquered, distributed and inhabited by Israel and the Lord grants Israel "rest" (נוח) from the enemies "surrounding" (מסב׳ב) her and all this in accordance with the promise made to the fathers (Jos 21:44-45)[130] to which Judg 2:12 becomes a natural sequence; because after these things the Israelites worshipped the gods of the nations around them, contravening the command in Deut 6:14, and provoked Yahweh to anger. Yahweh would also sell them into the hands of their enemies in accordance with the *Lex Talionis*. This, notes Blum, is so in as far as the *"Kernland"* is concerned because Joshua 23 and 24 deal basically with the periphery[131] and serve as an end to the Hexateuch with Joshua's promulgation of the "Torah of God" (24:26) in the DtrH.[132] Like Schmid, Blum finds the hand of the Dtr going back deeper into the Pentateuch than is normally held, but

---

128 K. Schmid, *Erzväter*, p. 97–98.
129 K. Schmid, *Erzväter*, p. 158–159.
130 E. Blum, *Kompositionelle Knoten*, p. 183. These are very important dtr vocabularies that are found also in the David and Solomon narratives; 2 Sam 7:1, 1 Kgs 5:4, 8:56.
131 E. Blum, *Kompositionelle Knoten*, p. 185.
132 E. Blum, *Kompositionelle Knoten*, p. 194–206.

begins with Exodus instead of Genesis, as Schmid does. He finds a perfect harmony of expression in Judg 2:8-10 and Ex 1:6-8 that he ascribes to the Dtr.[133] Blum does not only see the link between the book of Joshua and those before it but also those after it, especially Judges, and attributes this redactionary work to the dtr author.

In his article, *Gab es eine deuteronomistische Bewegung?* Lohfink warns against a wholesale attribution of texts to the Dtr on the basis that these texts portray the thoughts and are written in the language and style of that author, since his influence is to be found in a very wide range of texts. He will rather talk of a dtr school than of a movement (*Bewegung*) or a "*Bewegung*" in the sense of a school (or as it may turn out to be, a coalition). He agrees with Rainer Albertz (*Religionsgeschichte Israels in altestamentlichezeit 1*) and Frank Crüsemann (*Die Torah*) that the membership of the "school" did cut across social status to include courtiers, priests, members of the Davidic family, members of Judean middle-income families, and individual prophets, forming a coalition.[134] He, however, has no doubts in stating that in Deut 1-3 we are certainly not dealing with the introduction of the Deuteronomic Law, but rather with the beginning of the DtrH as Martin Noth has rightly pointed out. To this, he continues, can be added the conquest of the land (Jos 1-12) as belonging to the oldest dtr hand, which was written at the time of the reform of Josiah in "*Teilstücken*".[135] The aim of the school was the restoration of the twelve tribes of the nation of Israel under a single Davidic King worshipping the only one God in Jerusalem.[136] The importance of the contribution of Lohfink to the debate, in my estimation, is two-fold: on one hand he strikes a difference between a dtr corpus and traces of dtr thought or influence. Thus we can single out a dtr thought or language within a text without necessarily attributing the text to that author. On the other hand, he provides answers to the two

---

133 E. Blum, *Studien*, p. 102–103.
134 N. Lohfink, *deuteronomistische Bewegung?* p. 355. Lohfink further qualifies this group as „nationale und kultische Restaurationsbewegung der Joschijazeit" because of its aim and the fact that it was probably dissipated by the sudden death of Josiah and the marauding power of the Pharaoh sealed its doom so that it would no more exist in its original form (cf. p. 359).
135 N. Lohfink, *Geschichtstypologisch*, p. 152–155.
136 N. Lohfink, *Bewegung*, p. 357.

intriguing questions of identity and purpose of the dtr author; a coalition or school that cuts across social status with the common purpose of the restoration of the twelve tribes of Israel under the Davidic king around the Temple of Yhwh in Jerusalem. To this identity and purpose, Ansgar Moenikes, like many others, will seek to add the time frame.

Moenikers moves from the promise of "rest" to Israel as a key word in Deut 12 to 1 Kings 8 that is fulfilled in the achievements of the Davidic dynasty and Solomon's building of the Temple (1 Kings 8:56) with its attendant centralization of Yahweh's cult in Jerusalem to the reform of Josiah, who sought to return Israel to the *status quo* established by David (2 Kings 22-23). This provides a uniformed narrative that serves as a theological foundation of the cult-politics of Josiah.[137] Thus Deut 1 – 2 Kings 23 was put together at the time of the Josianic reform and an exilic redactor added 2 King 24-25:21 to the corpus.[138] This position does not differ in any practical terms from the proposition of Cross, Smend and Dietrich besides seeking to concretize that position.

If the influence of the dtr author is felt in Genesis and Exodus, why do exegetes follow Martin Noth by insisting that Deut 1-3 is the beginning of the DtrH? Walter Groß finds a simple means to respond to this relatively complex question. In the introduction to his commentary on the book of Judges, Groß confirms the hand of a dtr redactor (Dtr[R]) in the "Regenten" (Judges) narratives to link up the time of Joshua to that of the reigns of Eli, the sons of Eli and Samuel (p. 85). This redactor could either be the early Dtr behind Deuteronomy – 2 Kings or a late dtr author who joined the earlier history of Israel in (Genesis-) Exodus – Josua to that of the State in Samuel – Kings. What Groß might be saying in effect is that we have, on the

---

137 A. Moenikes, *Beziehungssysteme*, p. 79. Moenikes seeks to be more specific in his designation of the narrative in stating that: „Es liegt daher nahe, es als "Joschijanisches Geschichtswerk" zu bezeichnen; als Kürzel bietet sich "JoschG" an". This becomes a necessity as he identifies other levels of narrative materials such as: Efraimitisches Geschichtswerk (EfrG) from Jos 24 to 1 Sam 12 and Hiskijanisches Geschichtswerk (HisG) from 1 King 15 – 2 Kg 19 that the JoschG has incorporated into his work (p. 80). In this work we will avoid the entry into the diversity of sources and maintain the generally accepted position and nomenclature; DtrG or DtrH.

138 A. Moenikes, *Beziehungssystem*, p. 81.

one side, the narrative of the early history of Israel from the Exodus to the conquest of the land and, on the other, the reigns of Eli, his sons and Samuel that effectively introduce the monarchy and a united nation of Israel with its seat of government in Jerusalem. To create a flowing narrative out of these separate units, a dtr author has assembled the independent and sometimes legendary accounts of the individual regents as an appropriate linkage for his work. To this work a post-exilic dtr redactor (Dtr^S) added Jos 23 as an explanation for the uncompleted conquest of the land referring to the presence of the unconquered folks within the "*Kernland*" (2:22-3:4) as a test for Israel to learn the art of war.[139]

Lothar Perlitt narrows the argument down to Deuteronomy and its immediate context. He considers Deut 1-3 a co-ordination of the uncoordinated ideological and geographical material in Numbers and a theologization of the raw facts presented therein[140] that links up smoothly with the book of Joshua (as the Hexateuch). He naturally would not read it just as the beginning of Deuteronomy but that of a bigger block of texts that constitutes the work of the dtr historian.[141] Perlitt, thus, confirms the position of Martin Noth and the majority that the great work of history, put together by the dtr author, begins with the first three chapters of Deuteronomy.

On the whole Noth's position without excluding the possibility and the fact of the different stages of internal reduction in the DtrH holds sway in the debate. The primary work could have begun in the reign of Josiah as a propaganda material for the reform of the cult of Yahweh in Jerusalem and the return to the Davidic kingdom in its unified form with a later exilic updating or retouching as the case may be. Against this position stands Kratz who will not budge for a DtrH beginning from Deuteronomy to Kings, but proposes a gradual growth from the Hexateuch (Genesis – Joshua) to the Enneateuch extending from Genesis to Kings upon which the so-called

---

139   W. Groß, *Richter*, p. 82–87.
140   Perlitt notes that in the Numbers narrative (21:21-31) of the conquest of Zihon, Yhwh does not appear in the drama at all but in Deut 2 Yhwh ordains the fate of Sihon and gives the order with Israel at the receiving end (2:24-36). This in itself is an indication that the writer of Deut 1-3 has knowledge of the tradition to which he adds his own theological touch or interpretation. Cf. *Deuteronomium* 1-3, p. 161.
141   L. Perlitt, *Deuteronomium*, p. 157–163.

deuteronomistic author has stamped his reduction secondarily before it was split into the two parts of the Canon; the Torah and the Former Prophets.[142] Kratz argues that the classic dtr judgment of the kings of Israel and Judah on the basis of whether they did what was evil (mostly Israel) or what was right (basically Judah) in the sight of the Lord has as its criteria the unity of cult and place of worship and the oneness of Yahweh. Whereas the first (the place of worship) more strongly recalls Deuteronomy the second (oneness of Yahweh) derives its force from the dominance of the Decalogue in the Sinaitic law of Exodus – Numbers. Thus the first Commandment provides the literary connection of Samuel – Kings to the whole law in the Pentateuch, cited regularly as the Law of Moses[143], and therefore the framework of the Enneateuch. Of the two dtr ideas, the unity of the place of worship is the original scheme present in the annals of the kings and relates to the political history of the two kingdoms, the expansion which has the first commandment as criterion has to do with a later level of dtr redaction.[144] The dtr additions to Deuteronomy – 2 Kings presuppose the existence of the Enneateuch and the connecting speeches and theological interpretative texts in Josh 23-24, Judg 2-3, 1 Sam 12, 2 Sam 7, 1 Kings 8, 2 Kings 17, etc., argues Kratz, are only very late formulations imposed upon the Hexateuch. For Kratz "the beginning of the dtr redaction does not lie in Deuteronomy but in Samuel – Kings and from here extends backwards into (Genesis-) Deuteronomy, Joshua and Judges" and is, therefore, a confirmation of the old view of the Dtr additions to the Hexateuch.[145] The position of Kratz, simply put, is that the Dtr is only a late redactor who has stamped his connecting influence upon an otherwise extant and varied tradition through "a literary and historical theological connection. This revision, extending beyond individual books, speaks quite a uniform language which in many respects recalls Deuteronomy and the Deuteronomistic paranaesis of the law."[146] In the same vein, Jan Christian Gerz will vouch for the *"Priestly*

---

142 R. G. Kratz, *Composition*, p. 158.
143 2 Kings 18: 6, 21:8, 22:8f, 23:25.
144 R. G. Kratz, *Composition*, p. 162–163.
145 R. G. Kratz, Composition, p. 158 cf. C. Frevel, *Deuteronomistisches Geschichtswerk*, p. 80.
146 R. G. Kratz, op cit, p. 156.

Narrative Strand" from Genesis to Numbers and Deuteronomy 34, which singles out the non-priestly Moses narrative of Exodus 1 – Joshua 12 as the logical sequence of the exodus from Egypt to the Land of Promise that goes back before the *Priestly Narratives*.[147] This position, like that of Kratz, naturally rules out a DtrH beginning from Deuteronomy – 2 Kings.

In a recent work, Erhard Blum focuses on the self-reference formulations within Deuteronomy that point out that the book was conceived as an independent work from the Tetrateuch. In Deut 31:9, Moses is said to have written "this law" (התורה הזאת) which he gave to the Levitical priests who were responsible for the ark of the covenant of Yhwh and to all the elders of Israel, who were to read "this law" (התורה הזאת) every seven years before all Israel (v. 11). He then commanded the Levites who carried the ark of the covenant to deposit "this book of the law" (ספר התורא הזה) beside the Ark of the Covenant of Yhwh (v. 26). It is this Torah that Moses had set himself to expound in the land of Moab (Deut 1:5). This art of self-definition makes the book unique, for it is completely absent in Genesis – Numbers, but very much used in the legal documents of agreements between states in the ancient world. Deuteronomy being a *"Torah book"*, written by Moses and handed over to the Levitical priests, would mean that it can be cited on its own and or integrated into other works. In his own words, Blum returns to Martin Noth's theory of a DtrH that begins with a dtr edition of Deuteronomy which stands as an independent *"Torabuch"* from the Tetrateuch.[148]

Hermann-Josef Stipp, the latest to return to the issue of the date of Noth's DtrG, does so with the background of the Block or Göttinger Model which seeks to date the *Vorlage* to the period after the fall of Jerusalem – 580. He approaches the theme from the stand point of the clues that the concluding parts of 2 Kings bring to light. The important role, accorded King Josiah

---

147 J. C. Gerz, *Grundinformation*, pp. 278–281.
148 E. Blum, *Pentateuch – Hexateuch – Enneateuch*, pp. 83–89. Erhard Blum finds similar self-references in the book of Joshua which he expounds in his *Kompositionelle Knoten*, p. 203–204. The report in Jos 24:26 that Joshua wrote these words in the book of the "Torah Elohim", states Blum, does not imply a recording in the law of Moses but a new definition which includes the very writing of Joshua in a book, hence the Torah Elohim; the Hexateuch, which is not the same as the Torah.

in the tradition for his repentance, successful cultic reform and centralization of Yhwh cult in Jerusalem, produces an enormous conflict in the text bearing upon a discrepancy in the dtr ideology and theology. Josiah coincidentally finds a copy of the law – ספר התורה (2 Kings 22:8, 11) or ספר הברית (23:2, 21) during the renovation of the Temple and begins a religious journey of repentance and reform, which earned him dtr praise in superlative terms: *"Before him there was no king like him, who turned to the LORD with all his heart, with all his soul, and with all his might, according to all the law of Moses; nor did any like him arise after him"* (2 Kings 23:25). This exemplary act of the king is immediately followed by the comment that it did not placate the fierce wrath of Yhwh kindled against Judah for the provocations of Manasseh (v. 26).[149] Instead of the expected salvation that such a reform should have brought, the king dies in war at the hands of Necho of Egypt and the deportation of Judah seems a forgone conclusion, rendering fruitless the pious acts of repentance and cultic purification. This close-ended fate of Judah, opines Stipp, definitely portrays a pessimistic view of the material that Noth ascribes to the DtrG which indicates that the basic text at the root of the Books of Kings was different from their present tone which is a *"Kompromissprodukt"* (a product of compromise), born out of a gradual process of growth.[150] What can be deducted from the text itself, continues Stipp, is that the basic text upheld the person of Josiah and his reform as the sure hope of Judah, but the reality proved otherwise and is logical that the basic literary architecture of the work was laid down before 587 and was later expanded with the theological rationalization that puts the blame at the feet of Manasseh.[151]

---

149 H. J. Stipp, Ende bei Joschija, in ÖBS 39, p. 234.
150 H. J. Stipp, op. cit., p. 240.
151 H. J. Stipp, op. cit., p. 241–242. Stipp quotes the protest of the exiles in Egypt against Jeremiah and the cult reform as an indication that there was the need for the Dtr to defend his basic doctrine of the purity of Yhwh cult as the recipe for security and salvation against the pathological doubt of the people based upon their historical, personal experience. The proximity of the events of 587 despite the reform of Josiah was too negative an experience to foster an optimistic future (cf. p. 246). Shortly before this position, Wolfgang Oswald had posited 561 as the date of the DtrG that was expanded in the subsequent years. Cf. *Nathan der Prophet*, p. 272.

Martin Noth has good reasons to have singled out the text from Deut – 2 Kings as the dtr corpus, the basic work of which may have been written during the reign of Josiah. The work might have originally served as a propaganda tool justifying the reform of Josiah and legitimizing the efforts of the king. In its final form as it appears in the end text of the Biblical narratives, the DtrH is the product of an exilic author or an exilic trend of thought that seeks to explain the cataclysmic events in the history of Israel as the result of the disobedience of the kings and the people, symbolized by Jeroboam of Israel and Manasseh of Judah, but does not fail at one and the same time to transmit a message of hope at the end of the dark tunnel which he shared with his contemporaries. This great author had the quality of editing various components of the history to become, in one way or the other, a mirror image of the whole. For instance, the book of Judges revolves around a perennial cycle of sin-retribution-redemption. This becomes a mirror image of what will happen to Israel in the future with her constant disobedience to the law of the Lord despite the persistent warning of her prophets. Thus the retouching of the parable of Nathan and its placement within the context of the succession to the throne of David, the Succession Narrative (SN), brings out the fact of retribution for crimes or sins committed against the law of the Lord without losing sight of divine mercy that pardons, forgives and redeems. It is only by the appropriate and expert extension of the parable of Nathan by the dtr author to include the double prophecy of doom that this mirror-effect to the exile is achieved. For the purpose of this work, I have chosen a very small part of this great work as my theme and will, therefore, seek to narrow down the discussion to that part of the work instead of the whole. The parable of Nathan is found in the sub-section that is called the Succession Narrative (2 Sam 9 – 1 Kings 1) and it is to this section that I will now turn the attention.

3.1 The Succession Narrative and the Deuteronomist (Dtr)

It stands beyond any reasonable doubt that the books of Samuel and Kings, like those books before them, are composed out of previously independent blocks of narratives that have been brought together under the guise of an astute author to constitute a single whole. Under the scrutinizing eye of the critical reader such blocks as the Saul tradition of 1 Sam 1-15, the rise of David in 1 Sam 16-2 Sam 5, the succession narrative of 2 Sam 7-1 Kings 2, the history of the ark in 1 Sam 4-6, 2 Sam 6 (and possibly 1 Kings 8) and the chronological narratives of the kings of Israel and Judah in the books of Kings become readily identifiable. Each of these narratives would originally tell a story of its own and a good author or editor who has such a variety of texts at his disposal would naturally trim the edges and straighten up the curves or even intersperse them, as in the case of the history of the ark, to fit into his broader plan or programme. Our interest at this point will be centred on that block within which 2 Sam 12:1-15a is located.

The material that we have termed "Succession Narrative" (SN) in consonance with the trend of modern exegetical thought, 2 Sam 9-1 Kings 2, has within it other identifiable component parts that have been put together. The narrative in 2 Sam 13-19 depicts Absalom as its protagonist planning and executing his vendetta and revolting against his father, and could be captioned "the Absolom cycle", while 2 Sam 11-12 and 1 Kings 1-2 may constitute "the Solomon narrative". Leonhard Rost discovers, rightly, the pivotal point around which these two narratives rotate; the question of David's succession, as put in the mouth of the prophet Nathan, first in his plotting with Bathsheba and then before the king: "*Has this thing really been brought about by my lord the king and you have not let your servants know who should sit on the throne of my lord the king after him?*" (1 Kings 1:27) Effectively, the whole account, stretching from the childlessness of Michal in 2 Sam 6:20f to the death of David and consolidation of the reign of Solomon in 1 Kings 2, is a family saga geared towards responding to the pertinent question of the succession to the throne of David. Some analysts will prefer to call it "Court History" (cf. Flanagan and Van Seters), as it deals with the history of the Jerusalem court of David and the problems that David faced in maintaining his sovereignty over the united Israel.[152] As much as this portrays the facts at stake, it misplaces the

---

152 J. W. Flanagan, *Court History*, p. 177. Flanagan stretches this fact so wide as to make the revolt of Absalom the central point of the narrative, being the most severe threat to the sovereignty of David in Jerusalem. The story will flow without 2 Sam 11-12 and 1 Kings 1-2 but will woefully fail to explain how Solomon becomes the next king to sit on the throne of David in 1 Kings 3.

emphasis of the paramount theme of the narrative and leaves the reader in a blank space. The narrative will jump from 2 Sam 20 (leaving out the appendix of 21-24) to 1 Kings 3 with Solomon as king and acting as such without any kind of introduction at all. A redactor worth the name will not leave such an obvious *lacuna* in his work. The question of succession as depicted in 1 Kings 1 becomes the guiding principle of every action or inaction, it causes apprehension and agitated excitement and propels itself unto a high pedestal fit only for a climax to be reached when a new king successfully sits on the throne "after" David. The theme surfaces for the first time in 2 Sam 7:12 in the oracle of Nathan. With the exclusion of possible offspring of Michal, the choice silently swings from Amnon, executed by Absalom, to Absalom, who is killed by Joab, then to Adonijah, the usurper and, finally, to Solomon, who is enthroned as king upon the word of David. This would be the basic tradition inherited by the dtr author and how he uses it to recount the story is his quality as an author, who achieves "a skilful homogeneous literary masterpiece, perhaps the finest prose in the entire Hebrew Bible."[153]

The argument, that the SN in its present form and location in the Bible is either pro-monarchy (cf. Rost and von Rad) or anti-monarchy (cf. Van Seters), is definitely an understatement that disregards the historical circumstances and purpose of the author, be it a single person or a group of persons. It fails to distinguish between the original purpose of the work and the aim of the final editor who placed the work in his project and ironed it out to fit into his history. The work could have served as an apology at the time of Solomon's reign, but the fourth century author had certainly no need of an apology and a defence of the monarchy to have made that theme paramount in his work. The Dtr, in the texts that are undisputedly attributed to him, does not mince words in the condemnation of people and institutions that require his condemnation and would not hide his displeasure about anyone who sells himself "to do what is evil in the sight

---

A good story will not miss the origin of its most prominent actor and a good narrator will ensure that such a vacuum is filled up.

153 J. Van Seters, *Historiography*, p. 278. This is how Van Seters sums up the thoughts of L. Rost.

of the Lord" as he clearly demonstrates in the books of Judges and Kings. The materials at his disposal were enough to make him concentrate on other things than the choice of Solomon, the youngest son, over his elder brothers; Absalom, Amnon and Adonijah. David, the youngest of the sons of Jesse, was chosen over and above his seven other brothers with a simple and divine affirmation: *"...for the Lord does not see as mortals see; they look on the outward appearance, but the Lord looks on the heart"* (1 Sam 16:7). Moreover, the SN does not show any marked interest in Solomon as a person and King, as an apology would have done, but as a successor to the throne of David and the builder of the Temple of Jerusalem. He came to the throne not on his own merit but on account of the divine choice and election that the author with his usual refined sense of informed innocence hints upon at the announcement of his birth (2 Sam 12:24-25). His choice is not singular in being the youngest and least expected; the choice of David was exactly in the same manner.

The dtr author presents the traditions that he has inherited for the SN with a few interventions of his own for the purpose of portraying the divine hand that guides a frail human institution through turbulent times to its fulfilment. In doing so he employs 2 Sam 11-12 and 1 Kings 1-2 as a framework within which he inserts the history of turbulence at the court of David through which the humanly possible candidates to the throne are either liquidated or excluded to pave the way for Solomon, the son born to David in Jerusalem, to inherit his father. An author with the qualities of the Dtr would not let the origin of the silent hero of the narrative fall into oblivion. Therefore, he uses the Amonite war as a framework to narrate the adultery of David with Bathsheba, the murder of Uriah, the marriage of the two and the subsequent birth of the future king in 2 Sam 11-12.

3.2 2 Sam 12:1-15a and the dtr

One does not need a special form of training to realise that the narrative block of 2 Sam 12:1-15a stands out of tune with its surroundings. All through the history of David there is no single moment where David is accused of something evil; he is either not present at all at the scene of crime or it happens at his blind side. In this episode and for the first time in the whole narrative, David stands accused by a prophet on two counts of adultery and murder. This prophetic intervention, with its resultant prophecy of doom, has caused a flood of questions and responses by way of explaining the authorship and motive behind it. The literal critic simply considers this episode a later addition to the text. Rost identifies 2 Sam 12:1-7a and 13-15a as the "Nathan pericope", which is not a dtr material. It is the work of a courtier who sought to show that the sin of David had been forgiven and, therefore, could be said of Solomon; "And Yhwh loved him". He argues that the double threat in vv. 7b-12 breaks the flow of the narrative and has Absalom's revolt and the death of David's three sons at the sword in view. This could not have come from the same author as the Nathan pericope.[154] This model emphasizes that the SN was written during the reign of Solomon at which time the idealization of David was not in vogue, being a later concept, and the author did not have to concern himself with the preservation of that non-existent ideology. It holds the entry of Nathan at this point in the history as an exilic addition and served the purpose of proclaiming that: *"Der König hat bereut, und ihm wurde vergeben"* (the king has repented and he has been forgiven).[155]

Dietrich has become a prominent proponent of the redaction critical model with his proposition of a three-strata system of redaction within the chapter:

11:27a + 12:24b → a SN that is critical of David (The illegitimate son is Solomon.)
12:15b – 12:24a → a pro-David narrative (David's penance and death of the son)
11:27b – 12:15a → an independent prophetic tradition (DtrP)

The first level of redaction deals with the pure SN which is very critical of David and Solomon. It identifies Solomon as the son born out of wedlock

---

154 L. Rost, *Succession*, p. 77–78. Rost notes that the whole pericope can be lifted out of its present context without any difficulty. However, without it the long and detailed description of the sickness and death of the son of David (12:15b-23) makes no sense. The presence of the Nathan pericope acts as the needed catharsis to propel the narrative towards the fulfilment of the prophecy and gives the moral force of the whole.
155 E. Würthwein, *Thronfolge Davids*, 25f.

to David and therefore illegitimate. This has been toned down in the second level by the addition of the David-friendly narrative of the sickness of the son, David's penance, the subsequent death of the child and announcement of the birth of Solomon. To these two is a third level of narrative of a prophetic origin added by the DtrP who has reworked the material to fit into its environment by the addition of 11:27b and 12:15a as literary seams.[156] Timo Veijola goes further in his claim that the original narrative moved from 11:27b to 12:24a and that Solomon was the first son of the union between David and Bathsheba and, therefore, the fruit of adultery. It is only an addition of the second stratum to introduce a second son that could mitigate the dark shadow surrounding Solomon's birth.[157]

The traditional historical critical model proposes the Court History as the older material with the SN being a small part of the whole. The CH generally idealizes David and refrains from passing negative comments about him. The SN is a post-exilic addition to the DtrG with the purpose of countering the idealization of David that is paramount in the DtrH and serves to discredit David.[158] It is for this reason that the SN in many instances presupposes the CH but the CH does not portray any knowledge of the latter. In the David-Solomon narrative (SN), nothing good, but everything bad, is said about the two monarchs. It can only be the hand of an opponent to the monarchy at work in this block.[159] It is a labyrinth of incomprehension to have God quickly forgive the sins of David and proclaim the product of that union as the beloved of God.[160]

Do we really have before us an anti-David narrative? In any given historical narrative, even in the case of apology, what is narrated is not as

---

156 Cf. A. F. Campbell – M. A. O'Brien, *Unfolding the Deuteronomistic History*, p. 299.
157 T. Veijola, *Gesammelte Studien*, pp. 84–87. Veijola argues that the report of the birth of the illegitimate son curiously lacks a name, which is very unusual in Biblical narratives especially in the SN. However, if 12:24-25 makes up for this lack if it comes directly after 11:27a with the first part of 12:24 functioning as a resumption of the narration from 11:27a. This will make Solomon the name of the son born to David by Bathsheba, the wife of Uriah and therefore illegitimate.
158 J. Van Seters, *In Search of History*, 278.
159 L. Delekat, *Tendenz und Theologie*, p. 27.
160 L. Delekat, *Tendenz und Theologie*, p. 32.

important as how it is narrated. The events of 2 Sam 11 lay it bare that the bearer of the promise of an everlasting dynasty has endangered the whole project by committing adultery and murder and it takes no odinary person than the very prophet who proclaimed the good things to come who now confronts the king with his guilt. The sinner acknowledges his guilt, his sins are forgiven and he remains under the mercy of God, who accepts the son born after the forgiveness. The theme of divine mercy and benevolence resting upon the repentant sinner is never lost in the DtrH. It is in fact a paramount idea at the basis of that work.

Nowack, in the already quoted commentary, sums up, in concrete terms, the position of many scholars on 2 Sam 12:1-15a: the text is not just a later addition to the narrative but has in itself seen various stages of redaction. The obvious question to ask is: A later addition to which narrative? I would not like to consider it a later addition to the CH or even to the SN but as an integral part of the dtr reworking of a pre-existent historical tradition. In this view I am not looking at the material only as the SN of David but from the global view of the DtrH to which it belongs. This means that I am not giving preference to one model against another. Being all-inclusive, I am looking at the text as the product of a historical process that has sustained and preserved it in its state and context over the centuries. In doing so I give credit to the efforts of the various models and the various questions that constitute their starting points.

The Smend school of thought, symbolized by Dietrich, unearths a dtr redaction in the internal fabric of the pericope and ascribes it to the DtrP because of the emphasis on the prophetic role of Nathan.[161] The text brilliantly links up the past, the rise of David, with the present, the sins of David, which will account for the future turmoil in the royal family, and the fragility of the dynasty. These separate narratives may have existed independently from one another, but the dtr author has brought them together to constitute a complex whole as the history of Yhwh's folk. Moreover Nathan's double prophecy of doom is couched in too typical a dtr language to remove from that author.

---

161 A. F. Campbel & M. A. O'Brien, *Unfolding the Deuteronomistic History*, p. 299.

A hallmark of the dtr author is the strategic positioning of long or short speeches of the important personalities of the history at important moments of transition to look backward and forward interpreting the course of events and drawing practical conclusions for the future.[162] In many instances the author adds his own voice to the inherited material to bring out his judgement based upon his rule of conduct. Noth cites such examples as Joshua's brief address to the trans-Jordanian tribes in Josh 1:12ff, and his final speech to the house of Israel in 23, Samuel's address to Israel in 1 Sam 12 and Solomon's inauguration speech in 1 Kgs 8:14ff. Admittedly, Nathan's oracle has not caught the attention of analysts for it to be added to the list, but it serves much the same purpose as any of the aforementioned speeches in its triple glance at history. The language itself, as we will see below, is purely dtr and follows the classic formula of the dtr prophecy of doom.

Examples of prophecies or oracles of doom abound in the work of the Dtr to facilitate a comparison of their forms in order to give us a broad view of what happens in such prophecies and what is at stake in them. Avoiding superfluity, I will cite only three of such oracles for our purpose: Samuel and Saul in 1 Sam 15, the wife of Ahab and the prophet Ahijah in 1 Kings 14 and Ahab and the unnamed prophet in 1 Kings 20;

---

162   M. Noth, *Überlieferung*, p. 5.

1 Samuel 15:17-23 (NRSV)	1 Kings 14:7b-16 (NRSV)	1 Kings 20:39-43 (NRSV)
[17] Samuel said, "Though you are little in your own eyes, are you not the head of the tribes of Israel? The Lord anointed you king over Israel. [18] And the Lord sent you on a mission, and said, 'Go, utterly destroy the sinners, the Amalekites, and fight against them until they are consumed.' [19] Why then did you not obey the voice of the Lord? Why did you swoop down on the spoil, and do what was evil in the sight of the Lord?" ... [22] ... "Has the Lord as great delight in burnt offerings and sacrifices, as in obeying the voice of the Lord? Surely, to obey is better than sacrifice, and to heed than the fat of rams. [23] For rebellion is no less a sin than divination, and stubbornness is like iniquity and idolatry. Because you have rejected the word of the Lord, he has also rejected you from being king."	[7] Go, tell Jeroboam, 'Thus says the Lord, the God of Israel: Because I exalted you from among the people, made you leader over my people Israel, [8] and tore the kingdom away from the house of David to give it to you; *yet you have not been like my servant David*, who kept my commandments and followed me with all his heart, doing only that which was right in my sight, [9] *but you have done evil above all those who were before you* and have gone and made for yourself other gods, and cast images, provoking me to anger, and have thrust me behind your back; [10] therefore, I will bring evil upon the house of Jeroboam. I will cut off from Jeroboam every male, both bond and free in Israel, and will consume the house of Jeroboam, just as one burns up dung until it is all gone.... [12] Therefore set out, go to your house. When your feet enter the city, the child shall die.... [15] *"The LORD will strike Israel, as a reed is shaken in the water; he will root up Israel out of this good land that he gave to their ancestors, and scatter them beyond the Euphrates, because they have made their sacred poles, provoking the LORD to anger.* [16] *He will give Israel up because of the sins of Jeroboam, which he sinned and which he caused Israel to commit."*	[39] As the king passed by, he cried to the king and said, "Your servant went out into the thick of the battle; then a soldier turned and brought a man to me, and said, 'Guard this man; if he is missing, your life shall be given for his life, or else you shall pay a talent of silver.' [40] While your servant was busy here and there, he was gone." The king of Israel said to him, "So shall your judgment be; you yourself have decided it." [41] Then he quickly took the bandage away from his eyes. The king of Israel recognized him as one of the prophets. [42] Then he said to him, *"Thus says the Lord, 'Because you have let the man go whom I had devoted to destruction, therefore your life shall be for his life, and your people for his people.'"* [43] The king of Israel set out toward home, resentful and sullen, and came to Samaria.

In the first two oracles the prophets begin with a narration of what the Lord had done for the monarch as a basis for the requirement of his faithfulness to the God of Israel then name the sin of the king as a deviation and violation of the otherwise established trust. The method of a typical prophecy of doom in the DtrH would sound like: *X (the Lord) did all that for Y (the monarch) but Y has done this. Therefore X will do the following to Y (dynasty and people)"*. It would be necessary to analyse each of these examples to find the hand of the dtr at work in them.

3.2.1 Samuel and Saul

In all probability, 1 Sam 15 stems from a prophetic source with its image of Samuel, the prophet, as king-maker and mouth-piece of Yahweh. He gives the divine order to the king and he has to obey it to the word. A disobedience to the prophetic word can not be explained away with the flimsy excuse of the choice of the people or for the sake of a sacrifice. It is very likely that the late author has not touched the material here and has presented it just as he might have found it in its prophetic form or from the Saul-David narrative which has the tendency to emphasize, on one hand, the failure of Saul and, on the other, the success of David. Where Saul woefully failed, David gracefully fulfilled the command of Yahweh.[163] The background of the enmity between Israel and Amalek and the prophecy of doom against Saul is the cowardly act of Amalek in attacking the weary Israelites on their way out of Egypt (Ex 17:8-13). In this basic Amalek text, the faceless Amalek is pictured only as an aggressor who appears on the scene to cause havoc without *the fear of the Lord*. This event was to be written down in a book and not to be forgotten, because the Lord would avenge the atrocity.

The tradition, however, is given a formulation in Deuteronomy that makes it imperative for the monarch to obey (Deut 25:17-19). The presence of the command in Deut 25 is suspect. The chapter deals with domestic and moral laws but ends up with the call to avenge the crime of Amalek against Israel "when she (Israel) has rest from all her enemies on every hand". The only element that seems to connect this command to what precedes it

---

[163] In 1 Sam 29: 26 David names the marauding Amalekites whom he had conquered "the enemies of the Lord"

may be the command to use an honest measure; measure for measure, and stretching it from the domestic or individual to the national level as vengeance upon the enemy of Israel.[164] Without having to edit the material in 1 Sam 15 the author may have thrown back the command into Deut 25 to blow up the disobedience of Saul and justify his rejection as a violation of the Deuteronomic law; a favourite theme of the dtr, who further garnishes the command with one of his basic expressions: *"when the Lord your God has given you rest from all your enemies on every hand"* (v.19). In this way the dtr author has fashioned a hook out of Deut 25 that links Exodus 17 to 1 Sam 15. The unique command that was to be written down in a book (Ex 17:19) is now written down in the Torah (Deut 25) and must be obeyed (1 Sam 15).[165] The eponymous Amalek, even though a small group of people, becomes synonymous with and the short form for the enemy, whoever and wherever he may be, with whom Yahweh is constantly at war until he is no more.[166] Agag then becomes the prototype of Israel's arch enemy, who has no fear of God. Saul's inability to destroy him becomes an outright disobedience of the command of the Lord and warrants his rejection as king. His place will be taken by another, David, who will obey that command in accordance with the divine will as a mission accomplished.

---

164 There is hardly a reference to Amalek in the Old Testament that does not refer to him as an aggressor. Taking Exodus 17, Deut 25 and 1 Sam 15 for granted we might find this sense of aggression in the reference to the Amalekite who brings the news of Saul's death to David as "lifting the hand to destroy the Lord's anointed without fear" (2 Sam 1:14); Haman the Agagite (a descendant of Agag the Amalekite) plots the complete annihilation of Mordecai and his people (Israel) in the drama of the book of Esther. The defeat of Haman is a victory of Israel over her ancient enemy, Amalek (cf. B. Ego, *Israel und Amalek*, pp. 288, 414).

165 Tanner ascribes to Deut 25:17-19 a quality of backward and forward-looking in regard to Exodus 17 and 1 Sam 15 respectively. Deut 25:17 links up with 1 Sam 15:2 as a summary of the war between Israel and Amalek in Ex 17:8-16 while Deut 25:19 looks back to Ex 17:14 and prepares the ground for the future war of 1 Sam 15 upon the command of Yahweh himself. (cf. *Amalek*, pp. 92–93) That Israel is commanded to blot out the memory of Amalek from the surface of the earth is a unique command in the whole of Old Testament tradition.

166 C. Houtman, *Exodus*, p. 376.

3.2.2 Ahijah and Jeroboam

In the second instance, the king does not appear himself but sends his wife, disguised as a farmer. The "blind" prophet identifies her instantly according to the promptings of the Lord of which the reader has fore-knowledge. Once again, this story may have stemmed from the prophetic cycle for the important role that the prophet plays as a seer, king-maker and mouthpiece of Yahweh. The core of the original story could be deduced from the sending of the wife instead of the king himself and her misguided and unsuccessful disguise, suggesting a possible tension between the king and his former mentor (1 Kings 11:29-40) and the prediction of the death of the son of Jeroboam. The dtr has made use of these facts by extending the speeches of Ahijah to bring out the rejection of the monarch and the whole of Israel with him because of their sins of idolatry. The mention of the loyalty of David in v. 8b; "...*yet you have not been like my servant David, who kept my commandments and followed me with all his heart, doing only that which was right in my sight*", is simply the dtr yardstick for measuring all the kings of Israel and Judah who reigned after David.[167]

The presence of the statement requires a period when the idealization of David was already established and that could not have been before the exile. The implication is that the text has been reworked by an exilic writer. This author leaves us yet an editorial mark in v. 9; *but you have done evil above all those who were before you and have gone and made for yourself other gods, and cast images, provoking me to anger, and have thrust me behind your back*. This remark is definitely irrelevant in the present text considering the fact that Jeroboam was the first ruler of the northern kingdom. It is nonetheless important as the stereotypical condemnatory phrase of the Dtr as in the case of Omri and Ahab in 16:25 and 16:30 respectively. Vv. 15-16 raise the prophecy of doom from the royal level to the national and predict the exile of the whole of Israel putting the blame squarely at the feet of the king and upon the head of whole people. It is no longer the individual issue of whether the son would live or die, but rather the whole

---

167 Other such references could be seen in I Kings 3:6, 9:4, 11:4, etc. A singular exception to this note of uprightness is the famous blemish of 15:5; "... except in the matter of Uriah the Hittite."

nation would be driven into exile away from the land *"because of the sins of Jeroboam, which he sinned and which he caused Israel to commit"*. This is the core of the dtr theological explanation of the exile.

3.2.3 *The unnamed prophet and Ahab*

In the third instance, the prophet sets the scene for the king to easily pronounce judgment on him and then springs the verdict back unto the king himself in the similar manner as Nathan had done to David, from the point of view of the narrative if not historical sequence. The identity of the prophet in this narrative is not known, but that the king recognised him indicates that they may have previously had dealings with each other. Josephus identifies him as Micaiah ben Imlah, but this assertion could be a pure conjecture based upon Ahab's claim that Micaiah never had a good word for him but disaster (1 Kings 22:8).[168] Interestingly, the story does not mention the name of the particular "king of Israel" who is involved in the narrative. The fabricated story, in the form of an acted parable, flows smoothly, tactically hitting the nail on the head. The king's reaction to it, as would be expected, was quick and cryptic, but the prophecy of doom is still preceded by a short declaration of the sin of the king: *"Thus says the Lord, 'Because you have let the man go whom I had devoted to destruction, therefore your life shall be for his life, and your people for his people.'"* The image of Ahab in the war narrative is very positive; he has the support of the prophet in his refusal of vassalage and receives the promise of victory over Benhadad. There is no mention of an explicit or even implicit instruction on a *herem*. Therefore, this condemnation for sparing the life of "the man devoted to destruction" smacks of an independent narrative, stemming from opponents of the king. The Dtr has added it to his story and, at this position, in agreement with the generally negative picture he paints of the reign of Ahab.

Prophecies of doom in the DtrH, whether simply prophetic in origin or edited by the author, are hardly devoid of a narration of the transgression of their subjects. It is in this narration of guilt that the Dtr enters the story

---

168 Josephus, *Antiquities*, 8.391. Even without mentioning Elijah, Ahab's fierce critic, this narrative shows that Ahab's reign knew a number of prophets some of whom supported him and others who censured him.

with his own interpretation of history as a prologue to the fall of the monarch in particular and the fall of Israel in general. The same is true of the oracle of Nathan against David and his household.

3.2.4 *Nathan and David*

Acting upon the word of the Lord, Nathan approaches David with a juridical proposition that looks forward to the king's judgment. As in the case of the unnamed prophet and Ahab, the response of the king expresses his own condemnation. Herein lies the crux of the matter; Nathan comes before the king with the story and requires a judgment, the king promptly pronounces his judgment of the case and it is thrown back upon his own head. Armed with this story the dtr in his usual manner prolongs the prophetic oracle to make it reflect the past life of David and the future turmoil of his house (vv. 7b-12). The prophecy is introduced by what the Lord (X) had done for David (Y); I anointed you as king, I rescued you, I gave you… and would have added more (v. 7b-8) followed by the narration of the sin of David that violates the established confidence between him and Yhwh, prefixed with a question (v. 9): "Why have you despised the word of the Lord…?" Finally, vv. 10-12 present what the Lord (X) will do to David and his house (Y) because of this violation. This future action of the Lord against the house of David, in the usual manner of the Dtr, provides coherence in the whole narrative besides giving it a logical and moral basis.

As the analysis of the material at our disposal indicates, a number of critics consider Nathan's prophecy of doom (v. 7b-12) a "later addition" to "the narrative". The problem is how one defines *later*; exilic or post-exilic, and what *narrative* here refers to; SN or DtrH? Rost would even go to the extent of completely removing the oracle of doom from its surroundings. By removing vv. 7b-12 from the narrative, the reconstructed version of Rost would read:

> ¹Then Yhwh sent Nathan to David. When he came to him he said to him, "There were two men in a city, the one rich and the other poor. ² The rich man had very many flocks and cattle; ³but the poor man had nothing but one little ewe lamb which he had bought. He took care of it and it grew up with him and with his children: it used to eat of his morsel, drink from his cup, lie in his bosom and it was like a daughter to him. ⁴Now, there came a traveller to the rich man, and he loathed (pitied) to take from his flock and cattle to prepare for the wayfarer who

had come to him. But he took the lamb of the poor man and prepared it for the man who had come to him.

⁵Then David's anger was greatly kindled against the man. He said to Nathan, "As the Lord lives, the man who has done this deserves to die; ⁶ and the lamb he shall restore fourfold, because he has done this thing, and because he had no pity."⁷ Nathan said to David, "You are the man! ¹³ Then said David to Nathan, "I have sinned against the Lord." Nathan said to David, "The Lord has, on one hand, caused your sin to pass over, you shall not die. ¹⁴Nevertheless, because you have by this deed utterly scorned the Lord, the child that is born to you, on the other, shall surely die." ¹⁵Then Nathan went to his house.

In my opinion, the result of Rost's reconstruction of the story is an identification of the core material of the encounter of Nathan and David. It may constitute the kernel of the story at the disposal of the exilic author; the inherited tradition. As part of this inherited tradition, the exilic author also had access to the so-called SN or the narrative of the violent conflict at the court of David in Jerusalem that was geared towards the resolution of the suppressed question of which one among the many sons of the king would sit on the throne after their father. The Dtr then expanded this story by adding the double prophecy of doom (vv. 7b–12) to fit it into the future violence of 2 Sam 13-20, which he then placed together with 2 Sam 11-12 + 1 Kings 1-2 to answer the question of succession to the throne of David. With the addition of 11-12 at this opportune moment, the efficient author achieves the effect of the sinner who can not escape divine justice, even if he is the great King David himself and the bounty of divine mercy that is immeasurable for the repentant sinner. At the same time he silently and seemingly ignorantly prepares the scene for Solomon's succession with the apparent appendix of 2 Sam 12:24-25 that Yhwh loved Solomon. An isolation of the prophecy of doom (vv. 7b-12) from its context on the basis of the knowledge of the later events in the house of David will leave behind a dry, unsuited and meaningless narrative that belittles in so doing the authorial ingenuity of the sacred writer. It would take away, without impunity, the whole prophecy of doom, which in fact, forms an integral part of dtr oracles of this nature. To deny the Dtr the authorship of these verses and ascribe them to a later redactor would not reflect an objective representation of the material. Neither does the fact that this encounter with Nathan put David in a very negative light justify its separation from this writer. The author had access to a variety of material, one part of which was positive

and the negative. His integrity as an author is proven by his diligent use of both materials in constructing a single whole that would not in any way be too lopsided to be accepted as the history of his people.

The Dtr leaves no stone unturned in his portrayal of David as the chosen one of Yahweh; he is an excellent soldier, a marvellous king and a faithful servant in relying upon divine mercy. At the same time he does not fail to point out his frailties as a man, a husband and a father. In fact, the image of David in the DtrH without his faults would only make him too pure to be human and too human to be an angel. Such an image would woefully have failed as a paradigm for the exiled Jew, who would, despite the sins of the past, receive Divine Mercy, if he repented.

Thus far, one thing is clear: our pericope, in its uniqueness, is a pre-dtr material with a dtr addition and retouching. Besides 2 Sam 7, it is only here that a prophetic mediator stands between David and Yahweh in the entire Succession Narrative and it is only here that anything seriously unfavourable is said about the king.[169] This negative portrayal of David has prompted Flanagan to regard 2 Sam 11-12 as the work of a skilful redactor, whose interest was in Solomon and his succession to the throne of David.[170] This is not easily tenable because the reference to Solomon in vv. 24 and 25 comes almost as an after-thought or an appendix and could not have been the principal motive for the narrative. The author was not out to cover up wrong doing for the sake of glorifying his hero, neither was he out to destroy him by retaining the account of the same wrong doing in the narrative. The dark side of history shall not be glossed over, but can be told as it was with just a simple retouching to tone down the innocuous event to make it acceptable to a contemporary audience.

The classic narration of the heinous adultery and murder of David is neither too strange in the dtr corpus nor in Biblical tradition as a whole, which generally tends to humiliate its heroes by emphasizing their shortcomings. The end of such an exercise would be to give credit to divine grace and mercy, which accomplish great and sublime events through the

---

169 P. K. McCarter, *Plots, True or False*, p. 364. This remark certainly excludes 2 Sam 24:11ff since I have narrowed down the research to the SN, which skips 2 Sam 21-24 as an appendage to the narrative.
170 J. W. Flanagan, *Court History or Succession Document?* p. 176.

instrumentality of fragile human agents. Moses' death on the desert and his inability to reach the Land of Promise is blamed on his hitting the rock twice instead of commanding it to bring forth water for the murmuring people to drink. He stands condemned by God because he did not trust completely in him and did not give him the glory (Num 20:7-12). This notwithstanding, the stature of Moses as a prophet is said to be one of a kind, unique and unparallelled, *"whom the Lord knew face to face ... and who is unequalled ... in all the terrifying display of power that he performed in the sight of all Israel"* (Deut 34:11-12). In like manner, it is said of Samuel that all Israel knew that God was with him and let none of his words fall to the ground as a trustworthy prophet of the Lord (1 Sam 3:19-20). Yet the Dtr reports that God rebuked the great seer twice; first for being too slow to follow divine directive over the rejection of Saul (1 Sam16:1) and then for being too hasty in seeing the divine choice in Eliab, the brother of David, whom God had not chosen (16:7). The graphic description of the weakness of great leaders in the Bible is not lacking also in the New Testament. The primacy of Peter among the Apostles is not undermined in any way by his being called Satan by the master (Mk 8:33, Mt 16:23) nor by his triple denial of the Lord.[171]

In 1 Kings 1, David's impotence before Abishag is fully described, followed immediately by Adonijah's bid for the throne. The subtlety of the information is realised when one looks at the parallels: Moses' vigour had not abated at a hundred and twenty years (Deut 34:7) even as Abraham fathered Isaac at the age of a "hundred" (Gen 21:5). On the contrary, at seventy (2 Sam 5:4-5), David was impotent and therefore incompetent. This is clearly demonstrated by the attempt of Adonijah to take the place of his impotent father and the machinations of Nathan and Bathsheba to get the king to name Solomon as his successor. A nation cannot be ruled by an impotent king ("a dead wood") hence Solomon acceded to the throne before the death of his father. The same author, who reported the impotency of David and thus his playing second fiddle to the great fathers of Israel, will have no qualms of conscience retaining David's adultery and murder

---

[171] Mk 26:66-72, Mt 26:69-75, Lk 22:54-62, Jn 18:25-27: All the evangelists report Peter's denial of the Lord but, apart from John, they also emphasize his repentance and make that moment paramount in the story.

in the history despite elevating him unto that high pedestal as the ideal king of Israel. After all, it is at the point when the natural drive and inordinate vigour of a man desert him that he is at the end of his existence. The Dtr never portrays his heroes as super-human; they are ordinary human beings chosen by God for specific missions for the purpose of which missions he makes use even of their frailties and apparent failures.

Chapter 4. The text of the narrative

It is common knowledge that the LXX and some modern translations of the Bible, such as the New Revised Standard Version, read 2 Sam 11:27b with 12:1. This situation surfaces possibly on account of the wayyiqtol at the beginning of the narrative (וישלח) among other equally pertinent grounds. Biblical writers tend to use the *wayyiqtol* as a form of logical succession and consecution on account of its multifunctional purposes and, as much as possible, avoid making it stand at the first position in a narrative. A classic Biblical Hebrew narrative would begin with a *qatal* of a historic perfect or a *"wayhi"* and continue with a wayyiqtol or a chain of it which may be broken only for specific reasons, such as the insertion of a flash-back.[172] In the body of the narrative itself the *wayyiqtol* will consistently stay at the first position and has the function of a past tense.[173] It is, however, not out of place to find it at the beginning of a narrative as it is very technically associated with its function as a past tense. In such cases it may have a direct or indirect reference to a previous narrative. For example, 1 Kings 22 begins with a wayyiqtol (וישבו) in reference to a three-year period of relative peace between Israel and Aram: *Three years dwelt/passed* (וישבו) *without war between Aram and Israel*. This *wayyiqtol* takes the reader to the peace treaty of Ahab and Benhadad in chapter 20 where it links up very well to the double wayyiqtol at the end of v. 34: *So he made a covenant with him* (ויכרת־לו) *and sent him away* (וישלחהו). Thus the *wayyiqtol*, even though at the beginning of a narrative, functions in consecution to the events of two chapters before and stylistically connects the two episodes.[174]

---

172 P. Joüon – T. Muraoka, *Grammar*, par. 118.
173 W. Groß, *Wayyiqtol*, p. 35.
174 The development and usage of the waw-consecutive in BH makes an interesting study. Whereas some scholars at one end of the spectrum would posit the use of the waw-consecutive as a literary device used solely in the written language (so Rendsburg, 1981, p. 671) others at the other end suggest that it was a regular phenomenon in the spoken language as an indicative tense (so Blau, 1977, p. 23). Smith on his part rightly finds the waw-consecutive as, primarily, a literary style that belonged to the repertoire of scribal devices of the pre-exilic period, designed for presenting a series of past events. This technique would gradually be lost in the post exilic period as attested

On the face value, reading 11:27b together with 12:1 will provide a good ground for a textual unity. Fokkelman notes that the introduction of a new subject in "v. 27e" (*the Lord*) is a clue for the beginning of a new narrative and would therefore join the half verse to 12:1. At the same time he considers the self same remark found in the half verse as a summary of the whole of chapter 11, as a narration of *"that which David had done"*. It is this behaviour of David that literally provokes heaven and causes God to intervene.[175] This trend of thought is logical, but the summary of a chapter will serve its purpose better if left together with the chapter that it summarises. Uriel Simon draws attention to the fact that this literary device of ending one stage of a story with a sentence which alludes to the next stage is parallelled in the story of Samson; Judg 13:25, 14:20, 15:8 and 16:22. In the case of 2 Sam 11:27b, these words must be considered a complementing-by-contrast to the first part of the verse and on no account to be divorced from it and transferred to the beginning of the next paragraph.[176] Such penetrating remarks, standing at the close of a narrative block and constituting in themselves a device, are not alien to the Dtr School that is responsible for the present state of the story of David's adultery and murder. I will, consequently, maintain my position, as set out in the first chapter of this work, and read the two verses separately and in line with the Masoretic Text (MT) and aparatus.

For a good and legitimate reason, the Masoretic text or the received text of the Hebrew Bible breaks up the narrative after 11:27, indicated by the *petuha*, and leaves 12:1 to stand as the beginning of an apparently new episode that is however not independent but bound contextually and semantically to the two chapters preceding it. It can simply be said to be a new paragraph within the same narrative beginning with a waw-consecutive that gives room for it to be translated as "therefore".[177] It is in fact for the

---

     by passages in which the Chronicler parallels Samuel and Kings. Cf. Smith, *The Waw-Consecutive*, p. 24–27.
175 J. P. Fokkelman, *King David*, p. 71.
176 U. Simon, *The Poor Man's Ewe Lamb*, p. 212.
177 We will have to keep in mind that the division of the Biblical text into chapters and verses is a later development and not an integral part of the original text. This means that the consonantal text of the Hebrew Bible without chapter and verse division does not have to grapple with this problem at all.

specific reason that it is not a new and independent narrative that the piece begins with a waw-consecutive at the first position to indicate its linkage with what has gone before and picks up the protagonists of 11:27; Yhwh and David. If it were meant to be a new narrative, it would probably have had a *we-qatal* or *wayhi* at the first position,[178] with a possible introduction of the characters involved. It is all the more remarkable that the opening sentence of 12:1 states the personal names of the subject and both the direct and indirect objects: Yhwh sends Nathan to David, instead of resorting to the use of pronouns, even though no other grammatical element has intervened between 11:27b and 12:1. If the sentences were supposed to be read together, the author would naturally have avoided the monotony of repeating the subject or the indirect object in lieu of the economy of words in a narrative.[179] Syntactically, the name David has served in chapters 10 and 11 as the predominant subject who sends (10:2, 5, 7, 11:1, 3, 4, 6, 14, 27) and receives. In 11:27b the narrator presents *"the thing which David had done"* as the subject of the verb רעע in the sight of Yhwh. This basically ends the scene or paragraph in the narrative. The next paragraph picks up the genitive object of the previous sentence but this time with a different morphological function as the subject of the verb *send* with a completely new character, Nathan, as its direct object and David as the indirect object. This sending by Yhwh introduces the prophetic intervention which is completely new on the narrative level and sets the events in a new direction as a divine judgment upon the events of the previous paragraph or chapter.[180]

I have noted in the first chapter of this work that the style of the narrative is so constructed that one can easily carve out 12:1-15a from its position without disturbing the logical flow of the narrative. The comment; *"The thing that David had done was evil in the eyes of Yhwh"* permits v. 15b to be smoothly joined to 11:27b. This will be lost if the half verse is read together with 12:1 and, with it, the aesthetic beauty of the narrative

---

178 K. Schmid, *Erzväter und Exodus*, p. 1ff.
179 B. K. Waltke & M. O'Connor, *Biblical Hebrew Syntax*, 16.3.1a.
180 Even though the same lexeme or verb - שלח – is used in both 11:27b and 12:1 it is neither a *Rückverweis* nor *Vorweiser* and calls for a paragraph division since it initiates a completely new action in a new direction; in fact a new twist in the narrative that in itself is not an absolutely normal feature to the SN, namely, a prophetic intervention. Cf. W. Groß, *Bileam*, p. 178.

and its stylistic achievement. I cannot but agree with Von Rad that 27b is one of the three theological passages of the work and serves as a summary to the whole of the events of chapter eleven.[181] In this verse the author states his own view of the past events in the mode of a theological comment and prepares his audience for its logical sequence or consequence which he introduces with the *wayyiqtol* of consecution. The introduction of the new subject prepares the ground for the entry of the prophet or of some kind of intervention emerging out of a pure divine initiative as a response to the veritable question aroused by the theological twist: "What will the Lord do if the thing that David had done is evil in His eyes?" The phrase "to do what is evil in the sight of Yhwh" is a favourite creation of the Dtr that begins from Judg 2:11 and runs through the books of Kings almost as a slogan of a Judgment Formula for the kings of Judah and Israel.[182] Deftly inserting the comment at the end of chapter 11, the dtr author prepares his readers for some kind of condemnation and punishment that would reflect the fate of Israel at the end of the books of Kings, where the phrase achieves the height of its expression. Not even David, with all the favours received from Yhwh, is able to achieve the ideal of eschewing what is evil in His eyes.

4.1 Structure; 2 Sam 12:1-15a

The name nātān as the object of the verb *send* provides an *inclusio* in vv. 1a and 15a with the two verbs of motion, wayyābō' (he came) at the beginning and wayyēlek (he went) at the end with Nathan as the subject of both to demarcate the beginning and the end of the episode, respectively. As stated

---

181 Von Rad considers the reference in addition to 2 Sam 12:24 and 17:14 as the only explicit theological passages in the Succession Narrative. (*Cf. Hexateuch*, p. 198.) Also J. P. Fokkelman, *King David*, p. 71.

182 A cluster of the phrase is to be found especially in the books of Kings where it usually refers to the misdemeanour of the kings as against its instances in Judges which depict a communal behaviour of the people. In Judges, we meet the phrase in 2:11, 3:7, 6:1, with variants in 4:1, 10:6 and 13:1. In Kings, a condemnation of the kings of Judah is found in such positions as; 1 Kings 14:22*, 2 Kings 8:18, 27, 21:2, 20, 23:32, 37, 24:9 & 19 while the majority are directed towards those of Israel; 1 Kings 15:26, 34, 16:7, 19, 25, 30, 2 Kings 3:2, 13:2, 11, 24, 15:9, 18, 24, 28, 17:2.

before, this fact does not simplify the position of our pericope in any way. The wayyiqtols flow into the next pericope that begins with v. 15b and complicates the situation as the opening word, wayyiggōp̄, with Yhwh as subject, (*Yhwh struck the child that Uriah's wife bore to David*) links up smoothly both ideologically and semantically to 11:27b. Yhwh's striking of the child, so that it got ill, can be seen as the result of the evil that David had done, the deed that displeased the Lord. Considering the fact that 12:1, in like manner, has Yahweh as its subject, it is possible, to all intents and purposes, to skip 12:1-15a and read 11:27 with 12:15b without any grammatical or semantic distortion of any kind to the text: "²⁷ᵇ *The thing that David had done was evil in the eyes of Yhwh* ¹⁵ᵇ *so Yhwh struck the child that Uriah's wife bore to David, and it became ill.*" If the encounter of David with Nathan is an insertion into the broad narrative then the hand behind this insertion has done a perfect job by centering the whole work on the divine name. This play upon the divine name will be carried through to the final insertion of the purported divine act of renaming Solomon (12:25).

The sending of a prophet and the threat of pestilence as a result of Yahweh's displeasure are two attested phenomena in Biblical narratives, as stated before. The reader can jump over this pericope without losing the trend of the story. What will, however, be lacking here is a very well constructed narrative of artistic beauty and semantic perfection of an immense ideological value that arouses in its historical and actual audience an admiration for David, both as a king and as a man of God.[183] The Humble King

---

183 There are not many patterns to be found in the Bible to prove this point but the thinking of Abraham gives an indication that a man could be killed in order to liberate the wife from the marriage bond, thus making her free to be taken by another: "*Then it shall come to pass that seeing you, the Egyptians will say; this is his wife, and they will slay me but spare thee.*" (Gen 12:12). Hugo Gressman (*Altorientalische Texte*, p. 157) quotes a charm formula engraved on the pyramid of the Egyptian king Onas that reads: "Then he will take the wives away from their husbands whereto he wishes, whenever his heart desires them." Whether or not these two references could be taken as an example of the conduct of the ancient oriental monarch, one would still be justified to note that David acts like his contemporaries but at the same time is different from them. He does not simply take the woman regardless of her belonging to another man; rather, he sends her back home after sleeping with her so that as far as her husband is concerned the act is non-existent for

David bowing to the divine will, pronounced by the prophet, produces a fine demarcation line between David and the later kings of Israel in their relationship with their subjects, if not, in fact, of the whole Ancient Near East. The dtr author makes very conscious efforts to establish this difference and, thereby, enhances the character of David to make him fit into the role that lies at the core of the dtr image of the ideal king and is expressed in typical dtr vocabulary and language *("I have sinned against the Lord")*.

Dividing the pericope is not only cumbersome but also a high-risk enterprise. This is because 2 Sam 12:1-15a constitute a narrative unit, a continuous discourse or drama piece in a single scene, and any attempt to break it risks disturbing the flow of the narrative. All the same, an effective way of analysing the text will require short divisions to help us appreciate the dynamics of the linguistic style and ideological underpinnings that are behind the prophet-king dialogue in the unfolding of the tradition. I have, therefore, opted to divide the narrative on the basis of the sub-discourses paying attention to their lengths and, where possible, the change from one speaker to the other.

a. 1-4 → The story: introduction + a second degree narrative in durative mood (v. 2-3)
b. 5-6 → The judgement: a first degree narrative with punctual actions (monologue)
c. 7-12 → The prophetic word:
    7-9 – The accusation: a direct discourse + a question
    10-12 – oracle of doom: a predictive discourse – monologue
d. 13-15a → the concluding words: assertive and predictive discourses – dialogue

The existence of different methods of analysing Biblical texts makes it rather difficult for one to make a choice instead of facilitating it, since making a choice implies automatically rejecting another for one or the other reason. I will avoid choosing one method against the others and keep the eyes wide

---

    its lack of practical consequence (cf. U. Simon, *The poor man's Ewe Lamb*, p. 212). It is only when the consequence of pregnancy became an issue and he failed to push the paternity into Uriah's shoes that he sought to eliminate the man.

open as far as the achievements of the various methods are concerned in order to avoid mediocrity and lop-sidedness. What I imply by this saying is that I will, for example, not hesitate to make use of the critical apparatus of the literal critique, the dynamism of the historical and cultural milieu and its impacts on the text, the finesse of narratology and close reading, which have in one way or the other immensely contributed to the synchronic reading of the end text at our disposal. Because my aim is the end text, the other methods will be resorted to as each one of them contributes to the holistic understanding of the text as part of a whole.

4.1.1 The story: vv. 1-4

¹(Then) Yhwh sent Nathan to David. He came to him and said to him; "There were two men in one city, the one rich and the other poor. ²The rich man had very many flock and cattle, ³but the poor man had nothing except one little ewe lamb which he had bought. He took care of it and it grew up together with him and with his children: it used to eat of his morsel, drink from his cup, lie in his bosom and it was like a daughter to him. ⁴Now, there came a traveller to the rich man, and he loathed (pitied) to take from his flock and cattle to prepare for the wayfarer who had come to him. Instead he took the lamb of the poor man and prepared it for the man who had come to him.	¹וַיִּשְׁלַח יְהוָה אֶת־נָתָן אֶל־דָּוִד וַיָּבֹא אֵלָיו וַיֹּאמֶר לוֹ שְׁנֵי אֲנָשִׁים הָיוּ בְּעִיר אֶחָת אֶחָד עָשִׁיר וְאֶחָד רָאשׁ: ²לְעָשִׁיר הָיָה צֹאן וּבָקָר הַרְבֵּה מְאֹד: ³וְלָרָשׁ אֵין־כֹּל כִּי אִם־כִּבְשָׂה אַחַת קְטַנָּה אֲשֶׁר קָנָה וַיְחַיֶּהָ וַתִּגְדַּל עִמּוֹ וְעִם־בָּנָיו יַחְדָּו מִפִּתּוֹ תֹאכַל וּמִכֹּסוֹ תִשְׁתֶּה וּבְחֵיקוֹ תִשְׁכָּב וַתְּהִי־לוֹ כְּבַת: ⁴וַיָּבֹא הֵלֶךְ לְאִישׁ הֶעָשִׁיר וַיַּחְמֹל לָקַחַת מִצֹּאנוֹ וּמִבְּקָרוֹ לַעֲשׂוֹת לָאֹרֵחַ הַבָּא־לוֹ וַיִּקַּח אֶת־כִּבְשַׂת הָאִישׁ הָרָאשׁ וַיַּעֲשֶׂהָ לָאִישׁ הַבָּא אֵלָיו:

4.1.2 Analysis

V.1: The LXX, with a few other manuscripts, adds τὸν προφήτην to the name Nathan. This may clearly be an explanatory note to the name of the prophet and a possible later addition informed by 2 Sam 7:2 and 1 Kings 1:10 which describe Nathan as הנביא, "the Prophet". Remarkably, Nathan is in the whole of our pericope described without a title; a phenomenon which easily gives the indication that it was a household name at the court of David and required no qualification or introduction for clarity. The Lucianic Recension of the Septuagint (LXX^L) repeats the name of the prophet in the second part of the sentence; "*When Nathan came to him*", apparently for the purpose of clarity with the support of the Vetus Latina and the vulgate. What Nathan tells David generates other additions from scholars on the basis of the LXX^L, which has *anageilon dē moi tēn krisin tauten* (pass judgment on this case for me), that would look forward to the response of David in v. 5. This is supported by related readings in two Greek cursive manuscripts (Mss). Though this addition is lacking in the MT it is hardly to be considered secondary to the text as there is no good reason for a later addition. Its absence in the MT could, however, have been the result of haplography on the basis of *wayyōʾmer*, which would have occurred twice in the verse- "*When he came to him* **he said** *to him, Pass judgment on this case for me. And* **he said***: There were two men in one city…*" Thus the longer reading might have been the original from which a copier's oversight has produced the shorter.

The orthography of רָאשׁ (v.1c) in stead of רוֹשׁ may be a case of Aramaicism quite common in the MT. The א added to the qal participle is occasionally found on account of Aramaic, which was generally the spoken language.[184] MT reads *ləʿāšîr* (literary, *to a rich man or a rich man possessed/had*) in v. 2, which misses the definite article required for the expression of possession inherent in the particle (ל + def. article + name). A definite article would be expected to make sense of the nominal sentence (lə + hā + name) and may produce *lāʿāšîr* (literary, *to the rich man or the rich man possessed/had*)[185] as indicated by the definite article of the LXX (τῷ πλουσίῳ) to give the translational value of "*The rich man had….*"

In v. 3b, the text reads: וַיְחַיֶּהָ וַתִּגְדַּל ("and he kept her safe and she grew up" - two verbs). The Syriac has a single verb – וחיאהות - reflecting approximately the first verb of the MT (*and he kept her safe* or *preserved her in life*), while LXX expresses the same idea with three verbs - καὶ περιεποιήσατο καὶ ἐξέθρεψεν αὐτήν καὶ ἡδρύνθη ("*and he kept her safe and brought her up and she grew up*"). The first two verbs of the LXX may be variant renditions of וַיְחַיֶּהָ. On the basis of style, the MT looks more appropriate and convincing. The sentence can be broken into two phrases of three words each; *wayəḥayyehā wattigdal ʿimmô / wəʿim-Bānāyw yaḥdāw*. This is the shorter

---

184 Cf. P. Joüon - T. Muraoka, *A Grammar of Biblical Hebrew*, 80k.
185 T. O. Lambdin, Introduction to Biblical Hebrew, 18.

version, but it meets my unqualified preference.[186] Some Mss read ləbat̠ for Kəbat̠ at the end of the verse. This may be due to the typical problem of making a distinction between the letters "כ" and "ל" (*kaf* and *lamed*) in ancient Hebrew manuscripts. The idea expressed here is a comparison of the relationship between the poor man and his sheep to that of a father and his daughter. For this reason the MT is better preserved; "like a daughter". In the final verse (v. 4), the lə'îš of the MT is a probable scribal error in the vocalisation since the definite article calls for la'îš.[187] Our text uses three words in reference to the guest: הֵלֶךְ, אֹרֵחַ, אִישׁ (a traveller, a wayfarer and a man) respectively in the same verse. The LXX has πάροδος, τῷ ξένῳ ὁδοιπόρῳ (a combination of the Alexandrian and Lucianic texts) and ἀνδρί. The use of different terminologies for the single reality smacks of anonymity and underlies the fact that the identity of the guest is not important to the narrator of the story.

4.1.3 Interpretation

The writer does not lead his audience into the secret of what the Lord charged the prophet Nathan with. The otherwise confidant of the king, who had the singular privilege of sharing in the king's plan to build a temple to the Lord (2 Sam 7) now carries a dreadful message for the man who has reposed his trust in him. The enormity of his assignment calls for tact, skill and practical intelligence. For this purpose, he devices a simple but well thought out parable that catches the guilty king on the wrong foot and causes him to pronounce judgment on himself. The effectiveness of the story stems not only from the fact that David was used to passing judgment as a king and highest judge of the nation, but also from the prophet's knowledge of the king's past. As a former shepherd of the family flock, David identified himself quickly with the poor man and his love for his single ewe lamb and was prepared to send the callous, rich thief to his grave. This was a parable deducted from the life situation of its historical audience with a high degree of potency to achieve its aim.

---

186 McCarter identifies the possibility of the variant readings of the LXX as different renditions of the MT but prefers the short Syriac reading. On my part I find no fault with the MT. cf. *II Samuel*, p. 294.
187 P. Joüon - T. Muraoka, *A Grammar of Biblical Hebrew*, 138c.

The quality of Nathan as an actor in the SN plays a very important and reliable role in the present mission. In chapter 7, he was an eminent advisor to the king and had the freedom of movement in and out of the palace. His presence in this episode does not convey any aura of foreboding to the king, as would be in the case of Elijah and Ahab (1 Kings 21:20). The story he narrates has a natural quality that could have emerged from any level of the socio-religious strata or from any of the councillors around the king. One could say, in a modern situation, that a lawyer presents the case of a stolen livestock on behalf of his client and expects judgment in his favour. Vv. 1-4 present him as the man Nathan, without his official title as prophet; even though he has already been introduced to the reader as a prophet (7:2). His presence at the court of David does not raise any eye brow. He belongs there and the king would not suspect any thing in particular let alone a divine mission as the reason for his presence at that material moment. He, therefore, enters the presence of the king, as he would normally do, but this time he overwhelms the king with his parable. It is only when the king has given his verdict on the simply proposed legal case that Nathan turns coat and speaks in the name of the Lord.

Vv.1-3 set the scene and put the whole episode in perspective, building up the tension by means of opposition and repetition. The pericope opens with וישלח (he sent). The root שלח (to send) takes the reader quickly back to the previous chapter where it occurs twelve times. Nine of these occurrences are in the wayyiqtol form and six of them have David as their subject.[188] One would expect that David should have learnt from the weakness of Saul, whose successful general (then David himself) "led out and brought in Israel" (2 Sam 5:2) and subsequently became king in his stead, not to have weakened his contact with the soldiers. Ironically, at the height of his power, the king *sends out* Joab and the men *at the time when kings go out*

---

[188] The wayyiqtol forms are found in vv. 1, 3, 4, 6a & c, 14, 18, and 27. V. 6c has Joab as the subject while all the rest have David as their subject. The other three occurrences of the root שלח are found in v. 5 (*qatal*, with Bathsheba as subject), v. 6b (imperative issued by David) and v. 22 (*qatal*, describing David's action). In actual fact, only two occasions of the verb are not directly linked to David.

to war but he remains at home and *sends to take* Uriah's wife.[189] The verb *send* smoothly links up the current chapter to the two preceding it.

In 12:1, God is the one who sends to reproach David, who has "sent others" on mission or "sent to take" (ch. 11). With this verb (*send*) a dramatic contrast is set between the previous events and the current one. The stark narration of the evil deeds of David without any hint of a moral reproach takes a new turn. A moral conscience is not after all lacking in the narrative; there is at least one person who is not coerced into complicity for any imaginable reason. It is this person, the man Nathan that the text presents without a title. His presence provides the evidence that the king is not an absolute monarch, for there is a power beyond his, mediated by the prophet in the same way as Elijah would do to Ahab in the episode of Naboth's vineyard (1 King 21:17-24) and the nameless prophet to the same over Benhadad (1 Kings 20:35-42).

The first verse describes two men as citizens and then defines the opposition between them as one between a rich man and a poor man, who live in one city (with the sense of the same city[190]). In six tactical words, verse two describes the wealth of the rich man in terms of his many flocks and cattle. Besides these, no other indicator of his wealth is given. The description of the poor man begins with a negation and an exception; אֵין־כֹּל כִּי אִם (*nothing except*), and proceeds with the description of the ewe lamb which he had bought. The stative היה (*hyh*) highlights the permanence of the rich man's wealth, while קנה (*qnh*) delineates the possible difficulty with which the poor man could acquire the lamb; he did so, as it were, with his life's blood. קנה is used to express two basic ideas in Biblical Hebrew; to procure as the result of a mercantile activity or as inheritance and to acquire a progeny in the sense of giving birth. The commercial sense is what is very common in the Bible as in Gen 25:10, 47:19-23, Lev 25:14, Deut 28:68, Ruth 4:5-10, 1Chr 21:24 and Prov 4:5 (here it is used metaphorically as buying or acquiring wisdom). In Gen 14:19 & 22 the *qal* participle is used to mean "the one who acquires" or "creates" hence God Most High, the

---

189 Later on in the history we are told that for the sake of his safety the soldiers urged the king not to go with them to war lest he quenched the light of Israel, being "worth ten thousand of us." Cf. 2 Sam 18:3.
190 P. Joüon – T. Muraoka, A Grammar of Biblical Hebrew, 147a.

Creator. This emphasizes the creative quality of God who owns the universe as a result of his having acquired it by means of creation. Thus Eve's use of the same word to express the act of giving birth or acquiring progeny as a participation in the divine act of creation in Gen 4:1.[191] Nathan craftily uses *procure*, an expression that in one sense means "to buy" and in another "to give birth to", as the underpinning of the relationship between the poor man and his ewe lamb. The difference that is here underlined is not so much the transient nature of the poor man's property as against the permanence of the rich man's as the personal relationship of the two to their wealth. The narrative does not indicate how the rich man came by his abundance of wealth; whether by acquisition or inheritance. In this way the reader is left in doubt as to whether this miser of a man had any personal relationship to the property to which he clung so firmly that he was not willing to sacrifice even the smallest part of it. It, however, highlights the contrast by the insinuating description of the lamb's origin and activity in the house of the poor man in fourteen words, indicating the personal and emotional attachment of the poor man to his one and only acquired property.

It is striking to note that despite the economy of words, strictly observed in the story itself (61 words), the narrator has spent so many words (fourteen) describing the ewe lamb. The description can be divided into three parts;

a. the action of the man towards his ewe: *And he took care of it and it grew up with him and with his children*
b. the ewe in the house: *it used to eat of his morsel, drink from his cup, lie in his bosom*
c. the logical deduction from a & b: *and it was like a daughter to him.*

The piel of חיה has the connotation of a normal human nurture and preservation in life or physical protection. Its use with גדל implies a parent-child relationship, which is emphasized by the phrase *together with him and his children*. Thus the poor man is portrayed as going to every length to

---

191 The modern Italian language uses the term "procurare" to describe the act of giving birth to a child: "Ho procurato un bambino" – I have given birth to a son or a baby boy.

protect and preserve the lamb in life and bringing it up with the care of a father for his child, in this case, his daughter.

The LXX rendition seeks to emphasize this parent-child relationship in its double expression: *He kept her safe (or nourished her) and brought her up*. In putting it this way, the basis of a human relationship is established with the lamb, which is neither of the barnyard nor a pet but one with the poor man and with his children. The actions of the lamb in the house are captured in three verbs which have a strong reminiscence with 2 Sam 11:11 (אכל, שתה and שכב; *to eat, to drink and to sleep*) where they are put into the mouth of Uriah as a gentle protest to the king's bid to send him home for the night. The soldier bases his argument on the fact that the Ark and Israel and Judah remained in booths, his lord Joab and the servants of the king camped in the open fields; "*shall I then go to my house, to eat and to drink, and to lie with my wife?*". The poetic device of assonance on "-o" that the narrator employs makes the description so thematic that the reader does not miss its importance in the whole narrative:

mippittô tōʾkal	from his morsel she ate,
ûmikkōsô tišteh	and from his cup she drank
ûbəḥêqô tiškāb	and in his bosom she laid

To eat of the morsel and drink from the cup of the host is a human action of sharing in the family. This notion is crowned by the fact that she sleeps in his bosom- *ûbəḥêqô tiškāb*. Sleeping in the bosom of someone has a patently human sexual connotation, as in v. 8, or a filial relationship, as in Num 11:12; "*Curry them in your bosom as a nurse carries a sucking child*". This apt and even idyllic description of a familial relationship between the lamb and the poor man warrants the conclusion rightly deduced by our narrator that *it was like a daughter to him*.

At the end of the exposition, the narrator has successfully set the stage for the opposition between the rich and the poor man in a flowing chain of durative pasts, as would be expected in a classic narrative of a historical past. We are no longer dealing with just two neighbours but with two men completely different, one from the other. Whereas the rich man is emphatically detached from his plethoric wealth, the poor man is lovingly attached to his single ewe lamb. We may even talk about the poverty of the rich man against the wealth of the poor man. The long narrative time devoted to the poor man's ewe lamb in contrast to the tart description of the wealth of the rich man makes clear to the reader the irony of the whole story and what is to be expected; the callous slaughter of the lamb. The artistic subtlety of the prophet, who concocted the story, and of the writer, who has adopted it, reaches its height when the audience no longer consider the act as the stealing and killing of a sheep but the slaughter of the poor man's daughter.

The happiness of the poor man in his meagre wealth could have lasted but for the appearance of a new character in v. 4.[192] The verse begins with a wayyiqtol of movement (ויבא) that breaks the sequence of durative pasts in verses 1-3 and introduces a new activity and a new character (הֵלֶךְ), who is absent in the preceding three verses, as an element of disruption in the established idyllic order. It is the arrival of this stranger that sets the chain of events in motion.

To achieve the effect of the concealment of the parable from its application, the prophet resorts to anonymity by the three-fold designation of the visitor as a traveller, a wayfarer and a man (אִישׁ, ארח, הֵלֶךְ). The noun אִישׁ pervades the entire pericope, appearing in each section of the narrative. In v. 4, it appears three times in relation to each of the three men in the story in the same sequence as they appear: the rich man, the poor man, and the man who was visiting. In v. 5, it appears twice; first in the narrator's remark and then in the angry declaration of David against the fictional man. At this point David is only thinking of the rich man who is the perpetrator of such a heinous injustice. This builds up the suspense that awaits the dropping of the bombshell by Nathan in v. 7, constituting a strong link between the sections as tension and resolution. The anonymous and floating אִישׁ would find concrete and real life identification in David.

It is remarkable to note that the narrative time of the actual story is a single verse (v. 4). The prophet craftily leaves off the story, bluntly breaking the narration without a conclusion, and awaits David's angry outburst. It is highly probable that in whichever way the king might have reacted, the purpose of the prophet would have been served. That the prophet, a third person in the given circumstance, presents the case before the king implies

---

192 J. L. Ska, *Our Fathers have Told Us*, p. 24.

that the poor man had everything to lose if he were to insist on his legal rights against his rich neighbour and oppressor. The rich man could easily pay off the expected penalty and afterwards turn the life of the poor man into one of misery. In this particular instance, in fact, the wronged man lives no longer to be able to contemplate a legal action. As it were, David, "the callous rich oppressor", swallowed the bait by acting the righteous judge that he was expected to be and provided the ground for his own condemnation. He identified himself with the poor man in the injustice that he had suffered, showing the *ḥml* that he did not show while he had the chance. The ingenuity of the writer reaches its apex when his narrative accomplishes a melodramatic effect in the audience and the reader who are now poised to pronounce judgment on the guilty, the rich miser. The emotion of the audience is all the more justified because unlike the guilty miser, David has not only taken the poor man's supposed sheep; he has also killed the man, making the parable less repugnant than the actual behaviour of David. This has led Hugo Gressmann to conclude that the parable was not originally composed for the double crime of David but was already available and subsequently inserted into this context.[193] Whatever the case may have been, the effect of the parable is achieved by the ingenuity of the author who has inserted it at its present location.

---

193 H. Gressmann, *Oldest History Writing*, pp. 29–30. "The moving narrative with its exaggerated affection for animals, which ill befits Uriah's relationship to his wife, castigates only the violent action of the pitiless rich man; but David has not only taken the poor man's sheep, but on top of that has killed the man. Thus the parable was not composed for the present case but was already available and was subsequently inserted into this context. This also explains why the death sentence of David comes to be mitigated: You yourself shall not die, but your child; Nathan's judgment originally ran thus, probably because there was a historical justification for this. When the child born of David's intercourse with Bathsheba died, this was seen as the just punishment for the king's sin.

4.2 The judgment: vv. 5-6

| ⁵Then David's anger was greatly kindled against the man. He said to Nathan; As Yhwh lives, the man who has done this deserves to die; ⁶and the Lamb, he shall restore fourfold, because he has done this thing and he had no pity. | ⁵ וַיִּחַר־אַף דָּוִד בָּאִישׁ מְאֹד וַיֹּאמֶר אֶל־נָתָן חַי־יְהוָה כִּי בֶן־מָוֶת הָאִישׁ הָעֹשֶׂה זֹאת: ⁶ וְאֶת־הַכִּבְשָׂה יְשַׁלֵּם אַרְבַּעְתָּיִם עֵקֶב אֲשֶׁר עָשָׂה אֶת־הַדָּבָר הַזֶּה וְעַל אֲשֶׁר לֹא־חָמָל: |

4.2.1 Analysis

V. 5: The formula חַי־יְהוָה כִּי (hay-x-kî) is a derivative from "hay-x-nišba'-kî" (to swear upon the life of x that…) where the kî has passed into the sentence of imprecation without its original verb.[194] This is typical of Semitic languages as attested in the Akkadian or Cuneiform formula "nīš ilim" - (to swear an oath) by the life of a god. The solemn oath indicates the seriousness of the sentence to the person who utters it. David, in this instance therefore, meant that the man deserved to die for his callous lack of pity or compassion. If this were not the case, Nathan's reversal of the death sentence in v. 13 would have been absurd and superfluous since he had not pronounced it: *"Yhwh has also put away your sin; you shall not die."*

MT has אַרְבַּעְתָּיִם (*fourfold*) in v. 6 but the LXX reads ἑπταπλασίονα (*sevenfold*). The form is the feminine construct, the normal form even with masculine nouns, with a masculine plural ending. This is a characteristic of the Common Semitic period.[195] It would be logical to posit that MT has modified the text in the light of Ex. 21:37, as some scholars like McCarter do (*…the thief must pay five oxen for an ox and four sheep for a sheep…*).[196] But the major versions, Syriac, Acquila, Symmachus, Vulgate, Lucian, some Targumim and Josephus, agree with the MT, which imply the anteriority of MT over LXX. Remarkably, Targum Jonathan reads forty-fold. Coxon would prefer the LXX reading for the resonance it bears on the name of Bathsheba, the death of the son on the seventh day and the word play on בת in the narrative as a whole.[197] It is clear to us that Coxon

---

194 P. Joüon – T. Muraoka, *Grammar,* 165b & e.
195 P. Joüon – T. Muraoka, *Grammar,* 100d.
196 P. McCarter, *II Samuel,* p. 294.
197 P. W. Coxon, *A note on "Bathsheba" in 2 Samuel 12,1-6,* p. 250.

is reading too much more into the text than from it. For there is the probability that sevenfold is a later proverbial expression denoting a perfect restitution as reflected in Prov 6: 31: *"If they (thieves) are caught they will pay sevenfold: they will forfeit all the goods of their house."* It would make no sense for David to quote a later proverb when the amount of restitution was fixed by law and practised over the centuries.[198] Unlike Coxon, Seebass finds "fourfold" resonating in the death of the four sons of David; the first son born to him by Bathsheba, Amnon, Absalom and Adonijah as a better reason to maintain the MT.[199] Moreover LXX tends to increase figures generally.

McCarter proposes an emendation to the second part of the verse to avoid "the awkward shift from 'qb 'šr to w'l 'šr" (*because, and because*) in order to give the same translational value, *spare*, to ḥāmal in v. 4 and in v. 5. Thus he reads the possessive particle, *lw hml* (literally; *what belongs to him he spared*) for the particle of negation, *l' ḥml* (*he had no pity*). Given the fact that 'qb 'šr has the special nuance of "in recompense for" or the pejorative sense of "in punishment for",[200] I do not deem necessary such emendation without any textual support. The Masoretic Text has the same word in the two verses to express the same basic idea but that does not oblige the translator to do the same with a modern language. This may be an appropriate practice in poetry but very much out of place, if not counter productive, in narratives. Moreover, one may not have to emend the text in order to fit it into the modern thought and language pattern as it is not at all strange to find the play on the different meanings of the same word in a narrative. I am, however, convinced that the same translational value could have been assigned to the word if he had chosen "pity" instead of "spare" (... *he pitied to take from*... and "...*because he had no pity*). The tendency to emend a text does not always prove a true reflection of the poverty of the original language as the limitation of our own resources and understanding of it.

---

198 The declaration of Zacchaeus conforms to the dictates of the law: "Look, half of my possessions, Lord, I will give to the poor; and if I have defrauded anyone of anything, I will pay back four times as much" (Luke 19:8).
199 H. Seebass, *Nathan and David*, p. 204.
200 P. Joüon-T. Muraoka, op. cit., 170g.

4.2.2 Interpretation

The verb חמל is the binding element between this section and the previous one as it links the two speakers in both sections; Nathan in the previous section and David at the end of the current one. The prophet is portrayed completely in control of the situation with the king taking the cue from his words as a basis for his own reaction. The two verses constitute the response of David to the proposed legal case. The intensity of the reaction itself is a clear indication that the king had not penetrated the apparently harmless façade of the fictitious story. Considering it as a possible happening within his kingdom, the king passes the expected judgment.

David's angry outburst has opened volumes of discussions and caused great anxieties for translators. The main problem is the expression בֶּן־מָוֶת הָאִישׁ, literally, *a son of death, he*. Some scholars tend to consider it a virtual death sentence pronounced by David on a person to whom a death sentence does not apply.[201] McCarter does not consider this outburst a judgment at all but an expression of David's righteous indignation.[202] The law stipulates restitution of the stolen livestock or in the case where the thief is incapable of restitution that he is sold for the theft (Ex. 21:37). This is supported by the laws of the Ancient Near East as expounded clearly by the Codex Hammurabi in which the thief may be put to death only when he does not possess enough to make restitution.[203] David goes a step further than the stipulated law as Josephus indicates; "David called him a wicked

---

201 Philips considers it in the superlative sense of the word to mean "an arch villain" who is morally guilty but cannot be condemned under the criminal law. Cf. A. Philips, *The Interpretation of 2 Samuel xii 5-6*, p. 244.
202 McCarter considers it a characterization of the man's behaviour, not a condemnation of the person and compares it to such expressions as: ben-beliyaal and ish beliyaal, which in general terms would mean a scoundrel or a damnable fellow. Cf. *II Samuel*, 299.
203 E. Bergmann, *Codex Hammurabi*, pp. 4–5. § 8 states: "If a man stole either an ox or a sheep or an ass or a pig or a goat, if it belonged to the temple or if it belonged to the state, he shall return thirtyfold; if it belonged to another man, he shall return tenfold. If the thief does not have sufficient to make restitution, he shall be put to death." In his introductory note to the codex, James B. Pritchard indicates that Hammurabi may have promulgated his law code in 1726, being the second year of his 43 year reign of 1728-1686 (Cf. ANET, p. 163).

man who deserved to be punished with death after a fourfold restoration of the lamb."[204] Elsewhere in the Bible, the same expression is used with the implication of the death of the subject in question. In 1 Sam 20:31, Saul called David בן מות הוא, to which Jonathan responded: "Why should he die?" It is important to read the phrase within its context to arrive at its full meaning and implication. Saul certainly meant the death of David, but could not provide any good reason for it when challenged by Jonathan. The reader, however, knows the reason from the first part of the same verse: *"For as long as the son of Jesse lives upon the earth, neither you nor your kingdom shall be established."* In our verse, a similar scenario is depicted when David pronounces judgment without the needed premises. The narrator had, however, prepared the reader for this when he commented that the anger of David was greatly kindled against the man (literally, *his nose was heated very much against the man*). I would like emphasize that David's reaction does not need to conform to the law as he might not have had a written code before him. Even if he did have a written code, he acted under the impulse of anger, which would explain his deviation from it. Instead of being juridical I would rather look at the text as it is; a double sentence pronounced by David, which includes a death penalty, reinforced by an oath in the typical Semitic manner of pronouncing judgment.

Describing the rich man's attitude towards his own flock, Nathan uses וַיַּחְמֹל (*wayyiqtol*) with an infinitive construct. David's outburst puts enough emphasis on the word as to make it a key-word in the story. The problem of interpreters has been the exact relationship between Nathan's use of the verbal root of the word (*ḥml*) and David's use of the noun form in describing the action of the rich man.[205] The word instinctively takes the reader back to v. 4; the stealing and killing of the ewe lamb, the negative particle (*lʾ*) in this verse (v. 6) effects the contrast of emotions that is evident in the story; the pity of the rich man for his own goods, expressed by the durative sense of the *wayyiqtol* with infinitive, and his lack of pity towards his fellow man in the given situation (*qatal* for punctual action). In Hebrew, the *wayyiqtol* is a flexible tense form simply tagged as the inverted future and is commonly used in a narrative sequence that begins with a past or

---

204 Josephus, *Antiquities*, 7.150.
205 P. K. McCarter, *II Samuel*, p. 294.

perfect tense. The *wayyiqtol* then takes on the tense value of the perfect and is said to be "converted".²⁰⁶ Combined with the infinitive; the pure and a-temporal form of a verb, it expresses an action that is not limited in time. In this light, we could say about the text before us that the pity of the rich man is expressed as ingressive with an explicit beginning but no particular end, while his lack of it towards the poor man takes place at an explicit moment of time and is out and done with. In this way the rich man is depicted as a miser who pitied taking from his own flock, but did not show pity towards the poor man's lamb, which had been carefully described as a member of his family.

The Hebrew verb חמל denotes an action taken by a person who has a privileged position against the other and may even have the authority to condemn that subject to death.²⁰⁷ Among the many uses of the verb in the Bible, the action of Pharaoh's daughter classically demonstrates this meaning. She had every opportunity to condemn the baby (Moses) to death because he had already fallen under the sentence of death issued by her father, the Pharaoh, but she had compassion for him (ותחמל עליו) and took care of him (Ex 2:6). It is the attitude of the powerful towards the powerless. In this instance, the Egyptian maiden showed compassion towards the would-be shepherd of Israel while the shepherd of the flock of Yhwh, the king, acted without it. The pagan princess has what David, the king of Israel, did not have.²⁰⁸

---

206 T. O. Lambdin, Biblical Hebrew, 98a, P. Joüon – T. Muraoka, Grammar of Biblical Hebrew, 47a.
207 The "Einheitsübersetzung" translates חמל as "*Mitleid*" but Seebass prefers "*Erbarmen*". Mitleid, on one hand, with its basic meaning of "mit dir leiden", has the implication of a sharing of emotions among equals as in *cum passionis* (compassion). Erbarmen, on the other, has an implicit tone of a superior condescending towards an inferior, hence its use in connection with God towards human beings in religion (*miserere*). If one seeks the same translational values for the two occurrences then Erbarmen and Erbarmenlos would be the preferred alternatives in this context. Cf. H. Seebass, *Nathan and David in II Sam 12*, p. 204. The normal English usage will swing between mercy, on the high side, compassion, on the lower level and pity, somewhere between the two. Adrian Schenker opts for "Reue" in the first instance but falls back to Mitleid in the second. Cf. *Versöhnung*, p. 42.
208 G. W. Coats, *II Samuel 12:1-7a*, p. 171.

What we have here is a juxtaposition of a miser's pusillanimous self-pity and the human emotion of compassion. The result is a reversal of the human condition where the poor is more likely to steal or receive from the rich than the rich from the poor. The prophet chooses his words with precision in stating that the rich man took the lamb of the poor man in stead of describing it as stealing. Whereas the poor would *steal* from the rich, the rich would *take* from the poor. It is the action of the powerful and strong against the weak and defenceless and in this sense an abuse of power with impunity. This, naturally, demeans David and casts a slur on his idealized image in the Bible tradition as a whole and in the dtr tradition in particular.

Stuart Lasine sees in David's *"exaggerated"* response to Nathan's story on one hand, and his callous indifference towards Uriah on the other, an insight into the king's topsy-turvy emotions.[209] Fokkelman considers David as trying to play the judge without exercising the sobriety requisite for such an eminent profession. A good judge would neither need to explode with anger at a mere theft nor employ the forceful terms of an oath. But, being in a state of perturbation on account of his adultery and cynical murder, David exploded with all the energy at his disposal to maintain his own equilibrium as anger at an injustice that had been committed. "One execution counter-balances the other. David attempts to secure his own equilibrium in this magical-pathological way. The great satisfaction which he hopes to gain by the condemnation of another is meant to fill the emptiness brought about in David's soul by Uriah's liquidation."[210]

The positions of both Lasine and Fokkelman tend to play down the full import of the king's reaction towards the fictional rich man in favour of the ill-treated poor man. The displayed callous indifference and cynical murder are in direct contrast to his indignation at the report of unnecessary loss of life, which struck fear into his generals. This fact is proven by the instruction of Joab to the messenger in 2 Sam 11:19-22[211], garnished with

---

209 S. Lasine, *Melodrama as Parable*, p. 102.
210 J. P. Fokkelman, *King David*, p. 76.
211 S. Pisano, *Additions or Omissions in the Books of Samuel*, p. 54. In his analysis of the LXX additions to 2 Sam 11:22, Pisano concludes that LXX is expansionist while MT indicates the intelligence of the messenger of Joab

the report of Uriah's death. We are, inevitably, dealing with the morally wrong behaviour of a good-natured king who has gone wayward by committing adultery and in his bid to cover it up has added the more heinous crime of murder to it. The author of the story would like us to note that David's conscience is not dead; he still possesses a strong sense of morality. The prophet only needed to provide him with a projection screen in the form of the rich man for him to be able to stand outside himself and pass judgment on his own deeds.[212] He does not simply look at the case before him as the stealing and killing of a single sheep but an outright disregard for the right to property of a poor man by his rich neighbour. It is, on one hand, the violation and trampling underfoot of the poor man's right as a human being and, on the other, an abuse of power at its most outrageous height. Significantly, he pronounces the death sentence before the restitution in correspondence to his own crimes; murder of Uriah and marriage to Bathsheba. Violence will be punished by violence and damage not by its equivalent in restitution but fourfold as pacification for the sufferings of the poor man as a result of this brutal evil that he has to endure after which the wicked rich man has to be punished with death as a prevention against such acts in the future;[213] a sentence which effectively introduces the prophetic oracle that constitutes the climax of the pericope.

4.3 The prophetic word: vv. 7-12

The block consists of a long monologue of the prophet Nathan that stretches from v. 7-12 and is broken only by the response of David in v. 13. The discourse can internally be sub-divided into two distinctive parts: the prologue (v. 7-9) and the oracles of doom (v. 10-12).

---

in avoiding the anger of the king by providing quickly the message he would want to hear. This means that the king's tendency to be angry over the loss of life in the army was well-known and Joab, therefore, anticipated it.
212 J. P. Fokkelman, *King David*, p. 77.
213 A. Schenker, *Versöhnung*, p. 45.

4.3.1 The Prologue: vv. 7-9

⁷Nathan said to David, "You are the man! Thus says Yhwh, the God of Israel: I have anointed you king over Israel and have rescued you from the hand of Saul. ⁸I have given you your master's house and your master's wives into your bosom and have given you the house of Israel and of Judah; and if that were too little I will add as much more. ⁹Why have you despised the word of Yhwh, to do what is evil in his/my sight? You have struck down Uriah the Hittite with the sword and his wife you have taken for yourself as your wife but him you have killed with the sword of the Ammonites.	⁷ וַיֹּאמֶר נָתָן אֶל־דָּוִד אַתָּה הָאִישׁ כֹּה־אָמַר יְהוָה אֱלֹהֵי יִשְׂרָאֵל אָנֹכִי מְשַׁחְתִּיךָ לְמֶלֶךְ עַל־יִשְׂרָאֵל וְאָנֹכִי הִצַּלְתִּיךָ מִיַּד שָׁאוּל: ⁸ וָאֶתְּנָה לְךָ אֶת־בֵּית אֲדֹנֶיךָ וְאֶת־נְשֵׁי אֲדֹנֶיךָ בְּחֵיקֶךָ וָאֶתְּנָה לְךָ אֶת־בֵּית יִשְׂרָאֵל וִיהוּדָה וְאִם־מְעָט וְאֹסִפָה לְּךָ כָּהֵנָּה וְכָהֵנָּה: ⁹ מַדּוּעַ בָּזִיתָ אֶת־דְּבַר יְהוָה לַעֲשׂוֹת הָרַע בְּעֵינוֹ אֵת אוּרִיָּה הַחִתִּי הִכִּיתָ בַחֶרֶב וְאֶת־אִשְׁתּוֹ לָקַחְתָּ לְּךָ לְאִשָּׁה וְאֹתוֹ הָרַגְתָּ בְּחֶרֶב בְּנֵי עַמּוֹן:

4.3.2 Analysis

The LXX adds ὁ ποιήσας τοῦτο *(who has done this* or *who did this)* to Nathan's nominal sentence of the MT in v.7. This can only be an explanatory note and is, consequently, left out by the Lucianic recension as well as the Syriac. The correspondence of David's admission of his guilt in v. 13 to the brevity of Nathan's statement of condemnation in this verse (a two-word nominal sentence in both cases) is too apt to warrant the explanatory addition of the LXX. Whereas MT reads לְמֶלֶךְ (*as king or to be king*), the Syriac and some Targumim point the same consonants differently to read limlōk (*to rule over*). It pays to retain the MT even though the other does not change the meaning of the text in any substantial way. The Syriac and one cursive MS of the LXX add *"my people"* to Israel. This is a logical addition as a formula found mostly when God speaks about Israel or when one speaks in a solemn way about Israel in connection with God. A catena of this formulaic reference is found in 2 Sam 7:7-11, where each verse contains the phrase "my people Israel", with the exception of v. 9. Such a natural sequence could not have so easily been missed by the MT, if it had been there before. Consequently, the primacy of the MT over the LXX is beyond any doubt. Remarkably the verse is inexplicably missing from the

Qumran text despite its importance to the general understanding of the encounter between David and Nathan.[214]

V. 8: The Syriac reads *bnt* (*daughters*) instead of *bêt* (*house*) of the MT, LXX and Targumim. The argument in this verse is clearly the "many wives" that the Lord had purportedly given to David, which in itself is more by implication than by specific facts. The only daughter of Saul that David married was Mikal and Josephus refers to the many such wives as he had legally married.[215] David had married those many wives because he had inherited the throne of Israel, "house" of Saul, his lord. In this sense MT brings more clearly into focus the two notions of "house" than the Syriac, which is lopsided, despite McCarter's praise of it.[216] *The wives of your lord* (וְאֶת־נְשֵׁי אֲדֹנֶיךָ) is strange in the context, since the only known wife of Saul is Ahinoam, daughter of Ahimaaz (1 Sam 14: 50), who could wrongly be associated with Ahinoam of Jezreel, wife of David (1 Sam 30:5). The reference is however possible for, if Saul had a harem (for which we have no proof), it would be understandable for David to have taken possession of it as the lawful ruler of the nation after King Saul. Even though the text does not provide any proof for it, Ahitophel's advice that Absalom went in to his father's concubines (2 Sam 16:21) seems to suggest, among others, that the act concretized the fact that Absalom had taken over the house of his father as the new master. In like manner, the misunderstanding between Abner and Ishbaal on account of Rizpa (2 Sam 3:7-11) and the execution of Adonijah (1 Kings 2:13-25) might also point to the same direction; arrogating to oneself the wife of the deceased monarch is equated to usurping that position, especially when the person in question is in a position to lay claim to the throne. The point does not need to be stretched too far because it is nowhere evident that David required any such act for his legitimization and, therefore, does not resolve the awkward position of the assertion.

---

214 F. M. Cross, *Qumran Cave 4*, Band 12.
215 Josephus, *Antiquities*, 151.
216 P. McCarter, *II Samuel*, 295. For this verse McCarter claims originality for the Syriac contrary to MT and LXX in both the variant reading and the additions on the basis of its elegant chiastic prose, the lack of extant witnesses notwithstanding.

V.9: The different versions of the LXX have slightly different ways of expressing the opening word of the question in the MT – מַדּוּעַ. The Lucianic and Basilianic versions have *kai ti* (*and why*) while Vaticanus has *hoti* (*because*) and some Greek MSS and recensions of the Lucianic version have *kai ti hoti* (*why is it that*). The last of the three seems to be a combination of the first two and is quite a better way of expressing the MT's idea. The Lucianic and Theodosionic versions of the LXX further omit the tetragramaton while it is retained in the other versions in accordance with the MT. This is clearly an attempt to avoid the divine name becoming the object of the verb "despise", employing a euphemism (*dbr*) in its stead out of respect for the divine.

The phenomenon of "Sender" and "Messenger" produces a difference in the expression between the written word (kĕtîv) and how it is to be read (qĕrê). While the kĕtîv has *hr' b'ynw* (*the wrong thing in his eyes*), the qĕrê suggests *hr' b'yny* (*the wrong thing in my eyes*). Witnesses are divided between the two but whichever of the two one takes makes no difference, as it is absolutely normal for the prophet to speak in the first or third person singular in an oracle without any problem at all. He speaks *in persona* Yahweh. The Syriac, some Targumim and one Greek cursive text make the genitive of possession more specific by the addition of Adonay (*the wrong thing in the eyes of Adonay*) reflecting the classic dtr formula of X *did what was wrong in the eyes of Yhwh (Y)*.

4.3.3 Interpretation

The section is a monologue that stretches from v. 7 to v. 9 and serves as a prologue to the oracles of the next section. Those who may have known about the activities of the king in chapter eleven; courtiers as well as Joab, in particular, had all become his accomplices. It is only a single voice that has the courage to stand against the power of the monarch and it is of no wonder that the prophet of the promise now becomes the prophet of divine justice.[217] The prophetic formula כֹּה־אָמַר יְהוָה (v. 7) marks the beginning of the oracle as the words of the Lord in contradistinction to the first part of the verse, which are purely the words of the prophet himself. The וְעַתָּה of

---

217 G. Ravasi, *I Libri di Samuele*, p. 102.

v. 10 marks the end of the prelude and ushers in the prophecy or oracle of doom. The prologue provides the religious dimension to the sin of David as a sequence to the hint dropped by the author in 11:27b. As could be expected, the discourse develops rapidly until it is broken by the response of David in v. 13. The language is a discourse, both direct and predictive, punctuated with a question: *Why have you despised the word of the Lord to do what is evil in his (my) sight?*

Nathan picks the word from the mouth of David, having put him on the wrong foot, to drop the bombshell as he *removes the veil from the parable*.[218] A better narrative art than this one could not have been employed in that rightful moment. Ravasi notes that in Hebrew narratives the apparently gentle and smooth narration of events that ends up in a violent explosion of emotions is a prophetic technique to get the audience, the culprit, pronounce the desired judgment on itself, as in the case of the vineyard in Isaiah 5.[219]

When Nathan tells the king: "You are the man", he speaks in his own capacity as a man of God acquainted with the events of the court through divine revelation and is capable of bringing the king face to face with the reality of his own wrong doings. The אִישׁ, which has so far been open-ended and floating, is now concretised; David is the villain, whom he himself has justifiably, but angrily, condemned to death. The effect of the pronouncement is achieved more by the brevity of the MT than the longer version of the LXX, which adds ὁ ποιήσας τοῦτο: *the man who has done this*. The quintessential brevity of the double two-worded sentences; אַתָּה הָאִישׁ (You are the man) and חָטָאתִי לַיהוָה (I have sinned against the Lord), effectively demonstrates the wit of the narrator. Indeed, brevity is the soul of wit. Nathan then assumes his proper role as a prophet; the human medium through which the mind of God is made known in a given situation (in contrast to his active political role in 1 Kings 1:11-27). His acceptance of God's word and commitment to the divine promise of a Davidic dynasty lead him on to enter the palace as an outstanding man of God, overwhelm the king, and deliver the long oracle of doom with authority. Nathan does not concern himself with the correspondence of the elements in his fiction to the real life application. What appears important to him is the religious dimension of the sin of

---

218   cf. Fokkelman, *King David*, p. 77.
219   G. Ravasi, *I Libri di Samuele*, p. 103.

David. Vv. 7b-9 spell out the ground for the condemnation of the king and serve as the basis for the subsequent oracles. By introducing his speech with the typical prophetic or messenger formula *"Thus says Yhwh"* and placing it in apposition to *"the God of Israel"*, Nathan makes it clear to the king that he is on a mission of national importance and obliges the king to listen to him without any form of interruption. The case is no longer considered as adultery and murder committed against a private person that has to be judged and punished, but as a crime committed by the king of Israel against a poor and powerless subject and against God who is so strongly bound to the kingship of Israel under David. The language is consequently couched in a classic prophetic formula of a stereotypical condemnation in three parts:

Prophetic Stereotypical Condemnation(dtr)		Nathan's Condemnation of David
A list of the kindness of the Lord towards the subject characterised by the repetition of אנכי ("I") as in Amos 2:9-10 with verbs of giving as in 1 Sam 2:28.[220]	a.	I anointed you king over Israel (v. 7b: אנכי) I rescued you from the hand of Saul (v. 7c. אנכי) I gave you your master's house and your master's wives into your bosom...
An accusation of ingratitude often expressed by a (rhetorical) question introduced by מדוע ("why?") as in 1 Sam 2:29: *"Why do you trample my sacrifice and my offerings, which I have commanded in my habitation; and honour your sons above me, to make yourselves fat with the choicest of all the offerings of Israel, my people."*	b.	Why have you despised the word of the Lord? (v. 9: מדוע) You have struck down Uriah the Hittite with the sword. And his wife you have taken as your wife
A conclusion consequent to the two, which would usually open with ועתה ("and now" or "now then") as in 1 Sam 2:30; and Hosea 2:12.	c.	And now (ועתה) the sword shall never depart from your house (v. 10) I will take your wives before your eyes, and give them to your neighbour (v. 11)

---

[220] Pronouncing judgment on Israel, Amos lists among the deeds of the Lord; "Yet I destroyed the Amorites before them" and "I brought you up from the land of Egypt." In the accusation against the house of Eli, the Lord reminds him; "And I gave to your father's house all my offerings by fire from the people of Israel."

The anointing of David as king can be derived from one of three traditions: the people of Judah anointed him king over Judah in Hebron (2 Sam 2:4) and the elders of Israel over the house of Israel (2 Sam 5:3). Preceding all these, and most importantly for the current text, is the anointing of David by the prophet Samuel in 1 Sam 16:1-13. Here the prophet acts upon the divine directive as a pure instrument in the hands of God. This warrants the declaration of Nathan who makes Yhwh the subject of משחתיך. This declaration lays a strong emphasis on the divine origin of the Davidic monarchy; a favourite theme of the dtr.

By Divine election and kindness, David was anointed king over Israel and was saved from the hand of Saul, who threatened his life. The bitter relationship that developed between Saul and David has the victory of the young David over Goliath as its root and the song of praise that was sung to his glory as its culminating point. The soliloquizing of Saul that: *"They have ascribed to David ten thousands, and to me they have ascribed thousands; what more can he have but the kingdom"* (1 Sam 18:8) sets the stage for the confrontation. Beginning with this event a series of colourful manoeuvres are hatched by Saul in order to carry out his diabolic intentions of eliminating David, but they are all thwarted by equally glamorous escapes of the would-be victim, until David finally fled to the land of the Philistines in chapter 27. In v. 7 of our chapter, Nathan declares God the agent of that saving act from the hand of Saul. This is substantiated by the fact that eighty-five priests of Nob had to lose their lives for aiding and abetting in the flight of David from Saul (1 Sam 22:8).

The house and wives of his lord were given into his bosom and he would be given "as much more" if that was not enough; "he only needed to say so". There is no doubt about the fact that Yhwh had given the house of Saul to David. As the first ruler of the kingdom of Israel the nation can logically be said to be his house and his successor inherits that house. Literally speaking, David brought the only remaining members of the family of Saul (Mephiboshet and his son Mica) to his court so that the two *"ate from his table like any of the sons of the king"* (2 Sam 9:11). With the two at his court David had taken over the house of Saul, but the question about the wives of Saul remains a riddle and a hard nut to crack. Neither is Ahinoam ever listed among the wives of David nor Rizpah, concubine of Saul (2 Sam 3:7, 22:11) among his concubines. However if Saul ever had a harem, which is rather unlikely, David would have logically taken possession of it as the legitimate successor to the throne.

The mention of בית ישראל ויהודה (the house of Israel and Judah) as apparently two separate entities in this context tickles the ear of the reader. Phrased in this form, the remark occurs in only two other places; Ezek 9:9 and Hos 12:1 (*He said to me, "The guilt of the house of Israel and Judah is exceedingly great; the land is full of bloodshed and the city full of perversity; for they say, 'The LORD has forsaken the land, and the LORD does not see"* and *"Ephraim has surrounded me with lies, and the house of Israel with deceit; but Judah still walks with God, and is faithful to the Holy One"* NRSV). In these two instances they definitely refer to the two as separate entities. In our context, however, it conveys the idea of "the nation as a whole", the people of God that is ruled by David with a divine mandate. It is this unified body that the converse in Jer 31:31 speaks of as "the house of Israel and the house of Judah" with whom Yhwh will make a new covenant different from what he had made with their ancestors when he took them by the hand to bring them out of the land of Egypt. Seen in this light, the rest of the verse attains its expected force and effect; *"...and if that were too little I will add as much more"*. David had no ground at all to have acted in such a greedy manner, since God had given him every necessary proof to merit his blind trust in divine providence.

The accusation of Nathan looks at the background of David in the light of his present quality and standard of life, his social and religious status as king. It deals with the man who could say of himself a few years before: *"Does it seem to you a little thing to become the king's son-in-law seeing that I am a poor man and of no repute?"* (1 Sam 18:23). Thus if divine election has gratuitously made of him not only a wealthy man but also anointed him king (1 Sam 16:13) it is all the more incumbent on him to live by the dictates of the law of Yhwh, which forbids him to commit adultery and murder (Ex 20:13-14), if not for anything at all, at least as a sign of his gratitude towards God. Unfortunately, David has committed adultery with Bathsheba and murdered her husband. It has to be noted, once more, that in the parable itself, it was the lamb that was killed, but in the application, it is the husband who gets killed for the purpose of hiding the lesser crime of adultery. The reproach, therefore, comes in the form of a rhetorical question: *"Why have you despised the word of the Lord to do what is evil in his (my) sight?"* The accuser of David is neither Nathan nor Uriah; it is God himself, the defender of the poor, who is the object of the verb *despise* and, therefore, the accuser of David. He breaks through the fear and unnecessary awe that are naturally attributed to people in high positions to overlook or even condone their wrong doings and launches the attack against David in defence of the poor and oppressed (cf. Ps 82:3, 140:13). The phrase takes the reader back to the book of Judges where Israel consistently does what is evil in the eyes of Yhwh (Judg 2:11, 3:7, 12, 4:1, 6:1, 10:6, & 13:1) and looks forward to the persistent accusation of the kings of Israel and Judah for doing the same (1 Kings 14:22, 15:26, 34, 16:7, 19, 25, 30, 2 Kings 3:2, 8:18, 27, 13:2, 11, 24, 15:9, 18, 24, 28, 17:2, 21:2, 20, 23:32, 37, 24:9, and 19). This is the dtr voice accusing Israel and her kings of the sins that led to her exile. The same voice accuses David of adultery and murder and awaits his confession of guilt and forgiveness by the Lord.

V. 9 sums up the whole accusation against David in three statements on two levels; theological and moral. You have despised the word of the Lord, you have killed Uriah the Hittite and you have taken his wife to be your wife. C. Westermann wonders how v. 9a could belong to the "original" text given its high theological stance.[221] The sequence of the accusation, first theological and then the concrete event is typical of the dtr (Ex 32:8, Deut 9:12, 1 Sam 8:10ff).[222] The prophet states the murder of Uriah twice in a single verse (v. 9); the first in general terms and the second with concrete and detailed facts. David could have said that he was not the perpetrator of the murder, but the crime was committed according to his exact instructions and in despise of the word of the Lord. Since God has nowhere within the context directly spoken "a word" to David to this effect, it is difficult to find this word of the Lord that has been despised, unless one looks back automatically to the commandments of God in the Decalogue and as they are expounded in the book of Deuteronomy (Torah). By actively causing the death of Uriah, David has broken the commandment against murder (Ex 20:13, Deut 5:17). The whole affair with Bathsheba runs contrary to the two related commandments against adultery in Ex 20:14, Deut 5:18 and covetousness in Ex 20:17, Deut 5:21. Nevertheless, David is not

---

221 C. Westermann, *Grundformen Prophetischer Rede*, p. 100.
222 W. Oswald, *Nathan der Prophet*, p. 120.

simply accused of having broken the commandment of the Lord, which would direct the focus of the sin onto the sexual escapade gone sour and wild with a resultant murder, but of despising the word of the Lord.

The question as a basis for the accusation is made too programmatic for it to be without significance. John Van Seters notes that "the phrase *word of Yahweh* is consistently used in the DtrH in this situation to mean a specific oracle from Yahweh, given previously by the prophet".[223] He, however, does not go further to find this word but ends up with the assumption that it is in line with the Torah. Wolfgang Oswald takes up the discussion and posits that since obedience to the Torah does not play any role in the pericope, the dtr author advertently challenges his audience to search and find his basis in the context of the relationship between the monarch and his God. If the deed despises the "word of the Lord", then that word must exist somewhere. The reader would only have to look back at the promise of a dynasty to David in 2 Sam 7 by Yahweh through the medium of Nathan, the prophet, as the possible source of this word that is despised. God has promised to build a house for David and raise his offspring to sit on his throne when David's days are fulfilled. Now, the important question that could be raised, according to Oswald, is the underpinning of adding Bathsheba to the harem. "Was it the lust of having this particular woman as a wife or the fact of increasing the number of possible heirs to the throne that drove David into the marriage with Bathsheba?" asks Oswald. "Or was it just for the sake of legitimizing the son to be born?" Judging from the fact that the marriage with Bathsheba became an option only after the report of the pregnancy and the death of Uriah, Oswald opines, it would seem that the king's actions were motivated by the last two questions. Thus David has sought to secure his dynasty through devious human means instead of trusting in the divine promise of a lasting house. Oswald argues that the prophet could have appeared on the scene after the death of Uriah, but he did not. It is only when mother and child enter the royal house, as part of the family, that the prophet enters the scene to pronounce his judgment.[224]

---

223 J. Van Seters, Court History, p. 74.
224 The behaviour of the prophet Elijah in the case of Naboth's vineyard (1 Kings 21), follows the same example of Nathan in this episode. Elijah does not appear on the scene immediately after the death of Naboth but at the moment

Oswald realizes that this view may not be in accord with the exegetical position on the issue and so calls it the *Interpretatio Nathanica*.[225] Thus in the opinion of Nathan, David has despised and turned his back to the Lord who had brought him thus far and would alone ensure the continuity of his house. The sin of David the monarch is a breach of trust in his God and contempt for the word of the Lord in the show of ingratitude.

David's sin of ingratitude is two-fold: you have killed and you have taken. The combination of the two sins puts the king on the same level of wickedness as Ahab, who was confronted by Elijah; *"Have you killed and also taken possession?"* (1 Kings 21:19), and re-echoes the multiple occurrences of לקח in the "evils of the monarchy" stated in 1 Sam 8:13-17, as if to affirm the fulfilment of the word of the prophet (1 Sam 3:19). The emphatic position of אנכי and the suffix לך, with their repetitions, stress the source of David's wealth as the Lord, so that his sin is not only against the victim but also against God. The author then employs the use of oppositions in the form of a chiastic construction to highlight David's sins of ingratitude:

a. I anointed you to be king, v. 7c
    b. I saved you from the hand of Saul, v. 7d
        c. I gave to you the house and wives of your lord – and Israel and Judah, v. 8
        c¹. And his wife you have taken to yourself as your wife, v. 9c
    b¹. Uriah the Hittite you have smitten with the sword, v. 9b
a¹. Why then have you done what is evil in my eyes? v. 9a

The man who was oppressed by Saul has himself become an oppressor. David has returned evil for good; Uriah, the faithful soldier, has been slain unjustly, his wife has been appropriated by the king, and the word of Yhwh has been despised. God has been provoked into action and he is here, and only here in the whole of the succession narrative, the protagonist; the judge

---

    when Ahab goes to take possession of the vineyard. The difference, however, lies in the fact that Ahab did not order the death of Naboth. Jezebel organized everything without the knowledge of the king; hence the king is guilty only at the moment that he goes to take possession of the ill-gotten good, his sanctioning of the murder to his own advantage (v. 17-19).
225 W. Oswald, *Nathan der Prophet*, pp. 119–122.

will be judged, the robber shall be robbed. The verdict is logically introduced by ועתה (*now then*), which deduces a conclusion from the aforementioned accusations. This prophetic mode of calling the powerful to book abounds in the dtr work (cf. 2 Kings 14:7-16). In such instances the prophet is seen as a representative of the divine and constitutes a veritable force to check and balance the power of those in authority.

4.3.4 The oracle of doom: v. 10-12

[10]And now the sword shall never depart from your house because you have despised me and have taken the wife of Uriah, the Hittite to be your wife. [11]Thus says Yhwh: I will raise up evil against you from your own house; and I will take your wives before your eyes, and give them to your fellow and he shall lie with your wives in the sight of this very sun. [12]For you did it in secret but I will do this thing before all Israel and before the sun.	[10] וְעַתָּה לֹא־תָסוּר חֶרֶב מִבֵּיתְךָ עַד־עוֹלָם עֵקֶב כִּי בְזִתָנִי וַתִּקַּח אֶת־אֵשֶׁת אוּרִיָּה הַחִתִּי לִהְיוֹת לְךָ לְאִשָּׁה: ס [11] כֹּה אָמַר יְהוָה הִנְנִי מֵקִים עָלֶיךָ רָעָה מִבֵּיתֶךָ וְלָקַחְתִּי אֶת־נָשֶׁיךָ לְעֵינֶיךָ וְנָתַתִּי לְרֵעֶיךָ וְשָׁכַב עִם־נָשֶׁיךָ לְעֵינֵי הַשֶּׁמֶשׁ הַזֹּאת: [12] כִּי אַתָּה עָשִׂיתָ בַסָּתֶר וַאֲנִי אֶעֱשֶׂה אֶת־הַדָּבָר הַזֶּה נֶגֶד כָּל־יִשְׂרָאֵל וְנֶגֶד הַשָּׁמֶשׁ:

4.3.5 Analysis

V. 10: The phrase עַד־עוֹלָם (*for ever*) has the nuance of "a lasting basis". It appears in 2 Sam 7:13 where it triumphantly marks the extent of God's choice of the Davidic dynasty. Here, the same expression is turned against the house of David, which will be visited by the sword 'ad 'ōlām. Anderson interprets the expression in the sense of a limited span of time: "as long as David lives".[226] In v. 11, Yhwh threatens to take the wives of David and give them to his fellow, לְרֵעֶיךָ (*your neighbour, companion or fellow*). McCarter takes the form to be plural but since the word is רעה, the form is the singular construct of a noun III-ה with a second person singular suffix.[227] The basic meaning of the word is someone with whom one has something to do. It does not by itself indicate such a close affinity as a member of the

---

[226] A. A. Anderson, *2 Samuel*, p. 159.
[227] A. A. Anderson, *2 Samuel*, p. 159, has every good reason to insist on the fact that the word is singular in contrast to McCarter.

nuclear family.²²⁸ It is only when the story is considered in its global sense as part of the SN that its affinity to Absalom comes out clearly and compounds the problem of the literal critic.

4.3.6 Interpretation

The small block of two verses comprises a double-oracle of doom pronounced by Nathan that stands in direct opposition to the double-oracle of lasting dynasty in 2 Sam 7:12 & 16 where the sons of David and their sons would reign forever. The first sentence, v. 10a, is congruent with the charge of murder formulated around the word חרב (sword), taken from v. 9, where it is used twice in the repeated murder accusation. Practically speaking, David has an alibi; he was not on the spot and the content of his letter was possibly known only to Joab, who might not speak about it. Besides, it was unwittingly sent to the front by the victim himself, who could definitely not have read it, let alone known its content. In fact, apart from the Amalekite, who killed Saul (2 Sam 1:15), and the Beerothites, who killed Ishbaal (2 Sam 4:12), David was never on the scene of murder at all in the whole history. His opponents either died a natural death (Nabal) or at the hands of other people, usually, Joab.²²⁹ The victim here is a foreigner employed as a mercenary or a resident alien qualified only by his ethnic affiliation, with no lineage of any kind.²³⁰ He is technically a war victim of no extraordinary importance or an acceptable military casualty. His death attains meaning and importance in as far as his life or death constitutes a loss or gain respectively for someone else. In this sense, only one person stands to

---

228 Josephus renders the expression as "one of his sons". The sense is correct but it is too specific a rendition of the word.
229 B. Halpern, *David's Secret Demons*, p. 92.
230 Althann points out that the designation "Hittite" does not necessarily make Uriah a foreigner as it may merely mean that an ancestor of his may have come from one of the Neo-Hittite states of northern Syria, where Hittite civilization outlived the Hittite empire. Cf. R. Althann, *Uriah*, in ABD. W. Propp draws attention to the fact that Uriah has a Hebrew name even though he is tagged the Hittite. His name is derived from the Hebrew root that means "Yhwh is my light". Cf. W. Propp, *Exodus 19-40*, p. 487. In modern terminology, we would say that Uriah was not just a mercenary at the service of David but a Jew (Israelite) with a Hittite background.

gain from the death of Uriah, namely David. His alibi was apparently perfect, but his machination did not escape divine intelligence and retribution.

Seebass argues that since Uriah was loyally bound to the king as a military officer, David could just have taken the wife and constrained him (Uriah) to accept it. The text never uses the verb "steal" but "take" to describe both the action of the rich man and of David.[231] Above all, Uriah could still have been prevailed upon to receive compensation from the king instead of what the law stipulated if the adultery had been discovered. In a nutshell, the king did not really need to so desperately seek to cover up his guilt with a more heinous crime. That he went all the way to use the complex means instead of the simple ones at his disposal would mean that he found himself on an unfamiliar terrain.[232] The abuse of power here exhibited with impunity was neither the order of the day nor the hallmark of the character of David as

---

[231] H. Seebass, *Nathan und David in II Sam 12*, p. 205.

[232] U. Simon quotes the practice of *Adayie*, one of the regulations of hospitality in vogue among the Bedouin in the Beersheba district, as a background to the story of the poor man's ewe lamb. *Adayie* (attack) is a Bedouin form of legal theft. If a neighbour attacked the flock of another and flinched one head to prepare a feast for a guest, the act is called *adayie* and it is legitimate. But the practice had its own restrictions which rendered it common theft and punishable if not complied with: it applied only to small cattle; the guest should have arrived already and in the absence of the owner of the cattle; the owner must not be a stranger, who has taken refuge with the tribe; and immediately after the deed is done the owner must be informed. Excluded from the practice of *adayie* are: the ram (needed for breeding) the ewe with a bell or beads attached to its neck (a sign of the owner's special affection) the ewe reared in the tent, and one earmarked for the payment of a vow. Whoever takes anyone of these for *adayie* is liable to pay the owner back *fourfold*. He has likewise to pay the Zerka- the fee of the judge who sits on the case. Above all, and most importantly, *adayie* is only to be performed for the honour of a guest when the host is poor. The story before us does not give any indication of the practice of Adayie so we may not be able to conclude that it was in practice at the time of David. Even if it were the action of the rich man towards the poor contravenes the major prohibitions of the practice: the culprit is rich and has many flocks and cattle and the ewe is one raised in the tent with the owner's affection. "What arouses the indignation of the listener.... is the callousness with which the object of true affection of the weaker is sacrificed by the one whose enjoyment fades into insignificance when contrasted with the suffering it causes his fellow." Cf. *Juridical Parable*, p. 227–228.

king. Contrary to the exhortation of Abigail to David, the fugitive from Saul, in 1 Sam 25; *"for the Lord will make my lord a sure house, because my lord fights the battles of Yhwh; and evil shall not be found in you all your days (v. 28). ...my lord shall have no cause for grief, or pangs of conscience, for having shed blood without cause"* (v. 31), the king has sold himself to do what is evil in the eyes of the Lord. Evil has been found in him; he has shed innocent blood. Consequently, the sword that was used to smite Uriah will not depart from the house of David עַד־עוֹלָם (*for ever*). The phrase עַד־עוֹלָם, with its nuance of "a lasting basis", is a favourite term of the dtr. It appears in 2 Sam 7:13 where it triumphantly marks the extent of God's choice of the Davidic dynasty. Here, the same expression is turned against the house of David, which will be visited by the sword ʿad ʿōlām.[233] Anderson considers the expression to mean "as long as David lives".[234] This would be in line with Hannah's usage of the same word in 1 Sam 1:22: *"As soon as the child is weaned, I will bring him; that he may appear in the presence of the Lord, and remain there forever (*ʿad ʿōlām*)."* This sense would restrict the punishment to the lifetime of David and not beyond it. It, nevertheless, deviates from the normal biblical usage of the expression. Solomon's double usage of the word after causing Joab to be killed indicates the meaning of a lasting basis: whereas the blood of all those who had been executed by Joab would be upon his head and upon the head of the seed of Joab ʿad ʿōlām, unto David and unto his seed and unto his house and unto his throne shall there be peace ʿad ʿōlām (1 Kings 2:33).

Contextually, the sentence looks forward to the future and sums up the series of violent deaths that were perpetrated by the house of David against itself as the consequence of the king's own murderous act, confirming his own message to Joab: *"for the sword devours in one manner or another"* (11:25). The sword actually devoured three of his own sons; Amnon, Absalom, and Adonijah. In fact, all the major players in the Succession Narrative died violently apart from David and Nathan. This almost explicit reference to the future of the house of David has rendered the passage suspect in the eyes of many an exegete, especially of the literal critical school of thought. This verse constitutes one of the important links between the chapter and

---

233 J. P. Fokkelman, *Throne and City*, p. 268.
234 A. A. Anderson, *2 Samuel*, p. 159.

the previous one. In 11: 25 David's assertion stands as an anti-thesis to the authorial remark of v. 27b, leaving the audience in suspense as to what the outcome will be. The expected result of David's hypocritical response to Joab is now given; the sword that cuts in one moment here and in the other there will now find its victims in the house of David. The unjust judge consoles his accomplice in the execution of the crime, but the just judge awaits the right moment to pronounce a fitting judgment.

V. 10b introduces the second verdict; because David has taken the wife of Uriah the Hittite as his wife, God will bring evil in his house. The opening words, עקב כי, a particle of causality with a conjunction, provide room for two options of interpretation. On one hand, it could serve as the basis of the condemnation that precedes it in v. 10a (*The sword shall not depart from your house forever because you have despised me*) and, on the other, as the result of an argument that is yet to be stated (*Because you have despised me and have taken the wife of Uriah...*). As it is the verse division of the MT requires that 10b be read with 10a, but the sense and flow of the oracles call for 10b to be read together with v. 11.

עקב כי looks back to v. 6 as a response to David's rash judgment (אשר עקב) and provides the ground for the second oracle: the judge will meet his own judgment from the highest judge. The messenger formula "*kōh 'āmar Yhwh*" (Thus says the Lord) prefaces the verdict, reflecting v. 7. The hiphil participle of קום (raise) makes God the active agent of the evil (v. 11), which will befall the household of David for the evil (hr', v. 9), which he has done. God will take the wives of David before his own eyes and give them to his neighbour, who would lie with them before this very sun. The sin had been committed in secret, but its repercussion would be before the sun: in the open. Almost all the key words of our pericope appear in these two verses; vv. 11 and 12. רעה re-echoes "*to do what is evil in my sight*" of v. 9; לקחתי... ונתתי, "*I will take ...and give*" (v. 11) resonates "and I gave" (v. 8) and "you took" (v. 9). Despite God's double giving in v. 8, David has doubly taken in v. 9c and 10c. Therefore, God will punish him by taking and giving away in v. 11.[235] The עשית *(you did)* of v. 12 reflects לעשות *(to do)* of v. 9. The opposition between secret and open is underscored by the repetition of

---

235 J. P. Fokkelman, *King David*, p. 86.

השמיה in both verses contrasting בסתר (v. 12). Israel is mentioned here again to take the mind of the reader back to vv. 7 and 8 as an indication of the national dimension of the sin of David. He is not a private person but the anointed of God and ruler of His people. His punishment, therefore, must be witnessed by the whole nation.

The repetition of the messenger formula in v. 11a does not seem natural. It sounds strange that there is a completely new beginning for the oracle regardless of what had already been said by the prophet. It is no wonder that the Wellhausen school of thought (Literal Critic) holds these two verses, with their explicit references to the future events, as secondary. In fact, Wellhausen notes rightly that Absalom's going in to the wives of his father upon the advice of Ahitophel (16:22) was a political calculation of David as he had taken away all his wives except ten concubines (2 Sam 15:16). This is however seen as a fulfilment of the prophecy of evil in the house of David as a result of his adultery. It is a later addition to the text, opines Seebaß, as it is not exactly said in the prophecy in the same way as the death of Uriah is not mentioned in the story but is made a capital point in the prophecy of doom. These elements are later additions by the dtr author who has reformulated the purpose of the story.[236] To some extent, I agree with Wellhausen, Seebaß and their followers that these elements may be a later addition, but maintain the logical question of how later these elements are to the text before us. Working with the established hypothesis of a deuteronomistic school or Bewegung, I logically maintain the position that different elements were added to the text of the history at different times within the school itself, hence the question of later additions does not necessarily make the material non-dtr, unless one implies a period later than the Dtr.[237]

The connection between the prophet's explicit message and Absalom's revolt (2 Sam 15-18) has called for no small a discussion over the years.[238]

---

236 H. Seebaß, *Nathan and David*, p. 207.
237 H. J. Stipp, Ende bei Joschija, in Das Deuteronomistische Geschichitswerk, p. 250. Stipp identifies at least two levels of redaction in the closing chapters of 2 Kings built around two basic themes; the salvation of Judah on account of her faithfulness to the cult centralization at the time of Josiah and Manasseh as the escape goat bearing the guilt of the exile after 609 B.C.
238 L. J. Wellhausen, *Der Text der Bücher Samuelis*, p. 184. Wellhausen considers the two verses, vv. 10-12 a later interpolation.

The proponents of the literal critical approach consider the whole oracle (vv. 7b-12) a secondary and later addition to the text, while J. Van Seters ascribes it to the CH as an anti-monarchical document. The revolt is seen as God's way of punishing David for the murder of Uriah and a fulfilment of the oracle of Nathan. It is concretized by the advice of Ahithophel, whose counsel was compared to a divine oracle (16:23) that Absalom goes in to his father's concubines in a tent pitched on the palace roof, before all Israel and, of course, under the sun, in accordance with the word of the Lord: *"For you did it in secret; but I will do this thing before all Israel, and before the sun"* (v. 12). לְרֵעֶיךָ (*your neighbour*), however, does not, by itself, indicate such a close affinity as a member of the nuclear family. The basic meaning of the word is someone with whom one has something to do, hence neighbour, friend or companion. This, however, does not destroy the strong link between the prophecy and its fulfilment for, seen in this light, Absalom was an instrument in the hand of God to punish David for his crime against his fellow man, depicted by the causative sense of קום with God as the agent. The prophecy then becomes programmatic in summing up the events of David's life; from his rise to the oracle and from the oracle onwards. The practice of inserting such general and retrospective reflections at certain important moments in the history is a characteristic feature of the dtr writer and, according to Martin Noth, "has no exact parallel in the Old Testament outside this writer or group of writers, as the case may be."[239]

The Nathan pericope of 12:1-15a and indeed the whole David-Bathsheba-Uriah sequence without 12:11-12 will be like a decapitated snake. The forecast of trouble in the house of David is an essential component of the story in chapters 11-12 and this is especially true of 12:11-12.[240] In these two verses, the punishment for adultery is spelt out. It is actually the adultery that sets off the chain of events in the two chapters. Without the adultery, the murder of Uriah would have made no sense and without the death of Uriah, David could not have married Bathsheba; but without this marriage, the origin of the future successor to the throne would hang in the air. Could it have gone otherwise? The marriage of a war widow contravenes

---

239 M. Noth, *"The Deuteronomistic History"*, p. 20.
240 P. K. McCarter, *II Samuel*, p. 301.

no law except that the would-be husband is the brain behind the death of the soldier. To miss this point in the oracle of doom would leave the story without a link to its surroundings. Herzberg puts the issue in its right perspective when he states:

> ...the two threats each singles out one aspect of David's sin and relates it to definite events which occur later. God's righteousness is clearly shown forth in a way beloved of the deuteronomistic and "Wisdom" literature. The punishment fits the crime. This need not, of course, be a late composition, but the passage will certainly be a later development. The section would very easily lend itself to emphasis on points which were only implicit and to the consequent demonstration that Yahweh's justice is not suspended, even for the mightiest.[241]

4.4 The concluding words: vv. 13-14

| 13Then David said to Nathan, "I have sinned against Yhwh". Nathan said to David, "Yhwh has, on one hand, caused your sin to pass over, you shall not die. 14Nevertheless, because you have by this deed utterly scorned the enemies of Yhwh, the child that is born to you, on the other, shall surely die." 15Then Nathan went to his house. | 13 וַיֹּאמֶר דָּוִד אֶל־נָתָן חָטָאתִי לַיהוָה ס וַיֹּאמֶר נָתָן אֶל־דָּוִד גַּם־יְהוָה הֶעֱבִיר חַטָּאתְךָ לֹא תָמוּת: 14 אֶפֶס כִּי־נִאֵץ נִאַצְתָּ אֶת־אֹיְבֵי יְהוָה בַּדָּבָר הַזֶּה גַּם הַבֵּן הַיִּלּוֹד לְךָ מוֹת יָמוּת: 15 וַיֵּלֶךְ נָתָן אֶל־בֵּיתוֹ |

4.4.1 Analysis

V.13: The MT has a short break between the reaction of David (v. 13a) and the response of Nathan (v. 13b) which many MSS omit in order not to break the natural flow of the dialogue, but the presence of the gap does not disrupt the discourse in any significant way, it rather constitutes a helping note for the reader by removing the temptation to read the two sentences together without a feeling of the swift change of characters. This can be contrasted with the similar phenomenon occurring between v. 10 and v. 11 which we have identified as not too good an occurrence as it rather breaks the sense of the oracle. The response of Nathan to David has an asyndetic structure as an explicatory note; גַּם־יְהוָה הֶעֱבִיר חַטָּאתְךָ לֹא תָמוּת (*Yahweh has... "caused your sin to pass over"; you shall not die*) and draws attention to

---

241 H. W. Hertzberg, *I & II Samuel*, p. 314.

the emphatic position of *gam*. This effect is broken if a "*waw*" is added to the particle of negation as in the case of some fragments of Geniza (Cairo) and Tertullian. Wolfgang Richter describes *gam* as a simple particle or modal word which expresses the function of emphasis[242] on account of its position before the subject of the sentence which it introduces. Van der Merve takes it further by pointing out that in this specific case, as also in v. 14b, *gam* marks the beginning of two main sentences modified by infinitive absolutes (העביר and הילוד) in the same context and therefore; "*Gam* marks the referent of each element in its domain for focus, and in this way indicates the commitment of the speaker to the truth of the fact that each of the elements is (or may be) assigned a shared element C",[243] in this case, the message announced by the prophet.

V. 14 poses daunting challenges to interpreters on account of the presence of the word, אֶת־אֹיְבֵי (*the enemies of*) as the object of the verb *ni'es* (blaspheme). Who are the enemies of the Lord, if he has any? Has David blasphemed the Lord or the enemies of the Lord? A veritable means of answering these questions will be to find out if the word אֶת־אֹיְבֵי, found in the MT and in the major witnesses, originally belonged to the text. 4QSam has אֶת־דְּבַר יְהֹוָה (*the word of the Lord*)[244] and a Greek cursive MS (376) reflects אֶת־יְהֹוָה. These variants clearly point out that we are dealing here with a euphemism. It was an accepted phenomenon for scribes to employ euphemistic expressions for pious reasons without any motive of obscuring a text.[245] This could happen at the moment of writing or as a later emendation, because a word or phrase sounds offensive to the religious sensibilities of a people in a particular era. In 1 Kings 21:13 Naboth is said to have *blessed* (ברך) instead of *cursed* (ארר) God and the king and is stoned to death for that matter. Job would send for his sons and purify them after their feasts in case they might have *blessed* (*cursed*) God in the moment of their joyful celebrations (Job 1:5). In both instances the Divine name would have

---

242 W. Richter, *Grundlagen einer althebräischen Grammatik*, p. 191 in van der Merve, *The Old Hebrew Particle gam*, p. 14.
243 CHJ Van der Merwe, *The Old Hebrew particle gam*, pp. 194–195.
244 McCarter calls attention to the fact that the citation of the MT is in error since the supposed lamed in the photo used by de Boer is rather a shadow behind a small hole in the leather. Cf. *2 Samuel*, p. 296.
245 R. Yaron, *The Coptos Decree*, p. 90–91.

been the object of the verb "*curse*" which is advertently substituted with "*bless*", to avoid offending the religious sentiments of the reader.[246]

The aforementioned instances go a long way to prove that euphemisms are employed in the MT in order to avoid certain naked truths that might appear to offend the religious sensitivities of the believing audience. In the the current verse, the primitive text may have had אֶת־יְהוָה (Yhwh) standing as the direct object of the verb blaspheme, which subsequent manuscripts substituted with the euphemism in order not to leave the sacred name standing at a *positum non gratum*. This would account for the fact that independent textual witnesses employed different euphemistic words within the same context since the primitive text did not have one.[247] This phenomenon was not unique to Israel, but was a common practice in the ancient orient. R. Yaron compares the phrase with a similar usage in the treatment of a rebellious feudal lord, Teti, son of Minhotep, count of Coptos, in a decree of the thirteenth dynasty (18th century B.C.) "*His name shall not be remembered in this temple, according as it is done toward one like him, who is hostile toward the enemies of his god.*"[248] Thus the phrase can be understood in the causative sense as: *Since by this deed you have caused the enemies of the Lord to blaspheme* (LXX and Vulgate) or in the active sense as: "*because by this deed you have utterly scorned the Lord,*

---

246 In his article; *The Coptos Decree and 2 Sam XII 14*, Yaron does not find any proof for considering the euphemistic substitution of *berekh* (to bless) for expressions meaning "to curse" (as in the case of Naboth in 1 Kings 21:10, 13) or "to blaspheme" (Job 1:5, 2:5, 9) as the result of emendation since the apprehension against uttering an express blasphemy may go back to very early times. He further cites the "third alleged instance of *berekh* for "to curse" in Ps 10:3 on which Geiger, Ginsburg and Pfeiffer put much emphasis (cf. Pfeiffer, *Introduction*, p. 86). Here, according to Geiger et al, the original text which reads "he despises" and the euphemism "he blesses" are both preserved in the text, showing perhaps that the correction was written originally between the lines over the objectionable word. Yaron, however, finds support for the genuineness of *berekh* in the synonymous *hillel* in the parallel v. 3b and the fact that the pair *berekh hillel* occurs also in Jer 4:2, Ps 113:1-3, 115:17-18, 145:2 (Coptos Decree, p. 90).

247 P. K. McCarter, *II Samuel*, p. 296 McCarter quotes Geiger who has already in 1957 noted that the chief witnesses are euphemistic and the primitive reading is what the Greek Ms 376 presents.

248 R. Yaron, *The Coptos Decree*, p. 90.

the son born to you shall surely die. The scribal work would represent the causative sense, while its euphemistic application would be the active. The euphemistic variant will give the impression that the sin of David acquires an international dimension with the reference to the enemies of the Lord. If Yhwh has enemies at all, these will probably be foreigners within and without the confines of the land of Israel. By his action, the king has given God's enemies the opportunity to slander the God who has bound himself so closely to his kingship. Another question would however remain open: If the sin of David was committed in secret how does it give this public scandal? The clumsiness of the expression causes the reader an enormous perplexity, but Yaron is of the view that this perplexity is resolved by the comparison with the Coptos Decree since what matters after "is not the literal meaning of an expression but what the reader of average intelligence and knowledge understands by it."[249]

4.4.2 Interpretation

The final part of our pericope begins with a *wayyiqtol* (*wayyōmer*) and a change of speaker. David responds to the long speech of Nathan in an assertive language as a mortified man in need of forgiveness ("*I have sinned against the Lord*"). Remorse for sin comes after a long period of reflection and meditation, but the author does not lead his audience into the interior process of David's remorse. What matters to this writer is the candid confession of his sin. The quality of his remorse is, however, underscored by his use of the word חטא (to sin) against the Lord, which has so far not been used in the whole discourse. Thus the king now acknowledges that the accusations levelled against him are right and that his evil actions have not just been against Uriah as against God. Ottmar Fuchs notes that at the level of the parable David recognises and even names the options of compassion

---

249 R. Yaron, *The Coptos decree*, p. 91. M. J. Mulder (*Un Euphémisme dans 2 Sam XII 14*, p. 110) refers to Goslinga's critique of Yaron that the Coptos Decree constitutes no proof to our text. Mulder maintains that the Decree provides the evidence that the use of euphemisms was not restricted to Israel but was widespread in the environs and that the expression carried by the MT; נאץ את איבי יהוה, is euphemistic and has found its appropriate place in our text on account of the popular practice.

and justice that are at play in the short account but only as far as it concerns the other person and not himself. This depicts the hermeneutical problem of how one rightly identifies oneself with the biblical text; with the culprit or the victim? Nathan had to play the prophetic role of opening the eyes of David to the dual realities of his parable; the actors in the parable and their corresponding identity in the real life situation, before David could rightly identify himself with the corresponding fictional character in the parable, the rich, avaricious miser and criminal. This underscores the absurd but completely normal human attitude of identifying with the victim instead of the culprit.[250]

The cryptic accusation of Nathan in v. 7 and the equally cryptic admission of guilt by David in this verse have caused Hertzberg to rejuvenate the position of the literal critical method of Wellhausen and Rost that the original text moved from v. 7a to 13, leaving vv. 7b-12 as a later development. Hertzberg moves a step away from his predecessors in intimating that vv. 7b-12 need not be a later interpolation.[251] It may not be out of place to assume that the story might have undergone a redaction or even redactions, which placed much emphasis on the prophetic rebuke and David's admission of his guilt, before the re-working of the deuteronomistic author

---

250 O. Fuchs, *Praktische Hermeneutik*, p. 117. „Das Spannende an der Geschichte ist, dass David zwar die Optionen des Mitleids und der Gerechtigkeit selbst kennt und benennt, diese aber kritisch nur auf den Anderen, nicht auf sich bezieht. Nathan muss ihm eröffnen, dass er selbst der Betreffende ist. Das alte Problem: nämlich sich lieber mit den Opfern zu identifizieren als mit den Tätern und damit die eigenen Täterschaften in den „blinden Fleck" abzudrängen, wird so sehr verdrängt, dass erst ein explizites hartes Wort wie ein blitzartiges Licht diesen blinden Fleck aufzuhellen vermag. Erst jetzt kann er seine Situation wie den Text gleichermaßen authentisch lesen, nämlich wo er wirklich aus der Perspektiv der Barmherzigkeit und Gerechtigkeit steht. Damit identifiziert er seine eigene Identität im Gleichnis und umgekehrt."

251 H. W. Hertzberg, *I & II Samuel*, p. 313–314. Hertzberg considers the two pronouncements of Nathan (v.7b-12) an explanation of both past and later events of David's family: the anointing might refer to that of 1Sam 16 since it precedes the pursuit of Saul; the giving of his master's house to Saul's harem, which sets the tradition for Absalom's entry into David's harem and Adonijah's request for Abishag, which was interpreted as a bid for the throne. The devouring sword may refer to the death of three of his sons by the sword- Amnon, Absalom and Adonijah respectively.

or authors. While the oracles portray David as an ingrate, who has repaid evil for good, his response makes him completely different from such a king as Ahab, and, possibly, from the typical oriental monarch. At the end of the encounter with the unknown prophet, Ahab *returned home resentful and sullen* (1 Kings 20:43) but David, on his part, pronounces his guilt in two precise words: חטאתי ליהוה. More than just the two words, the Psalter makes this repentance paramount to the character of the man when it ascribes Psalm 51 to David and intimates that he composed it after the encounter with Nathan over the Bathsheba affair (v. 2).

Consequent upon David's repentance, Nathan pronounces the word of forgiveness in predictive terms: גַּם־יְהוָה הֶעֱבִיר חַטָּאתְךָ לֹא תָמוּת (*Yahweh has, on one hand, "caused your sin to pass over; you shall not die"*). He begins from where David left off; "Yhwh", prefacing it with גם for emphasis while looking forward to the second גם in v. 14b. God, a judicial authority higher than the king, is the subject of forgiveness and he reverses the death penalty pronounced by the king on himself. Since Nathan did not mention the death penalty in the oracles, the reader may have to presuppose that the two men understood that the punishment laid down for a man who had sexual relationship with a married woman was capital punishment (Deut 22:22) as is witnessed by the laws of the surrounding nations.[252]

In their dictionary of the Hebrew and Aramaic Old Testament of 1998, L. Koehler and W. Baumgartner define the hiphil of עבר as "cause to pass over" or "overlook guilt", among others. Notwithstanding the fact that the word could also mean "forgive sin", here it means more than just that. A sin of such gravity may not just be put away or forgotten; hence God causes the sin to pass over to someone else who, like the proverbial escapegoat, will bear the blood guilt of David. It would seem strange to the modern mind that the innocent child should bear the guilt of the parents' sin and carry a sealed death sentence: מות ימות (*he will surely die*).[253] But the prophet

---

[252] The Code of Hammurabi, § 129: "If the wife of a seignior has been caught while lying with another man, they shall bind them and throw them into the water. If the husband of the woman wishes to spare his wife, then the king in turn may spare his subject." Cf. J. B. Pritchard, *ANET*, p. 171.

[253] In the list of people excluded from the Assembly of God's people is found those born out of illicit union (Deut 23:2). This practice of exclusion is also found on the level of the family at the time of Jephthah the Gileadite (Judg 11). If this

explains: אֶ֗פֶס כִּֽי־נִאֵ֤ץ נִאַ֙צְתָּ֙ אֶת־אֹיְבֵ֣י יְהֹוָ֔ה בַּדָּבָ֖ר הַזֶּ֑ה (v. 14a), literally translated: *Because you have by this deed caused the enemies of Yhwh to blaspheme.* אפס has the quality of restricting a preceding material, offering clarifications, and in combination with כי restricting the immediately preceding clause.[254] In our text, it restricts the scope of the forgiveness and provides the grounds for the apparently contradictory pronouncement that follows in a causative manner (since or because), while the *figura etimologica*, the repetition of the root נאץ, gives emphasis to the declaration. David, the repentant sinner, is forgiven but the guilt of his sin still cries for expiation.

Nathan's pronouncement of the forgiveness of the sin of David and, at the same time, the announcement of the death of the child have for a long time caused unresolved problems for many a researcher.[255] The problem is compounded by modern translations that render the גם of v. 13 as a conjunction (also) with the role of an emphatic particle to the divine name. Oswald notes rightly that this problem loses much of its weight when one concentrates on the grammatical structure of the paragraph with the first גם playing the double role of an emphatic particle and protasis with the second גם in v. 14 as its apodosis, serving as a coordination and clausal adverb in a classic Semitic idiom; גם....גם, This would call for such a construction as "on one hand ... and on the other..."[256] in modern languages. Thus the two verses have to be read together for the full import of this form of construction to make a better sense of the death of the child despite the forgiveness of the sin. *Yhwh has, on one hand, caused your sin to be passed over, you shall not die. Nevertheless, because you have by this deed utterly scorned the enemies of Yhwh, the child that is born to you, on the other, shall surely die.* Seen in this light, the problem reduces to the barest minimum without being alien to Biblical thought and the dtr tradition. A parallel is found in Num 14:19-23, where the Lord forgives the sin of Israel upon the intercession of Moses but

---

practice was in vogue at the time of David, a thing that we have no reason to doubt, the situation of this son of David would have been very complicated on both levels; national and familial.

254 B. K. Waltke – M. O'Connor, *An Introduction to Biblical Hebrew Syntax*, 39.3.5e.
255 W. Dietrich, T. Naumann, *Samuelbücher*, p. 253.
256 W. Oswald, *Nathan der Prophet*, p. 115. C.f. Waltke – O'Oconnor, op. Cit. 39.3.4d.

avows that none of the rebels would see the Promised Land. Thus the sin is forgiven, but the guilt calls for a reparation or penitence, in the modern religious sense.

The death of the child, even if it might not be logical to the modern mind, is according to the author of the story a logical consequence to David's bid to broaden the base of his house and dynasty through violence as against the faithful reliance upon the promise of God, who alone establishes dynasties. By his deeds David has made himself culpable of the death penalty that he himself has pronounced, but his repentance makes him worthy of forgiveness. The repentant sinner must do reparation for his sins, as a rule. In the case of David, Uriah could not be brought back to life, and giving up Bathsheba would cause more social problems for the "victim" than would be acceptable, given the fact that the Dtr does not, in any way, make Bathsheba "a comrade-in-crime" with David. It would then not be out of place for David to give up the very reason for which he committed the murder as expiation: the son born to him. Oswald argues that since David has attempted to secure his dynasty through illegitimate means instead of relying upon the faithfulness of Yhwh, he has despised the word of the Lord, who alone could build him a house. The despotic act of snatching the wife of another man and securing the legitimacy of the child born out of the act through murder despises God who has promised to establish his dynasty for ever (2 Sam 7:11). The death of the child ensures that such a despicable act does not succeed and that the house of David is not built in such a manner at the expense of an innocent blood.[257] Regine Hunziker-Rodewald captures the point accurately in positing that Bathsheba was constantly linked to Uriah as her husband even at the birth of the child and implies that her marriage to Uriah was still legitimate. Hence that child, even though born to David, was still linked to Uriah and it is only with his death that Uriah falls permanently out of the narrative. It is only then that Bathsheba could be legitimized as the mother of the prince and future king.[258] Thus the fourfold restitution for the gruesome killing of Uriah by the sword of the Ammonites is achieved by the loss of the four sons of David: the unnamed son

---

257 W. Oswald, *Nathan der Prophet*, p. 123.
258 R. Hunziker-Rodewald, Die beide Söhne, p. 102.

of Bathsheba (12:14-18), Amnon (13:29), Absalom (18:15) and Adonija (1 Kings 2:25).[259]

Above all, and in accordance with the nature of prophecies of doom in the DtrH, notes Westermann, the death of the child is the patent sign that the prophet has proclaimed the word of the Lord. For the simple reason that the fulfilment of the prophecy of doom was in the future, a sign was always given in the immediate present as a confirmation that the judgment was from Yhwh. Westermann gives the following among others as the signs that accompany prophecies of doom directed towards individuals in the dtr tradition;

1 Sam 2:34 – the death of the two sons of Eli on the same day
1 Sam 15:28 – the torn hem of the robe of Samuel
2 Sam 12:14 – the death of the child born to David
1 Kings 11:30 – Ahijah's robe torn into twelve pieces
1 Kings 13:3 – The altar of Jeroboam torn down
1 Kings 14:12 – the death of Jeroboam's son the moment the queen enters the city

The texts, continues Westermann, show the original bond between the word and sign that constituted the prophetic judgment proclamation (prophecy of doom).[260] The death of the child is, therefore, an integral part of the prophecy of doom and must in no way be removed from the dtr author who has included it in his story.

Polzin identifies the use of two words otherwise unique to the DtrH in Nathan's reproach of David. In v. 9, God characterizes the murder of Uriah and the taking of Bathsheba as despising (בזה) Him and His word and Nathan emphasizes that David has "utterly scorned (נאץ) the Lord" by his deeds in v. 14. The only times in the whole Masoretic tradition that בזה is used with God as the object occurs here and in 1 Sam 2:30, a noted dtr passage. In the prophecy of doom against the house of Eli the Lord declares: *"...those who honour me I will honour, and those who despise (בזה) me shall be treated with contempt."* In the programmatic introduction to the

---

259 A. Schenker, *Versöhnung*, p. 49.
260 C. Westermann, *Grundformen*, p. 113.

song of Moses, God is said to have described the attitude of Israel towards him once they settled in the Land of promise in these words; *"For when… they have eaten their fill and grown fat, they will turn to other gods and serve them, despising (נאץ) me and breaking my covenant."* (Deut 31:20). This is re-echoed in the words of Yahweh to Samuel about Israel that has almost the same tone and language as Nathan's condemnation of David in this passage: *"…Listen to the voice of the people in all that they say to you; for they have not rejected you, but they have rejected (מאס) me from being king over them."* (1 Sam 8:7).[261] It is of great significance to note that all these references fall within the dtr corpus and reflect his important theme of Israel's persistent disobedience as a continuous rejection of Yahweh her God that will justify the exile and emphasize the need for repentance and a return to God.

The section ends with the usual Biblical mode of closing an episode, the departure of one of the parties (to his house) demonstrated by the wayyiqtol of movement, *wayyēlek*. After the episode of Saul's rejection in 1 Sam 15:34 the narrator closes the encounter as follows: וַיֵּלֶךְ שְׁמוּאֵל הָרָמָתָה וְשָׁאוּל עָלָה אֶל־בֵּיתוֹ גִּבְעַת שָׁאוּל (*Then Samuel went to Ramah; and Saul went up to his house in Gibeah of Saul*). Similar verbs of movement are used to express the departure of Baalam and Balak after their meeting in Num 24:25: "Then Baalam got up and went (ויקם -x- וילך) to his place, and Balak also went (הלך) his way." In 1 Kings 19:43, it is Ahab who sets out from the place of encounter homeward. Nathan's movement to his house contrasts his entering the house of David as a mission accomplished, while the name נתן concludes the episode even as it had initiated it. David acknowledges the supremacy of the power of God, wielded by the prophet, over his; having spoken the first word of the episode, Nathan says the last word and leaves at his own will. The supreme position wielded by the prophet in the social life of Israel is here brought to the fore. It may not be doubted that a prophetic hand is to be found at the background of this narrative, but the Dtr has made use of it as a frame work to pass judgment on Israel. As Nathan voices the ultimate sentence against David one hears the dtr voice pronouncing judgment and expecting the repentance of his contemporaries in order to let them embrace the forgiveness constantly offered by the Lord.

---

261 R. Polzin, *David and the Deuteronomist*, p. 129–130.

4.5 Summary

The crux of the matter is that Solomon inherited the throne of David as the second in the Davidic line of kings in Jerusalem. His mother was Bathsheba, who was previously the wife of Uriah, an officer in the army of David. The most legitimate, consequential and logical question to raise is how the wife of another man became not only the wife of David but also the mother of the successor to the throne. Such an important and, at the same time, interesting twist in a tradition cannot easily escape the ink of a good writer nor the eye of an interpreter of history, if he is worth the name. What will, however, make the story unique is how a particular author builds upon the tradition at his disposal to transmit the message that he would want his audience to receive. That later scholars see in the David-Bathsheba sequence an anti- or pro-monarchical trend is only a matter of the understanding of the individual interpreter and not the intention of the writer. The image of David painted in the story is neither as bright to make him an angel nor as dark as to bedevil him. He is simply a good-natured man and beloved king gone wayward on account of adultery and murder, but at the same time, possessing a morally active, good and sharp conscience that helps him to accept his fault and confess his guilt. In much the same way, considering the story as a legitimization of Absalom as heir to the throne of David will be a lopsided view of the sequence and basically out of place, as the announcement of the birth of Solomon comes almost as an after-thought or a matter of obligation and not as the main reason for the story. This report is only a leitmotif that launches the story into the future.

The whole affair of Nathan, calling David to order, places the prophet in a highly enviable position in relation to the king. This state of affairs makes some commentators consider the intervention a later addition to the text. But the story itself is not really strange in its context based upon the fact that David was only the second king in Israel and the first in the real sense of the word after the rejection of Saul. Saul's reign witnessed the bitter process of the separation of powers between king and prophet, with the prophet wielding the trump card. Nathan was not so strong and antagonistic towards David as Samuel was towards Saul, but at that period in the narration of the history the role of the prophet-priest as ruler of the people in place of Yahweh was not too distant. Above all, if at the time of Nathan there existed prophetic schools or guilds, as at the period before him (1 Sam 10:10) and after him (2 Kings 2:3), the nostalgia of those days would have played a significant role in keeping and cherishing such a tradition as the prophet, bringing the great king David to book. Not surprisingly, stories of this nature found in the MT are, but for one, narrated by prophets (cf. 2 Sam 12:1-15, 14:1-24, 1 Kings 20:35-43, Isa 5:1-7)[262] and three out of the four examples are found in the DtrH.

Seebaß notes with a good reason that the use of such terminologies as *the wives of your Lord, Uriah the Hittite you have murdered*, and *the God of Israel* in the story are the additions of the dtr author.[263] Coupled with this is the presence of such peculiar dtr terminologies as *'ad 'ōlām* and *na'as* with Yhwh as its object in relation to the Davidic dynasty. The emphasis on the divine origin of the kingship of David is a favourite theme of the Dtr and goes a long way to promote the image of the *Ideal King* in the tradition. To this end, the author utilises the fact of the prophet bringing the erring king to book as a promotion of that image when one sees in the powerful king a humble man who submits to divine reprimand with the prophet as an instrument in the hands of God and a mouth-piece of the Divinity.

The encounter of David and Nathan in this episode unfolds a very familiar pattern of social and relational dynamics of an encounter between two persons. In such a normal human encounter there is an action which is met with a reaction that in its turn produces a counter reaction. The process may be repeated depending upon the duration of that encounter. Thus David reacts (with anger) to Nathan's action (the parable) which provides the prophet the opportunity to pronounce judgment on the king (counter reaction). This calls for a second reaction from the mortified David which exudes the final counter reaction of forgiveness from the prophet. It is clear that the Dtr has inherited the story from his sources, but the hard nut to crack in this episode has been what the original story might have been and what possible additions have been made, if these are in some way traceable.

---

262 G. Ravasi, *I Libri di Samuele*, p. 103.
263 H. Seebaß, op. cit., p. 207.

Chapter 5. The David of the Dtr and the parable of Nathan

A browse through the work of the Chronicler gives the indication that the author had access to the work of the deuteronomist or had access to a parallel source which he had made use of to reconstruct the history of Israel as a repository of the message of hope that he intended to put across to his post-exilic audience.[264] The release of King Jehoiachin of Judah from prison (2 Kings 25:27-30), which was apparently the highest point of the message of hope of the dtr, did not end the exile and new answers had to be sought to meet the new questions of the day. The Chronicler picks up the strands from where the Dtr left off to give new impetus to the glimmer of hope in a vision that was on the verge of being shattered and consumed in the raging torrents of socio-political annihilation. In the usual manner of a writer with volumes of materials at his disposal, the Chronicler either adopted the whole or edited the sources to suit his plot and aim. However, and at complete variance with the dtr author, this writer left out the materials which would not easily serve his purpose or would obscure his aim and complicate the trend of his thoughts in a way that would inhibit the understanding of his audience. A comparison of 1 Chr 20:1-2 with 2 Sam 11:1-12:30 gives credence to this peculiar phenomenon in the narratives of the first book of the Chronicles. The similarity between the opening words of the two accounts is too glaring to be accidental and goes a long way to suggest that the Chronicler has edited the material in 2 Sam 11-12 by jumping from 11:1 to 12:30 and replacing the sending forth of Joab by

---

[264] Keeping in mind that all the great works of "historical writings" in the OT are first and foremost religious documents, composed for religious purposes at a given time in the history of Israel, it will be evident that the writer of the Chronicles "has in mind the postexilic period whose grave religious problems he was determined to face realistically and deal with as effectively as he knew how". (J. M. Myers, *I Chronicles*, p. xix). At the moment of the exile, the deuteronomist's appeal and programme had failed to save the nation, a new situation had arisen that confronted those who endeavoured later to pick up the pieces and begin all over again but the promises of Yhwh were still valid, however, requiring even more heroic efforts than earlier (cf. J. M. Myers, op. cit., p. xx).

David with Joab's going out (1Chr 20:1) apparently on his own accord but logically upon the authority of the king. In doing so, the Chronicler effectively omits David's adultery with Bathsheba and the gruesome details of the Ammonite war even as he avoids narrating the horrible murders in the house of the monarch but without departing from the narrative sequence of the Dtr in any remarkable way.

2 Samuel 11:1, 12:29-30	1 Chronicles 20:1-2
12:29-30 וַיְהִי֩ לִתְשׁוּבַ֨ת הַשָּׁנָ֜ה לְעֵ֣ת ׀ צֵ֣את הַמַּלְאֿכִ֗ים וַיִּשְׁלַ֣ח דָּוִ֡ד אֶת־יוֹאָב֩ וְאֶת־עֲבָדָ֨יו עִמּ֜וֹ וְאֶת־כָּל־יִשְׂרָאֵ֗ל וַיַּשְׁחִ֨תוּ֙ אֶת־בְּנֵ֣י עַמּ֔וֹן וַיָּצֻ֖רוּ עַל־רַבָּ֑ה וְדָוִ֖ד יוֹשֵׁ֥ב בִּירוּשָׁלָֽ͏ִם׃ ²⁹ וַיֶּאֱסֹ֥ף דָּוִ֖ד אֶת־כָּל־הָעָ֑ם וַיֵּ֣לֶךְ רַבָּ֔תָה וַיִּלָּ֥חֶם בָּ֖הּ וַֽיִּלְכְּדָֽהּ׃ ³⁰ וַיִּקַּ֣ח אֶת־עֲטֶֽרֶת־מַלְכָּם֩ מֵעַ֨ל רֹאשׁ֜וֹ וּמִשְׁקָלָ֨הּ כִּכַּ֤ר זָהָב֙ וְאֶ֣בֶן יְקָרָ֔ה וַתְּהִ֖י עַל־רֹ֣אשׁ דָּוִ֑ד וּשְׁלַ֥ל הָעִ֛יר הוֹצִ֖יא הַרְבֵּ֥ה מְאֹֽד׃	וַיְהִ֡י לְעֵת֩ תְּשׁוּבַ֨ת הַשָּׁנָ֜ה לְעֵ֣ת ׀ צֵ֣את הַמְּלָכִ֗ים וַיִּנְהַ֣ג יוֹאָב֩ אֶת־חֵ֨יל הַצָּבָ֜א וַיַּשְׁחֵ֣ת ׀ אֶת־אֶ֣רֶץ בְּנֵֽי־עַמּ֗וֹן וַיָּבֹא֙ וַיָּ֣צַר אֶת־רַבָּ֔ה וְדָוִ֖יד יֹשֵׁ֣ב בִּירֽוּשָׁלָ֑͏ִם וַיַּ֥ךְ יוֹאָ֛ב אֶת־רַבָּ֖ה וַיֶּֽהֶרְסֶֽהָ׃ ² וַיִּקַּ֣ח דָּוִ֣יד אֶת־עֲטֶרֶת־מַלְכָּם֩ מֵעַ֨ל רֹאשׁ֜וֹ וַֽיִּמְצָאָ֣הּ ׀ מִשְׁקַ֣ל כִּכַּר־זָהָ֗ב וּבָ֤הּ אֶ֣בֶן יְקָרָ֔ה וַתְּהִ֖י עַל־רֹ֣אשׁ דָּוִ֑יד וּשְׁלַ֥ל הָעִ֛יר הוֹצִ֖יא הַרְבֵּ֥ה מְאֹֽד׃
¹And it happened that at the turn of the year, the time when kings go forth (to battle), David sent Joab with his servants and all Israel with him. They ravaged the Ammonites and besieged Rabbah. But David remained in Jerusalem… 12:29-30 ²⁹ So David gathered all the people and went to Rabbah, and fought against it and took it. ³⁰ He took the crown of their king (*Milcom*) from his head. Its weight was a talent of gold and in it was a precious stone, and it was placed on the head of David. He also brought forth the spoil of the city; a very great amount.	¹And it happened that at the (time of the) turn of the year, the time when kings go forth (to battle), Joab led out the army. He ravaged the land of the Ammonites and came and besieged Rabbah. But David remained in Jerusalem. ²David took the crown of their king (*Milcom*) from his head, he found that it weighed a talent of gold and in it was a precious stone, and it was placed on the head of David. He also brought forth the spoils of the city; a very great amount.

In both texts, David remains in Jerusalem at the time that one would have expected him to be with his army. In the dtr version, this piece of information prepares the scene for the royal drama as it gives David enough time and space to commit adultery with Bathsheba, the wife of one of his officers, who was certainly at the warfront and therefore absent from home, and to plot the death of the soldier to be carried out at the siege of Rabbah and then move on to the battlefield to capture the city upon the invitation of Joab, who had already captured "a part of that city" – the royal city (v. 26-28). In the Chronicles, the adultery is absent as well as the invitation of Joab. The reader is left to imagine how David in a split narrative second is in Jerusalem and then at the head of the conquering army at Rabbah, capturing a city and wearing a crown. Under normal circumstances, this would have meant that the dtr writer had knowledge of the work of the Chronicler and had filled in the blank space to make the story coherent, but in this instance the historical background of both books favours the inverse; the Chronicler has definitely summarized the dtr historian by leaving out the part of the latter's narrative that would not serve his purpose. He omits the apparent duplication in the capture of the city of Rabbah (first by Joab – v. 26 – and then by David – v. 29) and the background to the parable of Nathan and consequently the parable itself even to the detriment of allowing the birth of Solomon, the successor to the throne of David, to fall into oblivion.

It will not be too far-fetched to posit that the adultery, murder and homicides that took place in the palace of the king were counterproductive to the image of David that the Chronicler intended to present, as a hero, to the post-exilic Israel, making it convenient for the author then to gloss over that part of the history.[265] Moreover, the interest of the writer was more in

---

265 The Chronicler gives a very unique position to David in his history; before David the material is scanty and presented as genealogies with the narrative part beginning with David, Yahweh's regent. For this author the kingdom of Israel belongs to Yhwh and he chooses whom he wishes to rule it. In his version of the covenant with David, the Chronicler reports Yhwh as saying; "I will set him over my house and my kingdom forever" (17:14) where in the report of the Dtr it states; "Your house and your kingdom shall remain firm before me forever" (2 Sam 7:16). Chr 29:11-12 ascribes greatness, power, glory, victory and majesty to Yhwh and adds "...yours is the kingdom and

the life of the nation than that of the monarch as a person.[266] Now, if the Chronicler, despite citing the book of Samuel or paraphrasing its content, as the case may be, or even using a different source that had the parallel story, could simply skip the narration of the sordid side of the life of David as a hero, why couldn't the Dtr have done the same? What compelling factor made the Dtr preserve those episodes, especially the prophetic rebuke, in his work? What kind of image did he intend to portray of the monarch that would not be tainted by the flip side of his character?

The third chapter of this work has sought to establish the patent links of the text of 2 Sam 12:1-15a to the DtrH from the level of the text and its content paying much attention to the dynamics of the prophecy of doom in the history. In the subsequent chapters I will endeavour to establish as far as possible the importance of the encounter between Nathan and David in the whole concept of the Old Testament tradition, especially the deuteronomistic history with particular reference to the role that the author assigns the prophet Nathan as a character and as an institution face to face with the authority of King David as a person and his kingship as an institution. I will open the discussion with David and his kingship before entering into the realm of the prophet Nathan since, it seems to me, that this particular prophet emerges in the lime light of the narrative only in the context of the divine election and protection of the dynasty of David.

5.1 The Kingship of David in the OT Tradition

Judges 21:25	Judges 21:25
בַּיָּמִים הָהֵם אֵין מֶלֶךְ בְּיִשְׂרָאֵל אִישׁ הַיָּשָׁר בְּעֵינָיו יַעֲשֶׂה׃	In those days there was no king in Israel; each man did what was pleasing in his eyes.

---

you are exulted above all". Thus the actual ruler of Israel is Yhwh who has chosen the house of David as his earthly regent for ever. If David sat upon the throne of Yhwh, then his kingdom will not end even though at the time of the Chronicler there was no king. It is probably the subtlety of leaving the revival of the Davidic monarchy open that made this writer consequent in omitting materials that would otherwise militate against this hope of revival. Cf. J. M. Myers, *I Chronicles*, p. lxxxi-lxxxiii.

266   J. M. Myers, *1 Chronicles*, p. 140.

The position of Judg 21:25 from the point of view of the canon of the OT and as the closing words of the book of Judges, makes the verse stand out clearly as a logical explanation or justification for the emergence of kingship in Israel, if not a worthy introduction to the monarchy as it did unfold in the books of Samuel-Kings. A critical look at the verse in its context, however, suggests that it is the work of a redactor who judges the exaggerations in the actions of the Levite (Judg 19) and the consequent reaction of the eleven tribes of Israel against the Benjaminites (Judg 20) from the background of the unity of the historical books as the Enneateuch or the DtrH. This implies that it is the work of a redactor putting his imprint on the material as a conclusion of the events of the book of Judges. This redactor, possibly, had knowledge or experience of the monarchy as an institution in Israel. He achieves his aim by leading his readers on to the feeling that the lack of centralized government in Israel gave room for each man doing what he felt good in his own eyes and in so doing also what was evil in the sight of Yhwh.[267] Thus the time before the monarchy was nothing but chaos that called for the institution of kingship as a centralized authority to restore order in the society.

Robert G. Boling sees the hand of a late redactor at work and affirms that "Added to the book in a period as late as the Babylonian exile (when kingship had come and gone), it meant that the time had arrived once again for every man to do what was right before Yahweh, without any sacral political apparatus to get in the way."[268] Boling posits the Babylonian exile as the date of the verse. In his commentary on the book of Judges, W. Groß goes further by looking at the interest of this redactor whom he identifies as the work of *"ein junges nachexilisches Erzeugnis Schriftgelehrter"*. The interest of this post exilic writer, according to Groß, was not so much the cultic practice of Deut 13:13-19, as that of a dtr author would have been, but a response to an ideal social scenario; the reaction of the sacral community of Israel in the face of evil committed by the inhabitants of one of their own towns. He achieves this by the tacit description of the shameful act of

---

267 W. Groß, *Richter*, p. 877. The converse of the statement follows automatically the dtr judgment formula of X doing what is evil in the sight of Yahweh and therefore attracting divine punishment cf. 2 Sam 12:9.
268 R. G. Boling, *Judges*, p. 293.

Gibeah and the role of Benjamin in the whole affair (20-21), while carefully keeping Judah silent in the background and concludes that in the absence of a king, each man did what was good in his own eyes, and, therefore, evil in the sight of Yhwh, by implication. The author in so doing succeeds in subtly raising the kingship of Judah onto a positive plain by discrediting Benjamin before all Israel, indicating that his interest in kingship was not that of Saul, the Benjaminite, but David the Judahite and even here not in the real king David but the idealised one.[269]

Whether this redactor was the Dtr or someone else before or after him, the comment and its present position fit very well into the history and concept of the dtr author; the remark functions both as a positive introduction to the institution of kingship in Israel and, conversely, as an accusation against doing what is evil in the sight of the Lord, characteristic of the period of the Judges and of the kings. "To do what is evil in the sight of the Lord" (עשה הרע בעיני יהוה) is a persistent chorus in the period before kingship, especially in the book of Judges. Beginning with Judg 2:11, the phrase runs through the narrative as a distinctive feature of the unfaithful life of the new generation of Israelites leading to their subjugation by one or the other nation, the cry of the people to Yhwh and the rise of a redeemer as a response from Yhwh. In all these instances the subject of the phrase is "the Israelites"-בני־ישראל (cf. Judg 3:7, 12, 4:1, 6:1, 10:6, and 13:1). In the books of Samuel and Kings, this stereo-typed form of judgment runs through the narratives with a conspicuous change of subject from the "Israelites" to the specific kings, beginning from Saul (1 Sam 15:19) to Zedekiah (2 Kings 24:19) without sparing even David (2 Sam 12:9). This change of subject places the responsibility of the sin of unfaithfulness and or idolatry at the feet of the kings, since they were the visible heads of the people and their wrong choices determined the loyalty or disloyalty of the people, whom they led, to Yhwh their God. This links the books of the Torah, Joshua and Judges smoothly to those of Samuel and Kings (Enneateuch).

Although surrounded by nations like Egypt, Assyria, and the Canaanite states that had been governed by kings for many years, kingship and a centralized form of government did not appear in Israel until much later,

---

269 W. Groß, *Richter*, p. 877–885.

about 1000 B.C. Biblical tradition has it that the people of Israel were led out of slavery in Egypt by Moses who served as their leader and "judge". As the time of Moses came close to its ebb, Yhwh explicitly ordered him to bring along Joshua into the tent of meeting (Deut 31:14) where he was commissioned by Yhwh as successor to Moses to lead the people into the Land of Promise (31:23). Such an order and commissioning are absent at the end of the life of Joshua who consequently left behind an assembly of twelve tribes precariously united by their ancestral heritage and religious beliefs, but without a centralized leadership. In the absence of a centralized point of reference and political authority the twelve tribes of Israel enjoyed a more or less independent existence. When attacked by a common enemy, however, they would join forces under the guise of special leaders chosen by God and called "Judges". Their office was not dynastic. They emerged as and when the necessity arose and had the mission of saving the tribes in that particular moment in history. The books of Samuel pick up the story from where that of Judges leaves off assigning the mission of the "Judges" to the priest Eli (1 Sam 1-2) and then to his successor Samuel (7:3ff) whose time of service witnessed the request by the people for a king: 1 Sam 8:5

וַיֹּאמְרוּ אֵלָיו הִנֵּה אַתָּה זָקַנְתָּ וּבָנֶיךָ לֹא הָלְכוּ בִּדְרָכֶיךָ
עַתָּה שִׂימָה־לָּנוּ מֶלֶךְ לְשָׁפְטֵנוּ כְּכָל־הַגּוֹיִם׃

...and they said to him: "Look, you are old and your sons do not walk in your ways. Now, set over us a king to judge us like all the nations".

This request ushered in the reign of Saul, the first king of Israel who was rejected by Yhwh in favour of David who succeeded in establishing the first dynasty in Israel.

The death of Joshua created a power vacuum that could not be filled because Yhwh had not given any directives to that effect. This lack of recognized leadership paved the way for the rise of the judges to fill the vacuum. In this form of sporadic leadership was embedded a natural problem that the text is silent about but which the reader with hindsight quickly appreciates: it ignores the dynamics of a developing society in which different social actors or groups are in constant inter-relationship with one another within a given geographical milieu and in a particular span of time. This inter-relationship could be beneficial or detrimental to one another. Thus as the various nations in Canaan or Palestine braced themselves for the natural process of growth in an area of limited resources there was bound to be an increase in the struggle for and control over the different meagre resources. With the increase in the frequency of attacks grew also their corresponding brutality and destructiveness based on the principle of the survival of the fittest. Observing the nature of leadership that was current among those nations around them, many in Israel would have felt the need for a more permanent form of leadership as an answer to those perennial attacks. Above all, the nostalgia of the days of the almost mythical figures like Moses and Joshua, whose presence as leaders chosen by Yhwh in the midst of his people induced profound awe in those same nations and neighbours of Israel, could not have so easily been forgotten. The text of the OT leads the reader to infer that the seed of uncertainty and discontent in this state of affairs that had already been sown by this power vacuum blossomed into the legitimate desire expressed in the famous offer of royalty to Gideon after his dramatic defeat of the Midianites and his unequivocal refusal to be king (Judg 8:22-23).[270]

The final straw that seemed to have broken the camel's back was when Samuel, the prophet-priest, was aging and his sons were found wanting in the area of leadership that Israel required at that crucial moment in the face of the Philistine threat. This was almost a play-back of the state of affairs in the last days of the priest, Eli, and the attitude of his sons towards the people and the cult (1 Sam 2:22-25). In the case of Eli, it led to the rejection of his house in favour of Samuel.[271] This time around, the people would no

---

270 Unlike the Dtr the author of the Gideon narrative avoids the use of the term מלך and prefers to express the idea of "rule over" with משל. The text further pitches human kingship against divine rule and might suggest a pre-dtr mentality of a theocracy. Without reading a monarchical or anti-monarchical tendency into the text one can clearly see the faithfulness of Gideon to his call by Yhwh to save Israel from the hands of Midian which did not necessarily imply a dynastic rule (cf. Groß, *Richter*, p. 455–457). The text, nonetheless, sits oddly in its context (so Campbell & O'Brien, *Unfolding*, p. 187) as Gideon in a classic orthodoxy rejects kingship in one breadth and in the other makes an ephod to which "all Israel prostituted themselves". Thus the passage begins with hope but ends with sin, so did the monarchy as a whole.
271 It seems Samuel tried to establish a dynasty of a kind by setting his sons as judges over Israel (1 Sam 8:1) which made them acquire a position different from that of the sons of Eli, who were priests (1 Sam 2:12-13). It is when

longer sit on the fence and watch the priestly family play with the future of the nation at their own whims and caprices. This inevitably led to the request for a king; *"(And) they said to him; look, you are old and your sons do not walk in your ways. Now, set over us a king to judge us like all the nations."* (1 Sam 8:5) The request opened a new chapter in the history of Israel. Until now the people of Israel considered themselves as God's chosen people, with God rather than a human being as their king, at least so the tradition would like it to be seen, exemplified by Gideon's rejection of royalty in the sense of a dynasty or kingly rule and Israel's self-designation as עם־יהוה (Judg 5:11, 1 Sam 2:24, 2 Sam 6:21, 2 Kings 9:6). Samuel, the prophet and the last Judge of Israel, acting as the apparent representative of the old school-of-thought in the face of the new ideology, warned the people against the dangers of having a human king (1 Sam 8:11-18).[272] In the end, however, he agreed to take the matter to the Lord who allowed Israel to have a king. But this king would have to be chosen by Yhwh and would be expected to make God's invisible rule over the people visible or at least to rule according to the word of Yhwh. In this way, the people had their "king", but God would continue to rule over them.

The Old Testament reflects both positive and negative evaluations of how well kingship worked for Israel. The first king, Saul, gained the acceptance of the people by being anointed by the prophet of Yhwh (1 Sam 10:1) and his acting under the influence of the Spirit of God (11:6) to win victory over the Ammonites (11:11). His reign marked the crossroads between what modern categorization of leadership patterns will call "charismatic leadership", symbolised by the towering figure of Samuel, and kingship, which had no precedence in the tradition of Israel and had not yet been rooted in it. Its institution was actually due to the failure of the former, symbolized by the inability of the sons of Samuel to tread the path trodden

---

they proved unworthy of this position in the eyes of Israel that the request for a king was born.

272 The story-line would want the reader to note the tension between the demand for a king and the obligation to remain faithful to Yhwh, the only king of Israel, as a natural reaction from the prophet but the time line of the narrative is clearly an exilic reflection on the kingship as a failed institution. Despite its necessity, it could not save the people from the exile because of its excesses and waywardness.

by their father. A problem was bound to surface as a result of the division of labour or separation of powers (religious and political) that did not exist at that time. The dominating figure of Samuel as the prophet of Yhwh and king-maker and the emerging personality of a kingly figure quickly erupted into a conflict of powers that set in progress the process of Saul's downfall. He was publicly rejected as king by Samuel in a solemn proclamation as the word of Yhwh;

יַעַן מָאַסְתָּ אֶת־דְּבַר יְהוָה וַיִּמְאָסְךָ מִמֶּלֶךְ

"... Because you have rejected the word of the Lord, he has (also) rejected you from being king." (1 Sam 15:23).

As if that was not enough, a rival figure appeared on the scene in the person of David to complicate the already difficult situation and disorganised the disorientated king. His anointing at the blind side of Saul by Samuel (1 Sam 16) and his military prowess in defeating Goliath to save Israel from utter disgrace (1 Sam 17) made him the favourite of all, leaving Saul at an absolute disadvantage. The natural human emotion of jealousy propelled the rivalry to the unnatural degree of Saul, neglecting his role and responsibility as the protector and ruler of the nation. He directed his attention and energy towards how to get rid of David. He embarked on a wild goose chase while his subjects (22:7-9) and even some members of his own household, like Michal (1 Sam 19:11-17) and Jonathan (1 Sam 20) rendered their support to David even at the risk of losing their own lives in so doing (1 Sam 22:14-19). He ended up a failure, falling at the hands of the Philistines on Mount Gilboa (1 Sam 31), but not before he had laid down the foundation for the tradition of kingship that would be built upon by his successor. The almost mythical stature of David in the conflict with Saul prepares the reader for his future assumption of power as the chosen one who enjoys the protection of the deity even to the extent of turning every danger upon his life into an advantage for himself and a disadvantage for his pursuer.

With the death of Saul and his undisputed successor, the road was paved for David to return to Israel from his place of refuge among the Philistines in Ziklag. Within a period of seven years and six months, he was doubly anointed king of Judah and of Israel at Hebron (2 Sam 2:4, 5:3-5). He enhanced his position as king of a "united Israel" with the conquest of Jerusalem, a neutral city to both Judah and Ephraim, which became his political capital. As a seasoned warrior and shrewd politician, he sensed the need for a religious base of support to provide him the unflinching loyalty of the people whose political will and confidence he had already gained. This feat, he accomplished by transferring the Ark of the Covenant to its special place in Zion that later became the Temple of Yahweh (2 Sam 6). David had the advantage of the absence of a conflict of power as the death of Samuel (1 Sam 25:1) had ended the competition that Saul had to face. He filled this vacuum on the religious front by offering sacrifices in place of the priests (1 Sam 6:17-19), as was normal in the period of kingship[273]. Besides, the representative figure of religious authority in Jerusalem, the Prophet Nathan, was basically a member of the court and advisor to the king, and Gad, the prophet, was simply tagged the Seer of David (2 Sam 24:11).

The reign of David is considered the glorious age of Israel and the best that kingship had to offer that nation. Under David, the Philistine threat of the west came to an end with the conquest of Meth'egamah[274], the Moabites

---

[273] As part of the dedication ceremony of the Temple, Solomon sacrificed (1 Kings 8:5, 62) and blessed the people (v. 55) even as Jeroboam would do in his turn in Bethel (13:1). It appears to us that the king in Israel had, among others, a priestly role. The episode of Saul sacrificing in the absence of Samuel in Gilgal (1 Sam 13) builds up tension between the two symbols of authority. The narrator does not specifically condemn one nor justify the other on the basis of the sacrifice as such. The impression that is created is that Saul usurped the priesthood, but that occurred only after he had waited for a whole week, according to the time set by Samuel (v. 8) and, in the fear of the people deserting him at a time that he was faced with an imminent Philistine attack. In that moment Saul took his destiny into his own hands by offering the sacrifice to ask for the favour of the Lord. It is only then that Samuel shows up to rebuke Saul for acting foolishly; not obeying the commandment of the Lord and so destroying his chances of establishing a dynasty for ever (v. 13). Even then the fact of sacrificing is not mentioned directly as the ground for his rejection if not in Saul's own way of describing it as "I forced myself to offer the burnt offering" (v. 12).

[274] Hans Joachim Stoebe cautions against the unqualified reference of Meth'egamah as a proper name or toponym. He points out that even ancient times there was the tendency to resort to place names or interpretations whenever there was the difficulty to decipher a word and "wörtliche Wiedergabe" was no help as in the case of נבעת אמה in 2 Sam 2:24. A resort to linguistic evidence might render it a proper name based upon the examples of Aramaic אמה meaning canal, Assyrish *meteg ammati* meaning "Straßen des Kusternstriches" (beach

paid tribute to him (2 Sam 8:1-2) and the coalition of Ammonites and Arameans was summarily defeated (2 Sam 10-12). With these victories, David became the master of the whole land east of the Jordan River and north of Damascus in Syria as far as the river Euphrates.[275] Yahweh's promise of rest from the nations round about Israel (Deut 12:8-11) was achieved under David and Israel became an independent nation for the first time, to be treated on equal basis with the other nations round about her, and set on the road to prosperity.

As an institution, kingship in Israel was a logical human choice resulting from the dynamics of a developing society but with a divine endorsement, and the best that happened to that institution was David. Despite his human failings and domestic troubles David as king was faithful to Yhwh and God rewarded him for his obedience and good intentions by promising him an eternal kingdom; *Your house and your kingdom shall be made sure forever before me; your throne shall be established forever* (2 Sam 7:16). This promise is central to the dtr concept of the kingship of David and is couched in a basic dtr language as we shall see later. David was succeeded by Solomon, his son, who fulfilled the promise of building a Temple to the Lord, but failed in faithfulness to the Lord and in the treatment of his subjects (1 Kings 12:4). Consequently, the flourishing kingdom of David was split into two after the reign of Solomon; the northern and southern kingdoms or Israel and Judah respectively (1 Kings 12:16-19). One king followed the other in disobedience to the Lord (I Kings 15:26, 16:30, 22:52-53, etc) except a few like Asa (15:11-13), Hezekiah (18:3) and Josiah (22:2) of Judah.[276] Because

---

road) or even the Phoenician variant of אם which may mean capital town. In the context of 2 Sam 8 the word might possibly refer to one of the Philistine hegemonies. Cf. *Das zweite Buch Samuelis*, KAT VIII 2, p. 242.

275 This fact seemed to have been emphasized as a fulfilment of the promise to the Patriarchs, especially to Abraham in Gen 15:18, where the Promised Land was supposed to stretch from the great River of Egypt to the Euphrates.

276 In the first book of Kings the trend is that the kings of Judah do what is pleasing in the eyes of the Lord, besides removing the high places, while the kings of Israel follow the abomination of Jeroboam by worshipping the idols of Dan and Bethel. This trend continues in the second book of Kings with the only difference that this time the kings of Judah join the train of unfaithfulness to Yahweh with the exception of a few like Josiah (22:2) making the doom of both states a foregone conclusion.

of the disobedience of the kings and the people, Israel's four hundred-year experiment with kingship came to an end with the exile of Israel to Assyria in 722 and of Judah in 587 to Babylon. With the exile, the socio-political institution of kingship came to an end, but the theology of the concept remained, nourished by the promise of an eternal kingship to David, which would be carried on by a designated member of the Davidic dynasty, the son of David. For the Dtr, the release of Jehoiachin from prison by the king of Babylon was the turning point in the history and the great event that was to keep the flame of the hope of restoration glowing once again.

This is how the biblical author or, at least, the dtr redactor of the history of kingship in Israel would like the reader to believe, but what was it like with David as king and why this vested interest in the man David and his kingship? The natural instinct to guide such an interest would be to polish up the character of the chosen hero in such a way that he would be beyond reproach, but the Dtr allows his hero to sink into the depths of sin and have a prophet condemn him in a way that turns him into a laughing stock in the eyes of the reader. What did this author hope to achieve with this mode of reproach? In my bid to find answers to these pertinent questions, I will delve into the narrative material at our disposal with my eyes more upon thematic issues than the generally set patterns of the structural division of the text. While I will, on one hand, gloss over details that do not immediately help in responding to our questions, I will, on the other hand, provide such ones as will throw the necessary light on them and serve the purpose of providing answers to those questions.

5.2 The kingship of David in the light of Nathan's oracle

There is no gainsaying that the name David plays a very significant role in biblical tradition whether OT or NT. While in the OT the name evokes very simply "the king" (המלך) as a title of specification and recalls the memory of the reign of David as the time of peace and prosperity for Israel, in the NT the name is generally preceded by "the son of" (υἱὲ Δαυίδ)[277] as a

---

277 Luke 18:38, 39, Mk 10:47, 48, Mt 9:27. I maintain the vocative case as it was the call for help or healing that depicts without doubt the identity of Jesus as the long awaited son of David, the Messiah and restorer of the dignity of man.

continuation of the reign of David in a messianic sense, wrought by the life and activities of Jesus. The stature of David as king and bearer of hope for Israel is systematically worked out to its highest point in the idealization of the monarch in the works of the Dtr especially in the books of Samuel and kings. The narrative material spreading from the sixteenth chapter of the first book of Samuel to the eighth chapter of the second provides a flamboyant description of the rise of David from his supposed anointing by Samuel (1 Sam 16) to his enthronement as king of Judah (2 Sam 2:4) and of Israel (5:3) and the consolidation of his power through the series of wars summed up in 2 Sam 8:1ff. Undoubtedly, the said narrative material is what the final redactor would like to present to his audience and it depicts the image of the would-be king of Israel that the writer presents to his readers. It is this image that in the end will justify the words of Nathan when he confronts David as the prophet of Yhwh impressing upon the monarch his past, his present and his future: ... *Thus says Yhwh, the God of Israel: I anointed you king over Israel, and I rescued you from the hand of Saul. I gave you your master's house, and your master's wives into your bosom, and gave you the house of Israel and of Judah; and if that had been too small, I would have added as much more...* (2 Sam 12:7-9).

5.2.1 The rise of David; 1 Sam 16-2 Sam 8

The fame of David precedes him even before he appears on the scene. He does not belong to the royal family of Saul and is an absolutely unknown figure in the unfolding story. A reader who follows the sequence of the Masoretic Text has no idea of who David is except if one follows the LXX which places the book of Ruth between Judges and Samuel. The book of Ruth closes with the genealogy that ends with the name "David": [21] καὶ Σαλμαν ἐγέννησεν τὸν Βοος καὶ Βοος ἐγέννησεν τὸν Ωβηδ[22] καὶ Ωβηδ ἐγέννησεν τὸν Ιεσσαι καὶ Ιεσσαι ἐγέννησεν τὸν Δαυιδ *(...Salmon became the father of Boaz, Boaz of Obed. And Obed became the father of Jesse who was the father of David."* Ruth 4:21-22). In placing the book between Judges and Samuel, the LXX causes a curiosity in the reader who looks forward to a new development around the name, possibly in line with the charismatic leadership of Judges or kingship in line with the suggestion at the end of the Book of Judges (21:25). This riddle is unravelled when the author unexpectedly introduces the said character into the scene after the failure of Saul to establish a dynasty. The MT, however, achieves suspense in an absolute way by avoiding any reference to David as such, but keeping the reader at his wits' end as he anxiously awaits a resolution of the kingless state of Israel by the introduction of a king; whoever that might be. The narrative makes it clear that the initiator of the choice of David was Yhwh and that he was to be anointed king in place of Saul, whom the Lord had rejected:

I Sam 16:1	I Sam 16:1
(Then) Yhwh said to Samuel: How long will you continue to grieve over Saul, since I have rejected him from being king over Israel? Fill your horn with oil and go forth;[278] I send you to Jesse, the Bethlehemite; for I have found myself a king among his sons.	וַיֹּאמֶר יְהוָה אֶל־שְׁמוּאֵל עַד־מָתַי אַתָּה מִתְאַבֵּל אֶל־שָׁאוּל וַאֲנִי מְאַסְתִּיו מִמְּלֹךְ עַל־יִשְׂרָאֵל מַלֵּא קַרְנְךָ שֶׁמֶן וְלֵךְ אֶשְׁלָחֲךָ אֶל־יִשַׁי בֵּית־הַלַּחְמִי כִּי־רָאִיתִי בְּבָנָיו לִי מֶלֶךְ׃

The actual reason for Samuel's mission to Bethlehem was because the Lord had found for himself a king among the sons of Jesse; a causal clause in a *dativus commodus*. This defines the future of the hitherto unknown son of Jesse and the dtr writer lays the foundation for the nature and identity of his hero upon which he will deftly build in the subsequent narrative. The narrator leaves his readers in suspense with Samuel rejecting the elder sons of Jesse one after the other with the only insight, which was actually a rebuke of the hasty prophet by God, that *"...the Lord does not see as mortals see; they look on the outward appearance, but the Lord looks on the heart"* (16:7). The suspense is compounded by the error of Samuel who apparently forgets the clear-cut instruction at the beginning of his mission; *"...and you shall anoint for me the one whom I name to you"* (v. 3c). Neither the physically obvious and imposing stature of Eliab, which was also the hall mark of Saul (9:2), nor the prerogatives of the first son sufficed to

---

278 Samuel was the agent of the anointing of both Saul and David. Remarkably, he used two different instruments in performing the anointing of the first two kings: while he anointed Saul with a vial (פך) he used a horn (קרן) for that of David (I Sam 10:1, 16:1 respectively); the same instrument that will later be used for the anointing of Solomon by the priest Zadok (I Kings 1:39).

make him the divine choice (v. 7) and in a sense any of the other six.[279] Only when Jesse had made seven of his sons pass before Samuel and had been told that the Lord had not chosen any of them did he reveal, as if it was an after-thought, that his youngest son was keeping the sheep; he was not even invited to the religious ritual – the façade of Samuel's presence in Bethlehem (v. 2)[280] – and had to be sent for upon the order of the prophet. The suspense is finally broken with the arrival of the said youngest son, who is coincidentally or naturally small (הקטן) in relation to his seven elder brothers, and his uniqueness is expressed in a three-step description in v. 12;

וְהוּא אַדְמוֹנִי - he was red, ruddy or healthy in complexion
עִם־יְפֵה עֵינַיִם - with fair or beautiful eyes
וְטוֹב רֹאִי - and good looking or handsome of aspect

In the words of McCarter, "the attribution of good looks is a traditional part of the biblical presentation of an Israelite hero or heroine, e.g. Joseph (Gen 39:6), David (I Sam 16:12), Esther (Esth 2:7), the infant Moses (Ex 2:2), and so on. The quality [of being fair, good looking or beautiful of aspect] is to be interpreted as a physical symptom of special divine favour."[281]

---

279 The rush action of Samuel in this chapter is an outright contradiction to his whole life and mission as a prophet and especially to his own pious pronouncement against Saul in 15:22; ...Has the Lord as great delight in burnt offerings and sacrifices as in obeying the voice of the Lord? Surely, to obey is better than sacrifice and to heed than the fat of rams" (NRSV). Fokkelman notes a double ellipsis in the story at this point first in Samuel forgetting to prepare for the sacrifice and secondly literally forgetting to wait patiently for God to show him the one He had chosen to replace Saul. This would have been in consonance with his original instruction; "I shall tell you who you are to anoint." What this double ellipsis demonstrates is that "Samuel cannot or does not wish to withstand the pressure that he has applied to himself by his tense anticipation and forces his own solution." J. P. Fokkelman, *Crossing Fates*, p. 120.
280 The sacrifice and sacrificial meal that was supposed to have led Samuel to Bethlehem, unlike in ch. 9, fall out elliptically in the narrative. Even though it can be taken for granted that the sacrifice took place, this fact demonstrates that the paramount issue at stake in the narrative was the anointing of the youngest son of Jesse as king of Israel and not the sacrifice, which was after all a ploy.
281 P. K. McCarter, *I Samuel*, p. 277.

A comparison of all these references makes it clear that the description of David stands out in its three-step quality. While Joseph was handsome of form (יפה־תאר) and of appearance (יפה־מראה), Esther was said to be beautiful of form (יפה־תאר) and good of appearance (וטובת מראה). Moses was simply described as good or handsome (טוב הוא). In the majority of such descriptions the emphasis is placed on "form" (תאר) and "appearance" (מראה). In I Sam 9:2, Saul is accorded a very different mode of description as young and handsome (בחור וטוב) with an emphasis on the fact that he was fully developed and vigorous but unmarried. David, for his part, is described in a completely unique and comprehensive manner that takes cognizance of his complexion, eyes and appearance. He is ruddy in the sense of a healthy complexion that makes him bold and capable of competition, with beautiful eyes to make him attractive or even astute and handsome to make him stand out of the lot. This is a checklist of physical qualities of leadership that would endear David to both the historical and future audience of the narrative and to the army as a born leader. It is worthy of note that the heaping of epithets of physical qualities upon David follows shortly after the unequivocal declaration of the narrator that Yhwh does not see as mortals do: He does not look at physical appearance but at the heart (v. 7). Going along with this principle we would say then that David did not only possess the inner qualities of leadership; he was also endowed with the physical extras.

If the youth was so handsome and endowed, why then was he overlooked by his own father and was treated as an after-thought? Fokkelman draws attention to the fact that the first thing known about this great hero of the narrative is the fact that he is haqqātān. He is not only the youngest but also small in comparison to at least the oldest son of Jesse. Thus his physical description constitutes another level of opposition that is at the centre of the narrative. Remarkably, David is described only when he appears on the scene and is seen for the first time by Samuel after he had been overlooked by his own father. Jesse "looked through the clouded spectacles of routine and thus found it difficult to distinguish the youth's uniqueness. Samuel, however, is in quite a different position (because) David's beauty, as a sign of his choosing, is evident only when the spotlight of providence is directed upon it."[282] With this the narrator of the story

---

282   J. P. Fokkelman, *Crossing Fates*, p. 131.

is set to unfold the sequence of events that would lead his hero on to the throne of Israel.

5.2.2 The anointing of David and entry into the court of Saul

Yhwh then ordered Samuel: קוּם מְשָׁחֵהוּ כִּי־זֶה הוּא - "Arise and anoint him, for this is he." In obedience to this divine imperative, Samuel arose and anointed David "before his brothers".[283] In consequence to the anointing the Spirit of Yhwh descended mightily upon David from that day onwards. Two events are supposed to have catapulted David into the corridors of power; his talent as musician, skilful in playing the lyre to soothe the tormented Saul and his killing of the giant Goliath as a milestone in the Israel-Philistine conflicts (17:48-51). The Spirit of the Lord departed from Saul and in its place an evil spirit (from the Lord) tormented him. The servants of Saul impressed upon him to seek someone talented in playing the harp to soothe him with music whenever the evil spirit descended upon him. The search led to the son of Jesse who is here described as;

...יֹדֵעַ נַגֵּן וְגִבּוֹר חַיִל וְאִישׁ מִלְחָמָה וּנְבוֹן דָּבָר וְאִישׁ תֹּאַר וַיהוָה עִמּוֹ
"...skillful in playing (string instruments), a valiant man, a warrior, prudent in speech, a man of form (handsome) and Yhwh is with him." (2 Sam 16:18)

In the second instance the giant Goliath of Gath taunted the Israelite army with the challenge of a duel that no one was able to accept for mortal fear. In the meantime, the young David was sent by his father to bring supplies to his three elder brothers at the front. This brought David face to face with the plight of Israel before Goliath. The young man rose to the challenge and ended the forty-day torment by killing the champion to avert the disgrace of the whole army of Saul. The achievement of this feat opened the way for him to be set at the head of Israel's war machine with the approval of all the people including even the officials of the royal court, עבדי שאול (18:5).

---

283 The text leaves another vacuum here unfilled as to the question of the elders of Bethlehem. In v. 5, Samuel asks them to sanctify themselves and go with him to the sacrifice but they are left out at the anointing of David in v. 13. Could they have been included in the expression בקרב אחיו "before his brothers"?

David quickly built bonds and ties in the palace of Saul which in addition to his own ingenuity and divine providence (18:10-11, 23:26-28) ensured his safety against the raging anger of Saul. His great friend Jonathan and wife Michal, both children of Saul, his mortal enemy, protected him against their own father (19:11-12, 20:1-42).

The anointing of David is normally ascribed to the prophetic redactor of the history (DtrP) who does not hesitate to present the authority of the prophet to make and unmake kings; having rejected Saul, the Prophet Samuel proceeds to anoint a successor, David.284 The whole event occurs in obedience to a divine order carried out by the prophet of Yhwh in secret, without the knowledge of the reigning monarch, just as would be in the case of Jehu (2 Kings 9:6). This redactor establishes the dignity of David by placing him on parallel but opposite lines with Saul, whom the prophet has rejected (15:23). The spirit of Yhwh comes upon David and remains, while the same spirit leaves Saul in a depressed state. Thus the doom of the one is spelt out while the fortune of the other begins to take root and shape. The description of David is augmented by no other person than one of the servants of Saul, who piles up epithet upon epithet in his bid to make the youngman acceptable to his master. In the words of that servant, David is not only a healthy and handsome youth with beautiful eyes but also a skilful musician, a valiant warrior and above all, prudent in speech (16:18). As if that was not enough, the array of the qualities of David is crowned with the fact that "Yhwh is with him". According to McCarter, this last epithet explains all the previous ones; David's strength, manners, looks and successes are the result of divine favour. The author of the narrative makes the servant of Saul innocently pronounce the words that in the end would become the leitmotiv running through the whole story of David. "David was successful in all his undertakings because ויהוה עמו; "Yhwh was with him" (18:14). With this style of presenting the material, the writer has created a condition in which the reader knows what the actors do not. In his limited knowledge the servant is happy to recommend to his master a young man on whom God's favour rests and Saul is eager to have such a

---

284 A. F. Cambel & M. O'Brien, *Unfolding*, p. 257. In this narrative the prophetic redactor places his stamp on this phase of the history claiming the mandate to establish and dismiss kings.

one because divine approval of the young man will ensure the success of the mission for which he had been chosen. Divine favour functions as the source of the success of David in his various capacities and undertakings and that produces, as its resultant effect, the admiration and love or even hatred of the people who come into contact with him. In Saul it functions in both directions. When David entered the service of Saul, he loved him greatly and made him his armour-bearer (17:21). It is only when he gradually comes to the realization of the full import of divine favour resting upon David that he will begin to fear him and turn to become his enemy from that time onwards (18:29).

The composite text of the MT that we have inherited allows David to enter the court of Saul as a musician to soothe the fits of the ailing king or as a valiant man at the head of the army. Whether as a musician or a soldier, the description of the qualities of David in v. 18 captures and justifies both ideas establishing at the same time the key concept of the subsequent narrative; "Yhwh is with him", and divine protection would lead the young man through the turbulent times ahead of him. It was Yhwh who chose him and it is Yhwh who will protect him. David is here presented as a young man, aesthetically handsome, endowed with physical qualities of leadership, chosen by Yhwh as the future king of Israel and upon him dwells the Spirit of Yhwh.

5.2.3 Divine protection of David against Saul

2 Sam 21-26 present David as the innocent victim of Saul's inordinate anger, armed with various opportunities to have ended the struggle by simply turning the tide against his pursuer, but David would not stretch out his hand against the Lord's anointed (24:6, 11, 26:9, 11, 23). In these stories, the narrator presents Saul as the capriciously wicked ruler who seeks to destroy the life of his perceived rival; the humble, pious young man who is also the future successor to the throne (26:21-25). This trend of events begins with Saul's anger over the ascription of thousands to him and ten thousands to David by "the women of all the towns of Israel" in 18:6-7, after David had prevailed over Goliath. The narrator enters the mind-set of Saul and presents his soliloquy triggered by the normal human emotion of jealousy; *"They have ascribed to David ten thousands, and to me they have ascribed thousands; what more can he have but the kingdom?"* (18:8b). The fear of

a rival to his throne possibly aggravated the ailment of Saul who sought to pinion David to the wall with the spear while the latter was engaged in his normal service of playing the harp to soothe the fits of his lord but as divine providence would have it, he eluded him twice (18:10-11). Saul then hatched a plot to let David fall at the hands of the Philistines. In the first place David was to fight "the Lord's battles" as a valiant man to win the hand of Merab, the elder daughter of Saul. When the time came for Merab to be given to David, she was given instead to Adriel (18:17-19). Michal, who loved David, became the next pawn in the hand of Saul to be used against David. He won her hand with two hundred foreskins of the Philistines in place of a marriage present without losing his life in so doing, as was perceived by Saul (18:20-27). In the meantime, the war with the Philistines raged on and David had more successes than any of the commanders of Saul (18:30), to aggravate the already tense situation between him and the king. Saul could no longer conceal his intentions and made public his plan to kill David (19:1) but Jonathan, Saul's own son, interceded for David and secured a solemn promise from his father not to harm David (v. 6). This promise did not see the light of day as another decisive victory of David over the Philistines wrought a bout of psychical instability in which state Saul attacked David but missed him, sticking his spear into the wall (v. 19). The die was now cast for the survival of the fittest. The first step was to kill David in his bed but Michal tipped him off and aided him to elude the guards of her father who were to ensure the success of the plot (19:11-17). David fled to Samuel at Ramah and the two proceeded to settle at Naioth. From then on the scene of the developing drama changes from the court of Saul in Gibeah to the villages of Judah and the surrounding *negev* (steppe, desert).

Saul sent three separate groups of messengers to capture David, but they all fell into a state of confused excitement (ecstasy) at the sight of Samuel standing at the head of the prophetic band. Finally Saul himself went to Naioth and also fell into ecstasy before Samuel for a whole day and night (18-24).[285] David escaped, but Saul returned to wait for the

---

285 Opinions are divided as to whether this episode belongs to the same prophetic redactor of the history of David's rise to power on account of such apparent inconsistencies as the saying in 15:35 that Samuel never saw Saul again before he died but here lies Saul a whole day and night before the eyes of the prophet

157

next opportunity. It was the feast of the new moon. David secured the permission of Jonathan to remain in hiding while Jonathan tried to find out what the intention of his father towards David was. The exchange between Jonathan and Saul resulted in the outburst of anger which left no doubt in the mind of the former as regards the fate of David:

> ³⁰Then Saul's anger was kindled against Jonathan. He said to him, "You son of a perverse, rebellious woman! Do I not know that you have chosen the son of Jesse to your own shame, and to the shame of your mother's nakedness? ³¹ For as long as the son of Jesse lives upon the earth, neither you nor your kingdom shall be established. Now send and bring him to me, for he shall surely die." (I Sam 20:30-31, NRSV)

The next morning Jonathan relayed the message to David and sent him off on his way. David fled to Nob, where he received provisions in the form of food and arms for the journey from the priest Ahimelech. Although Ahimelech was not privy to David's real motive (22:15) the king would later make him pay with his life and the lives of all the priests and people of Nob with the exception of Abiathar, who managed to escape death (22:20-23). David left Nob and went on his way from one village to another: from Gath (21:10-15) to Adullam (22:1-5) and Keilah, which he had to defend against the Philistines in order to save it (23:1-5), but had to leave that walled town to escape the planned expedition of Saul against it.

David entered the hill country of the wilderness of Ziph which now became the scene of the unfolding drama (23:14) as Saul sought him in vain, because God did not give him into his hands (v. 14b). At Horesh, two things happened to twist the narrative. On one hand Jonathan visited David,

---

(19:24). Again the verse provides an alternative explanation to the saying in 10:11 that Saul was also among the prophets and can hardly come from the same author. Wellhausen (*Prolegomena*, p. 267–268) considers the episode a secondary insertion while Grønbaek (*Aufstieg Davids*, p. 114, 264) finds a grammatical and semantic unity of the materials that contain such interviews as the craft of the compiler, an opinion shared also by Nübel (*Davids Aufstieg*, p. 32–33) on stylistic grounds. Analysing the different opinions, McCarter (*I Samuel*, p. 330–331) concludes that it is the work of a late writer who shared the prophetic perspective in the narrative and wanted to add Samuel to the list of the important citizens of Saul's kingdom who aided and abetted with David. In this sense, Jonathan would represent the state while Samuel represented religion or cult hence in our modern terminology; church and state.

encouraged him and even made a pact with him (v. 18) and on the other, some Ziphites broke the news of David's hide-out to Saul and offered to help him catch David (vv. 19-20). This led to the near capture of David by Saul and his men in Maon, had it not been for the news of the attack of the Philistines, hence the name "the Rock of Escape" – סלע המחלקות (vv. 25-28). From there, David fled to the strongholds of Engedi and remained there. After Saul had repelled the Philistines he returned to pursue David in Engedi (24:1ff). Here the tide would turn as the Lord delivered Saul into the hands of David "on two separate occasions". Approaching the Rock of the Wild Goats, Saul entered a cave "to cover his feet", i.e. to relieve himself (v. 4). It happened that David and his men were hiding in the interior of that very cave. It can be imagined that in a moment like this the king was certainly alone, giving David and his men every opportunity to settle the matter. Instead, David only cut off a piece from the corner of Saul's cloak (v. 5), and refused to raise his hand against the king "because he is the anointed of the Lord" (v. 7). When Saul had come out of the cave, David followed suit, called out to him and showed him the patch of cloth that he had cut as a sign of his pure intentions towards the king. Saul, in a moment of mortification, wept for his mistakes, promised no longer to harm David and caused him to swear not to annihilate his house when he became king. David did as requested and Saul returned home while David and his men remained in the stronghold (vv. 7-22).

In the meantime, Samuel dies and is buried at his home in Ramah (25:1). The narrative then turns our attention to the episode of Nabal, the rich, but mean property owner of Carmel and his beautiful and wise wife Abigail, who became David's wife (vv. 2-42). The tradition then reproduces another episode of Saul falling into the hands of David in the night as he slept in the midst of his soldiers in the desert of Ziph (a doublet?). The episode seems to be a return to the events of 23:15-28 which occurred in the wilderness of Ziph but brings together such important personalities in the story of David's rise to power as Abner, the commander of Saul's army and Abishai, the son of Zeruiah, the brother of Joab. Again David refused to either harm the unprotected king or allow his nephew, Abishai[286] to do so. Instead he

---

286 According to the Chronicler, Zeruiah, the mother of Abishai, Joab and Asahel was the sister of David. Chr 2:16. The brothers will play a very significant

took away the spear that was at the head of Saul and the water jar and left him sleeping with his soldiers (26:1-12). He then woke them up from a distance, gave back the spear and water jar as a sign of his faithfulness towards the king against the latter's unjust stance (vv. 13-16). The narrative ends with Saul's acknowledgment of his fault, David goes his separate way and Saul returns to his place (v. 25).[287] This departure of the two was to be the last as David went to serve Achish, a Philistine prince, and would not return until the death of Saul (27:2-3). Achish gave him Ziklag as his residence all the years of his sojourn (27:6).

The narration of David outwitting Saul in various ways to save his life is almost legendary and very much akin to a fairy tale. This narrative style endears David to the audience who identify with him in his peril, admire his heroic deliverance and share in his honour of not paying evil for evil received, as with the hero of a fairy tale. Thus the narrator successfully adds the missing part of the qualities of his hero; his beauty is not only physical but also interior. It is a sublime inner beauty to suffer injustice and refuse to avenge oneself when one has the opportunity to do so. The climax is reached when the wicked king meets his own death in battle as the text has already intimated in a prophetic fashion coming from the lips of David (26:10). The fall of Saul ends the opposing journeys of the rivals; one systematically comes closer to ascending the throne, while the other falls dramatically far beneath it. The author of this narrative has woven the story in such a manner that the hand of Yhwh is clearly seen active in every twist and turn in the events of David's rise to power. The rejection of Saul by Samuel opens the search for the next king of Israel who is selected by Yhwh himself at the appropriate time through his prophet, Samuel, as

---

    role in the rise of David especially in the civil war that will end every trace of authority in the house of Saul to give way to the establishment of the Davidic dynasty.

287 We are certainly dealing here with a doublet to chapter 24 that narrates the role of divine protection in the rise of David to power which will make the accusation of Nathan solid when Yhwh says; "I saved you from the hand of Saul" (2 Sam 12:7). In chapter 24 the words of Saul are explicit in referring to the future reign of David (v. 21) but here he makes only a vague reference to David succeeding in many things (v. 25) and suggests that this last was probably the earlier version that has been built upon in chapter 24.

the instrument of Divine choice. Contrary to human expectations, David is chosen by Yhwh over and above his seven brothers and is anointed king in Bethlehem (16:6-13). He is helped on his journey to the throne by some members of Saul's own family, Jonathan and Michal, and the religious figures of the day, Samuel and Ahimelech (21:1-6) but betrayed by the inhabitants of the Judaean town of Ziph (23:19-24). That notwithstanding, the protagonist of David's dramatic escape is Divine Providence, which saw to his safety, letting the pursuer fall "twice" into the hands of the pursued. The dtr redactor of the parable of Nathan looks back to these events when he calls David to book: *"Thus says Yhwh the God of Israel: I anointed you king over Israel, and I rescued you from the hands of Saul..."* (2 Sam 12:7). With this declaration Nathan makes it clear to David that it is to Yhwh that he owes his salvation from the hands of Saul who had the whole apparatus of the state at his disposal and yet could not fulfil his vow of killing the son of Jesse:[288] *wəʿattāʰ šəlaḥ wəqaḥ ʾōṯô ʾēlay kî ben-māwet hûʾ* (...And now, send and bring him to me for he is a son of death) 20:31. God is the only power who could have prevented Saul from carrying out such a solemn vow made to himself with Jonathan as a witness.

Besides this clear indication of the source of David's strength as Yhwh himself, the narrator also opens the window for his audience to glance through the wave of emotions that spread among the people in general. Samuel, Jonathan, Mickal and the priests of Nob gave their unqualified support to David, but the inhabitants of Ziph remained faithful to Saul and took steps to surrender David into his hands (23:19-24). Even though this

---

[288] The only thing that saved the life of David in the Wilderness of Ziph was because Saul received notice of the Philistine attack at the deciding moment of the chase when Saul and his men were closing in on David and his men. At that crucial moment in the narrative the reader could take a breadth of relief as Saul calls off the chase and moves camp to respond to the Philistine challenge (23:24-28). The narrator leaves the reader to conclude that Divine Providence has saved the day and David is for the moment free to live, giving glory to the "Rock of Escape", which happens to be one of the many divine attributes (cf. Ps 31). David will later confirm this fact when he speaks to the assassins of Ishbaal; "As Yhwh lives, who has delivered my life from every adversity..." (2 Sam 4:9) and Nathan will hammer home this point in his condemnation of David, making it clear that it was God himself who saved him from the hand of Saul in 2 Sam 12:7.

might not have been the general feeling on the ground it gives us a good idea of the possible political climate of the day. The Nabal-Abigail-David episode (25:2-42) points along this same direction, but this time it paints a picture of a divided house in which the rich master favours the king, while the wise wife sees a better future in throwing her weight behind the fugitive David. Her gamble prompted her quick and precise reaction which saved David from blood guilt, which would have carried blood feud in its trail (25:18-35), and won her a place in the royal court as the wife of David (39-42). It is clear then that Israel was split into two around two symbols of authority; the waning power of Saul and the rising one of David.

5.2.4 The elimination of Rivals to the Throne

With the death of Saul and his son Jonathan, the way was paved for the hero to assume the leadership position for which he had been predestined and anointed. Having mourned Saul and Jonathan "David inquired of the Lord" if he were to go into any of the towns of Judah, and if so to which one? The decision fell upon the ancient town of Hebron (Gen 23:19) and to Hebron he went with his two wives, Abigail of Carmel and Ahinoam of Jezreel (25:42-43), accompanied by his men and their families (2 Sam 2:1-2). The people of Judah came over to Hebron and anointed David king over the house of Judah (v. 4). David settled quickly into the new role by sending good-will messengers to Jabesh Gilead for burying Saul and Jonathan, promising them a reward and courting at the same time their loyalty as subjects (2:5-7).

In the meantime, the drama of the future of Israel took place on two fronts. While David settled in Hebron as king of Judah, Abner caused the initiation of the two-year reign of Ishbaal, son of Saul, as king of Israel in Mahanaim (2 Sam 2:8-10)[289]. The conflict between the two houses was

---

289 The writer is precise in stating how Ishbaal became king; Abner son of Ner, the commander of Saul's army, took him to Mahanaim and made him king. Thus he was neither the choice of Yhwh nor of the elders and lacked the anointing by a priest or prophet. He was simply an imposition on the people by the commander of the army. A possible mirror reflection of the kingship of Ishbaal may be found in the attempted usurpation of the throne by Adonijah with the help of Joab, 1 Kings 1:5-10.

born and would rage on until one emerges the stronger to submerge the other in his shadows. In the ensuing conflict, the narrator portrays David as politically astute, morally prudent and humanly up to the task. The armies of the two rulers engaged in the war of supremacy culminating in the battle of Gibeon. There, Abner son of Ner, the commander of Ishbaal's army sealed his own doom by killing Asahel, the brother of Joab, David's commander (2:23).[290] Later, Abner, who was gaining more popularity in the house of Saul, fell out with Ishbaal on account of a quarrel over Rizpah, a former concubine of Saul (3:6-8).[291] Abner's reaction to the accusation

---

290 The narrator purposefully builds up the character of Abner as a good-natured commander with a very high sense of brotherly feeling towards the men of Judah, the enemy at war. His desire to prevent a blood bath between the two opposing forces is constantly underscored. His call for a combat of twelve men each would probably have settled the issue had it not gone wild by the death of all the twenty four (2:14-16). Again he tried to prevent the death of Asahel by asking him to end the chase which he knew would definitely end in his death but was ignored and Asahel paid for his stubbornness with his own life v. 20-23. Finally, he prevailed upon Joab to accept a truce and to prevent a massacre of Israel v. 25-27. It is of no wonder then when David later trustingly accepts his proposal and sends him on his way in peace (3:21) and mourns his death (3:32-34). It seems to us that the writer does not lack a good word for anyone who aids David on his way up the throne of Israel even if that one is found at the opposing side of the dice.

291 From the face value this question comes out so naturally that it would seem a simple misunderstanding between the two men; "…Why have you gone in to my father's concubine?" (3:7) But in the nature of things and in biblical sense, the subject has a very high implication upon the rights of the king. A similar situation is played upon in the Solomon-Adonijah conflict where Adonijah lays claim to the hand of the concubine of David. Even though David did not touch Abishag, his concubine, Solomon used that as a pretext to have Adonijah executed on the accusation of treason (1 Kings 2:13-25). By this implication, Abner has usurped the right of the successor or is laying claim to the throne of Saul in that moment that he went in to Rizpah. The situation becomes critical with the background information that she bore two sons to Saul (2 Sam 21:8). A concubine who bears two sons to the king must have been a very important personality at the royal court. To make things worse the narrator has already prepared his reader for this conflict with the statement: "Abner was making himself strong in the house of Saul" (v. 6). The statement allows itself to be interpreted in different ways such as: Abner was growing stronger, gaining power or popularity in the house

was to defect to David with the intention of transferring the kingdom from the house of Saul to the house of David. After consulting with the elders of Israel and of Benjamin, the tribe of Saul, Abner went with twenty men to consult David at Hebron and left there to rally the whole of Israel to David (vv.12-21).[292] This happened while Joab was on a military expedition with the army. When he came back, he heard what had happened and how David had allowed Abner "to go away in peace" (v. 22). This did not please the commander of the army. Without the knowledge of the king, Joab son of Zeruiah sent messengers after Abner, brought him back, took him aside, stabbed him in the stomach and killed him in the same manner as he had killed Asahel, his brother (v. 26-30). David showed his displeasure against his nephew and commander of his army by criticizing his action, cursing him and publicly mourning Abner, whom he buried at Hebron (v. 31-39). The next casualty in the journey towards a united monarchy was Ishbaal, the rival king; he was assassinated by his own marauding captains, Baanah

---

of Saul, hence the fear of Ishbaal for his throne. Hentschel notes that even though in both examples neither Abner nor Adonijah saw their action as a step in the direction of their political ambitions they stood accused as usurpers by the respective kings (cf. *2 Samuel*, p. 13–14).

292 David accepted to make a covenant with Abner upon the single condition that he did not appear in his presence without Michal, the daughter of Saul, to whom he had been "engaged at the price of a hundred foreskins of the Philistines". The narrator clears David of any wrong doing in making this demand with reference to the bride price that he had paid to make her his legal bride (1 Sam 18:27). That he had not divorced her and that it was her father who had forced him out of the land seem to make it legal that he takes back his bride at his return. The condition was fulfilled when David sent messengers to Ishbaal and he in turn sent and took Michal from the house of Paltiel, her husband (1 Sam 3:13-16). There seems to be a legal practice at play that forces Ishbaal to act accordingly and help in so doing David's bid to the throne. Hentschel posits that it was within the confines of Oriental law for David to demand the return of his wife from Ishbaal. The double demand of David might suggest that David made the demand upon Abner, who fulfilled it, but in his bid to prove the virtue of David, the narrator has added a second demand from Ishbaal to make it legitimate and place David beyond reproach (*2 Samuel*, p. 14–15). The demand demonstrates without doubt the aspirations of David towards the throne of Saul as a son-in-law and the fulfilment brings him a step towards the goal of his long journey; the kingship of Israel.

and Rechab, who decapitated him and carried his head to David at Hebron (4:5-8). David responded by executing them and burying the head of Ishbaal in the tomb of Abner (4:12).

The death of Ishbaal removed the only impediment left in the way of David's rise to power and with the background work done by Abner before his death, the tribes of Israel were ready for the extension of the reign of David proverbially "from Dan to Beersheba" (3:10). All the elders of the tribes of Israel came to David at Hebron, made a covenant with him and anointed him king over Israel according to that which they said had been the promise of the Lord – 5:1-2:

> Then all the tribes of Israel came to David at Hebron, and said, "Look, we are your bone and your flesh.[2] For some time, while Saul was king over us, it was you who led out Israel and brought it in. The LORD said to you: It is you who will shepherd my people Israel; you who shall be prince over Israel." (NRSV)[293]

Having been accepted king over all Israel, David unfolded his plan for the future by acting quickly and decisively in providing a seat of government acceptable to both sides of his hitherto divided kingdom. He attacked and conquered the Jebusite stronghold of Jerusalem, established it as his capital and named it the city of David (5:6-10). He built an alliance with Hiram, king of Tyre,[294] and definitively settled the Philistine question with the two

---

293 The resort to this promise of Yhwh by the elders of Israel sits awkwardly in its context and its position here is made worse by the almost word for word repetition of the opening words of v. 1 and v. 3. Several explanations have been proffered in the course of time but the most convincing in, my view, is that the reference to "a promise of Yhwh" draws attention to chapter 7, the cornerstone of the dtr story of David's rise to power. These two verses, then, belong in the list of dtr expansion of the older narrative in anticipation of the oracle of Nathan in chap. 7 (so MacCarter, *II Samuel*, p. 131).

294 The friendship between Hiram and David at this point of the story raises chronological problems the solution for which can be deduced from the account of Josephus and 1 Kings 6. According to McCarter, the forty year reign of David does not admit Hiram as the king of Tyre who built David a cedar house. Since Solomon began in the fourth year of his reign to build the Temple and that coincided with the twelfth year of Hiram's rule (so Josephus, *Contra Apion* 1.126), the king of Tyre at the beginning of David's reign could only have been the father of Hiram, Abibalus (*Contra Apion*, 116-117). A dtr hand inserted vv. 11-12 as a link between the old material that possibly ended with v. 10 and formulated narratives that follow; the taking up of residence

battles of Baalperazim (5:17-21) and Rephaim (22-25). Before each of the two battles, David consulted the Lord (vv.19, 23 & 24) and acted according to the outcome of those consultations to make Yhwh the author of both victories. Then David concretized the position of his political capital by carrying the Ark of the Lord from Baalejudah[295] to Jerusalem and installing it at the place and in the tent that he had prepared for it (6:1ff).[296]

In the narration of David's rise to power, the final editor, and in all probability his source, presents in carefully chosen words and expressions a story that depicts David as a humble, intelligent and kind man on his way up the ladder of greatness, who does not harbour rancour nor pay evil for evil. He is practically not only innocent of all the deaths that take place in the process, but is also portrayed as openly showing his disapproval of them and personally mourning the dead when necessary. He is consistently placed far away from the scene of murder so that even though these murders or deaths, from the death of Saul and Jonathan to that of Abner and Ishbaal, bring him closer and closer to his destination, none of them can be imputed to David as a person. When the road is finally cleared for him to ascend the throne as king of both Judah and Israel, he takes shrewd and

---

in Jerusalem by David, his cedar house and the promise of a "house" in chapter 7, cf. McCarter, *II Samuel*, p. 145–146) and David's successes in settling the Philistine conflict once and for all (5:17, 8:1).

295 The procession of the Ark of the Lord from its place of rest to the City of David took place in two different phases; the first journey from Baalejudah to Jerusalem was broken up at the threshing floor of Nacon, at Perezuzzah, because of the death of Uzzah who took hold of the Ark to save it from falling. For fear of bringing death into the city, the Ark was left in the charge of Obededom for three months (6:6-11) after which period it was conveyed into the city amid sacrifices, dancing and festivities (v. 12-19). There is the probability that in the first phase a later account is imposed upon an earlier one to explain the sojourn of the Ark in the house of a Philistine before its entry into Jerusalem (cf. Hentschel, *2 Samuel*, p. 25–26) and the presence of faithful Philistines in Israel like the sixty-two sons and grandsons of Obededom who were Gatekeepers in Chr 26:4-8. We will, however, not want to enter into this discourse in the present work.

296 We have purposefully avoided the Ark Narratives which begin with its capture by the Philistines in ch. 4, the seven-month sojourn in the temple of Dagon in Ashdod resulting in a plague (5:2), its return to Bethshemesh by the Philistines (ch. 6) and its subsequent rest in Kiriath-jearim (ch. 7).

astute decisions that ensure the stability of his reign right from the onset. His choice of Jerusalem as capital was for reasons of both political expediency and tactical security; the neutrality and central location of the city made it easy for acceptance by the northern as well as the southern tribes. The city was located between the two factions of the nation, originally inhabited by the Jebusites, hence removing any possibility of interference from Judah or Israel. Above all, the natural endowments of the city made it a citadel with every possible advantage over the would-be external aggressor. David took the city with his men or we should say with his mercenaries who had been with him all through the days of trial at the hands of Saul. Thus neither Judah nor Israel could claim benefits or privileges for it.[297] His constant enquiry of the Lord before going out to war and the response of Yhwh to his inquiries put him forward as a Yhwh-fearing king who had the Lord at his side as against the apostate Saul who consulted a medium in the moment of need because the Lord did not answer him, for Yhwh had deserted him (1 Sam 28:7ff). The series of appropriate decisions at the beginning of David's reign is crowned with the ultimate religious act of transferring the Ark of Yhwh into the City of David (6:1ff). This single act made Jerusalem at once the political capital of the nation as well as its cultic centre and the king as both political and religious symbol of authority to look up to.[298]

The long journey from anointing to enthronement seems to arrive at its expected destination with the programmatic remark of the narrator: "And David became greater and greater for Yhwh Sabaoth was with him" (5:10).

---

297 In his bid to idealize the capture of Jebus (Jerusalem) as the work of a combined force of "all Israel" under the leadership of David (I Chr 11:4) the Chronicler misses the importance of the neutrality of the city. It is this neutrality that the text of 2 Samuel achieves with the statement that "The king and his men went to Jerusalem against the Jebusites" (5:6). Thus it was a personal conquest of David with the men who had been faithful to him in all his trials at the hand of Saul and who had come with him to Hebron in 2:3.

298 In the second phase of the transfer of the Ark there is no specific mention of a priest or prophet. Even though the presence of priests as bearers of the Ark can be taken for granted (v.3) it is the king who assumes the role of the religious leader in climaxing the long sequence of events aimed at the fulfilment of Moses' words about the place where Yhwh would choose to put his name (Deut 12:5) after he had granted rest to his people Israel (12:10).

The remark was, however, not to be the climax to the story of the rise of David to the throne of Israel. Were it to be, the story would have left the question about the purpose of the oracles upon which the reign of David is based still open and, therefore, redundant. An author worth the name will not permit such an oversight in a work otherwise carefully tailored to the event, hence the author and, to all intents and purposes, the dtr redactor leads his reader on to his perceived logical conclusion to the story, namely the promise of an eternal kingdom to David by Yhwh (7:1-17).

In 2 Sam 3:18 Abner cites an apparently non-existent oracle or promise of Yhwh: *"Now then bring it about; for Yhwh has promised David: Through my servant David I will save my people Israel from the hand of the Philistines and from all their enemies."* In the same vein, the dtr author, in his addition to the narrative, makes the elders of Israel base their argument for a Davidic rule upon a promise of Yhwh; *"…The Lord said to you: It is you who will shepherd my people Israel;(it is) you who shall be ruler (prince) over Israel"* (5:2).[299] These oracles gain a foothold when one reads them in the light of 2 Sam 7 and in the context of the dtr history of the rise of David.[300] Thus, coupled with the initial victory over the Philistines, the oracles prepare the ground for the promise of an eternal kingdom to the house of David as a sign of the eternal peaceful existence of the nation of

---

299 The declaration of the elders of Israel at the end of v. 1, literally translated; "Look, your bone and your flesh we are", is curiously interesting as it rather aptly describes the relationship between David and Judah instead of Israel. Nevertheless, its appearance at this point of the history and at Hebron or Mamre, the very first acquired property of Abraham (Gen 23:17-18), underscores the unity of the tribes of Israel based upon its ancestral ties to the Patriarch Abraham. It is this Israel that the warrior David had led in and out against the Philistines at the time of Saul, hence, the kingdom that Saul had ruled before him. It is the reversal of this unity in the revolts of Sheba (2 Sam 20:1) and Jeroboam (1 Kings 12:17) that spells out respectively the foreboding and eventual doom of the nation.

300 In line with the attribution of v. 18b to the Dtr by Veijola, McCarter reads the verse under the guise of David's victories and the promise of an everlasting kingdom in 2 Sam 7, putting emphasis on the use of the favourite dtr designation of David as "my servant David" (*II Samuel*, p. 116). Campbell and O'Brien cautiously agree with this position but add that though references to "my servant David" are normally late it does not apply to all as in the case of Ps 78:70 (Campbell & O'Brien, *Unfolding*, p. 285).

Israel, which is the cradle of the dtr thought and ideology. The promise of a dynasty to David comes as a free choice of Yhwh, but with the collaboration of the pious and obedient servant who is the object of that promise.

5.2.5 The Promise of an Everlasting Kingdom: 2 Sam 7

Now that the king was settled in his house in Jerusalem and Yhwh had given him rest from his enemies all around him (v. 1); the perennial Philistine problem had momentarily been laid to rest, he was preoccupied with a different thought; a house for Yhwh i.e. a Temple. David communicated his intention to the Prophet Nathan who encouraged him to do whatever was on his mind כי יהוה עמך -"for Yhwh is with you" (7:3). But in a nightly vision, the word of Yhwh came to Nathan for "my servant David" that he would not build a house for Yhwh. Instead, Yhwh would build him a house (v. 11); a son of his loins would sit on his throne after him who would build a house for Yhwh and Yhwh in his turn would "establish his kingdom for ever" (v. 13). He would be a son to Yhwh even as Yhwh would be to him a father (v. 14). If he sinned he would be punished like mortals do but "I will not take my steadfast love from him, as I took it from Saul, whom I put away before you" v. 15. The oracle concludes in v. 16 with the full expression of the celebrated promise to David:

וְנֶאְמַן בֵּיתְךָ וּמַמְלַכְתְּךָ עַד־עוֹלָם לְפָנֶיךָ כִּסְאֲךָ יִהְיֶה נָכוֹן עַד־עוֹלָם׃
Your house and your throne shall be made sure forever before me (you); your throne shall be established forever.

Then King David went in, sat before Yhwh and pronounced a prayer of appreciation and thanksgiving for all that the "Lord God" – אדני יהוה – had done for him even without his personal merit (vv. 18-29).

The current chapter is one of the episodes in the OT that have attracted a high degree of attention from researchers of every generation. In itself the encounter introduces the core elements of the DtrH and the hinge on which the whole ideology depends i.e., temple and dynasty. Even though some analysts would like to end the story of David's rise to power with the final note in 5:10,[301] the final text at our disposal does not permit this as it

---

301 J. H. Grønbaek, *Aufstieg Davids*, p. 35. Grønbaek argues that with the anointing of David in Hebron by the elders of Israel as king in place of Saul,

clearly crowns the journey of David's rise with the promise of an eternal kingdom to "the servant of Yhwh", a promise prefaced by the remark; *It happened that as the king settled in his house and Yhwh had given him rest from all his enemies around him,* v. 1.[302] This is a typical dtr note that hints at the promise of Deut 12:10-12 as the basis for the oracle of Nathan, introducing the basic elements of the oracle as a step towards the realization of Moses' words; attainment of rest and the building of a shrine to Yhwh. The position of 2 Sam 7 in the dtr work and ideology will be revisited in the next chapter. For the purpose of this work, the episode arouses my interest from yet another direction; it constitutes one of the three moments in the history in which David and Nathan are in dialogue and more also because this episode and 2 Sam 12:1-15 are private audiences of prophet and king in which oracles are pronounced with both oracles eliciting an attitude of prayer from David as an after-math (7:18-29, 12:15b-23). Suffice it at this stage of the work to say that the Dtr as the final editor of the text succeeds in expressing to his audience that the pious King David had a good intention of building a temple to Yhwh once he was settled as king in Jerusalem v. 1. Yhwh denied him the honour of a temple-builder (v. 5), but

---

the earlier story of the rise of David which began in 1 Sam 15 comes to its expected close. The writer concludes with the conquest of Jerusalem. Grønbaek continues that even if there might have been other traditions about the rise of David that the writer might have known about, these were of no importance to him. I am of a different view; the rise does not end here for it can only end with the consolidation of the king's authority in Jerusalem and the attainment of "rest" there.

302 The setting for the promise raises apparent textual problems for critics. Why should David be promised "rest" in v. 11 if he already has it in v. 1? And why should he still be at war from v. 8-12? What is more the Chronicler apparently recognises the inconsistency and avoids the reference to rest in his report in 1 Chr 17:1. Could the reference to rest be a marginal note to v. 11 that later found its way into the text, hence its absence in Chr 17:1? (So McCarter, citing the older critics like Wellhausen, Driver, Budde and Nowack, *II Samuel*, p. 193–195). This will not be an issue if one has followed the turbulent journey of David from following the sheep to a musician at the court of Saul, a fugitive in the villages and the desert of Judah and finally to be the king of a united Israel living in a cedar house in Jerusalem, with the Ark of Yhwh in its tent nearby. Rest is definitely a long and tortuous process that has already begun and will continue.

rewarded him with the promise of an eternal dynasty instead (v. 11) with an assurance that his successor, a son of his loins, would build the temple for the name of Yhwh (v. 13).[303] The narrative proceeds with an enumeration of the successes of David in a war of expansion or consolidation of his power as if to say that the assurance of Yhwh gave David the impetus to bring to fulfilment the ancient promise of rest from the enemy all around (Deut 12:10-12).

5.2.6 David at the height of his reign – 2 Sam 8-20

The king turned his attention onto securing the borders of his state. He embarked upon a series of wars that were meant to break the spine of the enemy and protect the young nation. He smote the Philistines and took Metheghamah (8:1), reduced the Moabites to a vassal status (v. 2), conquered Hadadezer of Zobah and the Arameans of Damascus, where he stationed garrisons (v. 3-6) taking a great amount of gold and bronze from the standard-bearers and from the towns of Hadadezer.[304] He destroyed the Edomite army in the valley of Salt and stationed garrisons throughout Edom (v. 13-14). The defeat of Hadadezer won David an ally, Toi of Hamath, who had long been at war with Hadadezer (v. 9). Toi sent his son Joram[305] to David with gifts of silver, gold and bronze (v. 10). These gifts and the spoils that he had taken from the nations he had conquered the king dedicated to the Lord (v. 11-12) who had given him victory (v. 14).[306] *"For Yhwh gave victory to/ delivered/ protected David wherever he went"* (v. 14). The narrator inserts in vv. 15-18 a list of David's officers or cabinet

---

303 We have before us a composite text that has its own historical process of growth and final dtr trimmings and additions that make it the bearer of the key themes of dynasty and temple that are so important to the dtr corpus. I will pick up this point and elaborate it in the next chapter.
304 The Chronicler is specific about the use of the bronze taken by David in this campaign; Solomon used it to make "the bronze sea and the pillars and the vessels of bronze." Chr 18:8.
305 Chr 18:9-11. The Chronicler identifies the king of Hamath as Tou and his son as Hadoram.
306 This collection of David's wars can on one hand easily be placed after 5:25 as a continuation of the Philistine wars and on the other be considered a probable summary of the Aramean war of 10:1ff.

ministers, as the case may be today, and then has David turn his attention to an important internal affair of his reign, namely the house of Saul. David had the only remaining member of Saul's family, Mephiboshet, the lame son of Jonathan, brought to the court so that he could show kindness towards him – ואעשה עמו חסד בעבור יהונתן – for the sake of Jonathan (9:1). He restored all the land of Saul to Mephiboshet to be tilled by his servant Ziba and his house, but Mephiboshet himself remained in Jerusalem and ate at the king's table like one of the sons of the king (v. 11). Then follows the full account of the Ammonite and Aramean war into which the adultery with Bathsheba and the murder of Uriah, the oracle of Nathan, the death of the son of Bathsheba and the birth of Solomon are inserted; 10:1-12:31.[307] This leads on to the tumult in David's household that culminates in the revolt of Absalom (15:1-19:8), the revolt of Sheba (20) and David's return to Jerusalem and the final restoration of peace in the land (21).[308]

In this block of narrative material, the reader has before him a source that has produced divergent opinions over the years. The two main opinions can be summed up as follows; in the first instance, chapters 11-20 are perceived to be part of a unit in which David is portrayed as a passive, excessively lenient and gentle king, submissive to the divine will and imbued with paternal affection even to the point of succumbing to the whims of his family and chief officers which accounts for his troubles (so Rost).[309] In fact, his troubles are the result of the reckless behaviour of those around him. The second stance posits a contradiction of the image of David in chapters 11-20 as the reason for the divergent thought. While a passive David is, without doubt, an apt description of the man in the narrative of 13-20, the same cannot be said of the David of 11-12. In 11-12, David is an actively callous "taker" of the wife of one of his elite soldiers and

---

[307] This part of the narrative is treated as a whole in the first chapter of this book and as portions in the relevant chapters as it constitutes the mediate and immediate context of the parable of Nathan.
[308] We have a complex conflation of narrative material here that I will not spend time analysing because it is beyond the scope of this work.
[309] P. K. McCarter, *II Samuel*, p. 289–290. For Rost, 2 Sam 9-20 and I Kings 1-2 are a unity that deals with the Succession to the throne of David or the so-called Succession Narratives (SN) cf. *Succession to the Throne of David*, 1982, p. 75f.

a cunning contriver of the death of that soldier. These two images are contradictory, if not simply incongruous, and could not have come from the same hand. But "the king who takes is the king of I Sam 8:11-17, about whom the prophet Samuel warned the people". This is very well in accordance with the image of kingship in the prophetic history that has Samuel rebuke Saul (I Sam 15:17-29) and Nathan David in 2 Sam 12:7b-12, argues McCarter.[310] The prophetic image of David, the callous, adulterous murderer stands as a preface to Absalom's revolt (13-20) to lay the guilt of the whole trouble at David's own feet. Thus we are faced, at least, with two different sources of material that have been conflated; one that presents David's reign in a glorified account and the other that seeks to dampen it; a probable prophetic edition of and addition to that material to explain the events of David's reign in the light of the prophetic judgment and oracle against David for his sins of adultery and murder. The dtr author has adopted both materials and incorporated them into his global work of the history without necessarily cutting out the part that speaks negatively of David. This is a clear indication that the Dtr does not distort history in his bid to present a hero worthy of the name and role that he assigns him even when the blunt truth might appear to be detrimental to the image of the hero that he takes pains to construct.[311]

---

310 P. K. McCarter, *II Samuel*, p. 290. The final editor of the material that we have brings his opinions to bear on the narrative that he presents by the introduction of theological grounds for the course of events in the history. For instance, in the narration of the rise of David to power, the leitmotiv is the fact that "Yhwh was with him". At the height of his power, the narrator makes every effort to explain the negative course of events leading to the tumult in the house of the monarch (13-20) as the result of the sin of David and the fulfilment of the oracle of Nathan against him and his house (12:7b-12). As we have noted in the first chapter of this work, the dtr author has inserted the David-Bathsheba-Nathan sequence into the narrative and properly at this particular point to serve as a background to the succession to David's throne, by providing the identity of the successor even before that theme becomes an issue.

311 In his commentary (*Das Zweite Buch Samuels*, p. 285) on the narration of the adultery, Hans Joachim Stoebe has this to say; „An sich läßt gerade die Kurze der Darstellung keinen Zweifel an der historischen Zuverlässigkeit des berichteten Ehebruchs; es handelt sich nicht um vage Gerüchte oder Rufmord, sondern um eine Tatsache, zu dem eine Tatsache, an der man mit Recht

It is worthy of note that as part of this collection of David's wars and in the midst of the difficult process of the resolution of the moral conflicts of the king's life and as a preparation for the seemingly insurmountable internal political turbulence of the young nation, the narrator credits David with the conquest of a fortified city, Rabbah (12:26-31). Halpern finds this remarkable because, except in the books of Kings (9th and 8th centuries), Biblical narratives are notoriously chary about attributing to kings the storming of fortifications. In Judges, elaborate plans and stratagems were required to overcome a defensive position or even the perimeter of a properly pitched camp as in the case of Gideon against the Midianite camp (Judg 7:16-23) and Ehud's assassination of Eglon (Judg 3:15-30). The taking of towns such as Jericho (Jos 6) and Ai (Jos 8:3-23) was carried out through treachery and trickery. This leaves the frontal attack of Rabbah by Joab and the elite group of the Israelite army and its eventual capture by David at the head of the whole army a unique victory.[312] With this victory, "David was the undisputed master, by treaty or conquest, of an empire that extended from Egypt to the Euphrates and from the Mediterranean to the Arabian Desert."[313] Thus, at the height of David's reign, the king performs an extraordinary military act of valour, captures a fortified city, but compromises his fame by taking for himself the wife of another man and that man was one of his own elite soldiers. At the height of his greatness, the fall of the king is prophesied. King David stands before the reader as a glorious conqueror and founder of a great nation, but, morally, he is a sinner hitting the lowest level that a man can hit far away from his God, when that God is Yhwh, the Righteous One. It is only his unqualified

---

Anstoß nahm. Das Alter des Kindes war nachzurechnen, und das es sich bei der Heirat des Königs mit der Kindesmutter nicht um einen großherzigen Akt landesherrlicher Witwenversorgung handelte, war ohnehin klar." In effect, the Dtr does not distort the truth.

312 B. Halpern, *Paths of Glory*, p. 77. The extreme difficulty of capturing a fortified city in those days, especially one with a tower, is expressed by the proverbial death of Abimelech in Judg 9:53, referred to by Joab in 2 Sam 11:21. The saying underlies the practicality of even the weakest of human beings being at an advantage against the strongest once they are high up the wall as in this case a woman, armed with an upper millstone, positioned high up the tower, kills Abimelech, the commander of a conquering army.

313 J. M. Myers, *I Chronicles*, p. 140.

repentance and the boundless mercy of his God that save him from death (12:7-13). The Dtr allows his hero to be human in succumbing to the sin of lust that adds murder to its repertoire but at the same time acknowledges his humanity, rises above it and humbles himself before Yhwh who shows him mercy and forgives him.

5.2.7 The last days of David: 1 Kings 1-2

The first book of Kings picks up the story from where second Samuel left off; King David is now old and so advanced in years that he requires special care to keep him warm.[314] For this reason his servants sought for the king a beautiful young virgin, Abishag of Shunem, to attend to him "but the king did not know her" (v. 1-4). In consequence, Adonijah presumed himself heir to the throne, being the first born among the remaining sons of the king. He was a handsome man, born next to Absalom and had never incurred the displeasure of his father (v. 6). With the blessing of Joab,[315] the commander of the army, and Abiathar, the priest, Adonijah organized a sacrifice ostentatiously for his own coronation as king, inviting all the sons of the king except Solomon. Besides Solomon, the prophet Nathan, Zadok the priest, Benaiah and the Cherethites and the Pelethites, David's elite soldiers and royal corp, were also sidelined. This state of affairs got Nathan quickly acting in complicity with Bathsheba to break the news to the aged king and coerce him to name Solomon as his successor. The plan emerged highly successful when Nathan entered at the right moment to corroborate the point of Bathsheba. The king renewed his oath to Bathsheba referring

---

314 The sequence of our narrative has carefully avoided 2 Sam 21-24, traditionally considered to be an appendix to the text. This is rightly so because the Gibeonite vengeance (21:1-9) and the reburial of the bones of Saul and Jonathan (v. 12-14), for instance, would fit in better to the beginning of David's reign than after the Absalom revolt.
315 With this final act of Joab that determines his future at the hands of Solomon, the negative image of the sons of Zeruiah reaches its apex; it was not enough to put the guilt of every murder along the path of David's rise to power at the feet of Joab, he takes sides against the future king of Israel, Solomon. Is this possibly a way of describing the sons of Zeruiah as part of a party at the court of David; the Judah faction rendering their support to Adonijah born in Hebron (cf. 2 Sam 3:4)?

to an earlier one he had sworn that Solomon would sit on his throne after him (vv. 29-30). He gave the expected order for Solomon to be led to Gihon riding the royal mule, there to be anointed by Zadok and Nathan after which they were to sound the trumpet proclaiming; "Long live King Solomon" (v. 34). He was then to be brought in to sit on the throne as king of Israel and Judah. This order was immediately executed by Zadok, Nathan, Benaiah, the Cherethites and the Pelethites, each playing their proper roles at the coronation ceremony. Zadok took the horn of oil from the tent and anointed Solomon, proclaimed him king and all the people amidst music and rejoicing brought him in to sit upon the throne of his father David. When the message reached Adonijah, his guests and accomplices deserted him and he himself sought refuge in the tent by taking hold of the horns of the altar until Solomon had promised to let him live, *"If he proves to be a worthy man, not one of his hair shall fall to the ground; but if wickedness is found in him, he shall die"* (v. 52). King David then exalted his son and heir to keep the commandments and statutes of Yhwh so that Yhwh in turn would establish his kingdom and that he would prosper (2:1-9). He concluded his final words by instructing Solomon on what to do to Joab, Barzillai and Shimei, after which the king slept with his ancestors and was buried in the city of David (v. 10).

If the chronological data of 1 Kings 2:11, corroborated by that of 2 Sam 5:4, is anything to go by, David would have been seventy years (and six months) old and definitely at an advanced stage of bodily ailment when the events of the succession unfolded.[316] We must keep in mind the importance that the Dtr normally attaches to the fact that at an advanced age his heroes remain mentally fit and physically active. At a hundred and twenty years, the sight of Moses was not impaired and his freshness or vigour had not eluded him (Deut 34:7);

וּמֹשֶׁה בֶּן־מֵאָה וְעֶשְׂרִים שָׁנָה בְּמֹתוֹ לֹא־כָהֲתָה עֵינוֹ וְלֹא־נָס לֵחֹה:

Moses was a hundred and twenty years old when he died; his sight had not grown dim and his vigour unabated.

---

316 An "advanced stage of arteriosclerosis", so Mordechai Cogan and De Vries (I Kings, p. 156) Note the Biblical age of man perched at 70 or 80.

The same can be said of Joshua who died at a hundred and ten years after his exhortation of the people and the renewal of the covenant – ועשר שנים בן־מאה – (Jos 24:29). On his part, Samuel, the last of the judges was old and grey – ואני זקנתי ושבתי - (1 Sam 12:2) but still active in the religious and political life of Israel. Like David, these three men are the major pillars of deuteronomistic heroism, but the last days of David are not glorified in the same way as the three. The glorified account of the age of Caleb Ben Jephunneh seems to function in the same light as a sign of the Lord's blessings for his faithfulness; at eighty-five he was as strong as when he was forty in every ramification of that age (Josh 14:10-11, Sirach 46:7). David was far below the age of these others, but practically senile, sick and inactive, besides giving the order for the choice of his successor and that, only after being pushed to it by Nathan and Bathsheba. His seventy years (and six months), however, reflects or falls into the span of proverbial age of man in wisdom literature expressed by Ps 90:10.[317]

> The days of our life are seventy years,
> or perhaps eighty, if we are strong;
> even then their span is only toil and trouble;
> they are soon gone, and we fly away.

The insistence in the text that David did not know Abishag seems to suggest that at seventy, David's youthful vigour had left him or in plain text, that he was impotent. This impotence spills over unto the physical and political arena where Adonijah decides that his time had come to be king and proceeds to usurp the throne while Nathan and Bathsheba manoeuvre to get the king take the final decision in favour of Solomon in order to protect themselves or cause the fulfilment of a supposed promise made to the son born in Jerusalem. The Dtr has no qualms of conscience letting his celebrated hero play second fiddle to the other major pillars of the history, while at the same time hailing him as the yardstick with which to measure the rest of the kings of Judah and Israel. This may probably be a way of indirectly opining that David was the greatest of the kings of Israel but above him were other greater leaders like Moses, Joshua and Samuel whose greatness were of a different level in their relationship with Yahweh, the God of Israel.

---

317 Unlike the Dtr, the Chronicler expresses the age of David positively as; "good old age, full of days, riches and honour" (29:28).

There is no simple explanation for the behaviour of Nathan and Bathsheba with regard to coercing the king to name Solomon as the successor to the throne. Whether the king had actually promised the throne to Solomon or not is not easy to prove, but the Dtr in a fine way has prepared his readers for this trend of events in hinting that Yhwh loved Solomon, probably among the sons of David, and Nathan named him Jedidiah (12:24-25).[318] What is clear to the reader is that there was rivalry at the court of David and the king was expected to take a decision to end the conflict, as indicated by the words of Bathsheba in v. 20: *And you, my lord the king, the eyes of all Israel are on you to tell them who shall sit on the throne of my lord the king after him.* In the last days of his life David is portrayed as old, feeble, indecisive and even malleable, at the mercy of Nathan and Bathsheba, the so-called Jerusalem party. We will pick up this strand again in the next chapter.

5.3 The image of David that emerges from the narrative

We are now in a position to confront the question; what kind of image does the final editor or the dtr writer paint of David, his hero, to his readers? At the end of his analysis of the text of David's rise to power, Grønbaek concludes that the fundamental intention of the author was to document that David was the legitimate successor to King Saul as the king of the whole of Israel after Yhwh had rejected Saul, and may date back to the time after the death of Solomon and the schism that followed.[319] Whereas this view may not be too far-fetched as far as the source of the material is concerned, it is no doubt clear that the final editor did not have any need of defending the legitimacy of the kingship of David over Israel. The succession of David to the throne of Saul with its legitimacy is an established fact that was already deep-rooted in the tradition. What this fourth century author

---

318 The text of the two verses is very difficult and raises so many questions but at its present position it serves as a preparation for the role that this son of Bathsheba was supposed to play in the events of the succession and as the Temple builder promised in chapter 7. Carefully but purposefully, the Dtr brings together all the players in the drama of the succession in the two verses; (Yhwh), David, Nathan, Bathsheba and Solomon.
319 J. H. Grønbaek, *Aufstieg Davids*, p. 260-261.

needed and has sought to portray with the material culled from his sources was to present an image of the man David that did and would endear him not only to the generation of the writer but more especially to a generation after generation.

At the end of the book of Judges, the dtr writer records a situation of lawlessness that stemmed from the absence of a substantive ruler of the emerging nation of Israel (Judg 21:25). This situation is partially resolved by the demand for a king and the subsequent anointing of Saul, but the Benjaminite fell short of the expectation of a king of Israel. Yhwh rejected him through the prophet Samuel, the very same instrument of his anointing. In his place He chose David, the young, handsome, endowed shepherd and warrior of Bethlehem in Judah, whom he protected against Saul and guided through thick and thin towards his final destination; enthronement as "king of a united Israel". While divine protection assured his success in everything that he undertook, David co-operated with the divine presence by taking astute and informed decisions at the right moments and in consultation with Yhwh that boosted his image before the people he ruled. In doing this, the authorial hand behind the narratives places the king beyond any form of reproach in order to present him as the obedient servant of Yhwh, the "founder" of Jerusalem and the initiator of the Temple-building project on Mount Zion, where he stationed the Ark of God. It is David as king who succeeds in bringing about the promised rest to the people of Israel by conquering all the nations round about her (Deut 12:10), making them his tribute-paying vassals, and is the only king in Israel to receive from Yhwh a promise of an everlasting kingdom under the rule of his line of kings (2 Sam 7:16). David was faithful to his God in every way possible but, remained human and as a human being in a moment of weakness, he committed adultery and topped it up with the murder of no less a person than one of his own elite soldiers (2 Sam 11). He, however, repented of his guilt when the prophet Nathan confronted him and Yhwh forgave him his sins (12:1-15). As a potent sign of the great mercy of God upon David, the second son born to him from that marriage acceded to the throne, with David living long enough to see this accomplishment (1 Kings 1:28-53). This son of David, Solomon, built the long awaited Temple in Jerusalem, which became the sign of the cultic unity of the nation of Israel and a fulfilment of the words of Moses, in accordance with the Deuteronomic and the deuteronomistic tradition (Deut 12:10-14).

The Dtr presents his reader with a character which can be said to be a complex whole; he is God's own choice, a young, handsome shepherd, a musician and a soldier, a king and a pious man who knows the depths of sin and the pain of punishment but also the beauty of the grace of repentance. At the moment of his election, the young David had the responsibility of caring for the family flock as a shepherd; a proverbial quality of a leader in Israel.[320] He quickly translated his bravery as a shepherd into the boldness of a warrior that won him the fame of a giant-killer (1 Sam 17). His physical and internal beauty coupled with his talent as a musician opened for him not only the gates of the palace but also the hearts of those who lived therein (1 Sam 18). In the fall-out with Saul, David is simply presented as a victim who did not pay back evil for evil but, constantly aware of divine providence, was even capable of sparing the life of his arch enemy and did not rejoice over the death of his foes. He enjoyed the sympathy and support of the prophet Samuel (19:18-24), Jonathan, the prince (20:1f), the priests of Nob (21:2-10) and, eventually, "the elders of all the tribes of Israel" with the unflinching support of Judah as a foregone conclusion (2 Sam 5:1-3).

The establishment of the reign of Ishbaal by Abner son of Ner constituted a hurdle along the road to a unified state and its crossing was a *"conditio sine qua non"*. The dtr deftly resolves this otherwise difficult impasse without allowing the hero to soil his hands by personally shedding blood as Abigail had intimated earlier on in 1 Sam 25:26-31. The deaths of Abner and Ishbaal bring David closer to the goal of inheriting the throne of Saul but in both cases he is far removed from the scene of crime and his innocence is categorically emphasized. The return of Michal, daughter of Saul, to David as his legitimate wife was not without her being wrested from Paltiel, her second husband. This marriage would justify David's claim to the throne of his father-in-law, in the absence of a living son who would

---

320 In royal parlance the verbs mlk (to rule) and rʻh (to shepherd) are almost synonymous as the ruler is also a shepherd of his people. In Jer 2:8 and Isa 44:28 shepherd is used metaphorically to express the idea of a ruler even as Yhwh is depicted as the shepherd (of Israel); Gen 48:15, Ps 23, 80:2.

have logically inherited the throne. This fact notwithstanding, the narrative exonerates David from every act of wrongdoing in demanding the return of Michal and does not even concentrate on that theme as a point of legitimizing David. When the time came for his enthronement it was all the tribes of Israel (כל־שבטי ישראל) or all the elders (כל־זקני) who assembled in Hebron and anointed David king (2 Sam 5:1-5) in place of Saul; thus making public what God had already accomplished in secret (1 Sam 16:1-13).

As a father, David loved to a fault and his leniency towards his sons contributed to the woes that visited his house even to the last days of his life. His *laissez faire* attitude towards Amnon in the aftermath of the abuse of Tamar caused Absalom to take the law into his own hands to avenge the crime that his father should have been quick enough to resolve (2 Sam 13:28-29). This encouraged the young man to eventually stage a coup d'état that resulted in his own death, but not before he had succeeded in widening the gulf of tribal differences that existed within the nation. In the end it was the combined effort of Nathan and Bathsheba that finally achieved the aim of "forcing" the seventy year old David to take the all-important decision of naming his successor to end the family feud over the throne. This is the image of David that runs through the story of his election and rises to greatness under the guise of divine presence and guidance. It is on the basis of this image that the Dtr confidently makes Yahweh address David as עבדי דוד – my servant David (cf. 2 Sam 3:18, 7:5, 7) and use that as the leitmotiv for judging all other kings of Israel and Judah (1 Kings 11:13, 33-34, 14:8, etc.). The servant motif has an epoch-making function in the Deuteronomistic work which links David to such figures as Moses and Joshua.[321] This is the image of the king who stands condemned by the prophet Nathan in the episode of 2 Sam 12:1-15a. I will now turn the attention to the person of the prophet and his relationship to the king in order to find out the rational behind his hard words towards the otherwise "pampered" hero of the narrative.

---

321 J. Van Seters, *Historiography*, p. 276.

Chapter 6. The prophet Nathan in the dtr corpus

Among all the prophets of the Old Testament, the abrupt appearance or introduction of Nathan into the narrative limelight is out of the ordinary and looks as if the prophet is simply smuggled into the narrative. Perhaps the only other comparable character to Nathan in the Biblical tradition as a whole is Melchizedek, king of Salem, "who is without father or mother or genealogy, having neither a beginning of days nor an end of life".[322] Nathan is an elusive and yet very important character in the narrative about David and his house or dynasty. He appears only three times in the narrative and disappears almost in the same way as he has appeared, namely, without a trace. Unlike Samuel before him or the later prophets, Nathan is not introduced in the normal sense of the word so that his parentage and origin are shrouded in a mystery. The one thing that the narratives bring across is that he was active only in Jerusalem and at the court of David and even there, he appears only three times each of which appearances constitutes a very important moment and a turning point in the narrative.

In his first appearance, Nathan plays a double role as a confidant or councillor to David and, as a prophet proclaims the word of Yahweh to the king who plans to build a temple for his God (2 Sam 7:1-17). As confidant and councillor, Nathan endorses the king's desire to build the temple (v. 1-3) but has to go back to reverse his position upon the word of Yahweh that hinders the building of a house for the Lord but promises a "house" to David, leaving the building of the temple to his successor, whose name the narrative leaves open (v. 4-17). In the second appearance, the hitherto confidant of the king turns out to be the bearer of evil tidings and announcer of an oracle of doom against that same house of the monarch (2 Sam 12:1-15a) and turns round to give a theophoric name to the new-born Solomon (12:25), while in his final appearance he is practically presented

---

[322] Hebrews 7:2-3. This is the writer of Hebrews' commentary on the passage of Genesis 14:17-24, where Melchizedek king of Salem appears out of the blue meets with Abraham, offers bread and wine and blesses the Patriarch, who in turn gives him a tenth of everything. He then disappears from the narrative as abruptly as he had appeared.

as an astute politician actively involved in a palace intrigue, scheming for David's endorsement of his preferred candidate, Solomon, against the odds and initiating his anointing and enthronement as king in place of David (I Kings 1:11-40). Two of the discourses of this prophet are proverbial in Biblical circles; "the oracle of Nathan" (7:1-17) and "the parable of Nathan" (12:1-15a) respectively.[323] Over and above these the narrator lets the key words of the so called "Succession Narrative" drop for the first time from the mouth of Nathan: *"...Did you not, my Lord the King, vow to your servant saying that; "Solomon your son shall be king after me and he shall sit on my throne?"..."* (1 Kings 1:13).[324]

The narrator or the Dtr, as the case may be, leaves his audience in a blank as far as the origin of Nathan is concerned at complete variance with Samuel, who comes just before him as prophet (from the point of view of narrative chronology), and in fact almost all the other prophets of the OT, who are identified with their fathers or hometown.[325] Besides these three appearances, the prophet Nathan falls into oblivion leaving questions about his origin and identity a matter of pure speculation; a devoted supporter of David, a fearless critic, an intriguing courtier working in favour of his protégé, a representative of the Jebusite group or a protagonist of the Jerusalem party.[326] It appears to us that what is important to the narrator of the stories

---

323 W. Oswald, *Nathan der Prophet*, p. 10. At this stage of my work the use of the phrase *"the oracle of Nathan"* can be very ambiguous. It will be used basically for the prophet's pronouncement in 2 Sam 7 but since his judgment against David and his house in 12:7-14 constitutes an *oracle of doom*, one has to take note of the context in order to be able to distinguish one usage from the other. On the whole I will endeavour to employ the nouns "salvation" or "doom" respectively as the mark of distinction whenever necessary.

324 L. Rost sees the key to understanding the whole work (the Succession Narrative) in these words. Cf. *The Succession to David's Throne*, p. 68.

325 In the case of Samuel, the whole background of the prophet is spelt out in the first chapter of the first book of Samuel where we note the names of his parents, Elkanah and Hannah, from Ramah. Later prophets are known for example as; Ahijah the Shilonite (1 Kings 11:29) Elijah the Tishbite (1 Kings 17:1), Elisha son of Shaphat (19:16) and Isaiah son of Amoz (Isa 1:1). With regards to Nathan, the only thing known besides himself is the name of his sons, Azariah and Zabud, who later entered the service of Solomon in 1 Kings 4:5.

326 In his *Nathan Narratives* (pp. 19–30), Jones H. Gwilym notes that the mention of Nathan together with such personalities like Joab, son of Zeruiah

was certainly not the identity or life history of the man called Nathan but the function of the prophet called Nathan in the narrative about David and his dynasty, the building of the temple and, probably, the King-Prophet relationship in the early monarchical period and in the broader work of the dtr history as a whole. In this sense, the manner of Nathan's introduction into the narrative is absolutely in line with the phenomenon of Biblical narratives where important elements and details are introduced only when they are necessary and irrelevant issues are simply glossed over in order not to obscure the main purpose of an episode. The aim of this chapter is to explore the position of the Nathan narratives in the light of the dtr tradition of David and Solomon with the view to finding reasons that will help us appreciate the role of this prophet in the broader history and how this role functions in our text; "the Parable of Nathan" (2 Sam 12:1-15a). In order to achieve this goal, I will first look at the current views expressed about each of the episodes and then, carefully observing the text itself, I will endeavour to throw light upon the extent to which the dtr author has been at work in these episodes and what fruits his activities have yielded. In doing so, I will constantly be guided by the pertinent question as to whether the Nathan episodes can be separated from the dtr history of David and the successor to his throne. The question becomes inevitable given that in these appearances the great themes of David, throne and dynasty, which are at the heart of the

---

and Benaiah son of Jehoiada in 1 Kings 1:7-8, where the patronym is in each case carefully recorded but left out with regard to Nathan and Zadok, hence the erroneous tendency among exegetes to link the two to a remnant of a pre-Israelite Jebusite cult. The exact position and function of Nathan at the court of David can best be determined by the functional definition of "Court-Prophet" in the light of the parallel with other court prophets in the ancient orient especially in Mari. According to Jones, the court-prophets of Mari were dependent upon the king and had the task of confirming and preserving the monarchy. Such a task sometimes demanded an intervention in the king's affairs to censure him; they spoke words that were not always favourable to the king, criticised his behaviour, and were taken seriously by the king and his court. Over and above these, they were messengers announcing what the gods had commanded. This parallel throws a lot of light on the enigmatic character of Nathan and his role at the court of David. We may even vouch to say that Nathan, the court-prophet was a counsellor consulted by the king in cultic matters and showed concern for the dynasty and its stability.

dtr credo, come to the fore. The consternation of these themes in the Nathan episodes brings us to a halt and to pose another question; "What does the dtr seek to portray with the character called Nathan?" Here, I will like to remain far removed from any suggestion that seeks to present Nathan as a representative of the Jebusite party at the court of David as the text at our disposal does not hint at any such position.

6.1 2 Sam 7; an overview

The accurate and almost perfect hallmark of the dtr writer identified by Martin Noth that this author ascribes short or long speeches to the heroes of the history at important moments of the narrative will warrant Nathan's oracle (2 Sam 7) an unconditional dtr tag as it looks both back and forth upon the history of Israel as a whole and upon the life of David in particular and predicts in so doing the building of the Temple by the successor to David's throne (Solomon) without mentioning the name of that successor.[327] But upon another level of consideration, Noth does not accord the passage a dtr authorship because it places the building of the temple in a negative light while the Dtr is generally in favour of the Temple and its building.[328] The question whether the oracle of Nathan puts the temple in a negative light cannot be answered with a simple "yes", given the fact that Solomon recalls the same oracle as the basis for the whole project of Temple-building (1 Kings 8:14-21). G. Von Rad considers the passage a pre-dtr text that probably dates back to the early monarchical period but which holds the key to the dtr theology of history.[329] Von Rad sees the real import of Nathan's oracle as the turning point in the history of Israel, where charismatic kingship gives way to the principle of a hereditary dynasty with Nathan's prophecy giving the assurance that the throne of David will endure forever.[330] The logical question that this assertion brings with it to the fore is; how does a non-dtr material become the

---

[327] Solomon's dedication speech, I Kings 8:14ff, a passage generally recognized as dtr, refers to this oracle as the basis for the whole project of building a Temple and the accomplishment of that project as the fulfilment of this oracle.
[328] Noth, *Überlieferungsgeschichtliche Studien*, p. 5.
[329] G. Von Rad, *Theologie des AT I*, p. 53f.
[330] G. von Rad, *The Problems of the Hexateuch*, p. 192–4.

medium through which "two" of the core elements of the dtr theology of history are expressed; the promise of Yahweh that a son of David would build the temple and that the Davidic dynasty would endure forever? If such a material is not dtr or predates this author, then the least we can say about it is that it either informs the dtr ideology or lies at the root of it. In both cases the two cannot be separated, hence later scholars do not consider the grounds of Noth enough justification for the passage to merit an unconditional non-dtr classification. This is not gainsaying the fact that Jerusalem as the city chosen by Yhwh as his "place of rest", the Temple as the appropriate *locus culti* and the dynasty of David as the Lord's own choice to last forever are the elements at the heart of the dtr theology and the basis upon which the whole ideology oscillates. These three themes or elements are intertwined in a chain of unity in which each one implies the others. It will, thus, be impossible for an author of such a high acumen to leave a chapter completely untouched in which a consternation of his great themes is set forth. The dtr author has certainly played a role in the final form of the text, as we have it in the Bible, to make the material present his favourite themes or even constitute the basis of them.[331] We will now take a bird's eye-view of some of the stances expressed about this chapter to see how they support or refute the position we have accorded it. In doing so we will not want to look at the totality of the rich mine of different ideas expressed about this chapter, but at a sample of representative positions; Frank More Cross for a dtr adoption and expansion of a traditional poetic material from different epochs; John Van Seters for a whole-sale ascription to the Dtr without reserve and P. K. McCarter Jnr, who sees the unity of the material in this narrative as the function of its dtr redaction. Thus, in one way or the other, a dtr hand is definitely at work in the narrative before us.

---

331 Leonhard Rost attempts to reconstruct the chapter by intimating that there might have been some old tradition ascribing what Solomon had carried out to a previous plan of David's. First, 7:1-4a was inserted and was followed by a direct revelation to David. A second step took place when this revelation was deleted and its content put into the mouth of Nathan who is to be thought of as the speaker. In the process the two revelations were moulded into a single unit, which indeed the catch-word "house" positively invited. Cf. *Succession*, p. 87.

Frank More Cross

Cross belongs to the group of researchers who are convinced that only historical reconstruction can yield a good picture of the David Narratives and this is also true of 2 Sam 7. In his work, "*Canaanite Myth and Hebrew Epic*", Cross seeks to establish the relationship between the promise of an eternal kingship to David and how David probably understood his own kingship to be. He notes a duality in the kingship of David in the sense that Judah is attached to him by a covenant of kingship (so 2 Sam 2:4 purports) and Israel by one in which he is designated nāgīd, commander of the twelve tribes in 2 Sam 5:1-3.[332] This consequently would suggest that David saw his kingship as a continuation of that of Saul, which did not depart in any significant way from the league of twelve tribes. It is clear, continues Cross, that David introduced a number of innovations into the setup of the league by choosing a neutral capital which he made the centre of cult, but even there "he chose Abiathar, a priest of the Mushite priesthood of Shiloh, to serve at his national shrine alongside Zadok, chief priest of the kingdom of Judah, once again knitting together the institutions of the league and his kingdom."[333] Hence, David's own conception of his kingship and the "Davidic Covenant" in its primitive, historical form was a slow process of innovation that stressed continuities between kingship and the constitutions of the covenant league. This mode of thinking, Cross opines, coupled with the conditional covenant of Ps 132, which certainly belonged to the early stages of the Jerusalem cultic liturgy, fits well within the context of the temporary state of the tent that David constructed to be the abode of the Ark of the Covenant. It fits not at all into the ideology of the dynastic Temple, the eternal dwelling of the deity, and the symbol of a permanent house or dynasty. This makes the notion that David intended to build a temple and the idea of divine adoption in 2 Sam 7:16-17 and Ps 89:20-38, which specify that under no condition will the house of David be thrown down, a misfit.[334]

If the idea of a temple building is a misfit at the time of David, then why did the prophet Nathan agree to the proposal in 7:3? Cross interprets

---

332   F. M. Cross, Canaanite Myth, p. 230.
333   F. M. Cross, *Canaanite Myth*, p. 232.
334   F. M. Cross, *Canaanite Myth*, p. 233.

Nathan's response to the king as a polite disagreement with the request and cites the examples of Micaiah's response to King Ahab in 1 Kings 22:15 and Jeremiah's to Zedekiah in Jer 28:5-11, where the meaning of the prophet's response was the direct contrary to what was said. The oracle of v. 5-7, Cross maintains, is meant to oppose the building of a temple permanently as the Ark was always associated with a tent shrine as in Shiloh. The formulaic pair 'ōhel/miškān is presumably an earlier poetic form of the oracle, designating the past shrine of the league in agreement with miškān/'ōhel of Psalm 78:60.[335] "The oracle of Nathan directed David not to violate the link between Tent and Ark of the league tradition. The historicity of the oracle of Nathan against the building of a Temple for the Ark is guaranteed by the evidence that David never built a temple. In effect, it testifies to David's acceptance of a limited kingship, which on other grounds appears to have been the case."[336] If David accepted a limited kingship and so did not build a temple, then how do we explain the juxtaposition of a prohibition of an action and a promise to fulfil the same act in a single breath? According to Cross; "The allusion to Nathan's oracle against a temple is only a minor element in the narrative, important chiefly to the modern historian who recognizes its anti-temple sentiment. All of this, vv. 1-7, is preliminary, as the new oracle formula in v. 8 shows."[337] The purpose and importance of the chapter come to light in what follows: vv. 8-11b review Yhwh's favour in raising David to kingship, 11b-16 focus on the *bêt David*, the dynasty of David which Yhwh will build. It is Yhwh himself who will establish the seed of David on the throne and this son will in turn build Yhwh's bêt. V. 14 proclaims the adoption of the king

---

335 J. Van Seters disagrees with Cross that the complimentary or contrastive word pairs that occur in these prose passages constitute any synonymous parallelism, which are the hallmark of Hebrew poetry. Cf. *historiography*, p. 272.
336 F. M. Cross, *Canaanite Myth*, p. 243. In any case Ps 132:2-5 records David's oath, which was to build a tent shrine or tabernacle for Jacob's champion; not a temple of cedar. Nonetheless, the final author does not leave the question as to why David did not build the temple for Yhwh open for speculations. He proffers excuses for David's inability to do so as (1) in accordance with Divine will and (2) on account of the many wars that surrounded him (2 Sam 7:13, 1 Kings 5:17).
337 F. M. Cross, *Canaanite Myth*, p. 246–247.

as a divine son and vv. 18-29, the prayer of David, are a dtr composition underlying the importance of the oracle, the promise of an eternal house to David. This prayer presumes and embraces the full composite text of the oracle which has bêt David as its central theme and is repeated seven times in vv. 11b, 16, 18, 19, 25, 27a,b.[338] "...David ...was promised a new kind of kingship and Israel granted a new form of hope. Actual history is telescoped in 2 Sam 7. While the promise was made to David, it is the house of David and the house of Yahweh that were bound together and promised eternity."[339]

The unity of 2 Sam 7 is the unity imposed on his sources by the mind and point of view of the dtr historian,[340] who has reworked the material at his disposal in such a way as to make it the cradle and carrier of his theological concepts. 2 Sam 7, intimates Cross, echoes the dtr theme of unconditional promise of the land in Moses' speech (Deut 1:8, 39) and Yhwh's address to Joshua (Jos 1:6) and the assertion of Yhwh to Joshua and Israel that he will never break his covenant with them (Jdg 2:1), re-echoed in Samuel's address; "For Yhwh will not forsake his people for his great name's sake." (1 Sam 12:22). All these find their natural culmination in the oracle to David vv. 13b-16. "The promise of the future thus is focused upon David, the servant of Yhwh, in a new and unique fashion in 2 Sam 7."[341]

The position of Cross may be summed up as follows; vv.1-7 are historical, reflecting the realities at the time of David. Vv. 8-17 are a dtr work bringing together a consternation of dtr themes that come before the chapter and might date from the time of Solomon. These two were preserved as poetry which the dtr has expanded in addition to vv. 18-29, which are a free composition of the dtr flowing from the composite text of the chapter.

---

338   F. M. Cross, *Canaanite Myth*, p. 247.
339   F. M. Cross, *Canaanite Myth*, p. 251.
340   F. M. Cross, *Canaanite Myth*, p. 252.
341   A favourite dtr minor theme and expression used repeatedly for Moses; "my servant Moses" (Jos 1:2, 7) or "servant of Yhwh" (Deut 34:5, Jos 1:1, 13, 22:2) and for Joshua; "servant of Yhwh (Jos 24:29, Judg 2:8) even as Yhwh often calls David; "my servant David" (2 Sam 3:18, 7:5, 8, 1 Kings 11:13, 32, 34, 36, 38, etc.).

John Van Seters

Van Seters takes a contrary view of Cross' method of identifying "poetry behind the prose reworking of the text and then (extracting) archaic elements (out) of the admittedly later work." This is because the method used by Cross is, in the view of Van Seters, arbitrary since the text of the chapter is prose and not poetry and "in no case does the text contain good synonymous parallelism, the hallmark of Hebrew poetry. The complementary or contrastive word pairs that occur in these passages are such a common feature of prose that they scarcely count as evidence of an original poetic source".[342] For Van Seters, 2 Sam 7 begins with the king having been given rest by Yhwh, his God, and proceeds to the king's expressed desire to build a temple for the deity. This mode of composing an account is very much in keeping with the widespread Near Eastern literary convention of first providing the annals of the king's wars and then his temple-building projects[343] and thus sets aside Noth's and Hermann's position of a *Königsnovelle* in the manner of the Egyptian tradition.[344] Van Seters identifies in vv. 4-17 a

---

342 J. Van Seters, *Historiography*, p. 272.
343 J. Van Seters, *Historiography*, p. 272. It must be noted that the account follows the capture of Jerusalem and the double defeat of the Philistines, even though that may have been just temporary (2 Sam 5) and the triumphant entry of the Ark into Jerusalem.
344 The *Königsnevelle* hypothesis has for a long time been appealed to as a Form Critical explanation to David's wish to build a temple to his God, beginning with Herrmann and Noth. The idea of the royal novelette was in principle to present a laudable plan of the Pharaoh, usually of building or renovating a temple, which has been carried through to its fulfilment. The formal element of the novelette was that the king sitting in state is divinely inspired to initiate the specific action. He reveals it to his high officials who praise the initiative based upon the wisdom of the Pharaoh as the physical apparition of the state deity, his father. The building project then is carried through to the glory of the Pharaoh. Critics of Herrmann's hypothesis argue rightly that the purpose of the royal novelette is not served in the case of David, which would have been to praise him for the accomplishment of a great feat. In fact it is the direct opposite that happens; the temple was not built by David. Besides, the role of Nathan within the story of David's expressed wish is at variance with the concept of a novelette because David seems to seek approval from Nathan. The dominant figure of Nathan as an intermediary between David and Yhwh drastically flaws the novelette by showing that David did not have a direct link to the divinity, a requirement for the Pharaoh, who was the son or the physical apparition of the deity.

report of a prophetic oracle of the type common in the redactional additions to the story of Saul and the dtr's presentation of the prophets in the books of Kings. These accounts generally begin with a question and are followed by a narration of God's dealings in the past with either the king or the people (Deut 31, 1 Sam 12). The current oracle does not conclude with a judgment but a promise (v. 10), making it an oracle of salvation in the manner of Jeremiah (1:10, 2:21, 18:9, 24:6, 31:28, 32:41, 42:10, 45:4). This, according to Van Seters, makes the reconstruction of an earlier oracle of Nathan out of vv. 4-7 with v. 8ff as a later addition by a redactor to give it a more positive character, as Frank More Cross would have it, untenable. Thus on the basis of form criticism, "the oracle as it stands with its affirmation of David's plan to build a temple, is a unity and the most original version of the account that we possess."[345] It is this affirmation or oracle of salvation that provides the ground for the prose hymn of vv. 18-29, hence the work of a single author. Van Seters explains the seemingly ambiguous question of v. 5 as a comparison of two different epochs of Israelite history; the time of temporary leadership under the judges when Yhwh's abode was transitory and the establishment of the monarchy (v. 8) with its subsequent subjugation of Israel's enemies (v. 9), so that Israel is fixed in its own place (v. 10), with God establishing a dynasty (a house) for her, so that the first member of that dynasty will build him "a house".[346] It is, therefore, not a rejection of temple-building as held by many like Cross.

The text is very consistent with its dtr origin, continues Van Seters, as seen in its repetition of basic dtr themes such as the election of Israel (thy people Israel) and the use of the term nāgīd to express the divine choice of a ruler over the people of Israel (1Sam 25:28-30, 2 Sam 5:2, 7:7). Above all, the chapter falls in line with the dtr scheme of dividing the history of Israel into three periods; the exodus and conquest, the age of the judges, and the rise of the monarchy. The dtr designation of David as "my servant David" parallels his use of the title "my servant Moses" and sets apart these two figures as the co-founders of the nation and marks off two important eras in Israel's history (Jos 1:2, 7, Deut 34:5, etc). The chapter, opines Van Seters, constitutes the centrepiece of a larger history, i.e. the

---

345 J. Van Seters, *Historiography*, p. 273.
346 J. Van Seters, *Historiography*, p. 274.

DtrH.[347] Since his main purpose was to prove the priority of the DtrH to the CH (court history) and to establish the relationship between the two, Van Seters finds it convenient to affirm that the chapter in its entirety is the work of the Dtr which the author of the CH uses to negate the legitimization of Solomon by citing it ironically in 1 Kings 1:35 with David as the subject of nāgīd instead of Yhwh and the establishment of the kingdom of David under Solomon only after the gruesome murder of Adonijah, Joab and Shimei and the expulsion of Abiathar.[348]

Van Seters does a great job in discovering the hand of the Dtr behind the unity of Nathan's oracle and its importance in the broad history, but his conclusion leaves much to be desired. He rather overlooks or even ignores the question of Nathan as a principal character in the unfolding of the central theme of the dtr theology. How did the author come by the name Nathan? Did he create the character arbitrarily or was he a part of his source material? Does the fact that the author does not find it necessary to introduce the prophet not imply that he was a household name, a well-known figure in the tradition, or was it to be construed as a spurious enigmatic character of a prophet that he had created and, therefore, did not vouch to give him an origin? Is he only a symbol? If so, why then does he make a figment of his imagination become the bearer and announcer of the core concept and ideology of his history? Could an author of his calibre have risked not being taken serious by his audience? In fact, the prophet Nathan can be viewed as the seam that knits together the different parts of the dtr theology of the election of David and his house, the choice of Solomon and the temple-building project.[349]

---

347 J. Van Seters, *Historiography*, p. 276–277.
348 J. Van Seters, *Historiography*, p. 288. Van Seters repeats this position in his contribution to *the Neue Einsichten und Anfragen zu Die sogenannte Thronfolgegeschichte Davids* (OBO 176, p. 81).
349 The importance of Nathan as an actor cannot be overstated in the tradition as far as the dynasty of David, the house of Yhwh and the existence of Israel as a nation are concerned. It is not for nothing that Solomon's anointing was to be carried out by Zadok the priest and Nathan the prophet. It would have been enough to choose one but the tradition allows the event to take place under the auspices of the two. Of course Van Seters might respond that it was part of the CHs mode of discrediting divine election that Solomon did not have, if that material can be attributed to the CH. I believe with the majority

P. K. McCarter Jnr.

After an elaborate discussion of the chapter, McCarter comes out with the conviction that, even though not all scholars agree that the unity of Nathan's oracle is a function of its dtr redaction, very few deny that the oracle occupies an important position in the larger dtr corpus. This fact, McCarter intimates, bears the implication that any discussion of the literary history of the oracle must logically begin with the assessment of its deuteronomistic character which in its turn demands answering the literal-critical questions of how extensively it was edited, the degree to which the editing was a factor in determining its present form and the purpose of the editor.[350] It is obvious that the two central issues of Nathan's oracle, temple and dynasty, are also central to the DtrH of Deuteronomy – 2 Kings. The prospect of a central sanctuary appears for the first time in Deut 12, linked to the day when Yhwh would give Israel *"rest"* (security from all her enemies) and that Israelites would begin to worship him only "at the place Yhwh will choose" (12:5, 11, 14). Until that time, everyone would do what seemed right to him (v. 8). Doing what is right in the eyes of the single individual, according to the dtr interpretation of history, runs through the tumultuous time of the judges (Judg 17:6, 21:25) and comes to be linked to the absence of a king in Israel (cf. also Judg 18:1, 19:1), until the promise of rest is achieved with the institution of kingship, namely, the kingship of David (2 Sam 7:1).

By presenting a catalogue of David's victories (2 Sam 8:1-14), directly after his prayer (7:18-29), the Dtr seems to suggest that through the efforts of David, the land will be pacified and the promised rest will be realized. Along with the achievement of rest, the central worship will begin at the place chosen by Yhwh to place his name and the temple will be built by the son of David (v. 13a) whose throne will be established forever by Yhwh (v. 13b). Thus when the promise of v. 13 is finally realized, the rightfully enthroned Davidic king in his peroration utters a benediction in reflection of

---

   that 1 Kings 1 is dtr and that the author has done everything possible to let Nathan be a part of the fulfilment of his prophecy and to enjoy the fruit of his labour with the enthronement of his protégé. If this character was imaginary, the dtr would have built a castle with cards which would have been blown away by the raging storm long before our time.
350 P. K. McCarter, *II Samuel*, p. 217.

Moses' ancient promise of "rest": *"Blessed be Yahweh, who has provided rest for his people Israel, just as he promised. Not one thing has failed to happen of all the good things he promised through his servant Moses"* (1 Kings 8:56).

To the question why David failed to build the temple, McCarter cites two dtr texts as the response that, without doubt, reflects the thoughts of that author. In 1 Kings 5:17-19, Solomon addresses the king of Tyre in a speech replete with deuteronomistic clichés explaining that the failure to build the temple was due to the many wars of David, the lack of peace at that epoch in the history and divine injunction that the son and successor of David would be the one to "build a house for my name". Now that there was no misfortune and the period of tumult had come to an end, Solomon intended to build the temple. David had prepared the ground for it by securing the confines of the land and now the work of building a temple could be executed. In the second instance, Solomon looks back to the days of his father in his dedication speech, which amounts to a dtr *midrash* on 2 Sam 7:1-17. He states that his father had it in his heart to build Yhwh a house. Yhwh approved of his intention but said he (David) would not be the one to build a house for his name. "Rather, your son, the issue of your own body, he will build the house for my name."[351] Hence there was an earlier refusal of temple building, emphasizes McCarter, but it was a temporary one, directed towards David because the time was not ripe. It was, however, approved for Solomon as the target of that vector of history.[352]

The very first appearance of the prophet Nathan, from the point of view of the Dtr, plays an important role in the history as a link between the turbulent period of the judges and the unstable years of Saul's rule on one hand, and the peaceful period of the blessed monarchy, which was the reign of David, on the other. Nathan's oracle belongs to the epic speeches of the DtrH which reflect upon the past and set the pace for the future.

---

351 P. K. McCarter, *II Samuel*, p. 219–220.
352 P. K. McCarter, *II Samuel*, p. 230 The Dtr author achieves the effect of the refusal and approval by the use of two pronouns in the emphatic position in 1 Kings 8:19 – *'attâ* and *hû'* - "Nevertheless, *you* will not build the house. Rather your son, the issue of your own body, *he* will build the house for my name." Thus the import is clearly the distinction between "you" (David) and "he" (David's son).

Just as Deut 31 prepares the ground for the conquest and distribution of the land, Jos 23 lays down a programme of life in the Promised Land and 1 Sam 12 inaugurates kingship, so also does the oracle of Nathan inaugurate the two dominant themes that will dictate the direction and pace of the history hereafter: Temple and Dynasty.

6.1.1 2 Sam 7; description and interpretation

As the different positions we have looked at indicate, the Nathan oracle plays such an important role in the overall history of the dtr writer that we will do this writer or group of historians a great deal of injustice if we fail to base our observations upon the text itself as a narrative piece or an episode; for it is only in doing so that we may be able to ascertain the fairness or otherwise of the different opinions held by the different schools of thought. In this work we will not analyse the chapter word for word, as commentaries abound which fulfil this purpose. We will rather choose particular aspects of the narrative that will enable us to locate the stamp of the Dtr and expound on the role that he assigns Nathan in the history and, if possible, the purpose for which the material is retained or composed by the dtr writer. We retain the traditional three-part structural division of the chapter in accordance with the Masora: vv. 1-3, which serves as an introduction to the whole chapter, 4-17, the dynastic promise and 18-29, the prayer of David.

Vv. 1-3 provide the introduction to the episode; the king is probably at home (in his cedar house – v. 2) and discloses to Nathan the prophet his future plans for the kingdom. The first verse is a very compact statement that contextualizes the entire account without leaving much room, if at all, for doubt about its dtr origin.

וַיְהִי כִּי־יָשַׁב הַמֶּלֶךְ בְּבֵיתוֹ וַיהוָה הֵנִיחַ־לוֹ מִסָּבִיב מִכָּל־אֹיְבָיו	Now, as the king sat (settled) in his house and Yhwh had given him rest from all his enemies around...

The narrative opens with the king sitting in his house as a worthy beginning of a historical narrative or even a legendary or mythological account of the past, in this sense, akin to the Egyptian Royal Novellette (as indicated by Hermann). In this particular context, the reference to the king sitting, settling or dwelling (ישׁב) in his house has more to express than just the act of sitting. The expression sums up the long and tortuous journey of David from Bethlehem to Gibeah through the towns and desert of Judah to Ziklag, as a war lord and fugitive, and back to Hebron, as the king of Judah, finally dwelling in his own house (palace) in Jerusalem as the "king of a united Israel". The saying entails also allusions to both the civil war between the house of Saul and David and the war of consolidation against the Jebusites and the Philistines of 2 Sam. 2-6. The verse bridges the history of David with the history of Israel by playing on the leitmotiv of the dtr *kerygma* placed upon the lips of Moses in Deut 12:10; *"When you cross over the Jordan and dwell in the land that Yhwh your God is giving to you and when he gives you rest from your enemies all around* (והניח לכם מכל־איבכם מסביב) *so that you live in safety..."* What is enjoined upon Israel once this rest is achieved is that she brings her offerings to the place where Yhwh will choose to place his name (v. 11); a cultic centre of the nation. This cultic centre could be achieved only when the Temple in Jerusalem is built as a historical fact. Consequently, the dtr author makes David preface his desire to build "a house" for the Lord with the Mosaic injunction expressed in a similar language but a different word order with David as the object instead of Israel; ויהוה הניח־לו מסביב מכל־איביו.[353] In this verse, the Dtr takes his readers back to the conquest of the land and introduces the key word of the next epoch in the history; בית as house of God (Temple) or a house for David (dynasty). It is my conviction that this verse is too deuteronomistic and programmatic not to have stemmed from that author and too apt a description of the composition of the dtr view of history. It is this author's introduction to the

---

353 Over the years scholars have noted the inconsistency or unrealistic position of the word "rest" in this verse. Because of the wars of 2 Sam. 6, "rest" will be a state too far removed from David at this point of the narrative. Above all, David is promised "rest" in v. 11, a fact which confirms the precarious nature of a state of rest in v. 1. The Chronicler seems to have noticed this inconsistency or his source did not have "rest" (Chr 17:1). While the word could have been a marginal note that found its way into the text at the wrong place (so McCarter, II Samuel, p. 191) the dtr author or school from whom the word possibly stems maintained it for a purpose. It could simply suggest that with the establishment of the king in Jerusalem and his temporary defeat of the Philistines the peace promised by Moses has been set in motion and will continue to its final realization.

material that he might have had before him. V. 2 tactically links the episode with the preceding chapter with its reference to the Ark of the Tabernacle of Yhwh that was housed in a tent in Jerusalem as a conclusion to the Ark narratives (6:17), while v. 3 returns to the leitmotiv of the story of David's rise, this time in the second person singular: כי יהוה עמך, "because Yhwh is with you". Nathan politely encourages the king to carry out his intentions because Yhwh is with him or because it was a laudable idea to build a temple to "the Rock of his Escape". The success of David is consistently ascribed to the fact that Yhwh was with him and it was Yhwh who granted him victory in everything he undertook. It is clear that the introduction to the oracle of Nathan is the handiwork of the Dtr who gives his hero the accolades that befit the image of a successful oriental monarch.[354]

Unlike the previous chapter which is a simple narrative, the narrative block of 7:1-29 is made up of a dialogue; David and Nathan (v. 1-3), two monologues; God and Nathan (4-16), and David at prayer (18-29). Remarkably, the author almost smuggles into the narrative the dialogue partner of David, Nathan, who is also the audience of Yhwh's monologue in vv. 4-16. Even though this character appears for the very first time in the narrative, he is not introduced in any way besides being given the tag of a prophet (הנביא) and he will not be introduced anywhere else. This lack of information on the prophet can only be understood as a possible indication that Nathan was such a normal sight at the court of David or that the name had been so well established in the tradition by the time it was adopted by the dtr redactor that an introduction was no longer required. On another level, the writer demonstrates his quality as a narrator by making David leave out the subject matter of the dialogue. David does not say that he will build a temple (בית) for Yahweh; neither does Nathan use the word in his acceptance. The reader is left free to come to the conclusion as an obviously logical one.[355] So it was logical to build a temple for the state deity once that deity had blessed his people with peace and tranquillity.

---

[354] The desire of David to build a temple, according to H. J. Stoebe, was natural; it has nothing so much to do with his legitimation as a natural course of events in the Ancient Near East. It was a symbol of wellbeing; stability and growth flowing from the blessing of the state god (cf. *Das Zweite Buch Samuelis*, p. 215).
[355] J. P. Fokkelman, *Throne and City*, p. 210.

The second part comprises vv. 4-17 and is the middle section of the narrative or the dynastic oracle. In relation to vv.1-3, which was an actual dialogue between David and Nathan, this part is a monologue by Yhwh addressed to Nathan in two parts; a short speech (5-7) and a longer one (8-16). The oracular or messenger formula of v. 5b, כה אמר יהוה (Thus says Yhwh) and its partial repetition in v. 8a allow the block to be divided into two, where vv. 4-7 constitute the temporary objection to temple-building and vv. 8-17, the promise of a house for David and Yhwh respectively. But the two parts take place in the same nocturnal vision with Yhwh as the initiator of the vision and Nathan its audience. Moreover, v. 5 finishes off with a question ("Are you the one to build me a house to live in?") that comes to be answered only in v.13a ("He shall build a house for my name...") to form a single unit.

The adversative *waw* (ויהי) at the beginning of v. 4 calls for a translational value of opposition, *but*, and makes it clear that Nathan's approval of the king's plan was not motivated by a divine fiat but by a personal good faith. In a move that directly reverses the formerly agreeable position of the prophet, the word of the Lord comes to Nathan that very night (בלילה ההוא) to be divulged to David, the servant of Yhwh; לך ואמרת אל־עבדי אל־דוד (*Go and say to my servant David*), a favourite dtr destination that, as we have seen before, puts David on the same pedestal as Moses. The message opens with a rhetorical question (v. 5c); הַאַתָּה תִּבְנֶה־לִּי בַיִת לְשִׁבְתִּי, (*Are you the one to build me a house to live in?*) The response is a clear negative as vv. 6-7 explain. Yhwh has never desired or requested a permanent abode from any of the "tribal leaders" of Israel since the Exodus from Egypt, besides a tent and a tabernacle.[356] Thus a quick narrative of the events from the exodus and conquest of the land to the reign of the Judges is given as the basis for the denial of temple-building to David before the actual epoch-making oracle of eternal dynasty and a permanent centre of cult. This quick run through the history does not make the denial any simpler, since it also glosses over the existence of a היכל יהוה – Yhwh's temple – in Shilo (1 Sam 1:9). Cross maintains that Yhwh's denial of the effort of

---

[356] שבטי ישראל in direct link to צותי לרעות את־עמי lends itself to be understood as tribal leaders whom the Lord chose or commanded to be shepherds of his people and therefore a reference to the days of the Judges.

David to build him a temple must have been firmly established in the tradition before the dtr author took it over and used it as the framework for the development of his basic themes with the historical fact that it was Solomon, and not David, who built the temple, as the proof for this position.[357] This was, however, not enough for the dtr author who resorts to different ways of defending David's inability to build the temple to his God (7:12-13, 1 Kings 5:15).

Lohfink notes in agreement with Cross that the virtue of David is at the background of Ps 132 (1-5) where the emphasis is placed upon the expressed desire or oath of David not to give sleep to his eyes until he had found a dwelling place for the Mighty One of Jacob. It is this virtue of David which forms the basis not only of Nathan's Oracle but also of Yhwh's consistent faithfulness towards Judah all through the history.[358] This position can be sustained in as far as the vow of David elicits another vow from Yhwh and justifies Yhwh's faithfulness to His own promise in an inner Biblical, inter-textual context without any resort to the date of the Psalm.[359] This vow notwithstanding, David did not build the temple

---

357 The fact that David intended to build a temple to his God at the beginning of his reign does not constitute a deviation from the norm nor a surprise element in the history. It was normal in the Ancient Near Eastern tradition that a successful king built a temple to his deity in recognition of the protection enjoyed and thanksgiving for the successes. Examples of such activities are not lacking in the ANET as in the case of the king of Mari, Yahdun-Lim, who built a temple to Shamash in Mari, named Egirzalanki ("the pride of heaven and the netherworld") after his successful campaign to the Mediterranean (ANET III, p 556). Even though it was seldom to have such a wish denied it is also not inconsistent with the historical texts. According to Michael Avioz, there are at least two examples of such denials affecting Zimri-lim and Naram-sin (cf. *Nathan's Oracle*, p. 19).

358 N. Lohfink, Studien IV, p. 26–27. The relationship between David's piety and Yhwh's faithfulness was so strongly established within the context of the oracle of Nathan that even if subsequent generations gambled with it, Yhwh would never abandon his faithfulness to David.

359 According to Hossfeld and Zenger Psalm 139 is post Deuteronomistic. Even though it refers to the Nathan oracle of 2 Sam 7, the Psalm has its digression in being conditional under the influence of the Priestly language and theology, and omitting the agency of the prophet Nathan. They could, however, imagine that before its inclusion in the Pilgrimage Psalms, it might have been

hence, as we have already noted, in 1 Kings 5:2-4, Solomon is made to give a plausible reason for David's inability to fulfil his own promise; because of the wars which his enemies surrounded him with. The explanation, without doubt, constitutes the dtr's effort to explain the fact that David was not the one who built the temple. The necessity of a later explanation of David's inability to build the temple goes a long way to indicate that the Dtr did not create the oracle of Nathan, it predates him and was so well fixed in the tradition that he could not edit it in any substantial way, hence the later expression of his own views.[360] Up to this point, we would say that the Dtr has made use of an existing material, the core of the oracle of Nathan, to prepare the scene for his main purpose; the promise of a dynasty and of temple-building.

Vv. 8-17 constitute the crux of the matter. The block is introduced by a double oracular formula as if God is quoting his own message; *"Now therefore, thus you shall say to my servant David: Thus says the Lord of Hosts"*. The reproduction of the two forms acquires a dynamic narrative beauty in the sense that while the first emphasizes the unique quality and identity of the receiver (my servant David), the second dwells upon the bearer of the message, the prophet Nathan, as a messenger of Yahweh and not the author of that message, in a typical prophetic mode of communication. He is told how to deliver the message by the very one who sends him (Yhwh Zebaoth). In vv. 8-9 the narrative flows vigorously with Yahweh narrating the personal history of David from his election to his kingly rule over Israel under the patronage of Yahweh himself, who has been with him (v. 9a). Yahweh is the author of the fortune of the shepherd boy who has now risen to the position of the king of Israel and it is only He who is capable of making him a great name like that of the great rulers of the

---

used in the Jerusalem temple liturgy. Cf. F. L. Hossfeld & E. Zenger, Psalmen 101-150, p. 617–8.

360 N. Lohfink, *Studien IV*, p. 28–29 Lohfink identifies vv. 1b, 11aß & 13a as the only additions that the Dtr1 made to the already extant oracle because it had been so fixed in the tradition that the author could just not afford to apply changes to it. Instead he produced his own versions of the oracle in three different places within the developing story; 1 Kings 2:4, 8:25 and 9:4-5.

earth (v. 9).[361] With v. 10, as also in v. 9c, the sense of the narrative changes from the past to the future;[362]

וְשַׂמְתִּי מָקוֹם לְעַמִּי לְיִשְׂרָאֵל	10a	I will fix a place for my people Israel
וּנְטַעְתִּיו וְשָׁכַן תַּחְתָּיו	b	I will plant them there and they will live there (beneath),
וְלֹא יִרְגַּז עוֹד	c	And will no longer go around
וְלֹא־יֹסִיפוּ בְנֵי־עַוְלָה לְעַנּוֹתוֹ כַּאֲשֶׁר בָּרִאשׁוֹנָה׃	d	Nor will evildoers afflict them any more like former days;
וּלְמִן־הַיּוֹם אֲשֶׁר צִוִּיתִי שֹׁפְטִים עַל־עַמִּי יִשְׂרָאֵל	11a	(and) from the days when I set up judges over my people Israel.
וַהֲנִיחֹתִי לְךָ מִכָּל־אֹיְבֶיךָ	b	And I will give you rest from all your enemies
וְהִגִּיד לְךָ יְהוָה כִּי־בַיִת יַעֲשֶׂה־לְּךָ יְהוָה׃	c	and Yhwh declares to you that it is Yhwh who will make you a house.

It is worthy of note that the promise that will follow has as its premise the fixing of a place for "my people Israel" (10a). The granting of rest to David is inextricably linked to the establishment of Israel as a nation and the protection of that nation against all her enemies who had disturbed her all through the period of the Judges (11a). Once that is done, David will

---

361 J. P. Fokkelman considers Yahweh's reaction an upsetting of our expectations in a radical manner by scrubbing David's hero status and quickly manifesting himself as the agent. The mortal who thought the initiative was his and adopted the stance of a sender by giving God a temple becomes the beneficiary and gains a certain degree of immortality through the reception of a lasting dynasty from God (*Throne and City*, p. 208).

362 Fokkelman presents linguistic data from Moses long speech in Deuteronomy and elsewhere in the MT to the effect that wqtl in speeches are mostly volitive or imperative or the continuation of such forms. Hence they are never perfect tenses but imperfect. Moreover, the wqtl-wqtl of 9b-c is the transition of a series of three preterit forms in the preamble (the past of David) to an exceptionally long series of wqtl forms in parts 7c-11b and 11c-13b (*Throne and City*, p. 225).

also be given rest from all his enemies (11b). This links up very well with the question that Yhwh asks in v. 7: "...*Did I ever speak a word to any of the judges (tribes) of Israel whom I commanded to pasture my people Israel saying; why have you not built me a house of cedar?*" In these verses, the dtr author, whose signature the text bears, draws our attention to the fact that the peace promised long ago (Deut 12), that eluded the Judges and Saul, will now be realised under David. At the same time the author links the fate of David to that of Israel; after all, the dynasty of David does not exist without the existence of Israel (cf. David as a paradigm of Israel in 12:1-15a). The bond of the two fates achieves on another level the unity of the text by referring to v.1b, the partial peace of David from his enemies, and giving it an extended meaning; peace for David as a king will not be achieved unless it is linked to the peace of Israel as a nation.[363] As a visible sign of this peace, Yahweh will make David a house (11c). Whether in reference to the temple or dynasty, the author plays on the word בית, but at the same time makes a difference in the choice of the verbs to accompany it. When it is in connection with the temple, the verb used is the normal one used in describing the action of building a house, בנה (v. 5c, 13a), but in relation to God building David a בית – dynasty – the verb used is עשה with the sense of doing or making. Thus Yahweh emphasizes his patronage of David by telling him; "You will not build me a temple (v. 5), rather I will make you a dynasty" (v. 11c). This declaration is the foundation of the great name that David acquires in the history. God steps out of the human terrain of physically "building" houses just as Hiram had done for David in 5:11; He will "make" David a house; he will establish his dynasty.

V. 12 expresses the full content of what Yhwh means by making David a house and constitutes, in all probability, the kernel of the oracle of Nathan:

> When your days are fulfilled and you dwell with your fathers, then I will raise your seed after you who shall come forth from your viscera, and I will establish

---

363 In his analysis of the dtr literature, N. Lohfink ascribes 2 Sam 7:1, 11aß to the Dtr as seams to connect the whole narrative (*Studien IV*, p. 28–9). In my view, the addition of the two verses does not only serve as seam but more importantly as the basis for the promise of a dynasty. The establishment of the dynasty of David was to serve as a custodian of the peace of Israel in her own land in fulfilment of the words of Moses in Deut 12:10.

his kingdom. ¹³He shall build a house for my name, and I will establish the throne of his kingdom forever.

Without doubt, vv. 12 & 13 hit the nail on the head and capture the central theme of the whole chapter. While Van Seters ascribes the chapter wholesale to the Dtr, Lohfink assumes that the author added 13a in addition to vv. 1 & 11aß in order to achieve the unity of the text.[364] The majority of critics, like T. Veijola, hold that the oracle was very well known before the Dtr writer incorporated it into his work.[365] This position makes a lot of sense because it is clear that the promise of the son of David inheriting him and moving on to build the temple is here a narrow one with an unnamed son of the king as the object. This kernel grows in the transmission of the tradition to become a dynastic promise that reflects the historical fact of the Davidic succession which the Dtr will gradually, but systematically, develop into the hope of the future Davidic king of a restored Israel. Yet the inconsistency between the oracle and its fulfilment in 1 Kings 1 causes the ears of its audience to tingle. According to the oracle, David ought to have gone to dwell with his fathers before the son of his loins, the future temple-builder, would sit upon his throne but Solomon was anointed king in David's lifetime. An author of the calibre of the Dtr would do everything possible to make the oracle conform to its fulfilment as he does elsewhere.[366] That he did not do the same thing in this episode points to the fact that the oracle was known as such and he had not taken liberties in altering it in any substantial way.

The rest of the passage is dedicated to the adoption of the king by the deity and the threat of punishing him if he went wayward (vv. 14-15),

---

364   N. Lohfink, *Studien IV*, p. 29.
365   T. Veijola, *Ewige Dynastie*, p. 73. In line with this trend of thought, Lohfink holds that vv1b, 11aß stem from the dtr redactor as seams to bind the narrative together. This same late writer or redactor also added v. 13a where the dynasty is bound to temple-building. The text was apparently well fixed and so well known in the tradition that the writer could not afford to make any further changes (cf. Studien IV, p. 28–29).
366   The additions of the same author to 2 Sam 12:7-15 were made to ensure that the oracle of Nathan conforms to its awaited fulfilment in the drama of David's family in 13-20. He could simply have done the same here if the tradition had allowed him that liberty.

possibly with the sin of Solomon as a background, and yet allowing the throne and kingdom of David to stand firm forever; *"Your house and your kingdom shall be confirmed forever before me, your throne shall be established forever."*[367] It is this promise that forms the centre of gravity to David's prayer of thanksgiving in vv. 18-29. The prayer is couched in a language that reflects the promise of a house to David (v. 18, 19, 25, 26, 27 and 29) in the broad context of Yahweh's choice of Israel (vv. 22-24).[368] Vv. 23-24 deal with the establishment of Israel as the people of Yahweh and reflect the future planting of Israel in her own place in vv. 9c-11b which in its turn goes back to the rejection of temple-building in vv. 5c-7c. In this way, the redactor of the material has successfully linked the thanksgiving prayer of David to its cause, the oracle, both thematically as well as in content.

My purpose for singling out this episode is to assess the role that the writer or in this sense, the Dtr, has assigned the character he calls Nathan the prophet in the broad history from the particular case to the general. In this first appearance the purpose has been the announcement of the dynasty of David that was to endure forever with its first successor building the temple for Yhwh. As much as the issues at stake are the two themes of Temple and Dynasty, the mode of communication, the messenger, is equally important. The author had a choice in the manner of presenting the message; some of the options that were open to him are inquiry or priestly consultation (as in 2 Sam 5:19), personal dreams (1 Kings 3:5-15) and prophetic vision (2 Sam 7:4). He chose the latter and a specific name attached to it, Nathan, even though he could also have chosen Gad

---

[367] J. P. Fokkelman links the appearance of the verb נאמן in this verse to 1 Sam 2:35, 3:20 and 25:28 to give the effect that just as a "trustworthy" priesthood is announced and pursued by God after the failure of the house of Eli with the appointment of a staunch prophet, Samuel, so also is a "trustworthy monarchy" appointed and recognized by God after the unsuccessful project of Saul.

[368] There is not much argument against the ascription of the prayer of David to the Dtr. Veijola, among others, notes that בית as dynasty runs through the prayer. V. 27 intimates that the courage of the man at prayer is because of the divine promise to build him a house; a reference to v. 11b and 16. This promise is then made more meaningful with the addition of 22-24 as a link to the fate of Israel by the redactor, the dtr (*Ewige Dynastie*, p. 74).

who is elsewhere designated as "David's seer" (1 Sam 22:5, 2 Sam 24:11). Nathan receives the message in a nocturnal vision and relays the message to David. What is more, this author makes his messenger appear not only once but three times in the life of a single monarch and all the three at very important moments of the king's life; at the beginning (7:1-17), at the height of his power (12:1-15a) and at the final days of his life (1 Kings 1). The oracle without such additions as the condition of v. 14 predates the Dtr and was, most probably, already connected to the prophet Nathan (vv. 8, 9, 10, 11, 12). The dtr did not have to create a fictitious character called Nathan to be the transmitter of the oracle. He has adopted both the message and the messenger. Judging from the time that this author may have put the narratives together, it may be logical to conclude that the kernel of the oracle of Nathan must have existed before the dtr writer, else it would not have made sense for that author to have done everything possible to defend the eternal dynasty of David at a time when that dynasty had practically ceased to exist. The probable span of time in which the oracle may have originated or at least become important would be either shortly after the death of Solomon, when the kingdom of Israel was split into the Northern and Southern kingdoms or around 722, when Judah still remained after the fall of Israel; Judah could still continue to exist only because of Yhwh's faithfulness to his promise. It may have been an appeal to unity around the Davidic king as a *conditio sine qua non* for the continuous existence of the nation. This might explain why v. 14 carries the threat of punishment for the erring king without losing the divine promise of an eternal dynasty, a fact that is missing in the parallel of 1 Chr 17:1-17.[369]

Could the promise of an eternal dynasty to David have existed in the tradition without Nathan's involvement? We think the answer is in the affirmative. The author of Psalm 89, a royal Psalm in which the post-Davidic Israelite king prays for deliverance from his enemies, seems to have had

---

[369] It will be an understatement to presume that the Chronicler had the same intention as the writer behind 2 Samuel 7 because in the former it stands clearly that the Davidic king was to sit upon the throne of Yhwh and rule over Yhwh's kingdom and answers the question of why the dynasty is accepted by Yhwh if he was opposed to the idea of kingship right from the beginning (1 Sam 12)? Cf. E. Aurelius, *Zukunft jenseits des Gerichts*, p. 216.

the promise from a different source that did not have Nathan as the messenger. The hymn introduces "a messianic oracle (vv. 20-38) that sharply contrasts with the king's defeat and humiliation set forth in vv. 36-46."[370] He, therefore, prays for deliverance with recourse to the promise made by Yhwh to his servant David as we know from our text, but with the variation that Yhwh spoke in a vision to his pious or devoted one, namely David (v. 20). Ahlstöm pleads for the independent existence of the tradition behind Ps 89 and therefore against the priority of the Nathan oracle (2 Sam 7)[371] but Hossfeld and Zenger see in Ps 89:36-38 a secondary text to the Psalm that functions as a commentary on the dynastic promise of 2 Sam 7:1-17 and an obvious dependence of the psalm upon the oracle of Nathan.[372] If one takes the line of thought of Ahlström, one would say that the dtr author could very well have had the two traditions before him but exercised his right of choice for one and not the other or, in line with Hossfeld and Zenger, he may have stuck to the prophetic tradition which provided him with the instrument of this all-important promise. The presence of the prophet in the tradition offered him the opportunity of a veritable link to the appearance of the same prophet in 1 Kings 1. In this way, the dtr author is making use of a phenomenon that comes to the fore and proliferates itself in Israel in the time of kingship until the exile; Prophecy as an institution. Before this time, Yhwh had communicated basically on the personal level with the patriarchs (except Joseph), Moses, Joshua and the Judges (through the *mal'ak*) with the exception of Deborah who was addressed as אשה נביאה - prophetess. With the attainment of statehood, God speaks no longer directly to the monarch nor through dreams (except Solomon, 1 Kings 3:5 & 9:2) nor Urim and Thumim but He sends prophets as messengers.[373]

---

370 M. Dahood, *Psalms II*, p. 311.
371 G. W. Ahlström, *Psalm 89*, pp. 182f. Ahlström opposes any attempt to consider Ps 89:20 a repetition or reformulation of Nathan's prophecy in 2 Sam 7:8f and therefore a priority of the prophecy over the Psalm. Instead he posits that the text could have had either a north Canaanite or a Jebusite liturgical origin since similar oracles existed in most Canaanite state temples. Cf. also J. H. Eaton, *Kingship and the Psalms*, pp. 121–122.
372 F. L. Hossfeld & E. Zenger, Psalmen 51-100, p. 582–583.
373 C. Westermann, *Grundformen*, p. 71.

Thomas Römer argues that vv. 1-17 echo a seventh century text which was reworked and extended by the Dtr.[374] This would imply that there was such an encounter as the one between Nathan and David over the temple-building wish of the king which the dtr has expounded to make it bear the mark of his traits. Veijola subscribes to the notion of two older sources that have been fused together by a redactor; v. 1a, 2-7 and 8-17 (without 11, 13 & 16) but assumes that the promise of a dynasty was originally a narrow oracular kernel referring to Solomon (v. 13a) which a late dtr redactor has broadened to include the whole house of David by the addition of v. 11b, 13 & 16 with the word-play on the double meaning of בית as the bridge that joins the two parts together.[375] Dennis McCarthy broadens Martin Noth's identification of the dtr hallmark of long or short speeches of the major characters or editorial comments of the author that sum up the history and project it into the future with the literary tools and compositional techniques of the dtr that make 2 Sam 7 a central text of the DtrG. He has produced the most thorough work that picks out dtr strands which purport that in David, and especially in this oracle, the "ultimate blessing" promised by Yhwh long before is realised.[376]

Lohfink states with very good reasons that the Nathan oracle regulates the whole trend of the dtr history. The promise of a never lacking lamb (ניר) for David is what justifies the continuous existence of Jerusalem and consistently keeps the Davidic dynasty going despite the unfaithfulness of the kings and their unworthiness to the extent of saving the city and the dynasty even when their fates seemed to be a forgone conclusion as the reigns of Joram (2 Kings 8:19) and Manasseh (2 Kings 21:9) clearly indicate.[377] The first appearance of Nathan serves as a prolepsis for the

---

374 T. Römer, *Historiography*, 67-77.
375 T. Veijola, *Ewige Dynastie*, p. 73–74.
376 D. McCarthy, *II Samuel 7*, pp. 132–137.
377 N. Lohfink, *Studien IV*, pp. 12–32. In his quest for the oracle that gave the dynasty of David its stability ("*Dauer*"), Lohfink begins his work with the dtr judgment formula that condemns Joram in such hard terms that the downfall of Judah appeared imminent in the eyes of the reader. "However, the Lord refrained from destroying Judah, for the sake of His servant David, in accordance with his promise to maintain a lamp for his descendants for all time" (2 Kings 8:19). This oracle, according to Lohfink, must have originated

story of Jerusalem and its kings, in particular, the history of Israel as an established nation, in general, and in fact for the unfolding of the DtrH from the reign of David to the fall of Jerusalem and beyond. Once the epic-making events of dynasty and temple-building have been announced, what remains is how this prophecy is going to be fulfilled. In the process, the Dtr presents his readers with a messenger who identifies himself or is identified with the message he carries, the prophet Nathan. It appears to us that the first oracle of the prophet dictates the trend of his own life (7:1-17). He is so completely dedicated to the cause and its development that all the two other contacts he subsequently has with the king are played out against the background of the dynasty's future. His confrontation of David after the Uriah affair was to set the records straight by initiating the repentance of the king in order to save the dynasty from self-destruction (12:1-15a) and he does not shy away from taking positive political steps to see to the installation of the son of David, whom he "believes" in all probability to be the chosen one of Yhwh (1 Kings 1). Thus neither the parable of Nathan and its resultant oracle of doom (12:1-15a) nor the zealous promotion of Solomon as successor to David (1 Kings 1) can be viewed outside the context of the oracle of Nathan (2 Sam 7:1-17).

In the work of the Dtr, Nathan emerges as a significant actor in the unfolding drama, who concretizes the dynastic promise that the Dtr has

---

at the time of Solomon since it had already served its purpose by the time of his death. If it is restated in the 6th century then it must have existed before the redactor who organized the materials, i.e. Dtr1 or DtrG. Conversely, if the Nathan oracle did not exist before, there is no way the Dtr1 would have referred so many times and solidly to it in Samuel – Kings (p. 30; Dynasty: 1 Kg 2:15, 24, 3:6f, 8:20; Temple: 5:19, 6:12, 8:16-21, 24). With the sin of Solomon and his death Nathan's oracle had seen its fulfilment and the Dtr1 does not refer any more directly to it. It is reframed in the Ahijah prophecy of 1 Kings 11:38, where Jeroboam receives an everlasting kingdom in the same way as David hence as successor to David's throne and had to obey the commandments as David had done. The house of David would, however, maintain Judah and Jerusalem. It could well be said that this is a second Nathan oracle and invariably, like Solomon, Jeroboam will even more quickly gamble with his choice and become the symbol of sin. It is only at the time of Josiah that the promise finally is set on its course towards its realization as he did not turn left nor right from the way of his father David, 2 Kings 22:2.

craftily made Abigail hint upon in a harmless manner (1 Sam 25:28-31) and proceeds to develop it into the core elements of the author's theology; eternal dynasty and eternal house of Yhwh in the eternal city of Jerusalem. Given that Nathan was already part of the tradition, the author has enhanced the image of the prophet to suit the role that he assigns him. We will vouch to say that even his initial endorsement of the king's desire to build a temple for the Lord and his later retracting upon the word of Yhwh are in consonance with the proper role of an enigmatic character that the writer assigns him; a fervent courtier with a keen political acumen and a faithful prophet of Yhwh, who does not hesitate to change his personal position for the primacy of the divine will.[378] This kind of behaviour from a prophet is in any case not strange in the DtrH. It is the same writer who reported the error of Samuel in rushing to the conclusion that Yahweh had chosen Eliab and was rebuked for it because the Lord had not chosen him (1 Sam 16:6-7) who now exacts an agreement from Nathan only to be turned down by a nocturnal oracle from Yahweh. Unlike Samuel who was rebuked for his presumption of divine choice, Nathan does not presume to speak the mind of God so that Yhwh is not hard on him let alone reprove him. He simply takes him into his service and sends him to David. The narrator thus subtly and purposefully increases Nathan's prestige as a prophet and instrument of the message of hope.[379] With this unique and even elusive character that he effectively calls הנביא – the prophet, the Dtr makes Nathan set the story rolling by the announcement of the epoch-making elements of Dynasty and Temple under the auspices of a Father-Son relationship between the deity, Yhwh, and the monarch, the Davidic lineage of kings, in a bond of unity that was supposed to last for ever. It

---

378 Wolfgang Oswald sees these two roles as conflicting and notes that the historical Nathan could have been one of the two but not the two at the same time; in which case one of the roles will describe the historical Nathan and the other will be a secondary development in the text (p. 251). In the long run, however, Oswald remains with the conviction that Nathan is very far removed from everything that historical plausibility can make him (*Der Prophet Nathan*, p. 258); he is unique in his appearances and exclusive or even elusive in his roles; the only prophet who belonged to the inner circle of the king.
379 J. P. Fokkelman, *Throne and City*, p. 212.

must be noted at this point that prophets in Samuel – Kings wielded an enormous degree of power which they exercised, albeit in silence or, we dare say, in secret.[380] It is not for nothing that all the three encounters of Nathan with the king took place either solely between the two or in the case of 1 Kings 1, in corroboration with Bathsheba, in the presence of Abishag in the king's chamber.

The oracle of Nathan does not have to be a creation of the dtr author. It could very well have been a natural conclusion to the Ark Narrative, given that the tent was a temporary and not a permanent abode of Yhwh. David may have made known his intention to build a final resting place befitting the deity of an emerging nation for the Ark of the Covenant; a feat that was conventional in the Ancient Near East. Since it was the order of the day for great kings to build temples to their gods it would have been a normal expectation from David to have accomplished this feat but he did not. To complicate issues, David is the first ruler of Israel to have achieved relative peace and was promised an eternal dynasty by Yhwh. The attainment of peace in the theological thought of Israel gives rise to the building of the temple, at least in a dtr view of history (Deut 12) and the promise of a dynasty was closely associated with the building of a temple in the Ancient Near east. Why then did David fail to build Yhwh a temple?[381] It is in this light that the prohibition of the temple-building to David and its approval for Solomon in the same narrative finds justification. The time

---

380 The king-maker, Samuel carried out the anointing of Saul on the blind side even of Saul's companion or servant (1 Sam 9:27-10:1) and that of David before the "restricted" group of the elders of Bethlehem and the family of Jesse. The promise of the ten tribes to Jeroboam by Ahijah was done secretly between the prophet and the candidate along the road (1 Kings 11:29-39) in the same way as Jehu's would be carried out secretly by the prophetic messenger (2 Kings 9:1-13).

381 There was a widely understood association between temple-building and the hope of divine sanction of the continuing rule of a particular monarch and his lineage in the Ancient world, as royal annals and building inscriptions of Ancient Near Eastern Texts have shown. The common denominator was simply permanence; the perpetuity of the reign of a particular monarch and the durability of the shrine that he builds for his deity. Thus the correlation of Temple and dynasty was not unique to Israelite thought, let alone dtr innovation. Cf. P. K. McCarter, *II Samuel*, p. 224.

was not rife for the building of a temple during the reign of David; he was too preoccupied with securing the confines of the nation to have had the luxury of embarking on such a pompous project.

The source behind this material, according P. K. McCarter, is a pre-deuteronomistic prophetic history of the early monarchy.[382] The material is then adapted by the Dtr on the basis of the known facts of the political and religious life of Israel as a nation from the ninth century to the exile. This author, who compiled his work about the sixth century, was aware that the successor of David, Solomon, built the Temple, the imposing symbol of Jerusalem that centralized the worship of Yhwh in that city. With such a source material at his disposal, all that the dtr redactor had to do was to add the final trimmings to fit it into the broad history; the granting of rest by Yhwh to Israel and David, and the building of a house for David and for Yhwh in the context of an eternal dynasty to be exercised by the sons of David; hence a legitimization or divine approval of the Davidic dynasty with Nathan as the instrument and mouth-piece of the deity. Wolfgang Oswald is of the view that it was perhaps very important for the 6th century author to emphasize the fact that David did not build the Temple even though he was blessed with the promise of an eternal dynasty. In the period of the Babylonian exile, when the Temple had been destroyed, it may have been necessary to dissociate the three great elements of Israelite theological thought; Temple, dynasty and city, since the association of these three elements could otherwise have been used as a counter argument to the expectation of a Davidic king to continue the eternal dynasty. Thus the lesson in this argument may have been that if David was promised an eternal dynasty before the building of the temple to Yhwh in Jerusalem, then that promise did not depend upon the temple and would be fulfilled independently of it.[383] The promise was in no doubt made before the building of the Temple and David was not the builder, but the hope of the future Messiah is hardly ever dissociated from a reference to (the New) Jerusalem or Zion - the mountain of the Lord (Isaia 2:1-4, 4:2-6, 9:5-6, 11, 62:1-3, Eze 40-44, 48:21-23, 35-40). It is only the "heavenly Jerusalem" that categorically has no Temple, sun or moon, because the Lord God himself is its Temple and the Lamb its light

---

382 P. K. McCarter, *II Samuel*, p. 223.
383 W. Oswald, *Nathan der Prophet*, p. 234.

(Rev 21:22). The importance of the link between Temple and dynasty in the political theology of Israel is in no way to be underrated and the messenger who brings them together in an oracle is the prophet Nathan. It is the same prophet whom Yhwh once again employs as the messenger of doom in order to bring the erring king to repentance and subsequently pronounce divine forgiveness and salvation upon the house of David.

6.2 2 Sam 12

The oracle of Nathan (2 Sam 7:1-17) opens a new horizon in the narrative by arousing the curiosity of the reader and gearing it towards its fulfilment; who would this son of David's loins be and how was he going to build the Temple of Yahweh and, above all, how was this eternal dynasty within a nation that lacked the tradition of a dynastic rule and in an era of bellicose neighbours eager to wrestle power from one another possible? The victory of David over the surrounding nations (8:1-10:19) quickly sets in motion the fulfilment of the oracle of Nathan, from the point of view of appointing a place for Israel and planting her firmly there without her enemies disturbing her any more (7:10), but that process has only a very slender neck that breaks under the joke of David's adultery with Bathsheba, the wife of Urijah. The double oracle of salvation (7:5-7, 8-17) that Nathan receives in favour of David and his house has its flip-side in the double oracle of doom (12:7-10, 11-12) that the same Nathan delivers to David as God's reaction to the king's double crime of adultery and murder before his final reprieve (12:13c-14). This intervention of punishment and pardon can better be appreciated with the oracle of salvation as a background. It is the unity of these two episodes that will give meaning to the events of 1 Kings 1, where Nathan plunges himself into practical and pragmatic politics to safeguard the throne for the "beloved of God". The בית that has played such a marvellous role in the climax of David's rise to power as house, dynasty and temple now becomes the very place from where the anti-climax begins (11:2) and the עד־עולם (forever) which triumphantly marks the extent of God's positive choice of this dynasty turns against the בית־דוד (house of David) which from now on will be visited by the sword עד־עולם.[384]

---

384 J. P. Fokkelman, *Throne and City*, p. 267–268.

As the episode of Nathan's second encounter with David is the main theme around which this whole work oscillates, we will no longer need to go into a detailed discussion of the encounter from the various methodological points of view, as this has already been taken care of in the second chapter. We will instead proceed to look at how the dtr author develops the stature of Nathan in the context of the promise of a dynasty and temple-building and the fulfilment of these two promises in narrative time mirrored against the character of a fiery prophet of Yhwh spewing fire and brimstone upon the very house that he would do everything in his power to protect. Before then, however, a glance at the major views on the parable of Nathan will facilitate our discussion.

Leonhard Rost, the literal critic, saw the fulfilment of Nathan's oracle in the birth and succession of Solomon to the throne of David. This direction permits his rejection of the oracle of doom (v. 7b-12) as long-winded and unnecessary; the result of a later addition by a redactor.[385] This redactor we have identified as none other than the Dtr or the Dtr School. John Van Seters takes a completely different view of the matter. For him 2 Sam 12 is the work of the same author of the David-Bathsheba episode and no amount of fiddling can make it a later addition or the work of a redactor. Nathan's intervention puts David on the same level as the other kings like Saul and Ahab, condemned by the Dtr for doing *"what was evil in the eyes of the Lord"*.[386] It is part of what he calls CH, a late exilic work that attacks the notion of an ideal king and an eternal dynasty of a messianic dimension, which has been inserted into the DtrH. Naumann proposes a practical and fair view of the parable of Nathan. In his view, the events of chapters 11-12 paint a picture of the two sides of the same coin; the mighty king without scruple and the humble man who bows down to the prophetic reproach. This emphasizes not only the ideal of the sinner who repents from his sins but also raises the prophetic function unto a high pedestal.[387] This leads the reader on to the high point of the presentation of the two main actors in the episodes; prophet and king, and prepares the scene for the entry of the successor to the throne. The oracle of Nathan

---

385 L. Rost, *Succession*, p. 77.
386 J. Van Seters, *Court History*, p. 73.
387 T. Naumann, *Exemplarischer König*, p. 166.

as well as the punishment of David smack of a dtr reformulation, posits Naumann, almost in affirmation of the position of Rost that holds that chapters 10-12 constitute the background of the successor to the throne of David; the parable of Nathan and its fulfilment end the adultery and its curse and pave the way for the birth of Solomon.[388]

6.2.1 2 Sam 12; description and interpretation

The oracle of Nathan (7:1-17) raised the narrative unto a new dimension with the reader looking out for its fulfilment pepped up by David's acts of statesmanship, both on the internal as well as the external spheres (2 Sam 8-10). On the level of internal politics, David settles the issue of possible rival claimants to his throne by domesticating the last surviving member of the Sauline lineage: he brings Mephiboshet to his court under the auspices of showing him *hessed* (kindness, or good faith) on account of his promise to Jonathan (9:1-13). On the external level, the victories chalked against the neighbouring nations initiate the final stage of the long journey towards peace. The Ammonites and Arameans, Israel's eastern and northern neighbours respectively, practically offer David the springboard from which to jump upon them in the final war of aggrandisement (10:1-11:1, 12:26-31). With these two events, David proves himself to be a just king, a victor ready to *"set Israel firm in its place"* (7:10), to open the way for the fulfilment of the eternal dynasty and the building of the temple. It is unfortunately at this very moment, when everything seems to move in the right direction that the unexpected happens; David takes advantage of Uriah's absence from home; he commits adultery with the wife of the military officer and schemes to have the innocent soldier killed in the battle for Rabbah (11:2-27). This obvious anti-climax in the story line creates a tension in the reader who expects a kind of reaction. The shameful conduct is unacceptable of David, whether as king or leader or even an ordinary man, let alone as the celebrated "servant of Yhwh" and bearer of the promise of an eternal dynasty. The tension is further heightened by the fact that neither the narrator nor the actors in the episode who are privy to the events express their opinions about the situation, leaving too many moral and

---

388 T. Naumann, *Exemplarischer König*, p. 164 and L. Rost, *Succession*, p. 80.

ethical questions closed or at least ignored. The story, however, ends on an ominous note "*...but the thing that David had done was evil in the eyes of Yhwh*" (11:27b). At last the reader can take in a quick breath in the hope that Yhwh himself is going to take the initiative to rectify the evil done to the poor man. The author then proceeds towards breaking the dead-lock by means of no other agent than the prophet of salvation, Nathan, who now enters the scene with the contrary mission of the prophet of doom.

Commentators find it easier to read 11:27b with 12:1 as a logical sequence to the narrative. In fact, removing the half verse (11:27b) from the rest of the chapter and reading it together with 12:1 leaves the narration of David's adultery and murder without any form of comment and would seem to suggest that it was the way kings behaved at that time, and therefore very normal.[389] We must, however, keep in mind that chapter divisions in the Bible belong to a later Christian tradition of facilitating the reading and citing of texts.[390] The Masora presents it in a different way; the theological comment stands at the end of the double crime of adultery and murder (11:27b) to induce the positive feeling in the audience that all is not lost, there is a power over and above that of the king who has taken notice of the events. If the text is read without chapter divisions, as the MT has it, the sending of a messenger by Yhwh, who has observed the actions and inactions of men and now enters into the history to offer a solution, takes

---

389 Both P. K. McCarter (AB) and A. A. Anderson (WBC) read the half verse of 11:27b with 12:1 but for different reasons. For McCarter, 11:2-12:25 is the work of a prophetic writer who inserted the David-Bathsheba-Uriah-Nathan sequence into an archival frame and set the finished composition in front of the story of Absalom's rebellion, which it serves as an interpretative preface (p. 306). Anderson, on his part places the encounter in the context of the SN, which stems from the time of Solomon as a legitimization of his reign and therefore serves the purpose of exonerating Absalom from the sins of David. Even though the adultery and murder could not be denied the repentance of David and his forgiveness and punishment frees the dynasty from the effects of David's sin (p. 160).

390 The work of facilitating the reading of the Bible was begun in the thirteenth century by Cardinal Langton, Bishop of Canterbury, who developed a system of dividing the biblical texts into books with chapters. This work was perfected by Robert Estienne between 1546-1551 in his printing presses located in Paris and Geneva.

the bull by the horn. The reader is not disillusioned at the end of "10-11", he is hopeful that Yhwh will act in an appropriate manner to rectify the situation. This is positively in accord with the whole message of the dtr author who goes to every length to assure his readers that Yhwh will, at the appropriate time, intervene in the fortune of his people.

The author gives his audience no clue as to what Nathan is supposed to tell David. He creates the situation where the actor knows more than the audience, the reverse of 1 Kings 1, where the reader is privy to the plan of Nathan and Bathsheba and knows exactly what they are going to say to the king, who is effectively kept in the dark. The expected ignorance of the audience creates a surprise element in the narrative when Nathan begins the discourse with a parable (vv. 1-4) that we have identified with Uriel Simmons as judgment-invoking and, logically, a Juridical Parable. In addition to this, the prophet does not declare from the beginning the main purpose of his visit. This puts David on the same level as the reader as both are kept in the dark and hence the reaction of David is paradigmatic to that of the reader in every generation. It is only when David pronounces the expected judgment that the prophet proclaims the word of the Lord. The attitude of the prophet in this episode is completely in line with the status that the dtr writer has accorded him. As in 7:2, his presence does not cause eyebrows to tingle, he belongs in the household and he engages the king in a discussion as a person with the right to making his point before the monarch. The difference in this instance is that, unlike in chapter seven, where the king asks his opinion, here it is the prophet who initiates the discussion. He narrates the parable, awaits the king's response and pronounces the oracle of doom that Yhwh has put in his mouth (12:7-14). The apparently natural and harmless nature of the parable effectively brings David's good nature to the fore enabling him to view the case from the perspective of his role as a judge. He consequently judges the rich man in emotionally exaggerated terms completely unexpected in a case of theft and with that judgment condemns himself (vv. 5-6) in a manner that greatly facilitates the mission of Nathan. David has fallen into the carefully-set trap and all that Nathan has to do is to close in upon him with his famous declaration; "*You are the man*" (v. 7b). Once the trap springs shut, Nathan does not give the king any time to reflect upon the implications of this self-accusation and judgment. He quickly proceeds with the preamble of what Yhwh has "given"

David, who is the receiver of Yhwh's giving, and the spite of Yhwh in David's "taking and killing" (vv. 7c-12).

The content of the preamble is an accurate and precise recapitulation of David's life story from his election and anointing to his establishment in Jerusalem as the king of both Israel and Judah in twenty-five carefully selected words (vv. 7d-8). The anointing logically precedes the salvation from the hand of Saul (v. 7) because for the Dtr and the reader of the narrative of David's rise to power, it is the prophetic anointing by Samuel (1 Sam 16) that legitimizes David as king and not so much the later double anointing of 2 Sam 2:4 by the people of Judah and 5:3 by the elders of Israel. In his generosity or in his capacity as the one who gives to David, Yhwh has given him three things in sequence; the house of his master, his master's wives, the house of Israel and of Judah (v. 8)[391], and if these were not enough, he would have added כהנה וכהנה (as much more). In snatching the wife of Uriah, David demonstrates an attitude of utter ungratefulness to his generous "Giver" by playing the greedy "Taker" instead of remaining the humble recipient of divine benevolence. This makes the sin of David, first and foremost, a violation (spite) of the good faith that exists between him and his God (v. 9). The theological sense of the sin is reported in the favourite dtr cliché and judgment formula (*Gerichtwort*) for all the kings of Israel and Judah preceded by a question and then the list of his evil deeds:

Why have you despised the word of the Lord to do what is evil in his sight?	9a	מַדּוּעַ בָּזִיתָ ׀ אֶת־דְּבַר יְהוָה לַעֲשׂוֹת הָרַע בְּעֵינַו
Uriah the Hittite you have killed with the sword	b	אֵת אוּרִיָּה הַחִתִּי הִכִּיתָ בַחֶרֶב
and his wife you have taken to be your wife	c	וְאֶת־אִשְׁתּוֹ לָקַחְתָּ לְּךָ לְאִשָּׁה
but him you have struck (killed) with the sword of the Ammonites (the sons of Ammon).	d	וְאֹתוֹ הָרַגְתָּ בְּחֶרֶב בְּנֵי עַמּוֹן׃

---

391 We are reading בית ישראל ויהדה (the house of Israel and Judah) as the totality of the nation which comprises Israel and Judah and not as two separate entities at different times. As regards the daughters and wives of Saul, we have dealt with the open questions that the assertion raises in the textual analysis and will not like to go back to them to create any form of unnecessary repetitions here.

By the fact of the sin itself, David has despised his God for doing what is evil in his sight (a) like the later kings of Israel and Judah, which will justify the calamity that will befall the nation. The narrator then catalogues the sins of David in three short phrases; you have killed Uriah with the sword (b) and have taken his wife to be your wife (c) but him you have struck down with the sword of the Ammonites (d). On one hand, "d" can be considered a repetition of "b" where detailed information comes to be added to the previous assertion.[392] In this sense, "d" specifies the death as coming from the hands of the sons of Ammon, who were actually responsible for carrying out the act that had been insinuated by David with the help of Joab. Thus "b" and "c" put the guilt of David in sequence; you have killed and you have taken, since the marriage takes place only after the death of Uriah.[393]

The punishment for the sins of David can be seen as simple logic or a chiastic construction. In the first instance (b-c), the sword will not depart from the house of David because he has *killed* (v.10) and his wives will be taken openly by his neighbour (v.11) because he has *taken* the wife of Uriah to be his wife. In the second variant (c-d) David has *taken* and has killed with the *sword* and so will the *sword* not depart from his house and his wives will also be *taken*.

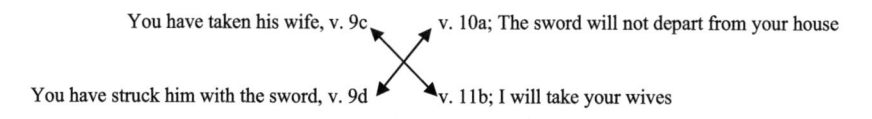

You have taken his wife, v. 9c   v. 10a; The sword will not depart from your house

You have struck him with the sword, v. 9d   v. 11b; I will take your wives

The sword will be punished by the sword but a violator will openly encroach upon the harem of David in a manner that is graphically described

---

392 According to 11:24, Uriah was most probably shot down by an archer, which will make the cause of his death not by the sword but by an arrow. Nevertheless, the sword is generally used in biblical sense as the instrument of death in wars.

393 J. P. Fokkelman subscribes to the first variant (b-c) which puts the most grievous of the crimes first but prefers to read v. 10a together with v. 9 and 10b-12 against the Masoretic verse division. In his opinion, it is misleading for the second "you have despised" of v. 10a and the second "you have taken the woman" of v. 10c to be joined to the punishment of v. 10a since this severely disturbs the structure of the oracles (cf. *King David*, p. 83).

219

in the text; Yhwh will raise up trouble against David from his own house for his "neighbour" will lie with his wives in the sight of "this very sun" (11), before all Israel (12b) and before "the sun" (12c). The only thing that fails in this vivid description of the events of 16:20-22 is the name of the violator of the wives (concubines) of David. This goes a long way to suggest that the narrator knew of Absalom's revolt without making the oracle in any way "secondary". The Dtr certainly had before him the various traditions and has composed the oracle in such a way that it responds to the subsequent events.

A comparison of the *oracle of Nathan* (2 Sam 7:5-17) and the corresponding *oracle of doom* (2 Sam 12:7-12) shows remarkable parallels or similarities that strongly suggest their possible common source. We will look at these similarities under the following guidelines: a. (rhetorical) question, b. Yhwh's past actions, c. Yhwh's future actions, and d. David's pious response.

a. The oracle of Nathan begins with the rhetorical question of 7:5c; *"Are you the one to build me a house to live in?"* The *raison d'être* of the whole encounter is hidden behind this simple device. David's desire to build Yhwh a house occasions the promise of an eternal dynasty. In 12:9, it is not rhetorical but a real question and does not stand at the beginning but after the historical background and encompasses the totality of the double sin of adultery and murder, and therefore the *raison d'être* of the second encounter with the prophet Nathan. The rhetorical question serves in the oracle of salvation the same function as the normal one in the oracle of doom; the vehicle that brings to light the reason behind the pronouncements of the prophet. In these questions the grounds that call for the presence of the prophet as the messenger of Yahweh are laid bare.

b. In chapter seven, the past deeds of Yahweh follow the rhetorical question and cover both his deeds towards Israel (vv. 6-7) and towards David (8-9) as the protector of the nation of Israel and its king. In chapter twelve, these deeds are concentrated upon the election and protection carried out by Yahweh with David at the receiving end of divine benevolence (vv. 7-8) and stand before the question, in contrast to the dynastic oracle. While in 7:9 the protection is against the enemies of David in general, in 12:7 the enemy is specified as Saul (מיד שאול) and David's rule over "my people Israel" (7:8) is purported in the two-aspect destination of "the house of Israel and of Judah" (12). Having produced a longer version of the divine benevolence towards David within the context of the chosen nation, the author now focuses on the narrow context of David, the shepherd boy who has become the king of Israel and of Judah by divine election and protection and yet has chosen to despise his benefactor. This logically calls for divine intervention in the present with consequences for the future.

c. As would be expected, the present or future divine action towards David in the oracle of salvation is benevolent; Yahweh will make David a great name (v. 9c), he will plant Israel in her own place (v. 10), he will give David rest (v. 11b) and will make him a house (v. 11c). The converse is what happens in the oracle of doom (*Drohwort*); the sword will never depart from the house of David (12:10) and his neighbour will lie with his wives before the sun (v. 11).

d. David's reaction to both oracles is the same except for the content. After the promise of an eternal dynasty David goes in and sits down before the Lord and prays in thanksgiving for the good news that he has received (7:18-29). The same attitude is observed after the oracle of doom but this time around he fasts and lies on the ground for seven days pleading for the life of the child who is supposed to die in his place (12:15b–19) and worships after the death of that child (v. 20).

The oracle of doom (2 Sam 12:7-12) is a mirror reflection of the oracle of salvation (7:5-16) with its corresponding repetition of the oracular or messenger formula in chiastic construction; 7:5, 8 and 12:7, 11.

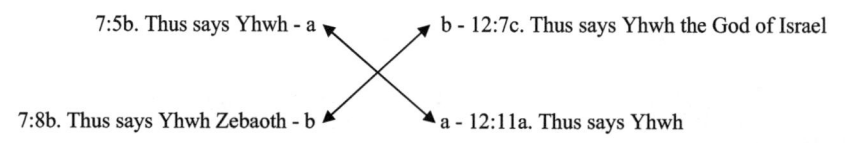

```
7:5b. Thus says Yhwh - a          b - 12:7c. Thus says Yhwh the God of Israel
                        ╲    ╱
                         ╲  ╱
                          ╲╱
                          ╱╲
                         ╱  ╲
                        ╱    ╲
7:8b. Thus says Yhwh Zebaoth - b    a - 12:11a. Thus says Yhwh
```

The chiasmus reverses the oracle of salvation in a close-ended form, absolutely sealing the doom of David. By reason of his evil deeds, David has turned upside down the promise of an eternal dynasty to his house which will now be visited by the sword for ever and he will die in accordance with his own statement of judgment against the nameless man of Nathan's parable. The reader now finds a just reaction to the impudence of David but at the same time notes the uncertainty that reigns over the whole narrative. What will happen to the divine promise? Will Yhwh's promise come to nought on account of the frailty of human will and inconsistency of behaviour in his ephemeral nature despite the permanence of divine nature and will? In the dtr tradition, the prophet is the medium through which Yhwh makes His will known and his pronouncements function as the resolution of tensions that have arisen in the course of history in order to give an impetus to the flow of events or set the account on the right track and in the right direction. It is this role that the prophetic presence at this moment in the narrative serves.

The phenomenon of prophecy is closely bound to the epoch of kingship in Israel and Judah. It was the means predominantly adopted by Yhwh to communicate with the kings. The prophet was accepted as and considered himself to be the messenger of Yhwh. In consonance with this basic conception, his message was introduced by the *messenger formula* known not only in Israel but also in the Ancient Near East; NN כה אמר (*Thus says NN* or *so NN has spoken*; depending upon the way the messenger decided to proclaim his message). According to Westermann, this messenger formula was developed before the time of writing of letters and appending of signatures.[394] The messenger rendered the message of the sender in a direct speech so that the force of that message was attained by the word for word repetition of the sender's instruction or demand. This implies that the messenger, at that moment of proclamation, represented the sender whose words he announced.[395] In some sense, the prophetic message was like the written letter of our time, continues Westermann, the

---

394 C. Westermann, *Grundformen*, p. 70.
395 This dynamic relationship of sender-message-messenger is true of many developing cultures. In many instances, as in the case of the Akan culture of Ghana, the messenger (Linguist) serves as a personification of the ruler, chief or king whose spokesperson he is. Any form of treatment meated out to the linguist is reconed as a treatment meted out to the sender's person and will be received as such. This message formula was very common in the Ancient Near East, states Westermann, and was even taken over in the written message, as the written letters represented the fixing of the oral message. Thus in old Babylonian letters we read; "Zu Y sprich: so (sagt) X ..." Cf. C. Westermann, *Grundformen*, p. 73.

prophet receives his mission, he is sent to a specific person(s) or place, he is asked to go and deliver that message, and he sets out to do just that. Such prophetic messages, directed against individuals, were issued on account of a breach of the social order where the victims were not in the position to defend themselves (1 Kings 21:17-19 cf. Ex 21:12) or against Yhwh (2 Kings 1:3-4 cf. Ex 23:13).[396] In 2 Samuel 12, David, the king, has gone against two traditional norms (Ex 20: 13 & 14), but his position as a king makes it almost impossible for any one to bring a case against him before a traditional court (where he will sit as the judge anyway). Above all, the wronged person, Uriah, is dead. Hence, Yhwh takes up the case and sends his messenger to charge the king on His behalf, with the authority to pronounce judgment as spoken by Yhwh himself. The prophet appears before the king as a messenger with the onerous duty of pronouncing a judgment that does not stem from him personally but from Yhwh. He therefore prefaces his judgment with the messenger formula; כה אמר יהוה which denotes the force of the message and commands the attention of its audience.

The double messenger formula within the speeches appears to be a typical dtr style of pronouncing judgment whether positive or negative. The oracle of the unknown man of God in 1 Sam 2:27-36 is a classic dtr explanation for a historical event as a fulfilment of the word of Yhwh. Abiathar, a priest of the Elide tradition is exiled to Anathoth by Solomon for taking sides against him in the struggle for the throne of David. By his action, Abiathar had called for his own death, but Solomon spared him because he had been faithful to David in his trials, serving him as his priest (1 Sam 23:6). The dtr author, however, ascribes the whole event to the fulfilment of the oracle of Yhwh concerning the Shilonite priesthood to which Abiathar belonged (1 Kgs 2:26-27). In that oracle, which is basically dtr, the oracular formula appears two times v. 27 and 30, following the classic pattern of that author:

---

396 C. Westermann, *Grundformen*, p. 94–95. In the books of Samuel and Kings prophetic oracles of judgment (prophetischen Gerichtsankündigungen) are without exception directed to individuals; they are never addressed towards groups of people, the whole nation or other nations (p. 98). It is only after Jeremiah that such prophecies are directed towards the whole nation or groups out of it (p. 99).

2:27 – Thus says Yhwh	2: 30 – Therefore the word of Yhwh the God of Israel
7:5 – Thus says Yhwh	7: 8 – Thus says Yhwh Zebaoth
12:7 – Thus says Yhwh the God of Israel	12: 11 – Thus says Yhwh

It appears to us that every time the Dtr resorts to a double oracular formula, the first recounts the events of the past, while the second concentrates on the present and or the future. 1 Sam 2:27 centres on the choice of the ancestors of Eli to be priests and the consignment of the priestly portion of the sacrificial victim to them as an introduction to the accusation of greed on the part of his sons as the present situation of the oracle (v. 29) while v. 30b states the contempt that awaits those who despise the Lord, in the future. 2 Sam 7:5 initiates the series of questions that prove that Yhwh never asked any of the leaders of Israel before David to build him a temple, culminating in his choice and protection of David (vv. 8-9a), but this state of affairs will change because Yhwh will make for David a great name (v. 9b) and will appoint a place for Israel and give rest to David (vv. 10-11a). Then he will build David a house (v. 11b) and the unnamed son who will inherit David will also build Yhwh a temple (v. 13). The formula is followed in 2 Sam 12 where vv. 7-8 recount the past deeds of Yhwh towards David and v. 11 the punishment that God will mete out to the house of David for despising him by adding murder to adultery.

Exegetes over the centuries have noted the apparent disjoint between the parable of Nathan (12:1-15a) and the reaction of David over the illness of the child (vv.15b-23). F. Schwally saw the hand of a late writer forcibly pushing David's pious behaviour into an old material and succeeds only in creating an absurdity in the narrative.[397] Ernst Würthwein assigns the purported reaction and subsequent birth of Solomon to the work of a writer at the court of Solomon who writes *ad maiorem Salomonis gloriam*.[398] Following this line of argument, Timo Veijola intimates that the original story moves from 11:27b to 12:24bß and that 12:1-15a and v. 25 are later additions to exonerate Solomon, who is actually the so-called first son of Bathsheba and therefore illegitimate. Others like P. R. Ackroyd argue that it will make a lot of sense to have David react in the way he did without 12:1-15a,

---

397 F. Schwally, *Der Prophet Nathan*, p. 155.
398 E. Würthwein, *Thronfolge Davids*, p. 24–25.

but it seems illogical that he would plead for the life of the child despite the absoluteness of the judgment stated in verse 14[399]; in reparation for his own sins of adultery and murder. This apparent lack of coherence between the prophetic encounter and the subsequent reaction of David makes the text suspect and raises the question of "originality". Hugo Gressmann points out that the account of the king's fasting and prayer reveals how David's inner struggles began to capture the narrator's attention – in his despair, the king is even thought capable of harming his own self. "Nothing is said here about any penitence of David such as should be expected after Nathan's appearance: thus we now have confirmation that the parable is foreign to the original text."[400] This assertion indicates the acceptance of the king's penance (12:15b-23) as an original part of the narrative and the parable of Nathan with its subsequent oracles (12:1-15a) a later addition. Which parts of the text are original and which a later addition? My own division of the text in the first chapter of this work has established that 12:15b can seamlessly be joined to 11:27b, leaving out the whole encounter of David with Nathan in 12:1-15a without distorting the narrative flow. This will, however, distort the whole dtr ideology of the house of David in the broad history and theology of election, sin, punishment and reconciliation mitigated by the prophet of Yhwh; in fact the text will lack a theological sense which will be contrary to the dtr style.

---

399 P. R. Ackroyd, *The second book of Samuel*, p. 113. In the opinion of Ackroyd, the original sequel to 11:27 is 12:15b for the style of the story here is less overtly theological than the Nathan section.

400 H. Gressmann, *Oldest History Writing*, p. 30–31. Gressmann finds it probable that the child born out of David's intercourse with Bathsheba died and was considered a just punishment for the king's sin, that is why the oracle of Nathan had to include that sentence as an appropriate threat to that effect (p. 30). Some scholars, like Veijola, believe that Solomon was the real offspring of the adulterous union between David and Bathsheba. To protect him from the stigma of such an origin, the story of the death of his older brother was invented. The problem that arises with this scenario is that 12:24-25 cannot be separated from 11-12 and no later editor would take such an interest in protecting Solomon at David's expense (so S. L. McKenzie, *King David*, p. 161). Gressmann's argument holds water; the story was extant and our author has included it in his work by placing it at an appropriate position in his history.

Much as various approaches seek to go beyond the surface, with the view to establishing what was before and what has been added to it, we will not approach the issue from the question of originality, as we find that practically overtaken by the trend of our time. Working with the premise that the Dtr has assembled the material at his disposal with the scope of narrating a story that is a complex whole, every aspect of the narrative is original as long as that author (or group of authors) has taken over that material or reworked it to fit into his framework or to demonstrate an aspect of his theme, whether major or subordinate. Thus the work, in its diversity of form and font, is original to the author who has shaped it into a single whole in the way that we find it today. In particular, there are indications in the text that the material itself is older than the dtr writer. For instance, the observers of David's self-mortification swing abruptly from "the elders of his house" (זקני ביתו) in v. 17 to "his servants" (עבדי) in vv. 18, 19 & 21, as if the two are the same group of people. However, the first group (elders) falls completely out of the text and does not appear anymore. While "servants" is frequently used in Samuel and Kings in reference to ministers or domestics of the royal palace "elders of his house" appears only in Gen 50:7, in relation to Joseph. This might reflect the state of affairs in the earlier stage of the monarchy where the authority of the tribal leaders still held sway and was quickly resorted to whenever the need arose (2 Sam 3:17, 5:3,). It is, therefore, highly probable that the term belonged to the older version that has been adapted and the Dtr for some unknown reason allowed the older form of expression to remain untouched.

In this episode the Dtr brings back the pious David on his rise to power filled with trust in "The Rock of (his) Salvation" (1 Sam 16 – 2 Sam 7). He mortifies himself in supplication for the life of the child as a loving father (v. 16), but accepts the divine judgment once it comes to pass (v. 20).[401] In

---

401 In the author's use of "*bqš*", Fokkelman (*King David*, p. 89) identifies David's vigorous attempt to mollify God to have mercy on the child. This appeal means that David still had a glimmer of hope that God might spare the life of the child and therefore positively seeks him; he radically alters his life. Such an act of penitence does not in any way point to oblivion of the oracle of doom; it rather buttresses the fervent hope and trust that David had in his God.

the meantime he learns a great lesson that is for all time valid for the whole human race; the immutability of death and the helplessness of man before that reality which is a one-way road that awaits all mankind. This lesson is expressed in his response to the curiosity of his servants in v. 20: *"But now he is dead; why should I fast (from eating)? I will go to him but he will not return to me."* "It is an answer which reveals much more than just simple resignation: it reveals the recognition of God's unwavering justice. Only submission is fitting for David."[402] While being a submission to the will of the divine, this attitude of David could also have been a sign of relief, because, after all, it was now clear that Yhwh had forgiven him. This peculiar behaviour of David was so completely out of line with the tradition of his day that one cannot imagine it being a figment of the imagination of a later writer; in this case the Dtr. The action stood out so clearly that the narrative audience could not help but question it. It may have been just as it was; David demonstrates his unconditional trust in the divine by his word and deed.[403] In his commentary on the episode, Walter Brueggemann sums up his thoughts as follows:

> This narrative portrays the remarkable pathos and freedom of David. That is the wonder of David, before whom Israel never ceases to be amazed. He has just been incredibly cynical, and Israel denies nothing of that. In the midst of David's cynical self-serving, however, there is a powerful grandeur about him. These verses show David's capacity for a human gesture that is marked by nobility. David knows when to weep and when to relinquish his grief. (Cf. Eccl 3:4)[404]

This admiration of David permeates the whole narrative which seems to suggest that despite the absolutely sordid behaviour of David expressed in the adultery, murder and the unsuccessful attempt to push the un-born child into the shoes of Uriah, the man now stands by the child with fasting and prayers to save him from the unavoidable death decreed by the prophet Nathan. And when he finally dies, David transcends the normal Semitic attitude of a great show of mourning. "Painful as his grief is, David moves quickly from the feeble realm of death to the vitality of life. He dresses, he

---

402 L. Rost, *Succession*, p. 79.
403 H. Gressmann et al, *II Samuelis*, p. 160.
404 W. Brueggemann, *First and Second Samuel*, p. 283.

worships and he eats (v. 20)."[405] This action cannot in any way be reckoned as a typical behaviour of David. The David of the Dtr is not simply a stoic but a man who shows emotions, especially when it is about the death of people dear to him. He mourned Jonathan (2 Sam 1:11-27) and wept so bitterly upon the death of Absalom that the victory that day was turned into mourning for his whole army (2 Sam 18:33-19:8).[406]

The death of the child has a purifying effect upon David or completes his process of purification, as it were. He washes, anoints himself and changes his clothes (v. 20). These physical actions of the hitherto fasting, mourning and praying monarch suggest a spiritual journey or attitude of purification for the sinner who is now forgiven and can take his place among the community of the redeemed. In fact the dtr author appears to say just this when he endorses for the first time the relationship between David and Bathsheba; *²⁴Then David consoled Bathsheba, his wife; he went to her and lay with her and she bore a son and he named him Solomon. And the Lord loved him. ²⁵So he sent a message by (through the hand of) Nathan the prophet and named him Jedidiah on account of Yhwh.* For once the narrator refers to Bathsheba by her own name and in apposition adds; "his wife".[407] She is no longer the wife of Uriah the Hittite nor is she a mere

---

405 W. Brueggemann, *First and Second Samuel*, p. 283. The reporter of the narrative, according to Brueggemann, makes his audience learn what Israel knows about David; he is greater than stories that we are able to tell about him. He persistently outdistances all normal expectations and all reasonable narrative renderings.

406 W. Oswald maintains that this attitude of David does not only contradict ancient and modern expectation but also freely contradicts himself and cites a check list of moments where David mourns at the death of people with meaning to him; Saul and Jonathan (2 Sam 1:17), Abner (3:31-35), his sons (13:31), Amnon (13:36f) and at the death of Absalom (19:1-3). This indicates that the attitude of David in this chapter was a particular and unique case and not a permanent change of character. Cf. *Nathan der Prophet*, p. 131.

407 It is remarkable that all through the story Bathsheba is neither accused with David nor punished for adultery. Victor A. Matthews (*The King's call to Justice*, p. 211) thinks that it is because the changes made in the adultery status by the Deuteronomic reform of Josiah's time provided that only the male partner was liable of the crime as a separate legal entity, the woman functioning legally as an extension of her husband or father. Whether this was the case or not it was David, the king with might, who sent for Bathsheba and,

instrument to quench the inordinate lust of David. This approval of the union between David and Bathsheba, in the eyes of the writer of the story, defines the status of this new son born to David by Bathsheba; he is legitimately conceived and born in wedlock. It is this new son who will later dominate the narrative and bring the promise of 7:1-16 to its expected fulfilment. In these two difficult verses (vv. 24-25) the author brings together the main actors of the story, Yhwh, Nathan, David and Bathsheba once again with the introduction of the next important actor in the drama; Solomon, as the one Yhwh loves. In bringing these characters together in a harmonious conclusion to the David-Uriah-Bathsheba sequence the author subtly but effectively portrays to his readers that David has acknowledged his faults and has been absolved of his sins; the guilt has been paid for by the appropriate punishment through the death of the son, David himself has done enough penance and Yhwh once more accepts the family and loves the son that is born through the union of David and Bathsheba, his legitimate wife.

With these two verses the author weaves a seam to join together David's fasting, the death of the child and the birth of Solomon (12:15b-25) to the parable of Nathan (12:1-15a) as its logical ending. The death of the child as a sign accompanying the prophecy of doom proves beyond any reasonable doubt the status of Nathan as Yhwh's faithful messenger. The same prophet who decreed the death of the child born to David by the wife of Uriah (vv. 14-15b) is once again sent by God to give a second name to the child born to David by his wife (v. 25). Stoebe notes that Yhwh is the subject of the idiom וישלח ביד which expresses modality with Nathan as its object, hence "*er ließ durch Nathan sagen*".[408] It is God who through the

---

    therefore, the accusation centres upon him. Any attempt to treat Bathsheba as a comrade in crime with the king would only succeed in weakening the impact of David's guilt in the narrative. What is more, which woman could have resisted the power of the king who had sent messengers to bring her to the palace? In any case she might have suffered in the same way as, if not more than, David at the death of the child because the life and status of the child changes her own life and status.

408 H. J. Stoebe, KAT, p. 300. The idiom has been at the heart of discussions from time immemoria. We will like to cite only one such point of view as expressed by Nowach's translation: "*Und er ward dem Prophet Nathan*

instrumentality of Nathan gives Solomon a second name. This sequence would seem to suggest that Solomon was the second or the next son born to David by Bathsheba but 1 Chr 3:5 makes him the fourth son. Thus we are here not dealing with a chronological sequence but a theological direction that is given to the narrative. Such a theological undertone would not only serve a legitimizing effect against critical minds but more also set the tone for the grace of forgiveness that reigns in the house of the monarch.[409] The family saga ends with the blessing of the birth of a second son who is legitimate and loved by God. At the same time, the author makes Yhwh the invisible hero of the story; it is He who moves the story forward with the renaming of Solomon.

The Dtr author broke off the narrative at 11:27b upon the divine name (what David had done was evil in the eyes of the Lord (יהוה-x-ב)) as having the last word and opened the insertion with Yhwh as the subject of שלח. In the same vein he rounds the story up with the divine name in 12:25b (*...so he named him Jedidiah because of Yhwh*) with the same formula as at the beginning (יהוה-x-ב). The formula is varied in v. 15b, the middle portion of the chapter, where Yhwh is simply the agent of the terminal illness of the son born to David by the wife of Uriah. Whether on the basis of ideology or semantics, the divine name regulates the flow of the narrative in every direction. In my view, this insertion into the war annals is an excellently constructed treatise of the Dtr to give a theological meaning to the unfolding history of David's house in relationship with Yhwh, who is the actual but unseen hero. It demonstrates "the amazing capacity of Yhwh to work more life at the border of death, to act in promise-keeping ways (7:12) just when the promise seems exhausted."[410] What should have constituted the

---

übergeben, und man nannte ihn Jedidja nach dem Wort Jahveh's" (*Bücher Samuelis*, p. 197). Nowach is correcting וישלח by adding a third person singular suffix to the verb to give the impression that Solomon was given over to the prophet. A number of exegetes over the years have resorted to this interpretation with its tendency to justify not only Solomon's succession but also Nathan's unexpected role in that event as the care-taker of the would-be successor to the throne of David. All the same this position reads too much more into the text than the narrative will warrant.

409 H. J. Stoebe, *KAT*, p. 311.
410 W. Brueggemann, *First and Second Samuel*, p. 284.

fall of David, the visible or human hero of the narrative, and the collapse of the promise of an eternal dynasty rather ends on the note of divine grace and the hope of good things to come "because of Yhwh". The close-ended chiasmus of the oracle of salvation and that of doom is once more open for the future and that only because of the Lord.[411] It is no wonder that tradition does not only ascribe Psalm 51 to David but also situates the psalm in the context of the aftermath of his adultery and murder (Ps 51:1).

With the birth of שלמה[412] (Solomon), or we should say with Ackroyd that with the return of peace into the house of David, as the sound of

---

411 The manner in which the dtr author makes use of the material at his disposal demonstrates his *"Anpassungsvermögen"* i. e. his rich repertoire of adaptation skills. In fact his insertions give the impression of the chameleon which changes its colour to suit the environment. In many instances he only inserts a phrase or two to join the narratives together (11:27, 12:24, 17:14) or simply lets one follow the other in the way he added 7:1ff to the Ark Narratives. Here, however, he breaks the war account into two and inserts the background story of the successor to the throne; a story which will fully blossom in 1 Kings 1.

412 P. R. Ackroyd, *Samuel*, p. 114. The name Solomon is connected with the Hebrew word šālōm, peace, well-being, prosperity: in this context it emphasizes the restoration of divine favour, and might also carry the sense of restitution. Karl A. Leimbach had earlier on (1936) expressed the name with the German equivalent, Friedrich, from the root *Friede* meaning peace (*Die Bücher Samuel*, p. 174). The position may be acceptable if it is only about the SOUND but not the etymology: šəlmoh is not šālōm. Veijola traces the etymology of the name שלמה to the Piel *ausgedrückten Tätigkeit* which can be rendered *unversehrt, ersetzen* (intact or replace) and explains it with the evidence of the kĕtîv - qĕrê. The verb for the naming of Solomon in v. 24 is third person masculine singular (ויקרא – he named) while the qĕrê retains the third person feminine singular (ותקרא – she named). Veijola argues that the disparity is an indication that there was an earlier version which reflects the earlier practice of the mother naming the child evidenced by the qĕrê upon which the later version of a male dominated society has been imposed with the masculine expression. In this light, the name would have been selected by Bathsheba, who then would have done so with her eyes on her recently dead husband, Uriah, as his replacement. Thus Solomon, according to Veijola, is actually the curiously unnamed first son of Bathsheba and the second name, Jedidiah, was a later addition to avoid the unavoidable connection to the murdered Uriah. Cf. T. Veijola, *Salomo – der Erstgeborene Bathsebas*, in David, Gesammelte Studien, pp. 87-91. Baruch Halpern goes further in defending this position

the name purports, the narrator takes his audience back to the war front together with David who is now ready to establish peace on the external sphere for Israel through the flexing of his military muzzles over Rabbah Ammon (vv. 26-31). Fokkelman notes the precise and deft strokes of the ink of the writer who has made use of the war annals to narrate the sordid behaviour of David and still succeeds in polishing up the character of the man in the eyes of his audience. This author, according to Fokkelman, was obliged to let the theatre of war; the cruelty, the atrocities and killings, affect the court of David so much so that the death of Uriah comes as a murder devised by David at the drawing-board with its accomplishment as the climax to the plot. This episode is so well woven into the framework that it is only after David's penance, mourning and marriage to Bathsheba that the announcement of the victory of David over Ammon can bring joy. The narrator effectively reverses David's remaining behind in Jerusalem by means of the invitation of the loyal Joab[413] that brought him to the front

---

by positing that the text witnesses, a number of Hebrew manuscripts, the Targum and Syriac are in accord with the qĕrê, meaning that the name Solomon was given by Bathsheba and indicated Uriah's replacement and therefore not the son of David. To buttress this point Halpern cites the exclusion of Solomon from the list of Adonijah's guests even though "all his brothers (1 Kings 1:9) or all the children of the king (v. 19)" were invited. He was excluded because he was not the son of the king and Bathsheba's action was purely out of self-preservation. Again, Ahitophel would have had no cause to throw his lot behind Absalom if his grandson, Solomon, the son of Bathsheba, was a prospective heir to the throne (*David's Secret Demons, Messiah, Murderer, Traitor, King*, Grand Rapids, 2002, p. 401–403). Halperns position is in our opinion a little too far-fetched since the narrative does not fail to indicate the paternity of Solomon (2 Sam 12:24-25). Hans Rechenmacher, however, argues that even though šlm is frequently used in personal names in association with its meaning of replacement, it is never employed with a deceased family member as its object (cf. *Althebräische Personennamen*, § 342, p. 142). It is clear that the etymological meaning of the name is still an open question and we may not be able to resolve it here.

413 The loyalty of Joab to David cannot be overstated in the narrative. He has conducted a very difficult campaign in the siege of Rabbah at a time when the king is busy revelling in his passionate desires in the comfort of his palace. While Joab is preoccupied with state affairs David is busy with himself even to the extent of making Joab his accomplice. That notwithstanding, Joab does not use it against David. He stays the victory at the last moment

(v. 27). Once David arrives at the front, he does what is expected of a warrior king; he captures the city, takes over its symbol of authority and returns to Jerusalem with the whole army (v. 31).[414] It is these deft strokes of the writer's ink that ensure the unity of the otherwise multifunctional text from various sources that he has brought together to constitute the history.

In the first appearance of Nathan, the relationship that already existed between David and Yahweh was concretized with the promise of an eternal dynasty. This relationship was jeopardized by David's disregard for moral decorum which occasioned the reappearance of the prophet to spew fire and brimstone upon the erring king. Despite the strain in the relationship and the outright difficulty of bringing a king to his knees, the prophet succeeded in re-establishing the wounded trust between Yhwh and the king for the simple reason of David's readiness to submit himself to the dictates of divine will. At the end of the encounter, the reader knows that even though the curse was yet to take effect upon the house of David, the hope of a better future had already begun to be realised in the birth of the "Beloved of Yahweh", Solomon. The fleeting appearance of Nathan at the end of the episode (v. 25) resets the oracle of salvation on the road to its fulfilment after its temporary halt. Through the intervention of Nathan, David is reinstated

---

and invites the king to come over in order to claim the glory and to silence the rumour mill that might have been boiling up in the city. After capturing the source of water to the city (v. 27), Rabbah had no chance of survival but he stopped short of initiating the last blow in order to honour his king with victory.

414 J. P. Fokkelman, *King David*, pp. 94–95. Despite the recognition that vv. 26-31 form part of the framework within which the author has inserted the "David-Bathsheba-Uriah triangle", Fokkelman intimates that the continuation of the story line here is a flashback because it does not give any time frame besides that of 11:1. We will rather maintain that vv. 24-25 provide information that extends beyond a season but which the Dtr writer has inserted as a concluding notice to the complete block of 11:2-12:23. This leaves 11:1+12:26-31 as a single block of narrative material. The flare of the author as a writer is clearly seen in the right choices he makes by way of where to begin the insertion and where to end it so that the emotions aroused in both blocks harmoniously coincide to satisfy his audience of different generations and epochs.

before the Lord, the dynasty is saved, and the would-be successor is born and endorsed by Yahweh.[415]

The image of Nathan that is portrayed here gives him the true stature of a prophet; obedience to Yhwh is the key to life or death and reveals a quality of the divine word that the prophet transmits; the same mouth that promised life promises death; a quality expressed by the image of the two-edged sword of the divine word before which every creature is naked and laid bare.[416] Moreover, it is a marked characteristic of the dtr (or the author of the SN as the case may be) to resort to the use of parables, whenever possible as a means to transmit his message.[417] In the hands of the Dtr, parables become the instrument with which the author breaks dead-locks in the narrative. They are the means to restore communication in difficult moments, as the case of the widow of Tekoa (2 Sam 14:1-24) and the unnamed prophet and Ahab (1 Kings 20:35-43) in addition to the parable of Nathan effectively indicate. With the parable, Nathan focuses on the conflict within the narrative; the king is led on to a rightful self-identification with the evil-doer instead of the simple, normal, human tendency of self-justification by identifying with the victim; he sincerely repents of his sins and is forgiven by Yhwh. The tension is resolved and the attention of the audience is once more focused on the fulfilment of the promise of an eternal kingdom to David pepped up by the short appearance of the prophet Nathan. It is no doubt that vv. 24-25 are the product of the dtr author, who prepares his audience for the future events of the succession. This author's definite knowledge of the successor to David requires that he prepares the ground for it and he does that in such a subtle way that the reader has the effect of an "aha-elateness" when the event occurs in 1 Kings 1. In the meantime the narrator leads his audience into the turmoil of the precarious life of the hero's family where the princes eliminate one another even before the succession becomes an issue at the court (13-19).

---

415 L. Rost, *Succession*, p. 78. Rost maintains that it is only when Nathan is brought into the otherwise loosely attached story of the death of the child that it becomes an important part of the whole narrative. The appearance of Nathan provides a definitive end to the adultery and the tension that it has created.
416 Hebrews 4:12-13.
417 L. Rost, *Succession*, p. 79.

This twist in the narrative sees to it that the candidates for succession are reduced to the barest minimum when the struggle for power takes centre stage in 1 Kings 1. Again the dtr author has craftily formulated this family tragedy into the oracle of doom (2 Sam 12:10) in order to tell his audience that the punishment of David for the killing of Uriah has been meted out to his family and not to the nation. While the evil that the subsequent kings did in the eyes of Yhwh always had a national effect and repercussions because it led the whole nation into sin (eg. 1 Kings 12:30), that of David was personal and familial and its punishment was also limited to that scope.[418] At the same time it arouses the feeling that the royal family is not capable of resolving its own problems without the help of an external force, which will be provided by no other person than the divine messenger at the service of the dynasty.

6.3　1 Kings 1

We now enter into what we will call a key chapter in the Nathan pericopae. In the first appearance of the prophet, David has been promised an everlasting throne before Yhwh. In a clear-cut expression, a son born out of the loins of David will sit upon his throne after him. The king, however, jeopardizes the throne by his adultery with Bathsheba and murder of Uriah, her husband, and occasions the second appearance of the prophet. This time around, the monarch is threatened with death for the sword, as the instrument of death that he has caused to cut short the life of Uriah, will in turn devour the royal house. It is only on the basis of the acknowledgment of his guilt before Yhwh that he is spared the death sentence that he has pronounced upon himself. The son born as a result of the crime dies in place of his father and another son is born, of whom it is said that "Yhwh loves", to bring to an end the crisis of relationship between God and king. The narrator then allows his readers an exclusive insight into the self-destructive lives of the sons of the king that makes one wonder which of them will in the end be left to succeed their father (2 Sam 13:1-19:8). The nagging question that remains open in the mind of the reader is whether the promise will be fulfilled at all and, if so, how

---

418　W. Oswald, *Nathan der Prophet*, p. 235.

this fulfilment will take place. The third encounter of Nathan with David resolves this uncertainty. Once again, it is the prophet of salvation and of doom who sets the ball rolling after a careful reading of the signs of the times. In the words of Walter Dietrich, a cunning Nathan sends the all-too-ready Bathsheba to the aged and weak David to lobby in favour of Solomon against Adonijah and he himself follows up to confirm Bathsheba's assertion until David finally pronounces the deciding words in response to the question of succession.[419] Thus, Leonhard Rost hits the nail on the head with his standpoint that this third appearance of Nathan holds the key to understanding the whole work that is termed "Succession Narrative".[420]

6.3.1 1 Kings 1: an overview

Given that so many before us have undertaken to research into the SN with the view to finding its beginning and end, its author, age and purpose, I will here sample the views of only four among the many authors that are relevant to my study; Leonhard Rost to represent those who consider 1 Kings 1 to be the end of the independent SN with chapter 2 as reverberations adopted by the dtr author; Otto Kaiser for those who posit a pre-dtr date; J. Van Seters who maintains the contrary stance of a post-dtr, anti-monarchical work of the court historian, and Timo Veijola for his reconciliatory position that the dtr redactional material in the episode provides theological basis for Solomon's succession. From the onset we will like to note that for the majority of researchers the ending of the SN is to be found in the assertion *"So the kingdom was established in the hands of Solomon"* (1 Kings 2:46). In this light 1 Kings 1 is treated as a build-up to this conclusion or the final events that lead on to this assertion and, therefore, one with 1 Kings 2. On my part, the Prophet Nathan does not appear in the second chapter, therefore, my interest is invariably in the first chapter and the second will be referred to so long as it helps us to understand the events into which we are delving.

---

419 W. Dietrich, *Prophetie*, p. 105.
420 L. Rost, *Succession*, p. 68.

Leonhard Rost

The opinion of Rost is justified in every way in considering the third appearance of Nathan not in isolation but together with the whole block of narratives that he identifies as the SN, adding that it plays a very important role in this body of narrative material. Rost takes over the final propositions of Steuernagel who identifies a unified narrative enshrined in 2 Sam 9-20 and 1 Kings 1-2 as the story of David's family, with a few insertions in 2 Samuel and 1 Kings 2. He adds 2 Sam 6:16 & 20ff and 7:11b & 16 to this block as the beginning of the succession story supporting his argument with "the investigation of the stylistic characteristics and religious conceptions within the block.[421] Rost maintains that 1 Kings 1 is the end of the story and that chapter two is only added as a concluding reverberation. In the opinion of Rost the chapter provides information about the writer's wishes and intentions, hence his method of working from here backwards to the beginning.

> The plot has much tension in it; it spurs its readers on and makes them hold their breath. And set in this framework - one could say with brutal insistence and frantic monotony – we have the insistent question: "Who shall sit upon the throne of my lord the king, and who shall reign after him?" Nathan's conversation with Bathsheba and their talk with David, David's order to Zadok, Nathan and Benaiah, and finally Jonathan's report to those banqueting around Adonijah's table, all centre on this question in agitated excitement. The whole action of the drama revolves around these disquieting words…This chapter, therefore, is the key to understanding the whole work.[422]

The all-important question is mooted by Nathan and is only answered successfully in 2 Kings 2:46; *"So the kingdom was established in the hands of Solomon."* But who could this son of David be who at the end sits upon the throne of his father? The answer to that question is enshrined in the narrative block of material found in 2 Sam 11:2-12:25, which provides detailed information about the successor, his mother and the prophet Nathan. Thus the background of the hero is inextricably linked to the appearance of the Prophet Nathan.

Rost notes that since the SN does not betray any knowledge of the later upheavals which plagued David's kingdom towards the end of Solomon's

---

421 L. Rost, *Succession*, p. 67–87.
422 L. Rost, *Succession*, p. 68.

reign, it is most likely a product dating from the beginning of the Solomonic period. The author may have been a courtier, but whether it was Abiathar or Ahimaaz cannot clearly be established. However, it was written *ad maiorem gloriam Salomonis* as indicated by 12:25 "and then the speeches of David (1 Kings 1:48) and Benaiah (v. 36-37) at his (Solomon's) accession to the throne require this conclusion."[423] Rost shares the opinion of Martin Noth that the author belonged to a circle at the king's court in Jerusalem, but where Noth posits a position which fundamentally approved the dynasty of David without accepting the way and manner in which the events around the individual successions were carried out,[424] Rost finds a pro-Solomonic authorship. In a nutshell, Rost maintains that 1 Kings 1-2 are an integral part of the SN, which the dtr historian has adopted and incorporated into his history. This block of narrative, which he terms Succession Narrative, is an independently unified work that is not part of a bigger whole.[425] The dtr author, according to Rost, added the introduction to David's Testament in 1 Kings 2:1-4, which is dependent upon the older passage of 2 Sam 7:12 & 14.[426]

In the course of this work, we have adopted a number of the positions that Rost has arrived at but, as far as the sequence of events is concerned, we do not think that the dtr additions of 2 Sam 7 predate the succession of Solomon to the throne of his father in 1 Kings 1-2. The insertions may rather have been informed by the events of the succession. In the same vein, David's testament (1 Kings 2:1-9) is the work of the dtr author and looks back to the dtr additions in 2 Sam 7 and, thus, cannot be older than that author. The dtr, we maintain, has reshaped the oracle of Nathan to reflect the reality of Solomon's unexpected rise out of the blue to succeed his father against the older and practically advantaged primogenitor, Adonijah, and that with the help of the prophet Nathan. Thus the narrative sequence naturally places the promise of a successor before the accession to the throne.

---

423 L. Rost, *Succession*, p. 105.
424 M. Noth, *Überlieferung*, p. 271.
425 L. Rost, *Succession*, p. 112–114.
426 L. Rost, *Succession*, p. 71.

Otto Kaiser
Kaiser researches into 1 Kings 1-2 with the view to establishing the relationship between the SN and the Deuteronomistic historical work.[427] He is of the view that the beginning of the SN is to be found in 2 Sam 2, because, for the narrative to be complete it should include the anointing of David at Hebron, the list of his children born there and the murder or executions of Abner and Ishbaal, hence 2 Sam 2-20 & 1 Kings 1-2.[428] In the opinion of Kaiser, 1 Kings 1-2 are the editorial linkage between the SN, with its pro-dynastic *Vorlage* and dtr redaction on one hand, and the dtr books of Kings on the other. 1 Kings 1, Kaiser opines, is an earlier work with a pro-dynastic redaction that can clearly be seen in vv. 30-37 with 37b, 46-48 as a later addition, but this pro-dynastic hand is not that of the Deuteronomistic historian.[429] The import of the pro-dynastic redaction was to explain why Solomon was made king in the life time of his father. The king made him his co-regent and automatic successor (v. 35b) and thus justifies the elimination of his opponents to the throne. The harmonizing hand of the Dtr, according to Kaiser, can be seen only in 1 Kings 2.[430] Thus in the opinion of Kaiser, 1 Kings 1 is not the work of the Dtr; the author has taken over the work of a pro-dynastic writer.

John Van Seters
Both J. Van Seters and Kaiser are in accord on the fact that 1 Kings 1 is not a product of the Dtr, but their reasons differ drastically. Van Seters maintains that the chapter is the work of the court historian (CH) who in his usual manner makes use of dtr material which he twists and bends in order to denigrate the royal ideology behind the reign of Solomon. He

---

427 This is the scope of his article; *Das Verhältnis der Erzählung vom König David zum sogenannten deuteronomistischen Geschichtswerk* in OBO 175, 94-122.
428 O. Kaiser, *Erzählung vom König David*, p. 95–99.
429 O. Kaiser, *Erzählung vom König David*, pp. 100–110.
430 Otto Kaiser divides the chapter as follows; v. 1-4 is the work of a late dtr redactor who resort to the "Formelschatzes seiner Vorgänger" in a free combination (p. 113–115), v. 5-9 is a pro-dynastic work to excuse Solomon's cleansing exercise (115-117), v. 10-12 is the typical Dtr notice (p. 111) and v. 15b & 24 are dtr, with v. 23 functioning as a doublet to v. 24 (p. 118).

considers the third appearance of Nathan, just as in the whole of the so called court history, an anti-monarchical work that could neither have stemmed from the early kingship nor from the political environs of the monarchy. The work rather dates from the time after the dtr historian, being the product of authors whose aim was to systematically denigrate the monarchy-friendly attitude of the DtrG in order to make the whole concept counter-productive.

Van Seters posits that over the years, additions have been made to the DtrH by a number of different authors of larger or smaller units. Such additions have also entailed editorial adjustments to make them fit, carried out by the same authors. The Court History[431] is one of such additions to the DtrH. This work, in the opinion of Van Seters, "is complete fiction, a late literary product, full of anachronisms and historical and chronological improbabilities, and no amount of fiddling by using multiple redactors can make it into history"[432] The CH is neither an apologetic nor a propagandist piece contemporaneous with David or with Solomon and it is no wonder that two irreconcilable images of David are portrayed in the tradition. The contradictory image of David in the CH and the DtrH, according to Van Seters, is only because of the existence of two different images in two different units of material stemming from two different epochs in two different circumstances. In the Dtr's judgment David is the epitome of the just and righteous king who was completely obedient to Yhwh and was the model for all subsequent kings to follow. For the author of the CH, the power of the monarchy corrupts itself and everything around it. Even David's reign was full of corruption and violence and was not worth aspiring to return to.[433]

---

431 J. Van Seters, *CH and DtrH*, p. 70. "Court History" (CH) is Van Seter's designation of what the majority following Rost refer to as the "Succession Narrative (SN). He accepts the limits set by Rost and von Rad to the work of the CH but with the addition of 2 Sam 2:8-4:12.

432 J. Van Seters, *CH and DtrH*, p. 71. David Gunn and Van Seters agree on the view that the CH is no history at all and to be read as a pure story which portrays an Israelite art of story-telling (cf. Otto Kaiser, Erzählung vom König David, p. 98).

433 J. Van Seters, *CH and DtrH*, p. 71–76.

Where Dtr texts can be identified with certainty in the CH, argues Van Seters, they cannot be later additions because they are presupposed by the CH and therefore earlier. For example 1 Kings 2:1-4[434] & 10-12 are undeniably dtr. The speech in 2:5-9 is not dtr, (it is CH) but is so dependent upon 2:1-4 that one requires various stratagems to save the priority of the CH. Similarly, 2:10-12 carry the Dtr's reignal formula of Solomon upon which everything else in the CH that comes after it depends. One of the characteristic elements of the reignal formulae in the DtrH is the name of the mother of the reigning monarch (cf. 1 Kings 14:21, 15:2, 15:10, etc.), but this element falls out conspicuously in the introduction of Solomon's reign (2:10-12). This lapse, according to Van Seters, means that the dtr author, as in the case of David and Saul, was oblivious of the information about the mother of Solomon.[435] It is the author of the CH who adds the information about the mother of Solomon, which was lacking in the DtrH. It is this same author who adopts a favourite dtr terminology, *nāgîd*, (usually with Yhwh as subject of the appointment as in 2 Sam 5:2) but in 2 Sam 6:21 and 1 Kings 1 in a totally derogatory fashion.[436]

The position of John Van Seters will lead us to the inference that since the Dtr did not know of Bathsheba, the mother of Solomon, that author could not have had anything to do with 2 Sam 10-12 and 1 Kings 1. Thus he assigns the last two appearances of the Prophet Nathan to the CH and removes them in so doing far away from the Dtr author. Now, if the CH is no history but fiction and the mother of Solomon, his conception and birth are only found in the CH, then is one saying that the origin of Solomon is no history but just a fiction? Such a position will require a lot more research to attract a following. We are convinced that the story about the origin of the successor to the throne of David could not have escaped the Dtr historian, if that author were worth the name and the fact that he might not have touched the material in 1 Kings 1 (cf. Rost) does not mean

---

434 J. Van Seters, *Historiography*, p. 279. David's parting moral advice to Solomon follows the pattern of Moses' charge to Joshua (Deut 31:7ff), Joshua's instruction to the people (Jos 23) and Samuel's warning to king and assembly (1 Sam 12). In each case, the leader is aged and about to die, and the instructions about keeping the law are in typical dtr terminology.
435 J. Van Seters, *CH and DtrH*, p. 79.
436 J. Van Seters, *CH and DtrH*, p. 90.

automatically that he had no knowledge of it, as he might as well have adopted the material without adding anything to it. But as the facts will indicate later, the Dtr has actually trimmed the edges of the material in 1 Kings 1 to make it fit into the history that he sets out to narrate.

Timo Veijola
The narrative material that surrounds the succession of Solomon to the throne of David is, in the opinion of Veijola, by no means unified; it is neither smooth nor free of contradictions, a situation that points to the work of a later redactor.[437] Veijola identifies a fine seam of redactional material that runs through the chapter with the goal of legitimizing the dynasty of David, in general, and the succession of Solomon, in particular. For instance in the royal language relating to the choice of Solomon, 1 Kings 1: 30 concords with v. 35 in the usage of the preposition תחתי (in my stead), while the rest of the narrative uses אחרי(ו) (after me/him). In the greater part of the narrative, symbolized by vv. 13, 17, 20, 24 and 27, Solomon is depicted as sitting on the throne after David his father i.e. אחרי(ו), which intimates that the succession occurred after the death of David. In addition to presenting the succession in the lifetime of David, v. 35 describes the kingdom in its separated form as "Israel and Judah" while the rest of the text consistently maintains "Israel" (vv. 20, 34) and, thereby, indicates that the whole of v. 35 is a later addition. Veijola also finds it questionable that in vv. 35-37 David could describe what should follow the anointing of Solomon and give instruction to that effect. It could only have come as a result of v. 40 and its reported version by Jonathan Ben Abiathar in v. 45, Veijola argues. In the same vein, Benaiah's response to David's instructions rather smuggles itself into the conclusion of the enthronement. It fits better after the anointing than before it and is a later addition.[438] Vv. 46-48 could not have originally been part of the response to Joab's question of v. 41 as that response may well have ended in v. 45, continues Veijola. The addition of these two verses to the response is the successful attempt of the late redactor to link the succession of Solomon to a promise made by Yhwh to David.[439]

---

437 T. Veijola, *Ewige Dynastie*, p. 16.
438 T. Veijola, *Ewige Dynastie*, p. 17.
439 T. Veijola, *Ewige Dynastie*, p. 17.

Vv. 30, 35-37, 46-48 belong to the same redactor and have the same aim which comes to light already in v. 30 where Solomon sits upon the throne on the same day; David is cajoled into swearing by the name of Yhwh to set Solomon on the throne "this day" (היום הזה) and at the end prostrates himself in thanksgiving to the Lord that He has granted him a successor to his throne with his own eyes seeing it. This redaction, according to Veijola, is about the theological legitimization of the dynasty of David[440] and has the aim of postulating that dynasty as an institution established according to the will of God.[441] While Otto Kaiser assigns these additions to a pro-dynastic author who precedes the Dtr, Veijola on his part finds clear links to the dtr author. In both 1 Kings 1 & 2, states Veijola, the redactor uses the word כסא (throne) in its extended meaning of "kingdom" or "dynasty" as the case may be (1:37, 47, 2:33, 45), makes references to an oath that Yhwh has sworn (1:30, 2:8, 42, 43) and crowns his triple use of וגם in 1:46, 47 & 48 with that of 2:5, the second part of "David's Testament".[442] On the basis of the arguments presented among others, Veijola concludes that the redactional materials in 1 Kings 1-2 stem from the same hand and this hand is none other than the Dtr author.[443]

It would be very strange that the dtr author who goes to every extent to provide theological meaning and purpose for the existence of the Davidic dynasty would fail to provide the same at the beginning of the reign of the celebrated successor to that throne. Such a blatant and obvious act of omission would have allowed the claim of Solomon to his father's throne to be shaky and baseless, if not detrimental in the face of active competition from the otherwise clear favourite to that throne, Adonijah. In my opinion, the project of the Dtr would make no sense and would definitely

---

440 T. Veijola, *Ewige Dynastie*, p. 18.
441 T. Veijola, *Ewige Dynastie*, p. 26.
442 The second part of "David's Testament", 1 Kgs 2:5-9, looks back to his rise to the throne with the murder of Abner (2 Sam 3:22-39) and Amasa (2 Sam 20:4-13) and his opponents in the event of the revolt of Absalom (2 Sam 16-19). Leonard Rost imputes this material to the author of the SN even as Van Seters considers it a later work of the CH and therefore post-Dtr. Contrary to both positions, Veijola finds enough reasons to assign the block to the DtrH.
443 T. Veijola, *Ewige Dynastie*, p. 26–27.

have come to nought if the author did not know of 1 Kings 1, as Van Seters purports, even though the position of Rost that the Dtr did not touch the material thereof could be tenable up to a point, as long as Rost does not negate the Dtr's knowledge of the tradition spelt out in the chapter. We will, however, subscribe to the stand of Otto Kaiser that the narrative is pre-dtr but concurs, in the long run, with Veijola that the hand of the Dtr is there to ensure that the edges of the material are trimmed to provide a theological basis for it, in order to make it conform to the promise of an eternal dynasty to David and the privileged position accorded Solomon by his theophoric renaming.

6.3.2 1 Kings 1; description and interpretation

We have before us a long and vigorous drama filled with tensions and resolutions in an episode that is played in different scenes at different locations. In fact, the whole chapter, as a drama, takes place on a single day, but brings together all the important characters of the royal court who, knowingly or unknowingly, make choices that will determine the course of their lives in the near future of the narrative. We will seek to divide the chapter into seven parts, on the basis of the time and locus (place) where that scene is played, in order to appreciate the natural development of the evolving drama with the shift from one locus to another.

- v. 1-4 – The exposition
- v. 5-10 – Adonijah's presumption
- v. 11-14 – Nathan and Bathsheba
- v. 15-37 – The successor is named
- v. 38-40 – Solomon is king
- v. 41-48 – Report by Jonathan Ben Abiathar
- v. 49-53 – Adonijah's capitulation

6.3.3 The Exposition: v. 1-4

The initial exposé of v. 1 is certainly not the introduction of a separate and independent narrative. It describes the last days of David who is simply referred to as המלך דוד (King David). Thus he is the same character that the narrative has dealt with up to this point, therefore, a continuation of the narrative of 2 Samuel.[444] Neither are any of the major characters whom we will meet in the unfolding drama introduced, thus giving credence to Rost's theory (see above) that 1 Kings 1-2 are the conclusion of the SN. In this exposition (vv. 1-4), the hitherto valiant man of vigour is here described as aged, weak and practically passive (he could not get warm under a pile of clothes); an object on whose behalf the servants must confer and take a decision (*a young virgin to lie in the king's bosom and keep him warm*). Despite the emphasis deliberately placed upon Abishag's physical beauty, "the king did not know her" (לא ידעה) - v. 4. We may be tempted to ask: what happened to the sexual impulse of the man whose inordinate sexual desire drove him to take the wife of his military officer and planned the death of the soldier in order to extricate himself from the web of intrigue in which he had been entangled? (2 Sam 11:4ff). The author of this piece has in this subtle way established an image of David that contrasts with the one of the parable of Nathan in which the rich man (the king) took the lamb which used to lie in the bosom of its poor owner (ובחיקו תשכב), 2 Sam 12:3, and slaughtered it for his visitor (his inordinate desire). Here lies David with Abishag in his bosom (בחיקך ושכבה), v. 2 and yet he did not "know her", v. 4:

ובחיקו תשכב → 2 Sam 12:3
ושכבה בחיקך → 1 Kings 1:2

The inversion of the word order seems to hint at the ominous nature of David's inability to know her and what the consequence will be. It is all

---

[444] This is directly in contra distinction to the opinion of Mordechai Cogan that given the numerous references to events in 1 & 2 Samuel, 1 Kings 1-2 is an independent narrative that bridges the reigns of David and Solomon, written by an author who was familiar with much of David's life but whose focus was the rise of the new king (*I Kings*, p. 166). It is clear to us that Cogan makes a marvellous analogy comparing the narrative here to a bridge. Since a bridge connects two points or loci (A-B) to ensure a smooth flow of thought or movement, the author already knew of what had gone before and after and, therefore, establishes the link between them. Hence the narrative will make no sense without its mediate and immediate past, to which the narrator looks for explanation of the present events as the basis for the future of his narrative. Thus the present narrative cannot be independent but dependent.

the more remarkable when we consider the fact that the king was at that point in time "only" seventy years old and as we have established in the previous chapter of this work (5.2.7) David was impotent at seventy and, inevitably, plays second fiddle to the great pillars of the history; Moses, Joshua, Samuel and even Caleb. The loss of David's virility adds a new twist to the story; just as the failing health of a modern head of state places his authority in question so also the failure of David to "know" Abishag brought on an emergency. He was no longer able to function as a king and therefore the choice of a successor had become critical.[445] As if acting upon a cue, or at least so the author would like it to look like, Adonijah jumps into action at this moment and makes his intentions to succeed his aged, impotent and languid father known. The whole drama of the succession is set rolling with this action of Adonijah as against the inaction of David and that in regard to Abishag, which will later spell the doom of the contender to the throne of David (1 Kgs 2:13-25).

6.3.4 Adonijah's presumption: v. 5-10

The choice of Adonijah to arrogate to himself the honour of kingship and his subsequent preparation towards the realization of his aim have a ripple effect within the corridors of power; by these actions, Adonijah sets a vigorous and fast-moving drama in motion that lasts within the span of a single day. With a simple but emphatic two-worded sentence, he sets forth his ambition; אֲנִי אֶמְלֹךְ (I will be king) The narrator has already betrayed his disapproval of Adonijah by describing his action as arrogant and presumptuous with the use of *miṯnasseʾ*, the hithpael participle of *nasaʾ*, which can be translated as: "he exalted himself continuously". The narrator establishes without doubt that the decision was personal and tantamount to a usurpation of the throne, since he arrogates to himself the authority of king-making and that not just once but day after day. Until now this position has been held and exercised by Yhwh himself, through his prophet, Samuel (1 Sam 10:1, 16:13). Nothing is said about the personal merits of Adonijah, besides being a handsome man, born after Absalom and not

---

445   G. Rice, *Nations under God*, p. 8.

having ever been reproved by his father, a remark that will suggest his *crown prince* position at court.[446]

The level of narrative material at this stage of the kingship in Israel does not provide the reader sufficient information for an objective position on the issue of succession, but it appears to us that primogeniture was the order of the day. With the exception of the interruption of Athaliah's usurpation, twenty kings succeeded one another upon the throne of David. Out of this number only two were irregular as far as the transfer of power from father to son, either primogeniture or the oldest living son, is concerned; Jehoahaz was succeeded by Jehoiachim, his brother (2 Kings 23) and Jehoiachin by Zedekiah, his uncle (2 Kings 24, Jer 37:1).[447] Since eighteen of the successions were the living oldest sons of their fathers and both irregularities were enforced by the Egyptians and Babylonians respectively, primogeniture was obviously, the preferred principle of succession. This makes the presumptions of Adonijah very well understandable, but his very first public act splits loyalties at the court of David[448] and provides room for the development of factions, if that was not already evident, which will lead to his own undoing. He invites Joab, the commander of the army, and Abiathar, the priest of the Elide lineage. In addition, Adonijah invites also all the royal officials of Judah and all his brothers, the sons of the king, to the sacrifice of sheep, oxen and fattened cattle at the stone Zohelet, near Enrogel, but

---

446 According to 2 Sam 3:2-5, Adonijah of Haggith was the fourth son born to David at Hebron; Amnon of Ahinoam, Chileab of Abigail, Absalom of Maacah, Adonijah of Haggith, Shefatiah of Abital and Ithream of Eglah. While the narrative leaves a lacuna with regard to Chileab, Amnon and Absalom were already dead (2 Sam 13-15), leaving Adonijah as the eldest of the existing sons of the king. His presumption then is not without good reason but the choice of the successor was not a close-ended affair for him to exult himself like Absalom. Beauty and lack of paternal reprove were no guarantee of succession even as they did not help Absalom before him.
447 T. Ishida, *The Royal Dynasties in Ancient Israel*, p. 154.
448 It is imaginable that Adonijah was aware of the developing opposition to his bid as successor to David that is why he categorically omits certain names from his list of invited guests. This action could be interpreted by those courtiers as being declared *persona non grata* with the risk of elimination at the appropriate time. The narrator has kept this fact out of the narration so that it comes as a surprise when Nathan initiates the counter move.

conspicuously leaves out Zadok, the priest, Benaiah, commander of David's elite corp, the prophet Nathan, Shimei, Rei[449] and Solomon.

The details of Adonijah's preparations are all set within the context of the day on which he makes his intentions known, but the reality is that he had already done the planning. Thus vv. 5-8 can be put in a parenthesis or, better still, rendered in the narrative past. He had procured himself chariots and horsemen with fifty men to run before him. This royal act reminds the reader of Absalom, who had done the very same thing in his bid to displace his father (2 Sam 15:1). Unlike Absalom, however, Adonijah had enlisted the help of Joab and Abiathar, and added the royal officials of Judah and the sons of the king to complete his list. The list of his invited guests was well thought out; the commander of the army, the royal officials of Judah, the priest and long-standing supporter of David[450] and all the sons of the king, apart from Solomon. Despite his thorough preparation, Adonijah commits an apparent omission that sets the casual reader of the text thinking; he struck out the name of Solomon (born in Jerusalem) from his list of the king's sons, left out Nathan and Zadok (active only in Jerusalem) as well as the "captain" of the Cherethites and the Pelethites, the faithful men who had been with and served David through thick and thin. "They were not with Adonijah", says the narrator, and could be understood as "they did not support him" and he, on his part, ignored

---

449 Practically nothing more is known about Shimei or Rei and they do not appear anymore in the narrative. This is perhaps a palpable indication that they featured in the tradition as presented otherwise it will not make sense for a redactor to add their names to the list. Dietrich's question marks raised on the position of Oswald point to the precise personal names that are mentioned in the events of the succession of Solomon as a possible indication of concrete events of the past embedded in the narrative (*Forschung an den Samuelbücher*, p. 277). His list leaves out Rei, the name which we find most conspicuous since the name does not appear anywhere else in the narrative.

450 1 Sam 22:20. The single survivor of the massacre of the priests of Nob by Saul, Abiathar fled to David and remained with him all through his struggles serving him as priest until Solomon would banish him to Anathot on account of his wrong choice of following Adonijah (1 Kgs 2:26-27). This banishment is for the dtr redactor of the books of Samuel and Kings in fulfilment of the oracle spoken against the house of Eli by an unknown man of God in Shiloh (1 Sam 2:22-36).

them.[451] As the story will have it, this political blunder and underestimation of human potentials and actions made the failure of his coup d'état a foregone conclusion. It is this same underestimation of human actions that led to his misjudgement in asking for the hand of Abishag in 2:13-25 to provide Solomon the needed excuse to order his death.

The main action of this scene comprises a single verse, v. 9; Adonijah sacrifices sheep, oxen and fatlings at the stone Zohelet near Enrogel and invites all his brothers and the royals of Judah. The scene of his sacrifice and possible coronation is chosen probably for its location and convenience of space. According to Mordechai Cogan, the spring Enrogel lay about 500m south of Jerusalem at the border point between the tribal allotments of Judah and Benjamin with an open area around it capable of accommodating such a gathering. The Serpents Stone or Zoheleth was a landmark at the time of the story but now is no longer identifiable.[452] Remarkably, it is the very location where Jonathan and Ahimaaz, the spies of David, waited for their information to be relayed to David during the revolt of Absalom (2 Sam 17:17). We may take it for granted that all his prime supporters were also present, but the actual intention of this feast is left out for the reader to conjecture. The many links that this coup d'état had with Absalom's revolt are, most probably, the narrator's patent mode of indicating that this was meant to be the coronation ceremony for Adonijah, but like its precursor, it was doomed to failure. The scene ends ominously with a second list of the uninvited which is the exact equivalent of the collaborators of Adonijah but this time around they are those who are closely associated with his father. It is this group of uninvited guests who will feature

---

451 It is clear that we have before us two parties that we might categorize as the Hebron and Jerusalem factions for the lack of an apt description in the text itself. While Adonijah was born in Hebron, Solomon belongs to Jerusalem by birth. Given the activities of Nathan in Jerusalem and Zadok's later role as the leader of the Jerusalem priesthood and the fact that this ancient Jebusite stronghold was captured by David and his men i.e. the Cherethites and the Pelethites (2 Sam 5:6), it seems Adonijah consciously sidelined those courtiers who were emotionally attached to Jerusalem and opted for those of Judahite origin and sensibilities. Whether there were other sons born to David in Jerusalem besides Solomon, and whether or not they were also invited are not stated anywhere and we may never know.

452 M. Cogan, *I Kings*, p. 159.

in the next scene and propel the drama forward. The following table illustrates the strength of the support base of each party:

Support base	Adonijah	Solomon
Military	Joab (+ army?)	Benaiah + elite corp
Religious	Abiathar (priest)	Zadok and Nathan (priest & prophet)
Political	Royals of Judah	?
Family	Sons of the king	Bathsheba (beloved wife of the king)

Despite the apparent advantage that Adonijah has over Solomon, the quality of the Solomonic camp and their close relationship to the aging king make them a powerful force to reckon with. It is this relationship that will eventually tilt the balance by craftly winning for itself the authoritative word of King David.

6.3.5 The counter plot: v. 11-14

As the course of events would have it, the prophet Nathan seems to have been the first to notice the dark clouds gathering around the court of David or is at least the first to make a counter move. He reacts with such astuteness and consequence that Adonijah is outwitted in his presumptions. He finds in Bathsheba a comrade in suffering and a willing collaborator; after all they were both unwanted guests at the feast of Adonijah and potential public enemies in the unfolding of events in the near future. We are left to imagine where the scene may have been played as the narrator does not find it necessary to indicate the locus of the encounter. We are free to imagine that it might have taken place at the residence of Bathsheba since Nathan takes the initiative by going to her. He employs the rhetorical style of exaggeration to drive home his point and ensures a quick acceptance of his view. In three effective steps he puts across his point and lays down his plan; Adonijah is king without the knowledge of King David, he has a good piece of advice that will save the life of both Bathsheba and Solomon and sends Bathsheba to David with the plan he has hatched promising to enter himself into the presence of the king to confirm her words. Even though the life of the prophet was also at stake, Nathan craftily avoids any form of reference to his own predicament and inherent advantage in the plan and plays upon the passion of a mother to save her own life and that of her son.

To ensure the success of the plot and encourage Bathsheba to carry it out boldly, Nathan assures her that he will come in to confirm her words while she speaks with the king. The crux of the plot was to hinge on an oath that the king had supposedly sworn to Bathsheba that Solomon would succeed him: *"Did you not, my lord the king, swear to your servant, saying: Your son Solomon shall succeed me as king, and he shall sit on my throne? Why then is Adonijah king?"* (1:13).[453] The real import of the plan was to cause the king to take the all-important decision of choosing a successor and that was to be achieved by the corporate report of the beloved wife and the faithful prophet at the service of the king, who bluntly claim that Adonijah "is king" on the blind side of the still reigning King David. The reader can assume at this point that Bathsheba hurriedly leaves on her mission while Nathan loiters about for a while.

The scene brings back into focus the main actors of 2 Sam 12:1-25, where Nathan rebukes David for his adultery and murder, announces the punishment commensurate with those sordid crimes but turns round to proclaim the return of the king to Yhwh's favour by the renaming of Solomon as Jedidiah, for the sake of Yahweh. Thus, this third appearance of the prophet is already prepared for by the events of the second. The narrator, however, does not provide his reader with any inkling of the issue of succession; neither does he make any reference to a promise of David to Bathsheba regarding Solomon as the future successor. Nonetheless, at the appropriate moment when a promise serves to diffuse the tension of succession, it is resorted to and is left with the aged and apparently weak David to either confirm or deny it. The said promise comes out of the blue

---

[453] The reference to this supposed promise is the cause of a variety of reactions from critics. Already in 1910, Hugo Gressmann had noted that this oath could not have been made by David earlier otherwise it would not make any sense for Bathsheba to have waited for the promptings of the prophet to take the necessary steps for its fulfilment. What is more she would not have required the assurance of the prophetic support in the presence of the king to ensure the success of the plan (*Die Schriften des Alten Testaments*, p. 194). Robert Alter remarks that the fact that we have no way of verifying whether David made this promise or whether it was a pious fraud that Nathan and Bathsheba are foisting on the old and failing king constitutes one of the intriguing aspects of omissions in biblical narratives (cf. *The Art of Biblical Narratives*, p. 98).

with Nathan using the root word for "king" or "reign" (מלך) four times in his instruction to Bathsheba (v. 13). In fact the multiple and almost redundant use of the word in the ensuing narrative leaves no room for doubt in the mind of the reader as to what the author wishes to communicate; the succession to the throne.[454] Thus the word becomes the leitmotiv on the lips of Nathan as he dismisses Bathsheba and on the lips of Bathsheba when she enters the presence of the king to carry out her mission.

6.3.6 The successor is named: v. 15-37

The scene now shifts from the encounter between Nathan and Bathsheba, wherever it might have taken place, to the chamber of King David. The presence of Abishag in the room does not in any way disrupt the mission of Bathsheba, thus indicating that Abishag had nothing to do with the contending parties and was no danger to the cause of succession.[455] Again, we have no idea of the protocol that was observed with regard to entry into the presence of the king unless we are to take it for granted that Bathsheba was the (beloved) wife of the king and had unrestricted access to her husband and that this condition was not affected by the presence of Abishag.[456] She

---

454 The root מלך is used sixty times in the fifty-three verses of this single chapter in its noun form and nine times in its verbal equivalent. In the middle portion of the narrative, vv.15-37, the word is used in almost every verse until it arrives at its apex when Adonijah recognizes Solomon as המלך שלמה (King Solomon) and demands an oath from him that he would not kill him with the sword (v. 51).

455 If the presence of Abishag serves its purpose, then the king must have received enough warmth from her intimacy with him and must be in a position to take the all-important decision that has brought Bathsheba into his presence. This returns to the importance of the initial information that the narrator has given his audience in vv. 1-4; the king required the presence of the maiden in order to keep warm.

456 The strict protocol observed in the palace of Ahasuerus does not help us much in painting a picture of the court protocol of the Jerusalem palace, especially at the time of David, coming out of a different land, epoch and tradition. We can only infer that however strict or relaxed it may have been, the favourite wife somehow had her way even as Esther did in the face of mortal danger (Esther 5:1-3). Fokkelman thinks that Nathan was aware of the fact that Bathsheba had an unrestricted access to her husband that is why he resorted to her to make the first entry before he goes in to confirm her report (cf. *King David*, p. 355).

enters the chamber and does obeisance to the king who asks her what she desires; a single-worded question of two syllables – ma^h-llāk - the consonants of which accurately play upon the theme of the whole drama because it sounds like *mlk*- to rule or be king.[457] Bathsheba takes the advice of Nathan but changes the mode of its presentation. The core of Nathan's plot was to be a double question: Did the king not swear to Bathsheba that her son Solomon would succeed him? Why then is Adonijah king? Bathsheba takes the cue but changes it to a narrative of what Adonijah has done without the knowledge of the king (mālak – he has become king – vv. 11 & 18) and ends upon the note that the eyes of all Israel are upon the King "to tell them who will sit on the throne of my lord the king after him" (v. 20). She subtly accuses the king of his inaction by reminding him of what fate she might share with her son after the death of the king should he fail to carry out his promise (v. 17-21). The force of the accusation is achieved by her cunningly listing the supporters of Adonijah without reference to the opposing party; all the sons of the king, Abiathar and Joab.[458] Thus, she and her son are isolated and can be saved only by the word of the king.

One notes immediately a variation in the supposed promise of David quoted by the two actors; Nathan and Bathsheba. Even though Bathsheba repeats the words of Nathan, she adds; "*My Lord, you swore to your handmaid by the Lord your God…*" (v. 17). This makes the said promise all the more solemn, but at the same time curious that Nathan left out the divine name in his version. Robert Alter posits that Bathsheba employs the style of an *incremental repetition* by lifting the promise unto a higher order of solemnity that opens the way for David to carry it further.[459] This actually

---

457 J. P. Fokkelmann interprets the short bi-syllabic question of David as his lack of desire or inability to talk much more but "his question "what do you want?" points inadvertently to the theme and thus already answers itself; for the consonants of *ma-lāk* echo the evil "*mālak 'Adōnīyāhū*" and even the vowels contribute to the effect." (Cf. *King David*, p. 355).
458 Putting Joab at the last position on the list causes the name to resound in the ears of the king, bringing memories of long years of rancour harboured in the heart of David, which will erupt in his final instructions to Solomon in 2:5-6, to which we would also add the execution of Absalom against the will of David (2 Sam 18:14).
459 R. Alter, *The Art of Biblical Narrative*, p. 99. That Nathan left out the divine name in his instruction is, according to Alter, because the Man of God was

produces psychological pressure on the otherwise inactive king who now realises that he is the only one who can decide the issue of succession and, at the same time, prevent the doom of his wife and son. With his ego boosted to the appropriate level by the court language of Bathsheba, David frolics in his prestige as the reigning king and will grasp the only choice left open for him. In the meantime, the narrator leaves his audience in the dark as to the actual reaction of David to the plea of Bathsheba and heightens the suspense by leaving it hanging and introducing the expected character who is to add salt to the narrative. In this scene, the reader notes a marked difference in the characterization of Bathsheba. In 2 Sam 11-12 she was practically the innocent object of David's lust and is either sent for (11:4), spoken about (12:9) or the object of David's consolation after the death of the son (12:24). The only exception to this passivity is the message she sent to David that she was pregnant (11:5). In this scene we meet for the first time a bold and active mother pepped up by her survival instincts and desire to save her son from impending danger, assured by the support of the prophet of Yhwh. She wakes up from her slumber, takes her fate into her own hands and enters the chamber of her senile husband whom she probes up by her cutting but well-measured words that will effectively coerce him into speaking the very words that will save her life and that of her son.

True to his words, Nathan arrives at the appointed time while Bathsheba is still speaking with the King. Whoever reports his arrival refers to him with his proper title, *the prophet*, to underscore his importance. He carries out the finesse of being in the royal presence as a loyal servant, falling prostrate in submission, and begins immediately to speak his part of the prepared speech without being asked by the King. While the scope of Bathsheba's repetition of the plot was based upon the dire strait of a worried mother and her son, in mentioning the guests of Adonijah as the sons of the King, Abiathar and Joab, Nathan raises the issue unto the political platform. He asks the King point blank if he has decreed that Adonijah be king in his stead. If not, then how come he has sacrificed today and invited as guests Joab, the commander of the army, and Abiathar the priest, who are eating and drinking before him and saying; Long live

---

perhaps nervous about taking His name in vain in case the idea of the pledge was a hoax.

King Adonijah? (v. 25). He then provides the list of the uninvited; *me, your servant, the priest Zadok, Benaiah son of Jehoiada and your servant Solomon*. The emphatic position of "me", appositioned to "your servant", finds its symmetry in "your servant Solomon" which encapsulates the list of David's faithful servants (v. 26). The incremental addition of Nathan to the planned message lays bare the political scenario of the two-party royal conflict. David has to react or his faithful servants will lose their lives. He finishes with another question that might even sound presumptuous unless his relationship with the King warrants it; *"Has this thing been brought about by my Lord the king and you have not let your servant know who should sit on the throne of my Lord the king after him?"* (v. 27).

The constantly servile attitude of Nathan and Bathsheba in their address of the King, in contrast to naming Adonijah as king, makes the latter automatically a usurper and induces the still reigning King David to react and save his own dignity even as he bears the onus of saving his faithful servants as well as Bathsheba and Solomon. The reaction of David allows itself to be interpreted in two directions; on one hand it underpins the absolute importance of Nathan in the narrative because the aged and evidently passive King David takes a decisive action only after the corroboration of the prophet to the message of Bathsheba.[460] On the other hand, as Michael Zach would put it, it portrays David as a fickle-minded old man who takes the all-important decision of succession so late in his life and under the influence of his emotions towards Bathsheba and the machinations of the prophet and not upon the good of the nation. He is only a tool in the hands of the cunning Nathan and Bathsheba who unduly manipulate him.[461]

---

460 The question that will bother the mind of the reader is why the prophet Nathan puts his life on the line for no other son of the king than Solomon. We may say that his life was already on the line since Adonijah had left him out of his list of favourites, but why only Solomon? Hugo Gressmann opines that the position of Nathan was natural because Solomon had been entrusted to him in his childhood, 2 Sam 12:25 (*Schriften des Alten Testaments*, p. 193).

461 M. Zach, *Die Ambivalenz des David-Bildes*, p. 72. Zach compares the decisiveness of David in his dealings with Bathsheba and Uriah on one hand and his indecision in the Adonijah-Solomon succession conflict on the other, and questions the actions of David at this moment since one cannot be certain whether he is acting consciously or simply under the influence of the prophet and his strong emotions towards Bathsheba, his wife. This leaves much room

The plan goes off when David takes the cue and acts probably better than expected; he has Bathsheba summoned, the reader is expected to assume that Bathsheba was silently dismissed from the presence of the king the moment Nathan entered and, therefore, was not privy to the discussions that ensued between king and prophet, and in the presence of enough witnesses, solemnly confirms the said vow which he now promises to fulfil *"this day"* (v. 30). We are inclined to believe that by this assertion David identifies fully with the said oath and removes, in so doing, any doubt in the mind of the reader about the "older" oath which now forms the core of the new. The problem that might have arisen with time is also resolved; David will act this very day. This action of David makes a difference between the two contestants; while Adonijah seeks power on his own accord, Solomon depends upon his father, King David. The king now causes Zadok the priest, Nathan the prophet and Benaiah, son of Jehoiadah, to be brought before him, he instructs them to seat Solomon on the King's own mule and lead him down to Gihon. There he is to be anointed by Zadok and Nathan, and be brought over to sit upon the throne of the king amid trumpet blasts and shouting; *"Long live King Solomon!" "You will go after him and he will sit on my throne and he shall be king in my place; for him I have appointed to be ruler (nāgîd) over Israel and over Judah."* To which Benaiah responds in the affirmation praying that Yhwh makes the throne of Solomon *"greater than the throne of my lord King David"*. Thus the said oath which, according to Alter, attained its solemn religious force by the incremental repetition of Bathsheba becomes, for Fokkelman, a reality opposing Adonijah in the moment when David transforms it into

---

for the ambivalence in the characterization of David in the SN. (p. 77). While we have no cause to doubt Zach's position, we see a conscious effort by the narrator of the story to leave his audience free to make up its opinion of David. He, however, does not provide any precise information that will influence the audience to form an unduly negative opinion of the senile king because, with the warmth received from Abishag, the king derives the needed energy to take the last most important decision as king and resolves once and for all the issue of succession. The instructions given for the anointing of Solomon and the reaction of David to the congratulatory messages of his courtiers at the end of the ceremony indicate that the aged man was definitely conscious of his actions and aware of its effects upon his dynasty and for the future of the nation (1 Kings 1:47-48).

a command in favour of Solomon, "which is then indeed fulfilled"[462] in the next scene. With this oath and the subsequent command, the king takes sides with Solomon and, thus, against Adonijah.

6.3.7 Solomon is King: v. 38-40

The scene is the climax of the whole drama and very unique in itself, because it is neither a dialogue nor a direct speech as in the preceding scenes. It is the narrator's own account of the execution of David's orders by his servants; Zadok, Nathan, Benaiah and the Cherethites and the Pelethites. Solomon is for the first time introduced into the drama but still as a passive character made to ride upon the king's mule and is led down to the Gihon, where the priest Zadok takes "the horn of oil" from the tent and anoints him. They blow the trumpets and all the people repeat the words of David (v. 34); "Long live King Solomon". The rejoicing of his following grows so loud that the earth quakes at their noise as they go up from Gihon.

In all these there is no report of Solomon acting or saying anything, rather everything is done on his behalf. The reader will logically make a mental comparison with the anointing of Saul and David. In both preceding accounts the protagonist is conceived as passive and on whose behalf the prophet acts. Saul innocently seeks the Seer for the purpose of consulting him about his father's lost asses and returns with the kingdom because the prophet had been waiting for his arrival (1 Sam 9-10). In the event of the sacrifice at Bethlehem, David was left out of the list, being the smallest of the sons of Jesse, occupied with his duty of tending the flock while his brothers line up before Samuel. It is only the insistence of the prophet that brings the chosen one to the sacrifice and to his anointing. There also David neither acts nor talks but everything is done on his behalf (1 Sam 16). This is in direct contrast to Absalom (2 Sam 15) and Adonijah (1 Kings 1:5-10) who make their own preparations as pretenders to the throne. In the question of kingship, the elect of Yhwh does not presume the position. He is led to it. The silence of Solomon in the struggle for power at the court of David is very much in accord with the developing tradition of kingship at the early stage of the nation of Israel.

---

462   J. P. Fokkelman, *King David*, p. 367.

The account is very short in narrative time and scrupulous in its precision of obeying the king's orders. The urgency in the flow of the language equals the haste that was required to beat out Adonijah's head start and every action in the narrative is geared towards that effect. In fact the scene ends with *all the people* playing pipes and shouting with great joy, described by a double paronomasia on *ḥll* and *śmḥ* and finishes with a powerful hyperbole; "The earth quaked/split with their noise" (v. 40). It is this earth-splitting noise that will initiate the next scene.

The mention of the Cherethites and the Pelethites makes explicit what hitherto has been implicit. The presence of Benaiah suggests the support of the elite corps that he commands; the loyal group of fighters who had remained faithful to David in all his trials before his installation as king, the same core group with which David conquered the Jebusite stronghold of Jerusalem.[463] It is this group of valiant men who guard Solomon to Gihon for his anointing and up from there into the city. Gihon, also known as the Spring of Siloam, in the Kidron valley, stands as a counter plot to Adonijah's choice of Enrogel and the fact that it was the main source of water to the city, was probably chosen to make for the maximum publicity and for its proximity to the palace to cater for space and time.[464] The location will

---

463 In this work we have drawn attention to the fact that the report in Chronicles (1Chr 11:4) simplifies the conquest of Jerusalem as the corporate work of the whole nation but 2 Sam 5:6 emphasises that the conquest was carried out by David and his men; to remove the possibility of any part of the nation claiming credit for the city; the City of David. Mordechai Cogan (*I Kings*, p. 162) links the origin of the name of this unit of mercenaries who remained loyal to David in most adverse circumstances with the island of Crete and the Philistines, noting the coupling of the two names in Ezek 25:16 and Zeph 2:5. The association in itself is a wonder even though probable that the name of David's loyal royal corps originated from the arch enemies of Israel; the feared "Sea Peoples". 1 Sam 22:2 gives the initial information about the base of the group of men who gathered around David; his brothers, his father's house and all who were aggrieved in one way or the other. From this humble base an army was built under the command of David and may have happened that in the unfolding of the history, mercenaries were hired who may have had foreign origin hence kĕrētî and pĕlištî.

464 Hugo Gressmann notes that why David did not cause the anointing to take place in the palace or in the tent of Yahweh remains an unresolved riddle (*Die Schriften des Alten Testaments*, p. 194), but we are of the view that it

make it difficult to place the "Tent", if it is a reference to that prepared by David for the Ark of the Covenant in the city (2 Sam 6:17). However, if we assume that Zadok had taken the horn of oil before going down to the Gihon so that מן־האהל (from the tent) explains from where he had already taken the horn, then this inconsistency would not arise. Once Zadok has the holy oil, Abiathar can not have it with him and the only anointing of the day takes place at Gihon. In the words of Fokkelman, "Now, as the oil cascades over his locks, we are reminded of the anointing of Saul and David."[465] It is in this context that the narrator's choice of words once more hits the apex of precision that the hyperbolic noise was made by "all the people", hence the acceptance of Solomon by all the people who were present.[466]

Despite the brevity of the narration and its precision in obeying the orders of David, a breach occurs in the execution of those orders. The report has it that Zadok the priest anointed Solomon and not Zadok and Nathan

---

was for the purpose of making the anointing a public action to counter the feast of Adonijah and at a location that would quickly attract attention to itself. Its proximity to the city makes for a shorter distance to be covered in respect to Adonijah's choice of Enrogel. Thus we have in the choice of Gihon, a symmetrical advantage to the opposing feast of the rival prince. This is however, not to play down the importance that a water source might have played in the mind-set of the Semitic people.

465 J. P. Fokkelman, *King David*, p. 371. This is in reference to the anointing of Saul and David in 1 Sam 10:1 and 16:13 respectively. It is this act that validates the kingship of Solomon; he is anointed with the holy oil taken from the Tent of Yhwh. We will like to once more add that the author makes a distinction between the two preceding anointings; while Saul is anointed with a פך השמן (vial of oil) David and Solomon are anointed with a קרן השמן (horn of oil). Thus Solomon's anointing corresponds better with that of David than Saul.

466 The contention of the so-called author of the Court History, according to J. Van Seters, that Solomon lacked divine election is certainly nowhere in the train of thought behind this narrative. In the opinion of this author, David made the choice in the presence of enough witnesses, he was anointed by the legitimate priest with the holy oil taken from the tent of Yahweh and acclaimed by all the people present, and who further followed him to his enthronement at the palace of the king. Cf. J. Van Seters, *In Search of History*, p. 288.

as David had ordered (v. 34). This leaves the question open why it was important for the narrator to put the two together in the instruction of David. Times have changed, we may imagine, and the days are gone when the towering image of the prophet Samuel made and unmade kings. Now cultic practice seems to demand that anointing is carried out by the priest and the prophet who was historically present remains as a witness of the priestly act. In that case, we would contend that the importance of the prophet was not so much for the validity of the anointing as for the choice of the actual successor, i.e. not cultic but political. Here, the prophet Nathan distinguishes himself immensely from the comparable Mari and Assyrian court or cult prophets of the Ancient Near East. While they were principally restricted to the cult centre, Nathan is only active at the court and where they communicated through written messages delivered by a third person, Nathan communicates in persona.[467] Of course, in Mari, prophecy was not restricted to temple personnel, but more especially the seers were lay persons who received messages for distinguished personalities of the society.

Nathan is present at the anointing, primarily, because the whole ceremony was the granting of his request by the king. He acted at the right moment to save the dynasty of David from falling into the hands of the usurper by encouraging the senile king to take the right decision and remained to see it carried through. After this final event that brings Solomon to the throne and its report in the next scene, the prophet Nathan falls abruptly out of the narrative line and into oblivion just in the same manner as he had abruptly entered the history. For many, Nathan's role in the political intrigue tarnishes his image as a prophet, a position that Rost captures in his work:

> Of course it must be admitted that Nathan seems all too entangled in worldly affairs to bring any great credit upon his vocation as prophet. But other prophets have intervened with greater or lesser force in the progress of history and in doing so have showed themselves to be at least as much "party men" as Nathan is here – a fact which did not detract from their prophetic activity and the respect given them as prophets.[468]

As far as I am concerned, Nathan is an important seam in weaving together the story of David's succession. My vested interest in this prophet, as

---

467 W. Oswald, Nathan der Prophet, p. 251.
468 L. Rost, *Succession*, p. 79.

Skah will put it, is neither for the study of details of his "psychology nor a verification of whether he is realistic or not. Because, in analysing biblical characters, critics use other categories by which they endeavour to specify the function of the characters with regard to the plot."[469] The function of Nathan acquires its shape and position only in the context of the succession to the throne of David in Jerusalem and hence, in the three chapters under review and every action or word of the prophet has its reverberation in the past, present or future of the history. Even though his renaming of Solomon in 2 Sam 12:25 is not explained, Peter R. Ackroyd precariously compares it to the double names of OT and NT personages, one of which may designate purpose or character as in the cases of Jacob-Israel (Gen 32:28) and Simon-Peter (Mt 16:18). In this sense, Jedidiah, Beloved of Jhwh, emphasizes the divine choice of this son of David and what Solomon was to be in the future, though curiously this name does not appear any more.[470] As the events of 1 Kings 1 unfold, the reader is no longer reminded of the already given clue, he is expected to read meanings into what he already knows and the active role of the prophet Nathan in the palace intrigue is not a surprise. Mordechai Cogan asserts that the main protagonists of 1 Kings 1-2, Adonijah and Solomon, are not mentioned in 2 Samuel "safe the reference to Yhwh's approbation of Solomon in 12:24-25, which plays no part in the present drama".[471] I am convinced that a seemingly innocent remark with such a grievous consequence could not have been made for nothing. The dtr author and narrator of the events has made use of the remark to foreshadow what was to happen later so that the audience will look back for meanings to explain the events of the present. This author was already aware of the succession story and its intriguing process and so has left his audience the chance of a hindsight provided by the presence of the prophet Nathan.

---

469 J. L. Skah, *Our Fathers Have Told Us*, p. 83.
470 P. R. Ackroyd, *Second Book of Samuel*, p. 115. Accroyd hints on evidence of throne and original names of the last kings of Judah in 2 Kings; Eliakim – Jehoiakim (23:34), Mattania – Zedekiah (24:17) and might suppose that Jedidiah was the original name and Solomon the throne name but this is only based upon pure conjecture.
471 M. Cogan, *I Kings*, p. 166.

6.3.8 Report by Jonathan Ben Abiathar: v. 41-49

The scene comprises three direct speeches; the almost rhetorical question of Joab (v. 41), Adonijah's address directed to Jonathan (v. 42) and Jonathan's long and comprehensive report of Solomon's anointing and enthronement (v. 43-48). The narrator craftily diverts the attention of his audience away from the expected enthronement scene at the palace of the king to the parallel feast of Adonijah, where another anointing (and possible enthronement) is awaited. Surprisingly, it is just as Adonijah and his guests finished eating (feasting), with no opportunity for anointing, that the earth-rending sound of Solomon's train was heard. The narrator constructs his narrative in such a way that the narrative events from the encounter of Nathan and Bathsheba to the anointing of Solomon take place within a time-frame of a dinner; a factor that might give us an inkling of the excellent organization of court life at the time of King David. It is the ability of this court system to provide a quick response to a situation of emergency that ultimately overtakes Adonijah in his own game.

Joab hears the sound of the trumpet and inquires what has brought the city into an uproar? At that very moment Jonathan Ben Abiathar arrives who could give an appropriate answer to the apprehensive military commander. The narrator, however, edges Adonijah between them so that the response is apparently not to the question of Joab but to Adonijah's. The latter acknowledges Jonathan as a worthy man who brings good news,[472] but the former counters that compliment indicating that this time around he brings only bad news and reports almost word for word the process of Solomon's anointing with the additional information that "Solomon now sits on the throne of the kingdom", the people have gone in to congratulate King David for his choice of Solomon and that the King has blessed the Lord for granting him a successor out of his own offspring who today sits on his throne before his very eyes. This addition proves that the succession was now a closed question that elicits the consequent reaction from

---

472 The praise of Jonathan is most probably in reference to his espionage for King David during the revolt of Absalom. In that event he and Ahimaaz, son of Zadok were responsible for the relay of the crucial information that was needed to work out the defeat of Absalom's plans (2 Sam 15:35-36, 17:17-22).

the guests of Adonijah; they all get up trembling and each one goes their own way (v. 49).

The speech of Jonathan has a quality of stating its conclusion right from the beginning. He opens his discourse with אבל, which could be translated as "alas" or "to/on the contrary" and immediately provides the reason: "Our Lord King David has made Solomon king." This was supposed to have made short work of Adonijah's self-confidence because, according to Fokkelman, it cancels his optimism that Jonathan had brought good news.[473] The rest of the report is clarification of what he meant by that naked summary of the event. We may take it for granted that Jonathan, like his father, was a supporter of Adonijah by the reception he received from the pretender, even though he was absent at that very moment to be able to bring the news of the counter event. That notwithstanding, he refers to King David in a very respectable manner as the centre of authority at court, who has made Solomon king. The words of congratulations pronounced by "the King's servants" reflect the affirmative response of Benaiah in the previous scene where Yhwh makes the throne of Solomon greater than the throne of King David, to make Benaiah's words a reflection of the sentiments of the courtiers (v. 47). At the same time he concludes his report by pointing to the fact that David acknowledges a higher authority than his own, Yahweh, the God of Israel, who has granted that his offspring sits upon his throne this day, and blesses Him for it.[474] One might think that the boldness of Adonijah coupled with the silence of David had led many

---

473 J. P. Fokkelman, *King David*, p. 374.
474 Fokkelman intimates that Jonathan might have been so swept along by the presuming air with which Adonijah, over a long period of time presented himself as David's successor that until that fateful day he had not realised the difference between Adonijah's and David's cause. Thus his report reveals a sincere loyalty to David which includes a willingness to continue recognizing the legal authority. In the view of Fokkelman, the narrative is created in such a way that there is a correspondence between the prophet Nathan and Jonathan in vv. 11-14, 22b-27 and 41-49 centring around the two names; יו/נתן (Jo/natan – Yhwh gives). The two men enter in all the three scenes to report on the unfolding events of the succession but it is the significance of their names and persons that serves as the most patent testimony of Solomon's kingship as a gift of Yahweh. Yahweh's interest transcends the opposition of the factions (*King David*, p. 376).

a courtier into the illusion of following a crown prince until the report of Jonathan lifted the veil of pretension from the face of the usurper. We see in their confused and trembling departure an unconditional acceptance of the authority of the aging King David and a shift in allegiance from Adonijah to Solomon.[475]

Veijola has remarked that the triple וגם (and also) which introduces the additional information of Jonathan in vv. 46, 47 & 48 does not in any way prove the haste with which the reporter gives his account (against Benzinger, 1899. 8, Sander, 1911. 24, Noth, 1968. 28) but provides a clear indication of a later addition to an existing narrative by the Dtr.[476] He argues that the response of Jonathan to the question of Joab ends logically in v. 45 with the sentence; *"This is the noise that you heard"* since the question of v. 41 was about that very noise or uproar; *Why is the city in uproar?* Vv. 46-48 link up smoothly with vv. 30, 35-37 and are built around the same theme of Solomon sitting upon the throne of David on "this very day", as a fulfilment of a vow purportedly sworn by David. It is this vow that Nathan and Bathsheba push David to fulfil in favour of their protégé against the legitimate crown prince. Once the vow is fulfilled, the pious David bows upon his bed in humble adoration to Yhwh to whom he attributes the accomplishment of the succession. This, according to Veijola, is the dtr *Bearbeitung* (revision)

---

475 David M. Gunn sees in the succession of Solomon a senile David caught up by the events of his youth. The aged David thinks that he has given up his throne into the hands of his son with the approval of the Lord and proceeds to worship but in actual fact the throne has cunningly been taken away from him by Nathan working together with Bathsheba. The promise upon which the choice of Solomon is based is non-existent; Adonijah has certainly not been made a king, even if his activities were geared towards that. All that we are witnessing here is an act of deliberate deception, an ingenious ploy by the Solomonic party, where David in his senility imagines that he is bestowing the kingdom but in actual fact it is being taken away from him, not by violence as in the case of Absalom but taken all the same. Thus ironically, it is the son of Bathsheba who brings to final expression the theme of seizure established originally by David's seizure of Bathsheba. Just as David took Bathsheba and secured his position by effecting the murder of her husband; so now Solomon takes the kingdom and reinforces his hold on it by having the heir-apparent murdered. Cf. *King David*, pp. 104–106.

476 T. Veijola, *Ewige Dynastie*, p. 16.

of the narrative with the view to a theological legitimization of the Davidic dynasty.[477] In reaction to this position of Veijola and my ardent desire to remain as close as possible to the text, I find it obvious that the *waw* + גם (the particle of coordination or conjunction) links up to what precedes it as a logical consequence, while maintaining its independent position in marking the final climax in the narrative.[478] Hence we posit that its three times repetition in vv. 46, 47, and 48 constitutes a three-step climax in the report: enthronement, congratulations and the King's thanksgiving:

46 וְגַם יָשַׁב שְׁלֹמֹה עַל כִּסֵּא הַמְּלוּכָה
Now, Solomon sits upon the throne of the kingdom.

47 וְגַם־בָּאוּ עַבְדֵי הַמֶּלֶךְ לְבָרֵךְ אֶת־אֲדֹנֵינוּ הַמֶּלֶךְ דָּוִד לֵאמֹר
Moreover, the king's servants have come to bless our lord King David saying...

48 וְגַם־כָּכָה אָמַר הַמֶּלֶךְ בָּרוּךְ יְהוָה אֱלֹהֵי יִשְׂרָאֵל אֲשֶׁר
And thus has the king said; "Blessed be Yhwh the God of Israel who...."

In all these three instances the particle of conjunction (*gam*) stands at the first position or the emphatic position and, according to van der Merve, marks the syntactic domain of the particle; the sentences that follow it, for focus (emphasis). In this regard *gam* marks the fact that a messenger is delivering his message[479] and the catch words in that message are marked by the emphatic position of gam. It facilitates the quick flow of the report by marking out the important elements in a cryptic or staccato fashion. We are in accord with Veijola in pointing out that the three verses are dtr additions to an existing narrative but we are also of the view that the triple expressions of *waw* + גם at the emphatic position in the three consecutive verses mark the important elements in the message that is hastily delivered for emphasis; the enthronement of Solomon, the congratulatory message of the courtiers and the thanksgiving of the aged King David. A short survey of the first Book of Kings shows that among the many uses of וגם in the book, the particle is found in the first position of sentences almost exclusively in the traditionally acknowledged dtr passages such as; 3:13, 8:41, 10:11, 14:24, 15:13, 16:7 and 21:23 besides 1:46, 47, 48 and

---

477 T. Veijola, Ewige Dynastie, pp. 16–18.
478 B. K. Waltke & M. O'Connor, *Biblical Hebrew Syntax*, 39.3.4c & 4d.
479 CHJ van der Merve, *The Old Hebrew Particle gam*, p. 159.

2:5 and supports Veijola's assignment of the verses to the dtr author and redactor of 1 Kings 1-2.

6.3.9 Adonijah's capitulation: v. 50-53

In the last scene of the drama, the unconditional acceptance of the will of the aging King David and consequently the choice of Solomon as the rightful heir to the throne has set the anti-climax of Adonijah's bid in motion by giving him out as a usurper. In mortal fear for his own life, the pretender goes over and takes hold of the horns of the altar demanding royal amnesty and pardon from Solomon: "Let King Solomon swear to me first that he will not kill his servant with the sword" (v. 51). The promise is given but on the ambiguous condition that he proves to be a worthy man. Solomon then has him brought before him, he does obeisance before the king and is dismissed by the simple two-worded imperative; "Go to your house" (v. 53). With Adonijah's acquiescence and conditional dismissal the palace coup ends, Solomon is king and, after the series of other related kingly decisions to be taken in the following chapter, the story is concluded in 2:46: *"So the kingdom was established in the hand of Solomon."* In the meantime the role of the Prophet Nathan ends with the enthronement of Solomon and the man of God falls out of the narrative limelight.

We may say that by his action, Adonijah seeks political asylum by the act of taking hold of the horns of the altar.[480] This brings the audience back to the advice of Nathan to Bathsheba "so that you may save your own life and that of your son" (v. 12) and the latter's emphasis on the issue; "Otherwise it will come to pass when my lord the King sleeps with his fathers, that my son Solomon and I will be counted as offenders" (v. 21). Now there is a reversal of roles and Adonijah is at the losing end. His request is temporarily granted when he comes face to face with his brother and does obeisance before the newly enthroned King Solomon. This obeisance

---

480 A typical Jewish altar was constructed according to Ex 27:2 with horn-shaped projections at its four upper corners, on which the blood of the sacrificial animal was daubed by the priest using his finger (Lev 4:25). Recourse to it as a means of asylum-seeking seems to have been a normal practice and is accepted by the king but the same act will be rejected when Joab attempts it in 2:28-34.

officially ends the rivalry between the two princes as an acknowledgement of the authority of Solomon and, therefore, a renunciation of his bid for the throne. The encounter is broken by the command of Solomon's authoritative word; "Go to your house" (v. 53). The crux of the matter here is not the question of who had the right to the throne but who was chosen for that position. The capitulation of Adonijah indicates that even though he was, at that moment, the eldest living son of David and the actual crown prince, succession to the throne was not simply the prerogative of primogeniture and Biblical tradition does not mince words on the issue of succession. In fact astuteness and good behaviour are praised, if not preferred to primogeniture. In broad daylight, Jacob robbed Esau of his birth right (Gen 25:29-34) and with the help of his mother, tricked his father Isaac to deprive Esau of the blessing due him (Gen 27). This made him the accepted heir to Isaac and the Patriarch of Israel. In another circumstance, the final blessing of a dying father turned to a time of reckoning for Jacob who denied Reuben the leadership position of the first born (Gen 49:4) and rather ascribed the sceptre to Judah and his house (49:10) because of his sin against his own father; he had gone up unto his father's bed (Gen 35:22). In doing so, Jacob side-lined also Simeon and Levi for their unpredictable wrath and violence (v. 5-9, cf. 34:30) and accorded the fourth son the leadership position.[481] The right person to rule or to be king is the question of whom Yhwh chooses through the instrumentality of his prophet.

6.4 Synthesis

At the right moment in the history of the monarchy in Israel when the successor to the throne of David becomes an open issue at court, in 1 Kings 1,

---

[481] In the so-called "Prism B" of the Babylonian and Assyrian texts, which recount "The fight for the Throne" of Assyria, Esarhaddon, the youngest son of Sennacherib was elected crown-prince with the approval of all the gods but his brothers pitched themselves against him in battle which he won against all odds and, subsequently, became king in the stead of his father. The practice of succession in the ANET makes it clear that primogeniture was not an automatic criterion for succession as in many instances the strongest or most able among the princes was the preferred choice. Cf. *ANET*, p. 298.

the author of the narrative has, carefully but adequately, prepared the mind of his audience as to how the heir is going to be chosen but not who he is going to be. According to Leonhard Rost, 2 Sam 6:23 and 9:1ff have made it clear that there is no competition from the Saulides since even Michal had died childless and Mephibosheth, the son of Jonathan, had been effectively domesticated by David.[482] The prophet Nathan has, in 2 Sam 7:11b-12, filled in the possible blank space in the course of events with the assurance that the successor would be from the loins of David, according to a divine oracle. 2 Sam 11-12 have seen to the introduction of Bathsheba into the court as "the beloved wife" of David and hinted at her second son as the *beloved of Yhwh* who is put into the charge of the prophet Nathan, intimate Gressmann and Rost. This son, Jedidiah or Solomon still drops out into the background, while the victory of Rabbah takes up the centre stage until he resurfaces in 1 Kings 1. In the meantime, other sons of David occupy our attention:[483] Amnon digs his own grave and is buried in it by Absalom (2 Sam 13) who in turn stages a coup d'état and meets his own death at the hands of the very man who pleaded his cause, Joab (2 Sam 15-18). 1 Kings 1 opens with another of the sons of David, Adonijah, flexing his muscles for the throne without the explicit approval of his father and thereby stands rejected as a pretender. This state of affairs reminds the reader of the choice of David when other sons of Jesse were the focus of attention until the youngest is brought unto the stage. There it was the prophet at the helm of affairs and that tradition is here not broken; the prophet exercises the role of a king-maker either at the background or at the forefront. In the same way, the elder sons of David are rejected, one after the other, until the choice falls upon the young Solomon, promoted by his mother with the active manoeuvre of the prophet Nathan and elected by the aged king as successor to the throne.

The three Nathan pericopae are undoubtedly connected directly or indirectly to the succession to the throne of David, with the prophet Nathan

---

[482] For Rost the childlessness of Michal meant that the continuance of the dynasty over all Israel was in danger, since David's sons so far were only the sons of the king of Judah. A child with Michal would have been a direct political link between David and the northern tribes. Cf. *Succession*, p. 86.

[483] L. Rost, *Succession*, pp. 98–99.

playing a very significant role as the connecting ligament that binds all the single episodes together. Guided by the divine word, Nathan limited the scope of the succession to the sons of David (2 Sam 7), he reappeared at the birth of Solomon whom he is said to have renamed Jedidiah, because of the Lord (12:25), and initiated the series of events that led to the enthronement of Solomon as king (1 Kings 1). We are of the view that the writer of 1 Kings 1 had other characters at his disposal who could very well have taken events into their own hands to aid Solomon's accession to the throne since their lives were also at stake. Two of such prominent characters were the priest Zadok and Benaiah, the commander of the royal corps. Thus the choice of Nathan as the initiator and leader of the counter coup that saw to the toppling of Adonijah has its own significance in the tradition. While Gressmann thinks that the prophetic movement took control of internal politics in an earlier period and even meddled in the affairs of the ruler,[484] we think that, at the time of David, kingship might not have completely weaned itself off the influence of the prophet, keeping in mind the role that Samuel had played in the life of Saul and in David's tortuous journey towards his establishment as king. On the level of the narrative sequence, Nathan takes over the role that Samuel had played in promoting the kingship of David and aids Solomon as the legitimate heir to the throne in fulfilment of his own prophecy, the word of Yhwh (2 Sam 7). Hence Nathan's active role in the palace intrigue, if not a simple fact of history, is in consonance with the character that the writer assigns the prophet all through the history.

Up to this point, I have narrowed down the scope of the research to three episodes where Nathan, the prophet, appears in the narrative and the significant role that these episodes play in the build-up to the succession to David's throne, but we are still not even an iota wiser with regard to the identity and development of this elusive character in the tradition. In none of the three episodes is the prophet introduced in the manner which we are used to in Biblical narratives; parentage or provenance, and yet he is the one character that the dtr author pitches against the great David and is able to bring the king to his knees. "*Nathan der Prophet*" is the title of

---

484   H. Gressmann, *Oldest History Writing*, p. 30.

Wolfgang Oswald's *Habilitationsschrift* of the year 2006 in Tübingen.[485] In this work, Oswald systematically treats the three chapters in which the prophet Nathan appears in the Biblical narratives, or we should say, in the Succession Narratives. He boldly enters into the intriguing field of identifying this elusive prophet with the initial stance that Nathan is not the only prophet who wielded authority over a king, but he is unique in being the only one who did so as a member of the court in a very close association with the king (Gath being the only one comparable).[486] He is a prophet who communicates the word of Yhwh and a counsellor actively involved in the political affairs of the nation and in both ways acts at the background or virtually in secret.[487] He may not have been a historical personality of the tenth century[488] but an *ideal-type* and a purely literary symbol of a prophetic figure of the seventh and sixth century B.C.[489] He was neither a Jebusite defender of the Yahwist religion nor the upbringer of the prince; a counsellor of David, nor a court or cult prophet, he was neither bound to any particular party at the palace nor was he the first of the prophets who pronounced judgment.[490] He is simply a fictional character created by a later literary genre that desired to have a messenger of Yhwh at the court of David and assigned to him various functions in different appearances. These functions include; refusal of David's plan to build the temple and the election of his dynasty for ever (2 Sam 7), the punishment of David for his guilt of adultery with Bathsheba and murder of Uriah to safeguard the legitimacy of the successor to the throne (2 Sam 12) and finally the initiator of the enthronement of that successor to ensure the stability of the reign of that dynasty (1 Kings 1).[491] He concludes that all the three episodes belong to the *Thronfolgegeschichte*, written hundreds of years after the event, with

---

485 Oswald has developed his Habilitationsschrift further into the book bearing the same title that appeared two years later. Cf. Section 2.2, p. 37–38.
486 W. Oswald, *Nathan der Prophet*, p. 255.
487 W. Oswald, *Nathan der Prophet*, p. 265.
488 W. Oswald, *Narhan der Prophet*, p. 263.
489 W. Oswald, *Nathan der Prophet*, p. 264–272.
490 W. Dietrich, *Forschung*, p. 274.
491 W. Dietrich, *Forschung*, p. 275, cf. W. Oswald, *Nathan der Prophet*, p. 274.

the image of the prophet Nathan as the means to prove the divine right of the house of David.[492]

In a nutshell, the Nathan pericopae are too explicit to be fictional, too concrete to be imaginary and yet too ambivalent to be the work of a single author. The sacred author has created such an elusive character that any attempt at identifying him remains a painful, brainracking exercise in futility. For this reason, I will rather expend my effort on finding out the interconnectedness of the three episodes in the context of the succession to the throne of David instead of seeking to establish the identity of the prophet. Do all three texts stem from the same hand (or two separate hands as Oswald purports)? What could have been the possible sequence of their composition? And why this particular character called Nathan?

6.5 The Nathan narratives seen together

In my effort to lay bare the interconnectedness of the three Nathan episodes, I cannot help but acknowledge my indebtedness to the literal critical method, especially as expounded by Leonhard Rost, for the necessary leads, but I will hold on deftly to a synchronic view of the End-text, which in itself does not exclude the historico-critical point of view. The three episodes have grown out of a historical milieu as an integral part of a literary product that functions in the context of a politico-religio-cultural environment so that the part does not exist independently of the whole. I will endeavour to eschew unnecessary repetitions that might amount to superfluity in the work, since the various episodes have already been analysed within their respective chapters. Instead, I will pick out those areas that require elaborations and add new inputs to those that will throw light on the current theme.

Mordechai Cogan virtually strips 1 Kings 1 of any trappings of history by modern definition since, as the general view of critics indicates, the writer betrays his bias in favour of Solomon right from the onset.[493] But it is this very aspect of the narrative that might accord it a historical basis in the light of biblical narratives; a pro-dynastic writer recounts the victory of the

---

492 W. Dietrich, Forschung, p. 275; a summary of Oswald's *Nathan der Prophet*, p. 264.
493 M. Cogan, *I Kings*, p. 166.

legitimate successor over a powerful pretender with equally potent support base. This author does not set out to write history in the modern sense of the word, but recounts in a flowing language and style the events that took place and how he understands them with his faith in Yhwh and his choice of the Davidic dynasty at the backdrop. The one aspect that is less contended is the fact that Solomon, a younger son born to the now aged King David in Jerusalem, inherited his father against the odds of older sons of the king. He was the son of Bathsheba, the wife of Uriah, whom David married under questionable circumstances. From the deuteronomistic author's point of view, Solomon built the long-awaited temple in Jerusalem (Deut 12:11, 1 Kings 6-8) and promoted Yahwism, at least, as the official religion of the State. His faithfulness to Yhwh was found wanting under the persistent temptation of diplomacy and political expediency (1 Kings 11:1-13). Besides, the toll that his elaborate building projects took on the people quickly quenched the flames of the euphoria that surrounded his rise to the throne and eventually set in motion the division of the nation (1 Kings 12:1-24) and its eventual collapse. Of all the three episodes involving the prophet Nathan, his active role in securing the throne for his protégé is the one that is least contended for its uniqueness and least affected by the insertion of additional materials. We are of the view that the historical probability of this active role in the process of Solomon's succession is at the basis of the two other appearances of the prophet, at least, in the form that we have them today. That is to say that the dtr additions to the two narratively previous appearances of the prophet are constructed with the succession of Solomon in mind.

Solomon's self-justification for commanding the death of Adonijah in 1 Kings 2:24 goes a long way to prove that the narrator, in this case the Dtr, knew of an account containing 2 Sam 7:11b, which belonged to an account by Nathan of a revelation made to him concerning the future of the Davidic dynasty and has linked it to the events of 1 Kings 1-2. We are inclined to believe that the genesis of the three episodes is the lobby of Nathan for his protégé.[494] The event is read backwards into the promise of an

---

494 In thinking along this wavelength we have benefitted from the method of Leonhard Rost who begins from 1 Kings 1 and works backwards to the origin and birth of the successor, where 2 Sam 11-12 provide the information

eternal dynasty (2 Sam 7:4-16) by a few deft strokes to make it reflect the succession of Solomon and his expected waywardness and punishment. Still, the dynasty of David would triumph because Yhwh had promised and Yhwh is faithful to his word even in the face of human failure. Since the dtr additions to the oracle of Nathan (2 Sam 7) bear the general durability of the dynasty (v. 11b), the almost specific reference to the reign of Solomon (v. 13) and the punishment with the rod of men (v. 14b-16) it will not be too far-fetched to conclude that the dtr writer has extended the oracle as a prophecy after the event, putting it in the mouth of the prophet Nathan. This would explain why the tradition behind the reference to the same promise in Psalm 89:20-38 has no link to the prophet Nathan; the Psalmist is concerned with the subject of the promise (Yhwh) and its object (David and his lineage), but not the instrument, hence, his preference of a vision (v. 20). The dtr author found in this narrative a dynamic prophet active at the court of David and who has no qualms of conscience lobbying for a particular son of David against another and succeeds in gaining the approval of the aged king to that effect. This yeoman's work was no mean achievement to play down and might very well have influenced the prophet's further appearances in the story of the succession of David. In case the prophet was already part of the tradition at the disposal of the dtr redactor of the oracle of Nathan in 2 Sam 7, the view that we identify with, the dynamism of the prophet in the political arena of 1 Kings 1 made it easier to place the additions of that author, which reflect Solomon's succession and reign, on the lips of this prophet. And if the name was not formerly attached to the tradition, here was the occasion to find a distinguished character worthy of that role in every sense of the word.

---

about his mother and his birth, v. 24-25. Oswald recommends the movement from 2 Sam 12 to 1 Kings 1 as a better way of reading the material in order to understand the stature of Nathan in the narrative and avoid the unnecessary inconsistency in the characterization of the prophet (*Nathan der Prophet*, p. 274). This recommendation is certainly the aim of the dtr author who expected his readers to take the narrative as a unity. It is for this very reason that he has edited the different narratives by providing the necessary linkages that serve as the foundation for the "future events" to connect the stories to one another. While agreeing with both positions, my stand gives priority to 1 Kings 1 as the motivating factor of the dtr additions in 2 Sam 7 and 12.

Nathan's portrayal in 2 Sam 7 is similar to that in 2 Sam 12; he is a prophet who executes God's commissions, whatever the cost. The prestigious position accorded him by the narrator in the pronouncement of the oracle in 7:5-16 as the ultimate word of the Lord favours his entry into the presence of the king as an outstanding man of God. Here he delivers the long oracle of doom with authority upon the overwhelmed king.[495] The similarity between the two oracles is glaring; they both contain a double messenger formula that links the past to the present and projects the result into the future. The theme of the oracles, like the third appearance in 1 Kings 1, is the dynasty of David and its continuity. Having pronounced the oracle of salvation geared towards the durability of the dynasty of David, the prophet Nathan is once again accorded the honour of balancing that oracle with another of doom aimed at leading the king on to repentance and thereby preserving his dynasty. The narrator accords Nathan a special function in the narrative; he is the one character who provides the theological stunt to the narrative and re-directs the trend of the events. He breaks the stalemate by causing the king to acknowledge his guilt and brings on course the process of fulfilling the oracle of an eternal dynasty to an otherwise human and morally fragile monarch.

The literal critic Hugo Gressmann is convinced that the parable of Nathan was not originally couched for the double crime of David, it was already available and the late writer has placed it there as an introduction to the judgment of David.[496] An author worth the name knows how best to utilise the bulk of information at his disposal to carry across his message. This author chose a subtle way of making the king judge himself before the prophet pronounced the oracle of doom upon his house, by means of a parable, whether that parable was originally couched for that moment or not. The Dtr, who has drawn the prophet into the promise of an eternal dynasty to David, concludes his insertion with the reprove of the monarch to give him a balanced image in the narrative; he is the only one who does not condone the evil deeds of the king (12:1-15a), even though he does not withdraw his service to him. The devotion of the prophet to the dynasty is there to be seen even in the moment of

---

495 J. P. Fokkelman, *Throne and City*, p. 212.
496 H. Gressmann, *Oldest History Writing*, pp. 29–30.

its deepest crisis. Despite his harshness in pronouncing the prophecy of doom, Nathan is not devoid of mercy towards the house of David, for he also declares the patent words of divine forgiveness (v. 13) and renames Solomon *"the beloved of Yhwh"* (v. 25) as a subtle introduction to the events of 1 Kings 1, where he appears as the legitimate choice of both David and Yhwh to rule in the stead of his father. In this way, the dtr author once again enhances the function of Nathan by linking him to one of the most significant leitmotifs of his narrative that will acquire its full import only when Solomon sits upon the throne of his father.[497] Nathan puts his head on the line for Solomon because he is the one whom Yhwh has chosen as the successor to the throne of his servant David. 2 Sam 12:24-25 are the dtr summary to the David-Bathsheba-Uriah sequence, necessitated by the author's knowledge of the events of 1 Kings 1. Taken in itself, this summary hardly fits into the framework of the siege of Rabbah, but such a remark is required for the future succession of Solomon to the throne of his father David. In this way the ingenuity of the author once more comes into play by preparing the minds of his audience for the events of the narrative future.

The narrator evolves a style of addressing David and Nathan that reflects the emotions he would like to transmit to his audience in the three episodes. We would like to demonstrate this style by means of tables:

---

[497] Leonhard Rost posits that the narrator has a passion of hinting at the future development by means of occasional leitmotifs whose significance does not become clear until much later in the narrative. He cites such beautiful and loaded but apparently harmless remarks as: "And Jhwh loved him" – 2 Sam 12:25, "But the king did not know her" – 1 Kings 1:4 and "Go to your house" – 1:53. The first acquires its full significance at the election of Solomon while the second will be used to eliminate Adonijah as an attack on the harem (2:13-25) and consequently, the response to the open-ended ominous dismissal of the rival. To this, Rost will also add that the only time that the narrator deviates from this habit and anticipates the development of his story is in 2 Sam 14:17; *"And Yhwh ordained to defeat Ahithophel's good counsel, so that Yhwh might bring evil upon Absalom."* Cf. *Succession*, p. 102.

2 Sam 7

Name	Mode of Address	Agent
David	המלך – v. 1, 2	Narrator
	המלך דוד – v. 18	Narrator
	עבדי דוד – v. 5, 8	Yhwh
	עבדך – 10x in vv. 18-29	Auto identification of
	דוד – 4x in vv. 18-29	David
Nathan	נתן הנביא – v. 2	Narrator
	נתן – v. 4, 17	Narrator

2 Sam 12

Name	Mode of Address	Agent
David	דוד – 13x in vv. 1-25	Narrator
Nathan	נתן – 6x in vv. 1-24	Narrator
	נתן הנביא – v. 25	Narrator

1 Kings 1:1-48

Name	Mode of Address	Agent
David	המלך דוד – v. 1, 28, 32 & 38, 47, v. 13	Narrator / Nathan
	המלך/ל – 31x: vv. 1, 2², 4, 10, 14, 15³, 19, 22, etc.[498]	Narrator et omnes
	אדני – v. 17	Bathsheba
	המלך אדני – v. 2	Courtiers
	אדני המלך – 15x: vv. 2², 13, 18, 20², 21, 24, 27², 31, 36, 37, 38²	Courtiers, Bathsheba, Nathan and Benaiah
	אדנינו המלך דוד – v. 43, 47	Jonathan Ben Abiathar
	דוד – v. 8,	Narrator
	אדנינו דוד – v.11	Nathan
Nathan	נתן – v. 11, 24	Narrator
	נתן הנביא – v. 8, 10, 22, 23, 32, 34, 38, 44, 45	Narrator, David, Jonathan

In the first appearance, David is addressed with his proper title as *king* by the narrator and as *the servant of the Lord* when Yhwh speaks of him. Nathan is introduced as *the prophet* by the narrator who subsequently refers

---

[498] In reference to David, המלך is used twenty-five times in vv. 1, 2², 4, 10², 14, 15³, 19, 22, 23, 25, 28², 29, 33, 34, 36, 38, 44², 47 and 48 while למלך appears six times in vv. 3, 4, 16, 23² and 31.

to him with his own name without title. The friendly tone of the narrative is the exact opposite of 2 Sam 12:1-25, where David and Nathan are consistently referred to with their own names without titles except in v. 25. In the third episode both David and Nathan are once again addressed with titles. David is constantly called *King David* by the narrator except in v. 8, in reference to David's own warriors and the servants, courtiers, Nathan, Bathsheba, Benaiah and Jonathan address or refer to the king as *my/our lord the king or my lord King David*.

This short survey helps us to come to the realization that the narrator or the dtr communicates a very powerful message by the mode of address that he chooses; David under the grace of Yhwh (2 Sam 7 and 1 Kings 1) is consistently addressed with royal and ministerial titles, while under the yoke of sin (2 Sam 12) he is referred to simply with his own name as if to say; "After all he is just like any other man." The fate of the king is also shared by the prophet, who rises and falls with him and his dynasty; while he is addressed with both his title and name in 2 Sam 7 and 1 Kings 1, he is simply stripped of every title in 12:1-24. It is only in v. 25, when Solomon is born, that he is called *the prophet* once again (a fact that is lost if one follows the LXX because of the explanatory note in 12:1). This mode of treating the king and the prophet indicates that Nathan is inevitably bound to the dynasty of David and its fate even as it expresses the fidelity of David to the prophet-king relationship that makes the king admirable to the dtr redactor of the history. It is no wonder then that Nathan would throw all caution to the wind and would not even hesitate to soil his hands for the sake of ensuring the stability of the dynasty of David.[499] Even before the temple was built, Nathan had promised the eternal durability of the Davidic dynasty and when the king jeopardized the kingdom by the guilt of adultery and murder, it was the same prophet who stepped in to provide the king the possibility of a second chance through his unqualified

---

[499] The bond between Nathan and the house of David was so strong that Leonhard Rost and Hugo Gressmann both conclude that Solomon was entrusted to the prophet in his childhood. Cf. *Succession*, p. 99 and *Schriften des Altes Testaments*, p. 193. While we will not foundamentally reject this view, we might not want to be that categorical as the narrative does not provide any such hint.

repentance and forgiveness. He crowned that ministry with the renaming of Solomon to conclude the mission of repentance and personally ensured the succession of this humble son of David when the royal house proved unable to heal itself of the burden of pride and self-agrandisement. Thus Nathan causes the fulfilment of two prophecies in the DtrH; the promise of Yhwh to build David a house in 2 Sam 7:11b and the inherent meaning of the second name of Solomon, Jedidiah, in 2 Sam 12:25b. The fulfilment of these two promises depends on Yhwh alone and that despite the unworthiness of the desolate royal house, as acknowledged by the prayers of David in 2 Sam 7:28 and 1 Kings 1:48.[500]

The three episodes have yet another noteworthy point in common; David at prayer. The piety of David does not go unmentioned whether in times of happiness or sorrow. At the end of the promise of an eternal dynasty for his house, David goes in and sits before the Lord in thankful prayer (7:18-29). When the son born to him by "the wife of Uriah" fell ill, he fasted and interceded for him and, even when he died, he went into the house of the Lord and worshipped. This attitude of prayer is repeated after the enthronement of Solomon as king in his stead; he bowed down in worship on his bed and prayed in thanksgiving. The Nathan pericope portrays the religiosity of David under three modes or attitudes of prayer; thanksgiving, intercession and worship. His trust in the Lord is clearly demonstrated by his boldness in daring to pray for the life of the child even though he knew that his death had been predestined according to the word of the prophet. He does not lose heart when his prayers are not heard, rather he concludes them with another level of prayer; worship. David remains practically the single character in the SN who constantly consults the Lord[501] and frequently refers to the divine purpose of human action and interaction. The Nathan pericope presents a very fine image of David; a grateful man whose success depends upon Yhwh his God, the repentant

---

500 W. Oswald, *Nathan der Prophet*, pp. 234–235.
501 Examples are not lacking in the stories of David's rise to power where he sought the divine will before undertaking expeditions or beating a retreat; 1 Sam 23:2, 4, 11-12, 2 Sam 2:1, 5:19. A remarkable example of the man David at prayer is his famous prayer that the Lord turns the counsel of Ahithophel into foolishness in 2 Sam 15:31.

sinner who surrenders his life into the hands of the Lord, against whom he has sinned, and the aged and frail king who acknowledges the divine hand that has guided his whole life and ensures him a successor. In all of these events, the prophet Nathan has been by his side as the spiritual guide and it is in this capacity that he provides him the needed push towards untying the knot of the issue of succession.[502]

---

[502] W. Oswald makes a distinction between David's inquiries of the Lord before taking specific actions and these three moments of prayer, where he is not the subject of his actions but at the receiving end of divine benevolence. It is with this David, who relies so completely on his God that he puts no price on his own choices, that Nathan correlates showing him the way of Yhwh; pronouncing judgment and mercy upon him and taking the challenge to set the fate of the king's house on the path predestined by Yhwh. Cf. Nathan der Prophet, p. 222.

Chapter 7. Conclusion: The parable of Nathan; a slap in the face of the dtr image of David?

The parable of Nathan with its attendant oracle of doom stands as the only moment in Biblical tradition in which David, the pious, righteous and ideal king of the dtr historian, stands condemned as a villain by a prophet. The condemnation follows the dtr pattern of judging the kings of Israel and Judah, especially the worst of them like Ahab and Manasseh, who did what was evil in the sight of Yhwh more than those who had gone before them (1 Kings 16:30, 2 Kings 21:2ff compare with 2 Sam 11:27, 12:9). This unique episode makes interesting reading and captures the full concentration of its audience, who, right from the beginning, is captivated by the witty parable ingeniously narrated by the prophet. The parable exudes a response from the king as a just judge who pronounces a just judgment. Unfortunately, that judgment is his auto-condemnation for the crimes of adultery and murder in which he has actively embroiled himself. The prophet proceeds immediately to pronounce an oracle of doom against the king and his house, presenting him as an arch villain who deserves nothing but the death penalty. The reader is left in a state of perplexity in his bid to reconcile the ambivalent image of David, on one hand, recognized as the ideal king of Israel and the yardstick with which all other kings after him are judged and, on the other, exposed as a villain and בן־מות - the son of death - i.e. one worthy only of death. Could the same author have presented the hero of his work as an ideal character and at the same time a criminal or has someone else smuggled this episode into the work in order to sabotage the otherwise impeccable image of King David in the DtrH?

The first chapter of this research has presented the context of the parable of Nathan and its resultant double oracle of doom like an archaeological field of research and has showed that there are three strata of narrative material woven together to construct the story of David's adultery with Bathsheba and murder of Uriah, which warrant the pronouncement of judgment against the king and, at the same time, his forgiveness by the prophet Nathan, and all these in the context of the siege and conquest of Rabbah. The frame-work is the battle of Rabbah (2 Sam 10:1-11:1 &

12:26-31) that could have been taken from the annals of King David. Into this account of the capture of the Ammonite city, the dtr author has inserted the report of the adultery and murder committed by David against Uriah's family (11:2-12:25). This narrator does not leave his audience in the dark with regard to the resolution of this moral evil, but the act of resolving the impasse is so placed that it could have gone one way or the other. On one hand, the sickness and death of the child born as a result of the illicit relationship could have been considered an appropriate punishment that would suffice for David's crimes. On the other, the intervention of the prophet and the judgment, consequently pronounced, will later be fulfilled almost to the letter in the tragedy of David's family (13:1-19:8). The narrator does not choose between the two options, instead he presents both and places them side by side in a uniform narrative that makes for an aesthetic and semantic beauty. The height of this beauty is achieved when one moves from what Yhwh would do as a follow-up to His displeasure on account of David's evil deeds (11:27b); He might send the prophet to David (12:1) or strike the child so that it gets sick (12:15b). The author opts for a third variant in presenting both options in his narrative without making it clumsy or ambiguous. That notwithstanding, the question still remains that if the Chronicler could overlook this blight on the moral life of the monarch (1 Chr 20:1-3), what hidden motive could this writer have had to maintain the blotch in his narrative while doing everything possible to portray David as the ideal king?

This perplexing question has been at a centre stage of Biblical scholarship over the years. The literal critical school of thought seeks to answer the question by positing that the parable is part of the SN, an identifiable unit in the DtrH, to which a later redactor has added 12:7-12 to make it reflect the self-destructive activites of the sons of David (13-19) as the effect of and punishment for the evil deeds of their father, David. The SN is in itself anti-monarchical and it is only the late redactor's addition of 12:24-25 that makes the material succeed as a legitimization of Solomon and therefore it was written *ad maiorem Salomonis gloriam*.[503] John Van Seters takes the argument further and proposes that the DtrH idealizes David in a manner that

---

503 E. Würthwein, *Thronfolge*, p. 7.

justifies the hope of a Messiah who would come from the dynasty of David as a future reality, if not present. This document gave shape and identity to the community of the exiled Jews at least from the early period onwards. In the post exilic period, however, there arose an anti-monarchical tendency that sought to subvert this identity in its bid to discredit any possibility of reviving the monarchy.[504] To sabotage or even nullify this perspective of history, this post exilic tendency, symbolized by the "Court History", takes up the concept of an ideal King David and submerges it in a quagmire of evil, intrigue, adultery and murder to smear the royal house in such depth of rot that it is no longer worth aspiring towards. It is this author then who is behind the parable of Nathan and its double oracle of doom against David and his house. The work is not history but the figment of the imagination of this post-exilic writer which has been added to the otherwise pro-David and pro-monarchical DtrH to dent the image of the Ideal King David, carefully created and meticulously defended by the exilic author.[505]

Modern opinon varies remarkably from the literal critical position on the parable of Nathan and especially on the SN which is seen as an integral part of either the DtrH, with the scope of finding meaning to the unimaginable catastrophy of the loss of nationhood in the 6th century and offering hope to the exiled Jew or the Enneateuch (Genesis – 2 Kings), which narrates the story of Israel from creation to the exile. Beginning with the unparalleled discovery of Martin Noth of the variety of materials spanning from Deuteronomy to 2 Kings that this exilic author (or group of authors) has gathered together to recount the history of Israel in the light of her obedience or disobedience to the word of Yhwh her God, the discussion becomes all the more vivacious with different writers finding different and single units within the big whole which were written for particular and specific objectives. McKenzie finds in the block of material stretching from 1 Sam 16-1 Kings 1 an apologia written in favour of the Davidic dynasty. This evidently makes 2 Sam 11-12 estranged in its environment since the report of the adultery and murder committed by David is, according to McKenzie, definitely not an apology and, therefore, a later addition.[506]

---

504 J. Van Seters, *Court History and DtrH*, pp. 91–92.
505 J. Van Seters, *In Search of History*, p. 290.
506 S. L. McKenzie, *David's Enemies*, p. 39.

Whybray responds to this problem by positing that this addition was made to produce the sense of cause and effect in the narrative,[507] but Anderson combines the two positions on the basis that an apology does not need to be a distortion of history to achieve its aim, rather it has to appeal to what is already known or believed. At the same time, it has to reshape and supplement the shared information, beliefs and hopes. The adultery and murder that were committed by David will not go away, but could be told in a less critical manner by the introduction of the necessary twist to the account in order to make it acceptable to its audience. Therefore, the material is part of the Solomonic apologia and predates the deuteronomistic historian. The author has only toned down the venom inherent in the narrative and made it innocuous; the adultery and murder have been forgiven and the dynasty is rid of the guilt of David so that the successor could gloriously be announced in vv. 24-25.[508] Yet others will neither consider the parable of Nathan an anti-monarchical nor apologetic material. Naumann finds in 2 Sam 11-12 a unified material that pre-dates the dtr writer. It is neither anti-David nor anti-monarchy but a prophetic prologue to Absalom's revolt and a paradigm of political ethic.[509] E. Blum concurs basically with Naumann on this point but goes further to add that the overriding theme of the narrative is the internal stability of the Davidic monarchy.[510] My research has proven that the stability and durability of the dynasty of David is at the heart of the DtrH and that the writer of the history associates the prophet Nathan so closely with this theme that every move he makes in the narrative serves to guide and protect the dynasty. Hence the parable of Nathan achieves its full meaning only when it is considered as part of the DtrH to which it belongs and within which the fullness of its meaning and purpose unfolds.

The Dtr demonstrates his worth as an author with the unique quality of developing the significant single blocks that constitute the history into the mirror image of the whole and that is true of the parable of Nathan. A basic concept of this author is the vicious cycle of *sin-punishment-repentance-forgiveness* that is only broken by divine mercy as the lot of the

---

507 R. N. Whybray, *Succession Narrative*, p. 23–24.
508 A. A. Anderson, *2 Samuel*, p. 166.
509 T. Naumann, *Exemplarische König*, p. 166.
510 E. Blum, *Geschichtsschreibung*, p. 22–23.

people of Israel (cf. especially the book of Judges). This cycle rears its ugly head even in the life of the celebrated King David and it is again divine mercy that saves him and his dynasty. In this light, the parable of Nathan and its oracle of doom becomes a mirror image of the whole history; David who has freely received everything from Yhwh does what is evil in Yhwh's eyes (2 Sam 11:2-27) and will be punished in accordance with the prophetic word of judgment (12:7-12) and in line with the *lex talionis* (Deut 19:21, Lev 24:18-20, Ex 21:23-25). He repents of his sins and is forgiven by Yhwh who does not annul his promise of an eternal dynasty to him. The parable of Nathan cannot be a degradation or denigration of the king and the man David because its purpose is to open up the door of mercy to the wayward monarch. Unlike the Chronicler, who overlooks the palace intrigue probably for its potential of portraying David as a criminal, this writer has retained the sordid story by providing it the necessary twist to emphasize the effectiveness of repentance and divine mercy that does not fail despite human weakness. The last word of Nathan for the dynasty is not death but forgiveness, not rejection but the love of Yhwh. David has been reinstated and even though the prophecy of doom will plague his house in the near future of the narrative, the birth of Solomon already provides the needed light at the end of the tunnel (12:24-25). It is the dtr author who has made use of the juridical parable as a strong and effective mode of bringing the king to judge himself and, in so doing, to recognize his guilt and avail himself to divine mercy and forgiveness.

Taken on its own, Nathan's condemnation of King David will seem completely out of place in the Biblical tradition since it is the only time that the Ideal King is completely and officially reduced to a condemned criminal. As part of the DtrH, however, the presence of the prophet is justified as a logical sequence to the misdeeds of the king and the corrective presence of the prophet of Yhwh performing his official duty both as the voice of the voiceless and instrument of divine mercy and, above all, as the divine messenger guiding the royal house of David; the house that has received the promise of an eternal dynasty and yet is saddled with the burden of human frailty. The writer assigns the prophet Nathan the important role of the human agent of Yhwh guiding the royal family towards the fulfilment of the divine promise of an eternal dynasty by raising him up to a stature comparable to that of Moses, Joshua and Samuel. Just as Deut 31 prepares the ground for the conquest and distribution of the land, Jos 23 lays down a programme of life in the Promised Land and 1 Sam 12 inaugurates kingship, so also does the oracle of Nathan (2 Sam 7) initiate the two dominant themes that will dictate the direction and pace of the history hereafter: Temple and Dynasty. Yhwh will establish Israel in her place (v. 10) and will raise up a successor to David (v.11-12) who will build a temple for His name (v. 13). In this oracle, Yhwh links up the future of David's house first to the acquisition of peace for the house of Israel and then to the building of the Temple to His name. In David, the ancient promise of rest will be realized. The exilic dtr author may have used this promise as a point of encouragement to the exiled Jew to hold on firmly to the hope of the future Davidic King because the destruction of the temple does not negate the promise of an eternal dynasty since that promise was independent of the temple; for David did not build it and still received the promise of an eternal dynasty.[511] Nathan's belief in the promise makes him a living witness of it because, being the messenger, he so inextricably identifies himself with the message that his subsequent appearances set the promise back on course in moments when all seemed to be lost.

The ideological, semantic and thematic similarities between the oracle of salvation (2 Sam 7) and the corresponding oracle of doom (2 Sam 12) place the dtr influence on the two prophecies beyond any reasonable doubt. The Dtr employs the use of questions in such oracles as the means to explain unequivocally the presence of the prophet, he then follows it up with the enumeration of Yhwh's past benevolence towards the audience (Y), the present wellbeing or ungratefulness of Y and the future action of Yhwh towards Y. My findings have also proven that the use of the double messenger formula in the body of such oracles is a typical dtr style (1 Sam 2:27, 30, 2 Sam 7:5, 8, 12:7, 11). The dtr author (or movement) thus enhances the character of Nathan whom he has taken over from the tradition and puts into his mouth his additions to the two prophecies, making him the linkage in the narrative of the DtrH.[512] The second appearance of the prophet, besides being the divine mandate, can also be

---

511 W. Oswald, *Nathan der Prophet*, p. 234.
512 W. Oswald, *Nathan der Prophet*, p. 234–235.

understood in the context of Nathan's self-identification with the message he has proclaimed; the dynasty of David that is to last forever is endangered by the king and needs to be given a push in the right direction to set it back on course. It is in this light that his third appearance as a "lobbyist" at the court of David (1 Kings 1) also acquires its full significance. His conviction that Solomon, the humble son of David, was the divine choice had already been prepared by the second name he had given him in 12:25. At the moment that it became clear to him that the senile David was too slow or even incapable of choosing a successor to end the crisis of inheritance that had kept the royal family in its firm grip, the prophet entered into active politics to promote the cause of Solomon in order to save the dynasty from imminent self-destruction. By this action, the dtr historian has made Nathan the connecting ligament between the three episodes and the significant player in his history. We dare say that the vested interest of the Dtr in the character called Nathan and the stature that he has accorded him may very well have been inspired by the role that the prophet played in the enthronement of Solomon. This stature is read backwards into the two other appearances that from the point of view of narrative chrononlogy precede the enthronement.

Remarkably, the three Nathan pericopae paint a fine picture of David as a pious man who has complete trust in Yhwh, his God. Each encounter of the prophet with David ends up with the king expressing himself in an act of prayer before Yhwh and that under three different aspects; thanksgiving, intercession and worship respectively. After the promise of an eternal dynasty pronounced by Nathan, David recognizes his unworthiness and Yhwh's free choice of his family and prays in thanksgiving (2 Sam 7:18-29). When the son born to him by Bathsheba fell ill upon the word of the prophet, the king fasted and prayed for a whole week, interceding for his son. The death of the child did not cause him to despair, instead his mode of prayer changed from intercession to worship in humble acceptance of the Divine will (12:16-20). In the same way, at the accomplishment of the royal order for the enthronement of Solomon, the aged and senile David bowed in worship on his bed blessing Yhwh, who had granted that his son sits on his throne with his own eyes seeing it (1 Kings 1:47-48).

The image of David that is portrayed by the dtr author in the whole history can be summed up in the description of the then youngman by the servant of Saul who does everything possible to make him acceptable to his master: he is a healthy and handsome youth with beautiful eyes, a skilful musician, a valiant warrior, prudent in speech and above all Yhwh is with him (16:18). To this pregnant description we can also add that he was above all a pious man who knew the depth of sin and the grace of forgiveness and freely relied upon his God in confident trust, especially in times of need, and was never abandoned. In the character called David, the Dtr presents the enigma of the imperfection of the perfect man; at the height of his power, David captures a fortified city, but falls at the same time as deep as a human being could fall into sin and is saved only by divine mercy. In that moment of sin, he is also portrayed as the paradigm of humanity in every age; quick to condemn the fault of others but slow to realize their own mistakes. David quickly notices the fleck in the eyes of the rich man of Nathan's parabl,e but is blind to the beam in his own eyes (Mt 7:3). That is exactly what he is, a human being with great qualities and equally great faults, he is no angel but a real human being. It is for that very reason that the promise still remains valid, because it does not depend solely upon David, the human recipient, but especially upon Yhwh, who has bound Himself to his dynasty and will see to it that it continues ʿad-ʿôlām. In effect, it is neither David nor Nathan who is the protagonist of the Nathan pericopae but Yhwh, the silent and invisible hero and the idealization of David is not because he was superhuman, but that he humbly accepted the prophetic guidance in his moments of moral difficulty.

The Dtr presents David as an idealized perfection of a king, chosen by Yhwh himself to lead Israel on the tortuous path towards nationhood at a crucial moment of that journey. As a political leader, David achieved a degree of unity for the nation which enabled him to conquer the nations around her, establishing the ideal boundaries of Israel in an epoch of relative peace, achieved by virtue of his victories. As the leader of a religious nation, the people of Yhwh, he was obedient to his God, whom he regularly consulted, submitting himself to the directives of the divine oracle and the prophetic guidance. David was a pious warrior-king who relied not so much upon military might as upon divine mercy and will, especially in the deepest moments of his life (2 Sam 12:13, 16:12). It is this pious King David who fulfils the promised rest for the house of Israel (Deut 12:10). Nonetheless, David was still a man and sinner before Yhwh, but even in his moments of sin he did not drag the whole nation with him.[513] He quickly accepted his guilt when confronted by the prophet Nathan and was forgiven. The parable of Nathan brings to the fore the human nature of David, indicating in so doing how deep that nature can fall and how much it depends upon divine mercy to once again be lifted up. It is not a slap in the face of the dtr image of David, as critics will want it to be, but the portrayal of the most important dtr doctrine; the depth of divine mercy towards its erring human objects. The Nathan pericopae as a unit is the compendium of the dtr theology and, in fact, the short form of the whole Biblical theology. It is the practical demonstration of God's faithfulness in the face of human frailty and infidelity; a paramount theme at the core of Judeo-Christian theology of salvation. The unflinching faithfulness of God is, however, not without justice: he promises punishment to the erring offspring and punishes David for his sins, but the dynasty will still remain ʿad-ʿôlām. The justice of God punishes the one who dishonours Him, but his mercy is not taken away forever; for his promise endures despite the frailties of his human agents (Psalm 103). It is Yhwh himself who is the condition upon which his promise is based and, as long as He lives, that promise will endure.[514]

---

[513] This image of David will be tainted dramatically if 2 Sam 24 is taken into consideration. There the king orders a census against the humble protest of Joab and incurs the wrath of Yhwh but when he was presented with three choices of punishment; a seven year famine upon the land, a three month flight from his enemies or a three day pestilence in the land, he chose pestilence in the land which cost seven thousand lives rather than flee three months before his foes. His sin caused the innocent sheep to suffer (2 Sam 24:17).

[514] The promise of Land to Abraham was sealed with Yhwh alone "passing through" the bisected sacrificial victims, without Abraham doing the same (Gen 15:17). The normal practice would have been that the two parties to the covenant walk between the bisected pieces of the victims to seal the oath of faithfulness. In this instance, the certainty of the promise was the fidelity of Yhwh over and above that of Abraham, the human partner of the covenant, since it was only the presence of the Divine that passed through the prepared pieces.

Bibliography

Ackroyd, Peter R., *The Second Book of Samuel*, London-New York et al., 1982, Cambridge University Press.

Ahlström, Gösta W., *Psalm 89, eine Liturgie aus dem Ritual des leidenden Königs*, Trans. by Hans-Karl Hacker, Lund 1959, Gleerup.

Alter, Robert, The Art of Biblical Narrative, New York, 1981, Basic Books -*The David Story*, A translation with Commentary of 1 and 2 Samuel, New York, 1999 W.W. Norton.

Asante, Emmanuel, *Towards an African Christian Theology of the Kingdom of Onyame*, Lewiston – New York, 1995, Lampeter.

Aurelius, Erik, *Zukunft jenseits des Gerichts, eine Redaktionsgeschichtliche Studien zum Enneateuch*, (BZAW 319) Berlin-New York, 2003, de Gruyter.

Avioz, Michael, *Nathan's Oracle (2 Sam 7) and its Interpreters* (BHTE 5) Bern – New York, 2005, Peter Lang.

Bailey, Randall C., David in Love and War (JSOT Sup 75) Sheffield (1990) JSOT Press.

Baker, John, *The Prophetic Line*, the Genius of Hebrew Religion, Edinburg, 1980, St Andrews Press.

Bauer, H. – Leander, P., *Historische Grammatik der Hebräischen Sprache des Alten Testaments*, Hildesheim, 1962, Georg Olms Verlag.

Bergmann, Eugen, *Codex Hammurabi*, Textus Primigenius, Editio Tertia (SPIB 51) Roma 1953, Pontificium Institutum Biblicum.

Bernini, Giuseppe, *I Libri di Samuele*, ed. Boccali Giovanni M. (Novissima Versione della Bibbia dai Testi Originali) Milano, 1975, Edizione Paoline.

Bietenhard, Sophia K., *Des Königs General: die Heerführertradition in der vorstaatlichen und frühen staatlichen Zeit und die Joabgestalt in 2 Sam 2-20 und 1 Kön 1-2*, OBO 163, Göttingen, 1998, Vandenhoeck und Ruprecht.

Blass, Friedrich – Debrunner, Albert, *A Greek Grammer of the New Testament and other Early Christian Literature*, Chicago, 1961, University of Chicago Press.

Blenkinsopp, Joseph, *Geschichte der Prophetie in Israel*, Von den Anfängen bis zum hellenistischen Zeitalter, übersetzt und mit einem Ausblick versehen von Erhard S. Gerstenberger, Stuttgart-Berlin-Köln, 1998.

Blum, Erhard, *Studien zur Komposition des Pentateuch* (BZW 189) Berlin-New York 1990, Walter de Gruyter.

Birch, Bruce C., *The First and Second Books of Samuel* (NIB 2) Nashville, 1998, Abingdon Press.

Braulik, Georg (Hg.) *Das Deuteronomium*, Frankfurt am Main, 2003, Lang.

Brooke, George J. & Römer, Thomas, ed., *Ancient and Modern Scriptural Historiography*, (BETL CCVII) Leuven, 2007, Leuven University Press.

Campbell, Anthony F. – O'Brien, Mark A., *Unfolding the Deuteronomistic History*, Origins, Upgrades, Present Text, Minneapolis, 2000, Fortress Press.

Carlson, Rolf A., *David, the chosen King*, A tradition-historical approach to the second Book. Of Samuel, Stockholm, 1965, Almqvist & Wiksell.

Coffman, James B., *Second Samuel* (Old Testament Series) Texas, 1992, Abilene Christian. University Press.

Cross, Frank M., *Canaanite Myth and Hebrew Epic*, Essays in the History of the Religion of Israel, Cambridge – Mass – Harvard, 1973, Havard University Press.

De Moor, Johannes C., *The Rise of Yahwism*, the Root of Israelite Monotheism (BETL 91 Revised and Enlarged Edition) Leuven, 1997, Leuven University Press.

De Pury, Albert. & Römer, Thomas, (Hrsg.) *Die sogenannte Thronfolgegeschichte Davids*, Neue Einsichten und Anfragen (Orbis Biblicus et Orientlis 176) Freiburg/Schweiz & Gottingen 2000, Univesitätverlag Freiburg-Vandehoeck & Ruprecht - Israel constructs its History, Deuteronomistic Historiography in Recent Research, (JSOT Sup 306) Sheffield, 2000, Sheffield Aacademic Press.

Dietrich, Walter, *Prophetie und Geschichte*, Eine redaktionsgeschichtliche Untersuchung zum deuteronomistischen Geschichtswerk (FRLANT 108) Göttingen, 1972, Vandenhoeck & Ruprecht.

Dietrich, Walter. et Herkommer, H. (Hrsg) *König David* – biblische Schlüsselfigur und europäische Leitgestalt, Stuttgart, 2003, Kohlhammer.

Dietrich, Walter et Naumann, Thomas, *Die Samuelbücher* (EdF 287) Darmstadt, 1995 Wissenschaftliche Buchgesellschaft.

Eaton, John H., *Kingship and the Psalms* (JSOT 12) London, 1976, SCM Press.

Ego, Beate, *Israel und Amalek*, Übersetzung und Kommentierung von Targum Sheni als Beitrag zur Auslegung des Ester Buches, Tübingen, 1993, Mohr Siebeck.

Eynikel, Erik, *The Reform of King Josiah and the Composition of the Deuteronomistic History*, (Oudtestamentische Studiën) Leiden – New York – Köln, 1996, Brill.

Evans, Mary J., *1 and 2 Samuel* (NIBC Old Testament series 6) Massachusetts, 2000, Hendrickson.

Fischer, Georg – Backhaus, Knut, *Sühne und Versöhnung*, (Die Neue Echter-Bibel 7) Würzburg, 2000, Echter Verlag.

Fokkelman, J. P., *Narrative Art and Poetry in the Books of Samuel*, vol. 1, King David, (Studia Semitica Neerlandica) Assen, The Netherlands, 1981, Van Gorcum & Comp.

- *Narrative Art and Poetry in the Books of Samuel*, vol II, The Crossing Fates, (Studia Semitica Neerlandica) Assen, The Netherlands, 1986, Van Gorcum Assen/Maastricht, Dover, New Hampshire.

- *Narrative Art and Poetry in the Books of Samuel*, vol. III, Throne and City, (Studia Semitica Neerlandica) Assen, The Netherlands, 1990, Van Gorcum Assen/Maastricht.

Gesenius, Wilhelm, *Hebräische Grammatik, völlig umgearbeitet von E. Kautzsch*, Hildesheim-Zürich-New York, 1983, Georg Olms Verlag.

Gertz, Jan C. (Hg), *Grundinformation Altes Testament* (UTB 2745, 2. Auflage) Göttingen, 2007, Vandenhoeck & Ruprecht.

Gressmann, Hugo, *Die älteste Geschichtsschreibung und Prophetie Israels*, vom Samuel bis Amos und Hosea, Göttingen, 1910, Vandenhoek & Ruprecht.

- *Die Schriften des Alten Testaments*, zweite, stark umgearbeitete Auflage, Göttingen, 1921, Vandenhoeck & Ruprecht.

- *Altorientalische Texte zum alten Testament*, Berlin, 1926, de Gruyter.

Grill, P. Severinus, *Das Alte Testament im Lichte der Literar- und Textkritik* (HS 10) Wien, 1957, Domverlag.

Grønbaek, Jakob H., *Die Geschichte vom Aufstieg Davids*, Copenhagen, 1971, Copenhagen University.

Groß, Walter, *Die Satzteilfolge im Verbalsatz alttestamentlicher Prosa*, untersucht an den Büchern Dtn, Ri und 2Kön, (Forschungen zum Alten Testament 17) Tübingen, 1996, Mohr Sieberg.

- (Hg.) *Jeremiah und die „deuteronomistische Bewegung"*, (Bonner biblische Beiträge; Bd 98) Weinheim, 1995, Beltz Athenäum.

- *Verbform und Funktion. wayyiqtol für die Gegenwart? Ein Beitrag zur syntax poetischer Althebräischer Texte* (Arbeit zu Text und Sprache im alten Testament 1) St. Ottilien, 1976, Eos Verlag.

Gunn, David, M. – Fewell, Danna N., *Narrative in the Hebrew Bible*, (The Oxford Bible Series) Oxford 1993, Oxford University Press.

Habel, Norman, *Literary Criticism of the Old Testament*, (Old Testament Series) Philadelphia 1971, Fortress Press.

Halpern, B., *David's Secret Demons*, Messiah, Murderer, Traitor, King, Grand Rapids-Michigan-Cambridge, 2004, Eerdmans Publishing Company.

Häusermann, Hans W., *Studien zur Englischen Literarkritik, 1910–1930* (Kölner Anglistische Arbeiten Band 34) New York, 1938, Johnson Press.

Heller, Roy L., *Power, Politics, and Prophecy*, the character of Samuel and the Deuteronomistic interpretation of Prophecy, New York – London, 2006, T & T Clark.

Heym, Stefan, *Der König David Bericht*: Roman, München, 1972, Kindler.

House, Paul R., ed. *Beyond Form Criticism*, Essays in Old Testament Criticism, Indiana, 1992, Eisenbrauns.

Houtman, Cornelis, *Exodus 2 7:14-9:25*, Kampen, 1996, Kok.

Ishida, Tomoo, *The Royal Dynasties of Ancient Israel*: A Study of the Formation and the Development of Royal-Dynastic Ideology (*BZAW 142*) Berlin – New York, 1977, de Gruyter.

Jenni, Ernst, *Die alttestamentliche Prophetie* (*Theologische Studien* Heft 67) Zürich, 1962 EVZ Verlag.

Jones, Gwilym H., *The Nathan Narratives*, (JSOT Sup 80) Sheffield,1990, JSOT Press.

Joüon, Paul – Muraoka, Takamitsu, *A Grammar of Biblical Hebrew* (Subsidia Biblica 14/I & II) Roma 2000, Editrice Pontificio Istituto Biblico.

Kaiser, Otto, *Studien zur Literarturgeschichte des Alten Testamentes* (Forschung zur Bible 90) Würzburg, 2000, Echte-Verlag.

Keys, Gillian, *The Wages of Sin, A Reappraisal of the Succession Narrative* (JSOT Sup 221) Sheffield, 1996, Sheffield Academic Press.

Koch, Klaus, *Was ist Formgeschichte? Methoden der Bibelexegese*, Auflage 4, Neukirchen-Vluyn, 1981, Neukirchener Verlag.

Kolb, Edward, David, Geschichte und Deutung, Ein Lese- und Arbeitsbuch in einfacher Sprache, Freiburg, 1986, Walter-Verlag Olten.

Kirsch, J., *King David*, The Real Life of the Man who Ruled Israel, New York, 2000, Ballantine Publishing Company.

Kratz, Reinhard G., *The Composition of the Narrative Books of the Old Testament*, Trans. Bowden John, London, 2005, T & T Clark.

Lambdin, Thomas O., *Introduction to Biblical Hebrew*, 10th printing, London, 1991, Darton, Longman and Todd.

Lohfink, Norbert, *Studien zum Deuteronomium und zur deuteronomischen Literatur V* (SBA 38) Stuttgart, 2005, Katholische Bibelwerk.

- *Studien zum Deuteronomium und zur deuteronomistischen Literatur IV* (SBA 31) Stuttgart, 2000, Katholische Bibelwerk.

- *Studien zum Deuteronomium und zur deuteronomistischen Literatur II* (SBA 12) Stuttgart, 1991, Katholische Bibelwerk.

- *Das Deuteronomium, Entstehung, Gestalt und Boschaft* (Ephemerides Theologicae Leuvaniensis 68) Leuven, 1985, Leuven University Press.

Lyke, Larry L., *King David with the Wise Woman of Tekoa: the resonance of tradition in parabolic narrative*, (JSOT Sup 255) Sheffield, 1997, Sheffield Academic Press.

McKenzie, Steven L., *The Chronicler's use of the Deuteronomistic History* (Havard Semitic Monographs 33) Atlanta, 1986, Scholars Press.

- *King David*, A Biography, Oxford, 2000, Oxford University Press.

Mittelstaedt, John R., *Samuel* (The People's Bible) Milwaukee, 1993, Northwestern Publication House.

Nahkola, Aulikki, *Double Narratives in the Old Testament*, the Foundation of Methods in Biblical Criticism (BZAW 290) Berlin, 2001, de Gruyter.

Nelson, Richard D., Double Redaction of the Deuteronomistic History, (*JSOT Sup.* 18) Sheffield, 1981, ISOT Press.

Nissinen, Martti. – Carter C. E. ed, *Images and Prophecy in the Ancient Eastern Mediterranean* (FRLANT 233) Göttingen, 2009, Vandenhoeck & Ruprecht-Ed., *Prophecy in its Ancient Near Eastern Context*; Mesopotamian, Biblical and Arabian Perspective (SBL Symposium series 13) Atlanta, 2000, SBL Press.

Noll, Kurt L., *The Faces of David*, (*JSOT* 242) Sheffield, 1997, Sheffield Academic Press.

Noth, Martin, *Überlieferungsgeschichtliche Studien*, Die sammelden und bearbeitenden Geschichtswerke im Alten Testament, Dritte unveränderte Auflage, Tübingen, 1967, Max Niemeyer Verlag.

- *The Deuteronomistic History*, (JSOTS 15) Sheffield, 1981, ISOT Press.

Nowack, Wilhelm D., *Handkommentar zum alten Testament, Richter, Ruth u. Bücher Samuelis* (Göttinger Handkommentar zum alten Testament 1. Abteilung, Die Historischenbücher 4) Göttingen,1902, Vandenhoeck & Ruprecht.

O'Brien, Mark A., *The Deuteronomistic History Hypothesis: A Research* (Orbis biblicus et orientalis 92) Göttingen, 1989, Vandenhoeck & Ruprecht.

O'Connor David – Silverman, D. P., *Ancient Egyptian Kingship* (Probleme der Ägyptologie 9) Leiden, 1995, Brill.

Orji, Chukuemeka, *And Yahweh delivered David Wherever he Went*, composition and redaction criticism of 2Sam 1-8, Rome, 1998, Pontificia Univ. Gregoriana.

Orton, E. A. (trans.) et Gunn, David M. (ed) *Narrative and Novella in Samuel*, (*JSOT* 116) Sheffield, 1991, Almond Press.

Petersen, David L., *The Roles of Israel's Prophets* (JSOT Sup 17) 1981, JSOT Press.

Pisano, Stephen, *Additions or Omissions in the Books of Samuel*, The significant Pluses and Minuses in Massoretic, LXX and Qumran Texts, Freiburg, 1984, Universitätverlag.

Pfeiffer, Robert H., *Introduction to the Old Testament*, New York, 1941, Harper.

Polzin, Robert, *David and the Deuteronomist*, A Literary Study of the Deuteronomic History, Part Three, 2 Samuel, Indiana, 1993, Indiana University Press, Bloomington & Indianapolis.

Pritchard, J. B., *Ancient Near Eastern Texts, Relating to the Old Testament*, Princeton – New Jersey, 1969, Princeton University Press.

Pyper, Hugh S., *David as Reader*, 2 Samuel 12:1-15a and the poetics of fatherhood (Biblical Interpretation Series 23) Leiden, 1996, Brill.

Ravasi, Gianfranco, *I Libri di Samuele*, ciclo di conferenze tenute al Centro Culturale S. Fedele di Milano, Bologna, 1993, EDB.

Rechenmacher, Hans, *Althebräiche Personnennamen*, (Kehrbücher orientalischer Sprache Vol II/1) Münster, 2012, Ugarit Verlag.

Rice, G., *1 Kings, Nations under God*, a commentary on the book of 1 Kings, Grand Rapids Michigan, 1990, Erdmans.

Richter, Wolfgang, *Exegese als Literaturwissenschaft*, Entwurf einer alttestamentlichen Literaturtheorie und Methodologie, Göttingen, 1971, Vandenhoeck & Ruprecht.

Robinson, Gnana, *Let us be like the Nations*(International theological commentary) Edinburg, 1993, Handsel Press.

Rost, Leonhard, *Die Überlieferung von der Thronnachfolge Davids*, (Beiträge zum Wissenschaft vom alten und neuen Testament 42) Stuttgart, 1926, Kohlhammer - *The Succession to the Throne of David*, Sheffield 1982, Almond Press.

Rudnig, T. Alexander, *Davids Thron*, Redaktionskritische Studien zur Geschichte von der Thronnachfolge Davids, BZAW 358, Berlin, 2006, de Gruyter.

Sandy, Brent D., *Plowshares and Pruning Hooks, Rethinking the Language of Biblical Prophecy and Apocalyptic*, Illinois, 2002, Intervarsity Press.

Schäfer-Lichtenberger, Christa, (Hrsg), *Die Samuelbücher und die Deuteronomisten* (Beitrag zur Wissenschaft vom Alten und Neuen Testament 10) Stuttgart, 2010, Kohlhammer.

Schenker, Adrian, *Versöhnung und Sühne*, (Biblische Beiträge, N. F. 15) Freiburg, 1981, Schweizer katholische Bibelwerk.

Schmitz, Barbara, *Prophetie und Königtum*, (FAT 60) Tübingen, 2008, Mohr Siebeck.

Schmid, Konrad, *Erzväter und Exodus*, Untersuchungen zur doppelten Begründung der Ursprünge Israels innerhalb der Geschichtsbücher des Alten Testaments, (Wissenschaftliche Monographien zum Alten und Neuen Testament 81) Neukirche 1999, Neukirchener Verlag.

- *Literaturgeschichte des Alten Testaments*, Eine Einführung, Darmstadt, 2008, Wiss. Buchges.

Schniedewind, William M., *Society and the Promise to David*, The reception history of 2 Samuel 7:1-17, Oxford, 1999, Oxford University Press.

Schorn, Ulrike – Büttner, M. ed., *Theologie in Prophetie und Pentateuch*, Gesammelte Schriften (BZAW 310) Berlin, 2001, de Gruyter.

Seiler, Stefan, *Die Geschichte von der Thronfolge Davids* (2 Sam 9-20; 1 Kön 1-2) Untersuchungen zur Literarkritik und Tendenz (BZAW 267) Berlin, 1998, de Gruyter.

Ska, Jean L., *"Our Fathers Have Told Us"*, Introduction to the Analysis of Hebrew Narratives (Subsidia Biblica 13) Roma 2000, EditricePontificio Istituto Biblico.

Smith, Mark S., *The Origins and Development of the Waw-Consecutive*, Northwest Semitic evidence from Ugarit to Qumran (Havard Semitic Studies 39) Atlanta, 1991, Scholars Press.

Sperry, Sidney. B. (Ed.) *Covenants, Prophecies and Hymns of the Old Testament*, The 30th annual Sidney B. Symposium (Sperry Symposium Series) Salt Lake City, Utah, 2001, Deseret Book.

Stipp, Hermann-Josef (Hrsg), *Das deuteronomistische Geschichtswerk* (ÖBS Band 39) Frankfurt am Main-Berlin-Bern-Bruxelles-New York-Oxford-Wien, 2011, Peter Lang.

Talmon, Semaryahu., *Literary Studies in the Hebrew Bible*, Form and Content, Collected Studies, Jerusalem, 1993, Magnes Press, Hebrew University.

Tanner, H. Andreas., *Amalek der Feind Israels und der Feind Jahwes, eine Studie zu den Amalektexten im Alten Testament* (TVZ Desertationen) Zürich, 2005, Theologischer Verlag, Zürich.

Thomson, L. Thomas, The Origin Tradition of Ancient Israel, *JSOT* 55, Sheffield, 1987, Sheffield Academic Press.

Tov, Emmanuel, *Textual Criticism of the Hbrew Bilble*, Second Revised Edition, Minneapolis & Assen, Netherlands, 1992, Fortress Press, Minneapolis & Royal Van Gorcum, Assen.

Uffenheimer, Benjamin, *Early Prophecy in Israel* (Publications of the Perry Foundation for Biblical Research in the Hebrew University of Jerusalem) Translated by David Louvish, Jerusalem, 1999, Magnes Press.

Van der Merwe, C. H. J., *The Old Hebrew Particle gam*, A syntactic description of gam in Gn-2Kg, (Arbeit zu Text und Sprache im alten Testament, Band 34) Edited by Richter Wolfgang, 1980, St Ottilien, Eos Verlag.

Van Seters, John, *In Search of History*, Historiography in the Ancient World and the Origins of Biblical History, New Haven – London et al, 1983, Yale University Press.

Van Staaldunine-Sulman, Eveline, *The Targum of Samuel*, Kampen, 2002, Theologische Universiteit.

Vanoni, Gottfried, *Literarkritik und Grammatik*, Untersuchung der Wiederholungen und Spannungen in 1 Kön 11-12 (Arbeit zu Text und Sprache im Alten Testament 21) St. Ottilien, 1984, Eos Verlag.

Veijola, Timo, *Das Königtum in der Beurteilung der Deuteronomischen Historiographie*, Eine Redaktionsgeschichtliche Untersuchung (Suomalaisen Tiedeakatemien Toimituksia Series B198) Helsinki, 1977, Suomalainen Tiedeakat.

- *Die Ewige Dynastie*, David und die Entstehung seiner Dynastie nach der Deuteronomistischen Darstellung (Suomalaisen Tiedeakatemien Toimituksia Series B193) Helsinki, 1975, Suomalainen Tiedeakat.

- *David*, Gesammelte Studien zu den Davidüberlieverungen des alten Testaments (Suomen Eksegeettisen Seuran julkaisuja 52) Göttingen, 1990, Vandenhoeck & Ruprecht.

- *Verheissung in der Krise*, Studien zur Literatur und Theologie der Exilzeit anhand des 89 Psalms (Suomalaisen Tiedeakatemien Toimituksia Series B 220) Helsinki, 1982, Suomalainen Tiedeakat.

Vermeylen, Jacques., *La Loi du Plus Fort, Histoire de la rédaction des récits davidiques de I Samuel 8 à I Rois 2* (Ephemerides theologicae Lovaniensis/Bibliotheca 154) Leuven, 2000, Leuven University Press.

Vervenne Marc – Lust, J. Ed, *Deuteronomy and Deuteronomic Literature* (Ephemerides theologicae Lovaniensis/Bibliotheca 133) Leuven, 1997, Leuven University Press.

Von Rad, Gerhard, *Studies in Deuteronomy* (Studies in biblical theology 9) London, 1956, SCM Press.

- *The Problem of the Hexateuch and other Essays*, New York, 1966, McGraw-Hill Book Company.

- *Old Testament Theology*, The Theology of Israel's Historical Traditions, Vol. 1, Edinburgh, 1968, Oliver and Boyd.

Wagner, Andreas, *Prophetie als Theologie*, Die *so spricht Jahwe*-Formeln und das Grundverständnis alttestamentlicher Prophetie,(FRLANT 207) Göttingen, 2004, Vandenhoeck & Ruprecht.

Waltke, Bruce. K. – O'Connor, Michael, *An Introduction to Biblical Hebrew Syntax*, Indiana, 1990, Eisenbrauns.

Wallis, Gerhard. Hrsg., *Von Bileam bis Jesaja*, Studien zur alttestamentlichen Prophetie von Ihre Anfängen bis zum 8. Jahrhundert v. Chr., Berlin, 1984, Evangelische Verlagsanstalt.

- Hrsg., *Zwischen Gericht und Heil*, Studien zur alttestamentlischen Prophetie im 7. und 6. Jahrhundert v. Chr., Berlin, 1987, Evangelische Verlagsanstalt.

Welch, Adam C., *Prophet and Priest in Old Israel*, Oxford, 1953, Blackwell.

Wellhausen, L. Julius, *Der Text der Bücher Samuelis*, Göttingen, 1871, Vendenhoeck & Ruprecht.

- *Die Komposition des Hexateuchs und der Historischen Bücher des Alten Testaments*, Berlin, 1963, de Gruyter.

Werlitz, Jurgen, *Studien zur Literarkritischen Methode* (BZAW 204) Berlin, 1992, de Gruyter.

Westermann, Claus, *Grundformen prophetischer Rede* (Beitrag zur evangeliscen Theologie 31) München, 1964, Kaiser.

Whiston, William (Trans), *The New and Complete Works of Josephus*, with commentary by Maier, Paul L., Grand Rapids 1999, Kregel Publications.

Whybray, Roger N., *The Succession Narrative, A Study of II Sam 9-20; I Kings 1 and 2* (SBT 9) London, 1968, SCM Press.

Wolff, Hans W., *Studien zur Prophetie* – Probleme und Erträge mit einer Werkbibliographie (Theologische Bücherei 76) München, 1987, Kaiser.

Wolfgang, Oswald, *Nathan der Prophet* (Abhandlungen zur Theologie des Alten und Neuen Testaments Band 94) Zürich 2008, Theologischer Verlag Zürich.

Würthwein, Ernst, Studien zum Deuteronomistischen Geschichtswerk (BZAW 227) Berlin-New York, 1994, de Gruyter.

- Die Weisheit Ägyptens und das Alten Testament, (Schriften der Philipps – Universität Marburg 6) Marburg 1960, N. G. Elwert Verlag.

Zach, Michael, Die Ambivalenz des David-Bildes in II Sam 9-20, I Kön 1+2 (Beiträge zur judischen Studien 19) Oldenburg, 2006, Bis Verlag der Carl-von-Ossietzky-Universität.

Zimmerli, Walther, *Studien zur alttestamentlichen Theologie und Prophetie* (Theologische Bücherei 51) München, 1974, Kaiser.

Articles and periodicals

Ackroyd, Peter R., "The Succession Narrative (so Called)", *Int* 38 (1981) 383–396.

Amit, Yairah, "The Dual Causality Principle and its Effects on Biblical Literature", *VT* XXXVII 4 (1987) 385–400.

Baines, John, Kingship, Definition of Culture, and Legitimation, *PdÄ* IX (1995) 3–48 - The Origins of Egyptian Kingship, *PdÄ* IX Leiden (1995) 95–156.

Blenkinsopp, Joseph, "Theme and Motif in the Succession History (2 Sam XI 2ff) and the Yahwist Corpus", *VT* 15 (1965) 44–57.

Blum, Erhard, Der Kompositionelle Knoten am Übergang von Josua zu Richter, Ein Entflechtungsvorschlag, *BETL* CXXXIII (1997) 181–212.

- Pentateuch – Hexateuch – Enneateuch? Woran erkennt man ein literarisches Werk in der hebräischen Bibel? *BETL* CCIII (2007) 67–97.

Bodner, Keith, Nathan: Prophet, Politician and Nevelist? *JSOT* 95 (2001) 43–54.

Bodenheimer, Alfred, Gottes Erwählter, Davidsherrschaftlegitimation und Dynastiegrundung, eine Reflexion, ausgehend von Stefan Heyms Roman "Der König David Bericht", *Neukirchner Theologische Zeitschrift* 17 (2002) 20–30.

Coats, George W., "II Samuel 12:1-7a", *Interp* 40 (1986) 170–175.

- "Parable, Fable, and Anecdote, Storytelling in the Succession Narrative", *Interp* 35 (1981) 362–382.

Cornelius, Izak, Aspects of the Iconography of the Warrior Goddess Ištar and Ancient Near Eastern Prophecies, *FRLANT* 233, 15–40.

Coxon, Peter William, "A Note on 'Bathsheba' in 2 Samuel 12,1-6", *Bib* 62 (1981) 247–250.

Daube, David, "Nathan's Parable", *NT* XXIV 3 (1982) 275–288.

Delekat, Leinhard, Tendenz und Theologie der David-Solomon-Erzählung, *BZAW* 105 (1967) 26–36.

Dietrich, Walter, Von den ersten Königen Israels, Forschung an den Samuelbüchern im Jahrtausend, Zweiter Teil, *ThR 77 Heft 3* (2012) 263–316.

- Tendenzen neuester Forschung an der Samuelbüchern, (BZWA/NT 10 Folge) in Schäfer-Lichtenberger (2010) 9–17.

Eckart, Otto, Der Zusammenhang von Herrscherlegitimation und Rechtskodifizierung in Altorientalischer und biblischer Rechtsgeschichte, *ZAR* 11 (2005) 51–92.

Eynikel, Erik, The Parable of Nathan (II Sam. 12, 1-4) and the Theory of Semiosis, *BZAW* 294 (2000) 76–90.

- The Portrait of Manasseh and the Deuteronomistic History, *BEThL* CXXXIII (1997) 233–261.

Flanagan, James W., Court History or Succession Document? A Study of 2 Samuel 9-20 and 1 Kings 1-2, *JBL* 91, (1972) 172–181.

Fontaine, Carole R., The Bearing of Wisdom on the Shape of 2 Samuel 11-12 and 1 Kings 3, in the Feminist Companion to the Bible 5, Ed. Athalya Brenner (1994) 143–160.

Frevel, Christian, Deuteronomistisches Geschichtswerk order Geschichtswerke?, *BThS* 58, (2004) 60–95.

George, Mark K., Ywh's Own Heart, *The Catholic Biblical Quarterly* 64, no. 3 (2002) 442–459.

Grabbe, Lester L., Ancient Near Eastern Prophecy from an Anthropological Perspective, In Prophecy in Its Ancient Near Eastern Context: Mesopotamian, Biblical, and Arabian.

Perspectives, *SBL Symposium Series 13*, Ed. Martti Nissinen (2000), 13–32.

Gressmann, Hugo, Narrative and Novella in Samuel, Studies by Hugo Gressmann and other Scholars 1902–1923, Trans. David E. Orton and Ed. David M. Gunn, *JSOT* 116 (1991) 9–58.

Groß, Walter, Das Richterbuch zwischen deuteronomistischem Geschichtswerk und Enneateuch, in Hermann-Josef Stipp, Hrsg. *ÖBS 39* (2011) 177–205.

Gubler, Marie-Luise, Bathsheba – oder: Wie ist Gott? *Neukirche Theologische Zeitschrift* 17 (2002) 31–44.

Gunn, David M., The Story of King David, Genre and Interpretation, *JSOT* 6 (1967) 207–242.

Halpern, Baruch, "Paths of Glory", Shame and Guilt – The Uriah Story as the Hinge of Fate, in Schäfer-Lichtenberger, C., Die Samuelbücher und die Deuteronomisten (2010) 76–91.

Haran, Menahem, The Books of the Chronicles of the Kings of Judah and of the Kings of Israel: What Sort of Books were they? *ZAW* 4525, (1999) 156–164.

Ho, Craig Y. S., The stories of the Family Troubles of Judah and David: A Study of their Literary Links, *VT* 49 (1999) 513–529.

Hunziker-Rodenwald, Regina, Die beiden Söhne, Sprache, Sinn und Geschichte in 2 Sam 10-12, in C. Schäfer-Lichtenberger, Die Samuelbücher und die Deuteronomisten (2010) 94–104.

Kessler, John, Sexuality and Politics: The Motif of the Displaced Husband in the Books of Samuel, *CBQ* 62 (2000) 209–223.

Lasine, Stuart., Melodrama as Parable: The Story of the Poor Man's Ewe-Lamb and the Unmasking of David's Topsy-Turvy Emotions, *HAR* 8 (1984) 101–124.

Lohfink, Norbert, Die Gattung der historischen Kurzgeschichte in den letzten Jahren von Juda und in der babylonischen Exils, *ZAW* 90 (1978) 319–347.

- Geschichtstypologisch Orientierte Textstrukturen in den Büchern Deuteronomium und Josua, *SBAB 31*, (2000) 75–103.

- Gab es Deuteronomistische Bewegung? *BBB* 98 (1995) 313–373.

- Narative Analyse von Dtn 1,6–3,9, *SBAB* 38 (2005) 57–110.

Kerygmata des deuteronomitischen Geschichtswerks, *SBAB 12*, (1991) 125–142.

Matthews, Victor H., The King's Call to Justice, *BZ* 35 (1991) 204–216.

McCarter, P. Kyle, Plots, True or False, The Succession Narrative as Court Apologetic, *Interp* 35 (1981) 355–369.

McCarthy, Dennis. J., II Samuel 7 and the Structure of the Deuteronomic History, *JBL* 84 (1965) pp. 131–138.

Moenikes, Ansgar, Beziehungssysteme zwischen dem Deuternomium und den Büchern Josua bis Könige, *ÖBS* 23 (2003) 69–84.

Mulder, Martin J., "Un euphémisme dans 2 Sam XII 14?", *VT* 18 (1968) 108–114.

Müllner, Ilse, Blickwechsel: Batseba und David in Romanen des 20. Jahrhunderts, *Biblical Interpretation* 6, 3/4, (1998) 348–366.

Nicol, George, David, Abigail, and Bathsheba, Nabal and Uriah, Transforamtion within a Triangle, *SJOT 12* (1998) 130–145.

Nicol, George G., David, Abigail and Bathsheba, Nabal and Uriah, Transformations within a Triangle, SJOT 12 (1998) 130–145.

Noll, Kurt L., Deuteronomistic History or Deuteronomic Debate?- A Thought Experiment, *JSOT* 31 vol. 3 (2007) 311–345.

Novick, Tzvi, Amaleq's Victims (~ylXxnh) in Dtn 25, 18, *ZAW* 119 (2007) 611–615.

Noort, Ed, Josua und Amalek: Exodus 17:8-16, *CBET* 44 (2006) 155–170.

Philips, Anthony, The Interpretation of 2 Samuel xii 5–6, *VT* 16 (1966) 242–244.

Perlitt, Lothar, Deuteronomium 1-3, im Streit der Exegetischen Methoden, *BETL LXVIII* (1985) 149–163.

Petersen, David L., Defining Prophecy and Prophetic Literature, *SBL* 13, 33–44.

Redford, Donald B., The Concept of Kingship in the Eighteenth Dynasty, *PdÄ IX* (1995) 158–184.

Roberts, Jimmy J., The Enthronement of Yahweh and David: The Abiding Theological Significance of the Kingship Language of the Psalms, *CBQ* 64 (2002) 675–686.

Römer, Thomas, Das deuteronomistische Geschichtswerk und die Wüstentraditionen der Hebräischen Bibel, in Hermann-Josef Stipp, *ÖBS 39* (2011) 55–88.

Schmid, Konrad, Das Deuteronomium innerhalb der "deuteronomistischen Geschichtswerke" In Gen – 2 Kön, *FRLANT 206*, 193–211.

Seebass, Horst, Nathan and David in II Sam 12, *ZAW* 86 (1974) 203–211.

Simon, Uriel, The Poor Man's Ewe-Lamb, An Example of a Juridical Parable, *Bib* 48 Sheffield (1978) 19–62.

Silverman, David P., The Nature of Egyptian Kingship, *PdÄ IX* (1995) 49–94.

Schwally, Friedrich, Zur Quellenkritik der historischen Bücher; Der Profet Nathan, *ZAW* 12, Herausgegeben von D. Bernhard Stade (1892) 153–157.

Shamesh, Yael, Measure for Measure in the David Stories, *SJOT 17* (2003) 89–109.

Stipp, Hermann-Josef, Ende bei Joschija, Zur Frage dem ursprünglichen Ende der Königsbücher bzw. des deuteronomistischen Geschichtswerks, *ÖBS 39*, (2011) 223–267.

Valler, Shulamit, King David and his Women, Biblical Stories and Talmudic Discussions, in *The Feminist Companion Bible 5*, Ed. Athalya Brenner, Sheffield (1994) 129–141.

Van Seters, John, Problems in the Literary Analysis of the Court History of David, *JSOT* 1 (1976) 22–29.

- The Court History and DtrH: Conflicting Perspectives on the House of David, *OBO* 176 (2000) 70–93.

- The Deuteronomistic History: can it avoid death by redaction? *BETL* CXLVII, 213–222.

Vanoni, Gottfried, Anspielungen und Zitate innerhalb der hebräischen Bible, *BBB* 98 (1995) 383–91.

Veijola, Timo, Verheissung in der Krise, *STTAASF*, 197 (1977).

- Davidverheißung und Staatsvertrag, *SFEG* 52 (1990) 128–159.

- Salomo – der Erstgeborene Bathsebas, *SFEG* 52 (1990) 84–105.

Vorster, Willem S., Readings, Readers, and the Succession Narrative: An Essay on Reception, *Sources of Biblical and Theological Study*, Ed. Paul R. House (1992) 395–406.

Wolff, Hans Walter, Das Kerygma Des Deuteronomistischen Geschichtswerks, *ZAW* 73 (1961) 171–186.

Wharton, James A., A Plausible Tale, Story and Theology in II Samuel 9-20, I Kings 1-2, *Interp* 35 (1981) 341–354.

Würthwein, Ernst, Die Erzählung von der Thronfolge Davids – theologische oder politische Geschichtschreibung, *TS* 115 (1974).

- Die Weisheit Ägyptens und das Alte Testament, Rede zur Rektoratsübergabe am 29. November 1958, Marburg (1960) 1-17.

Yaron, Reuven, The Coptos Decree and 2 Sam XII 14, *VT* 9 (1959) 89–91.

Commentaries

Anderson, Arnold A., *2 Samuel*, WBC 11, Dallas, 1989, Word Books.

Boling, Robert G., *Judges* (AB 6A) New York-London et al., 1975, Doubleday.

Cogan, Mordechai, *I Kings* (AB 10) New York-London et al., 2001, Doubleday.

Dahood, M., *Psalms II* (AB 17) New York-London et al., 1968, Doubleday.

Goldingay, John, *Psalms 42-89* (Baker commentary of the Old Testament, Wisdom and Psalms) Grand Rapids, Michigan, 2007, Baker Acad.

Groß, W., *Richter* (Herders Theologischer Kommentar zum Alten Testament) Freiburg-Basel-Wien, 2009, Herder GmbH Freiburg.

Hentschel, Georg, *2 Samuel* (KAT 34) Würzburg, 1994, Echter Verlag.

Hertzberg, Hans W., *I & II Samuel*, A Commentary, London, 1964, SCM Press.

Hossfeld, Frank-Lothar & Zenger, Erich, *Psalmen 51-100* (HThKAT) Freiburg-Wien-Basel, 2000, Herder.

- *Psalmen 1001-150*, HThKAT, Freiburg et al., 2008, Herder.

Leimbach, von Karl A., *Die Bücher Samuel*, Die Heilige Schrifft des Alten Testamentes 3,1) Bonn, 1936, Hanstein.

McCarter, P. Kyle, *I Samuel* (AB 8) New York-London et al, 1980, Doubleday - *II Samuel*, (AB 9), New York-London et al., 1984, Doubleday.

Myers, Jacob M., *1 Chronicles*, (AB 12) New York, 1965, Doubleday.

Propp, William H. C., *Exodus 1-18*, (AB 2) New York, 1999, Doubleday.

Stoebe, Joachim H., *Das Zweite Buch Samuelis*, mit einer Zeittaf. von A. Jepsen (KAT 8, 2) Gütersloh, 1994, Gütersloher Verlag.

Dictionaries

Alexander, Pat, et al., *The Lion Encyclopedia of the Bible, Life and times, meaning and Message, a comprehensive guide*, Sydney 1986, Lion Publishing.

Barnet, Sylvan – Berman, Morton – Burto, William, *A Dictionary of Literary, Dramatic, and Cinematic Terms*, Boston (1960).

Danker, Frederick W. & Bauer, Walter, *Greek-English Lexicon of the New Testament and Other Early Christian Literature*, Chicago 2000, Chicago University Press.

Freedman, David N., et al., *The Anchor Bible Dictionary*, New York-London-Toronto-Sydney-Auckland 1992, Doubleday.

Koehler, Ludwig & Baumgartner, Walter, *A Bilingual Dictionary of the Hebrew and Aramaic Old Testament, English and German*, Leiden-Boston-Köln 1998, Brill.

Electronic Media

Bible Works 7.0 - 00104582.